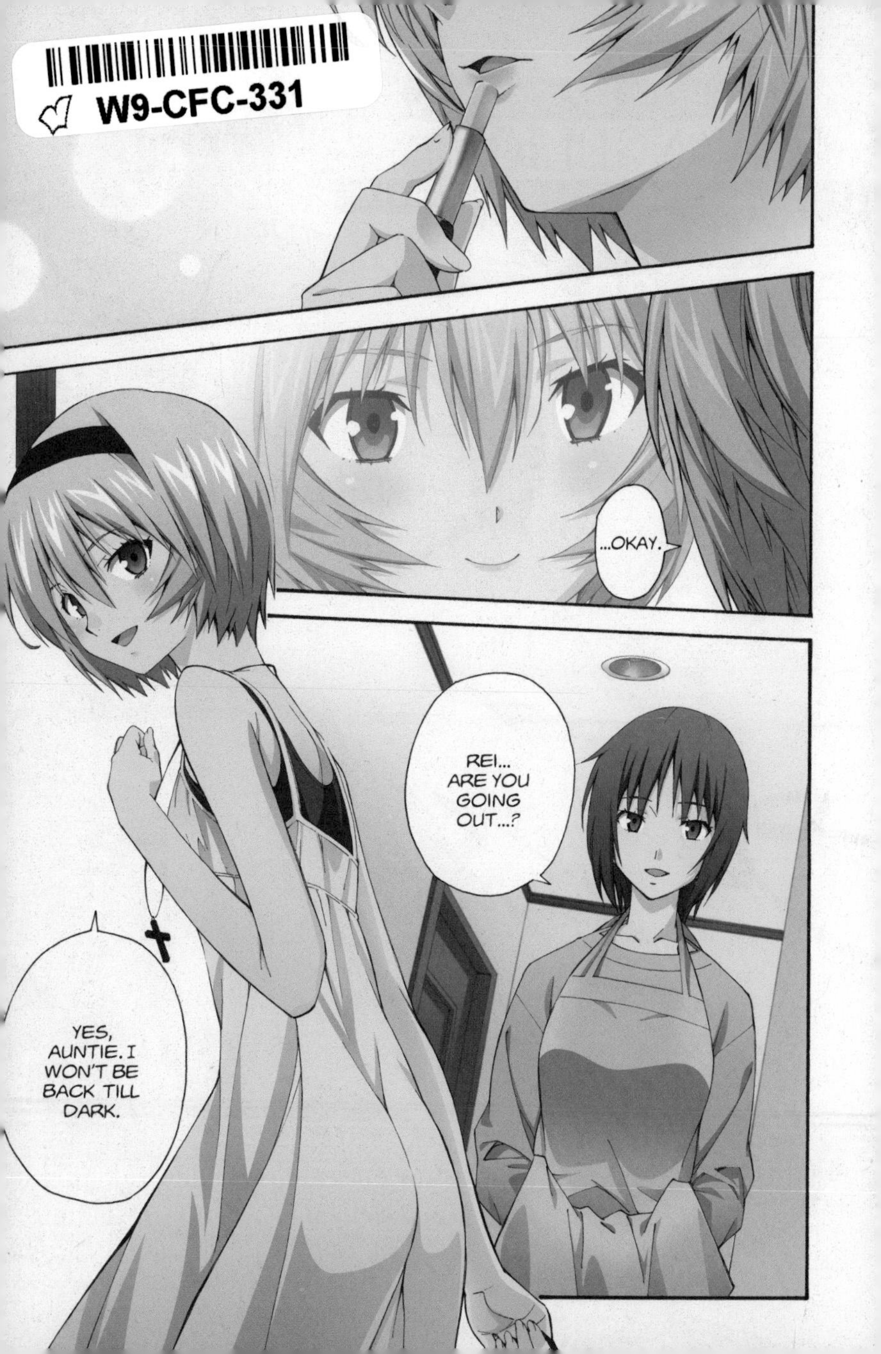
...OKAY.
REI... ARE YOU GOING OUT...?
YES, AUNTIE. I WON'T BE BACK TILL DARK.

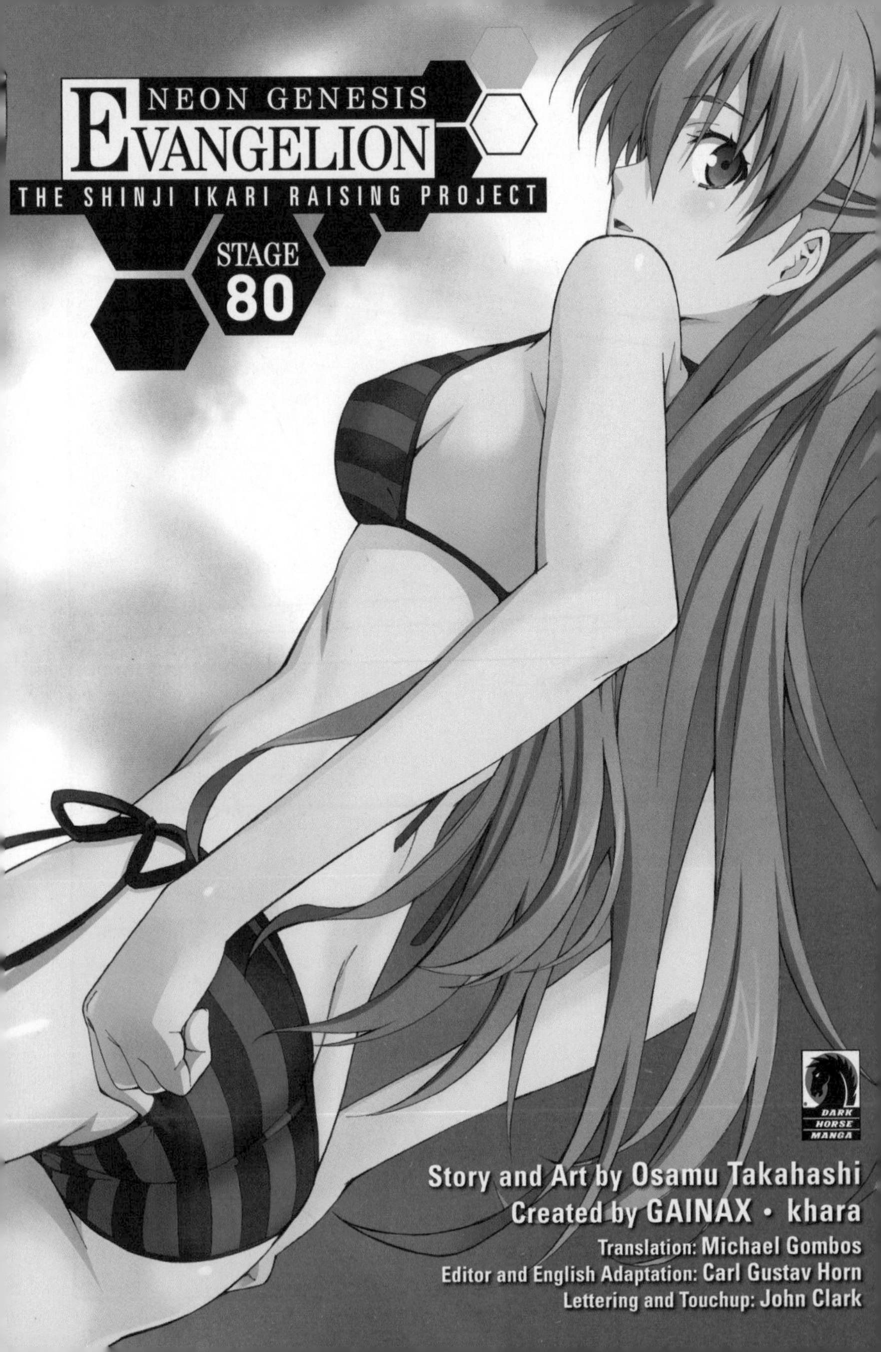

NEON GENESIS EVANGELION
THE SHINJI IKARI RAISING PROJECT

STAGE 80

DARK HORSE MANGA

Story and Art by Osamu Takahashi
Created by GAINAX • khara

Translation: Michael Gombos
Editor and English Adaptation: Carl Gustav Horn
Lettering and Touchup: John Clark

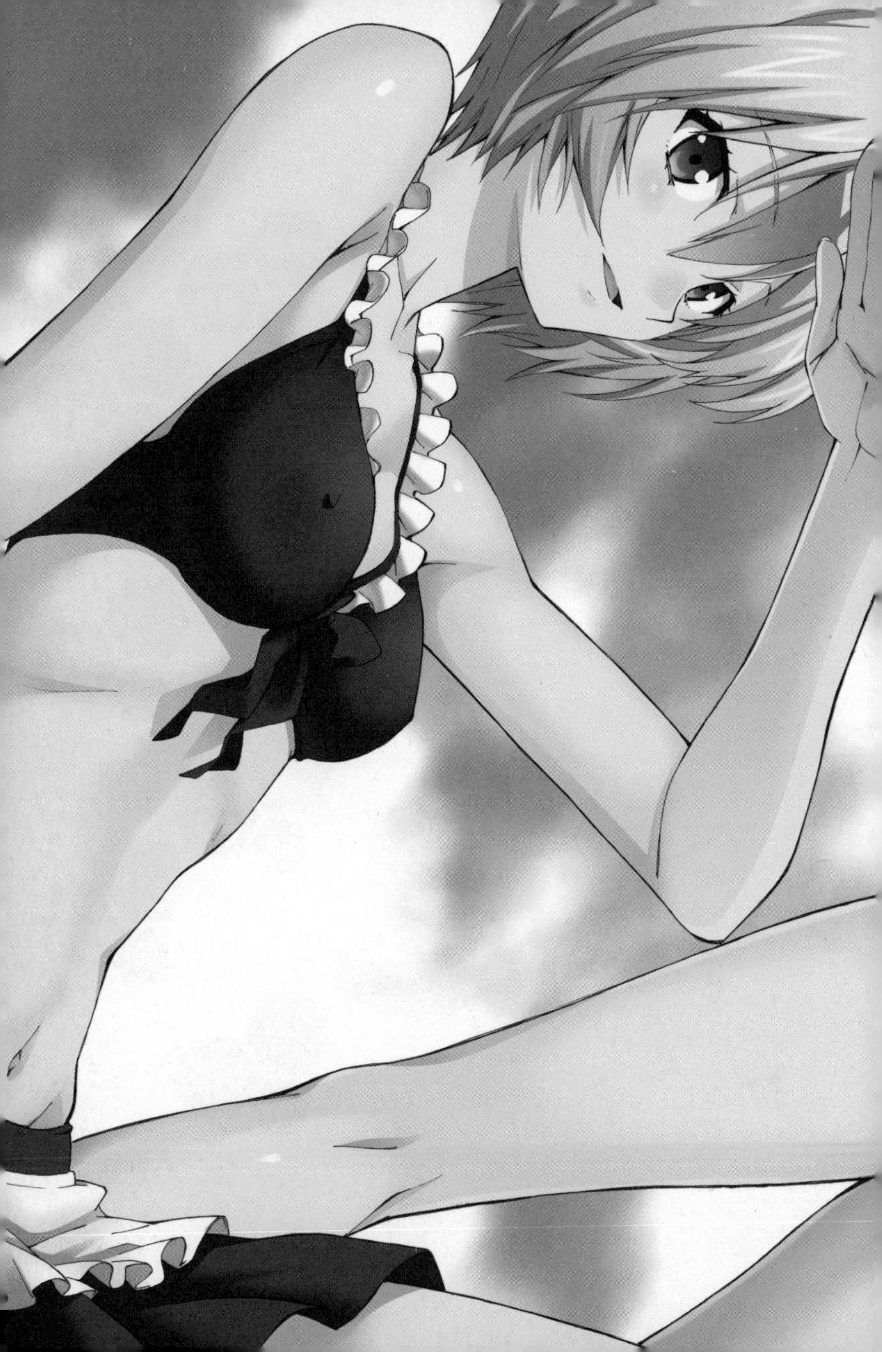

NEON GENESIS EVANGELION

THE SHINJI IKARI RAISING PROJECT

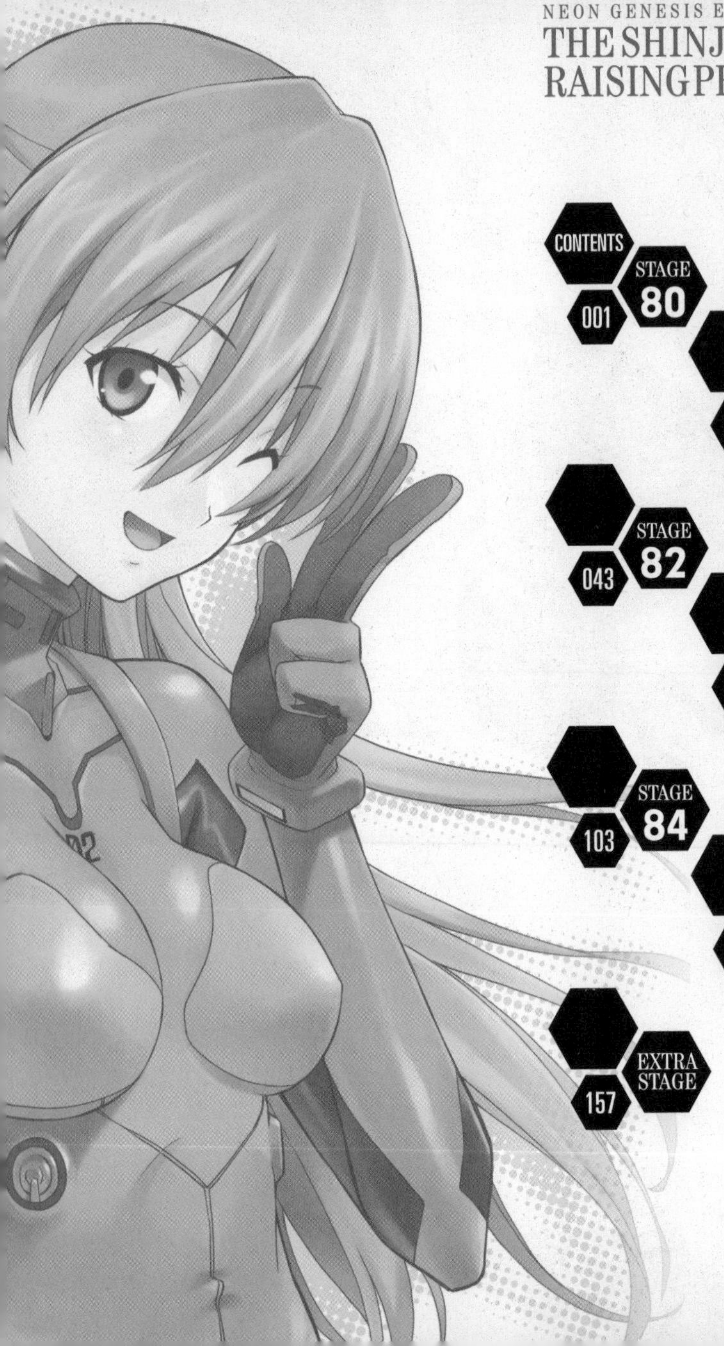

CONTENTS

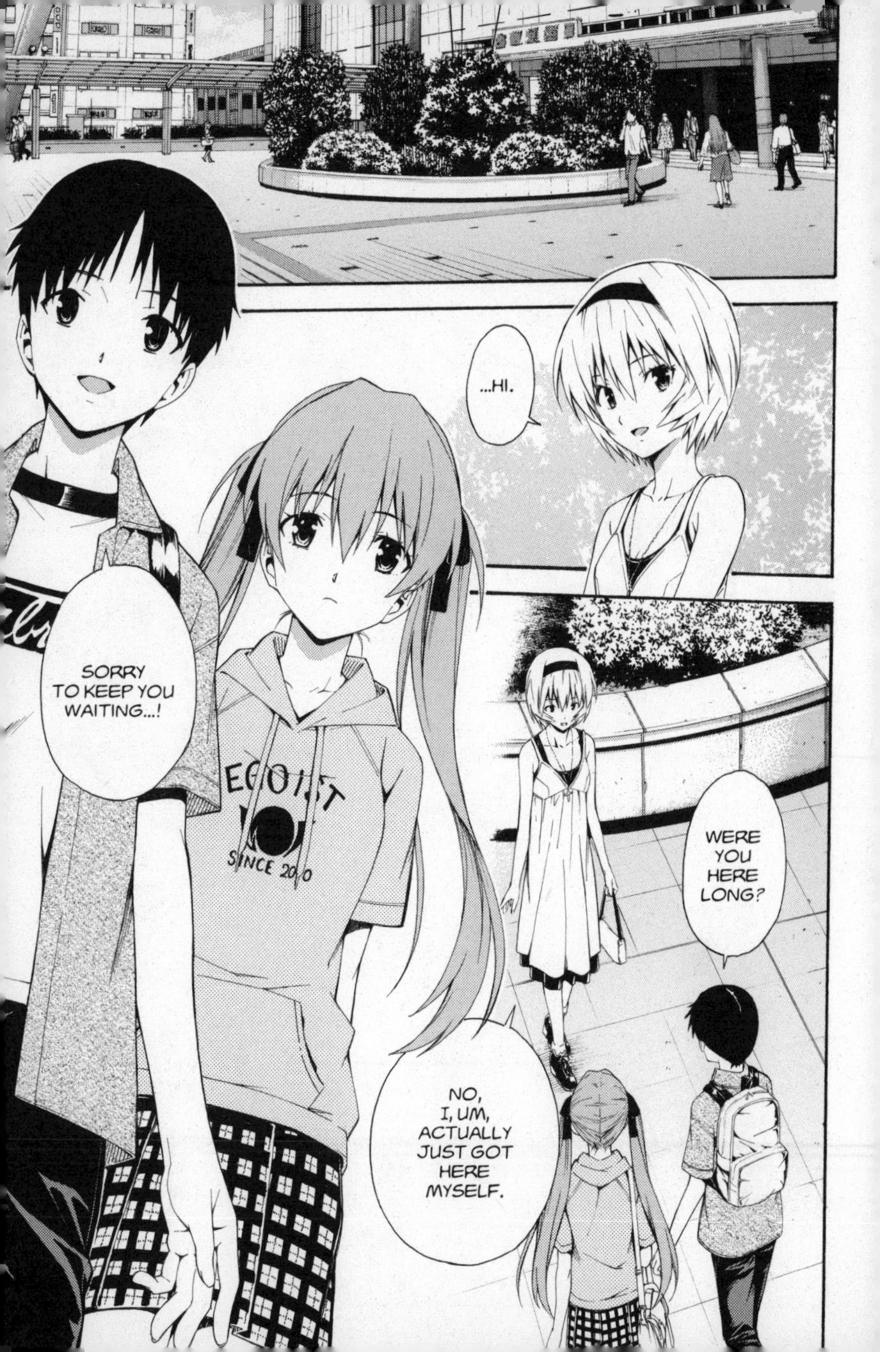
...HI.
WERE YOU HERE LONG?
NO, I, UM, ACTUALLY JUST GOT HERE MYSELF.
SORRY TO KEEP YOU WAITING...!
EGOIST SINCE 2010

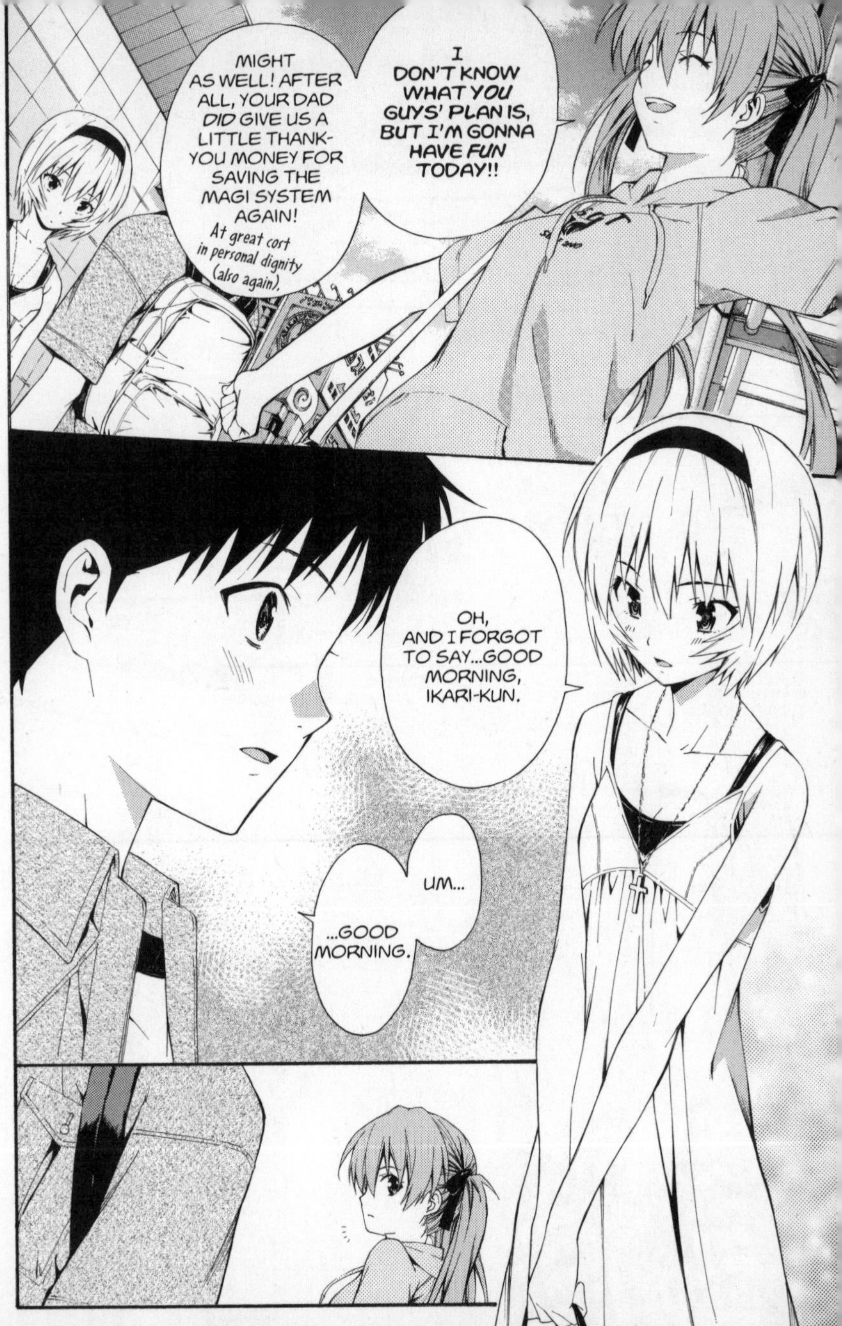
I DON'T KNOW WHAT *YOU* GUYS' PLAN IS, BUT I'M GONNA HAVE *FUN* TODAY!!
MIGHT AS WELL! AFTER ALL, YOUR DAD *DID* GIVE US A LITTLE THANK-YOU MONEY FOR SAVING THE MAGI SYSTEM AGAIN!
At great cost in personal dignity (also again).
OH, AND I FORGOT TO SAY...GOOD MORNING, IKARI-KUN.
UM...
...GOOD MORNING.

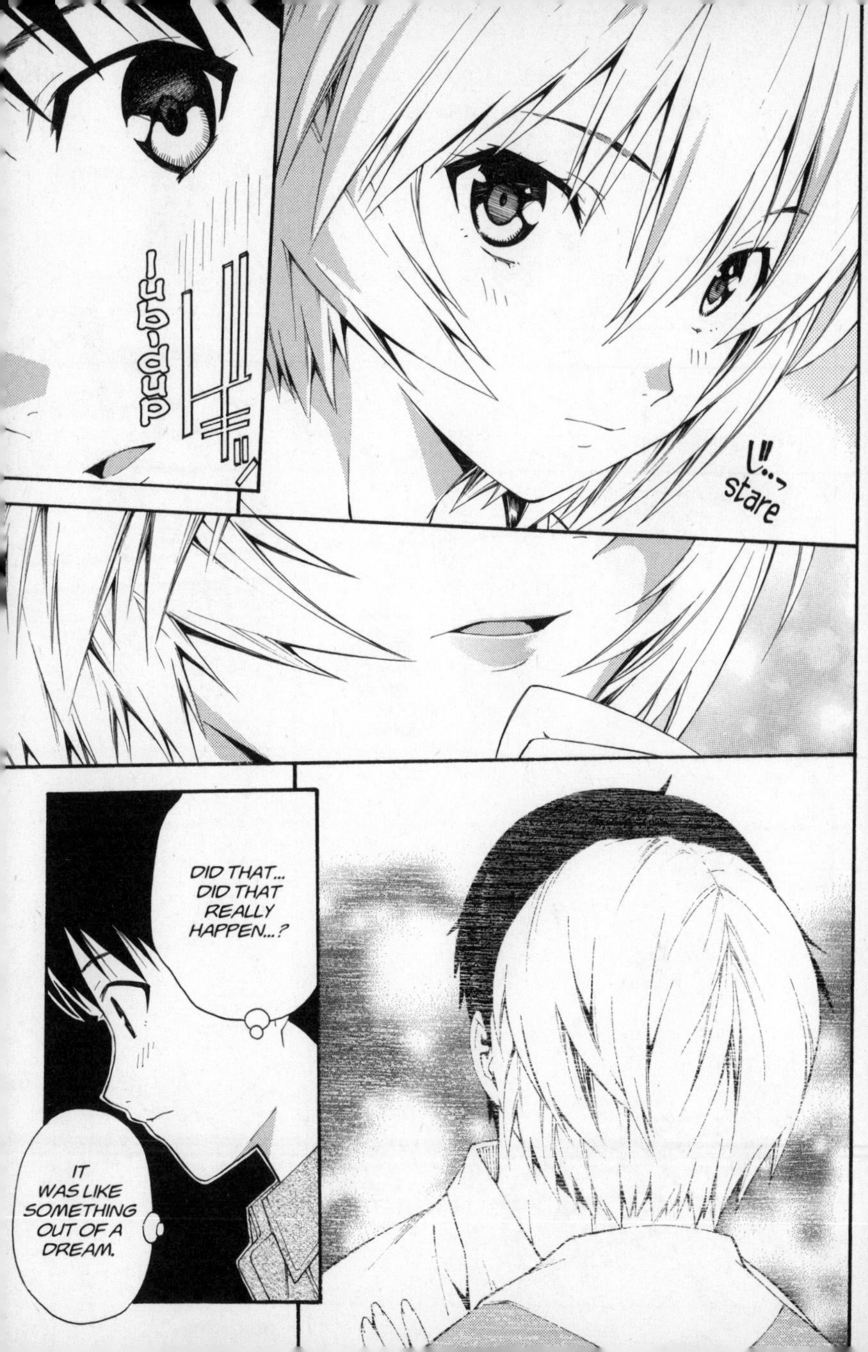
stare
lub-dub
DID THAT... DID THAT REALLY HAPPEN...?
IT WAS LIKE SOMETHING OUT OF A DREAM.

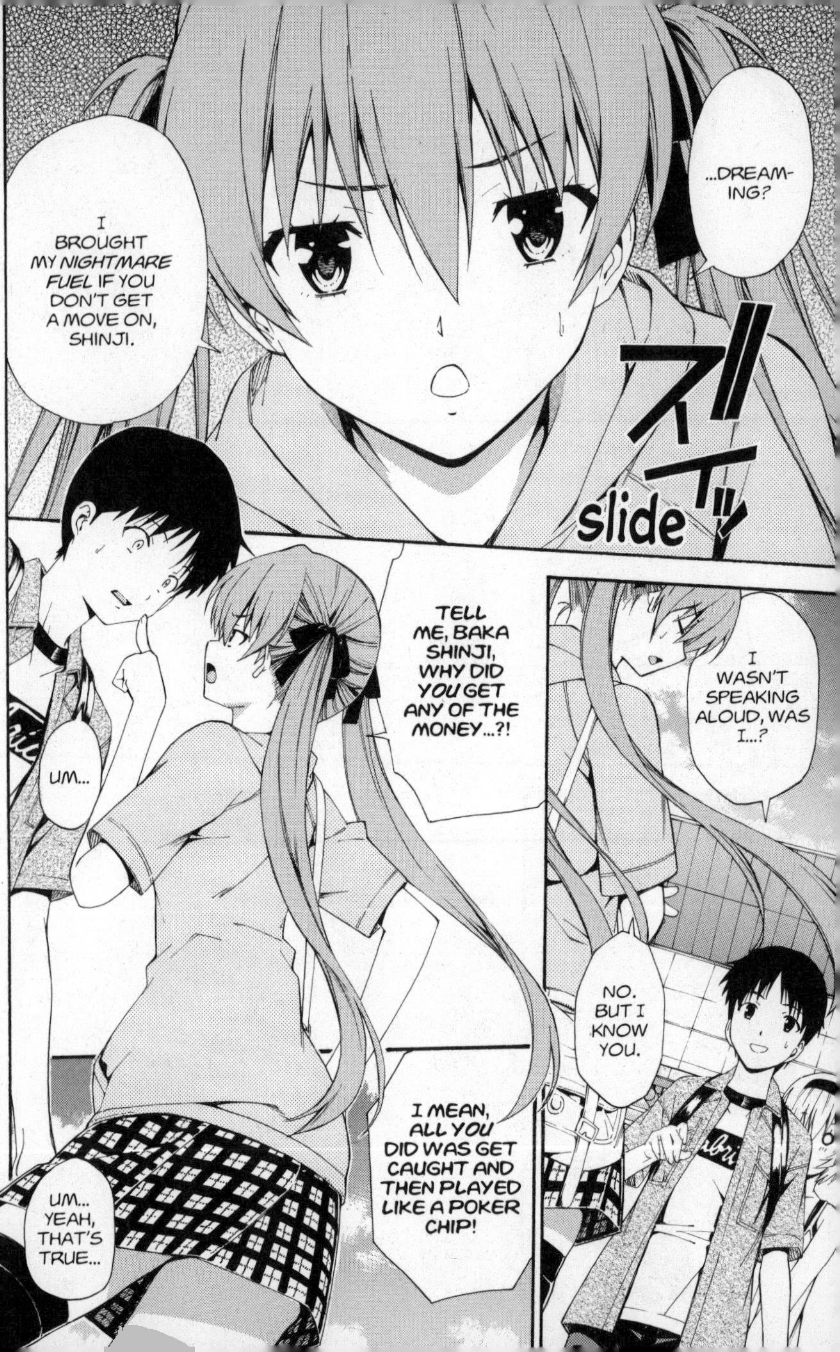
...DREAMING?
スイッ
slide
I BROUGHT MY NIGHTMARE FUEL IF YOU DON'T GET A MOVE ON, SHINJI.
I WASN'T SPEAKING ALOUD, WAS I...?
NO. BUT I KNOW YOU.
TELL ME, BAKA SHINJI, WHY DID YOU GET ANY OF THE MONEY...?!
UM...
I MEAN, ALL YOU DID WAS GET CAUGHT AND THEN PLAYED LIKE A POKER CHIP!
UM... YEAH, THAT'S TRUE...

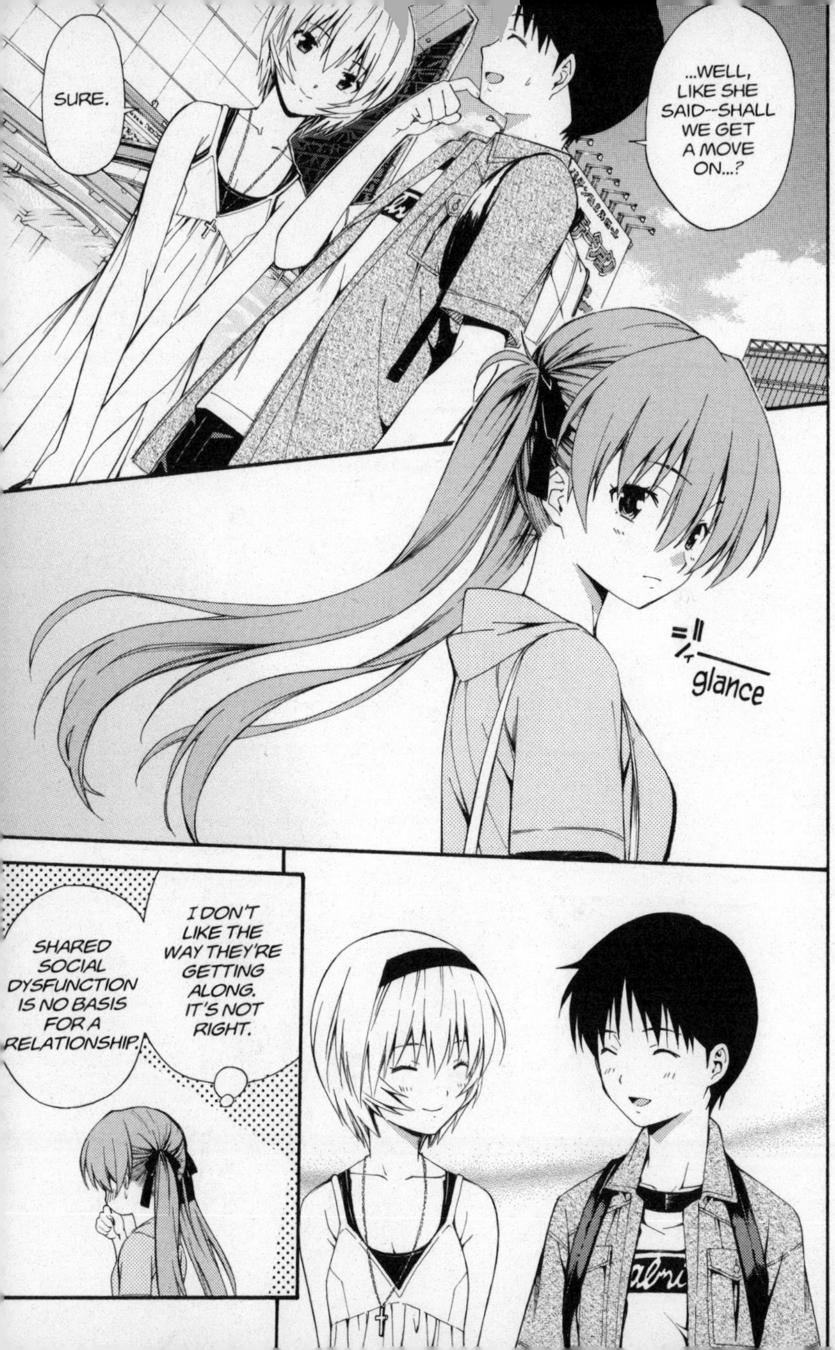
...WELL, LIKE SHE SAID--SHALL WE GET A MOVE ON...?
SURE.
glance
I DON'T LIKE THE WAY THEY'RE GETTING ALONG. IT'S NOT RIGHT.
SHARED SOCIAL DYSFUNCTION IS NO BASIS FOR A RELATIONSHIP.

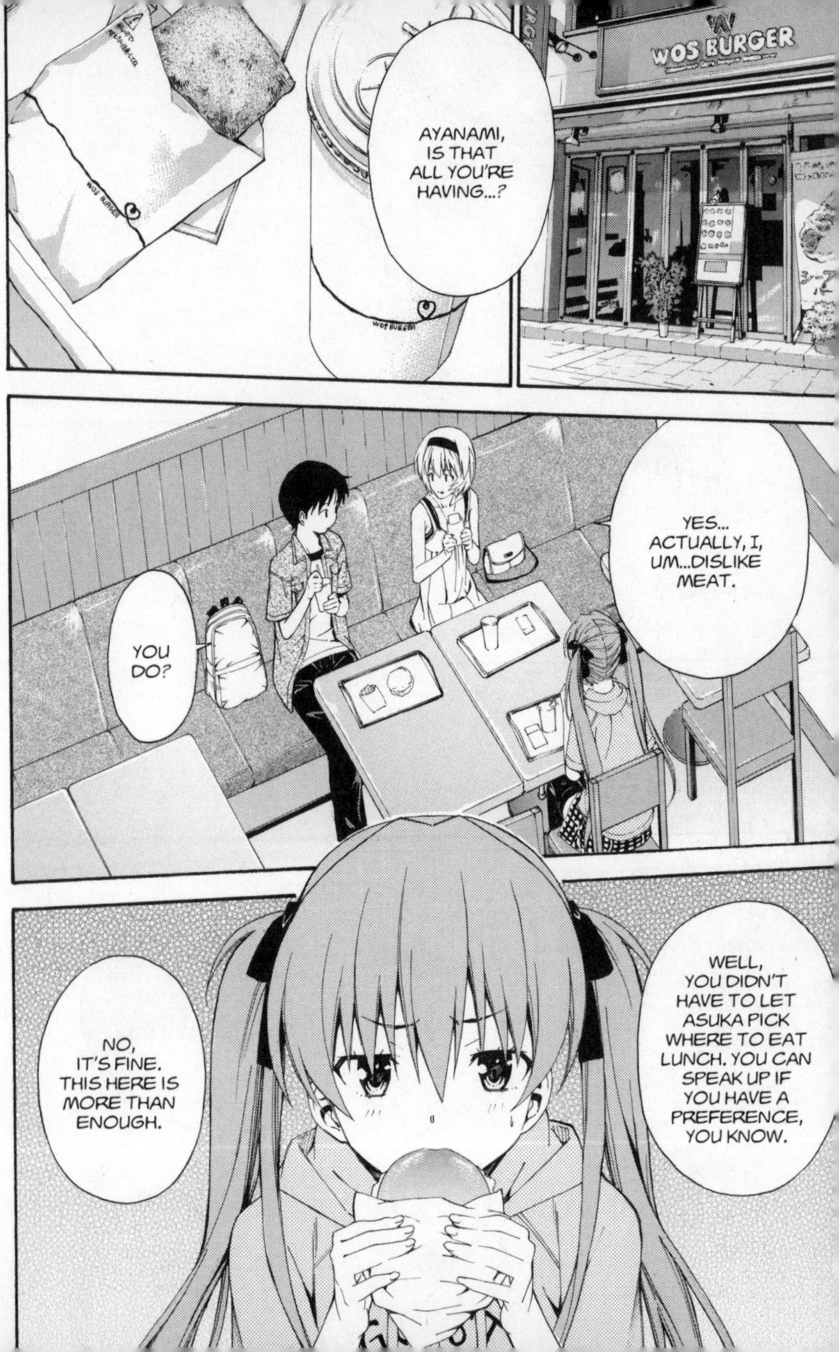
WOS BURGER
AYANAMI, IS THAT ALL YOU'RE HAVING...?
YES... ACTUALLY, I, UM...DISLIKE MEAT.
YOU DO?
WELL, YOU DIDN'T HAVE TO LET ASUKA PICK WHERE TO EAT LUNCH. YOU CAN SPEAK UP IF YOU HAVE A PREFERENCE, YOU KNOW.
NO, IT'S FINE. THIS HERE IS MORE THAN ENOUGH.

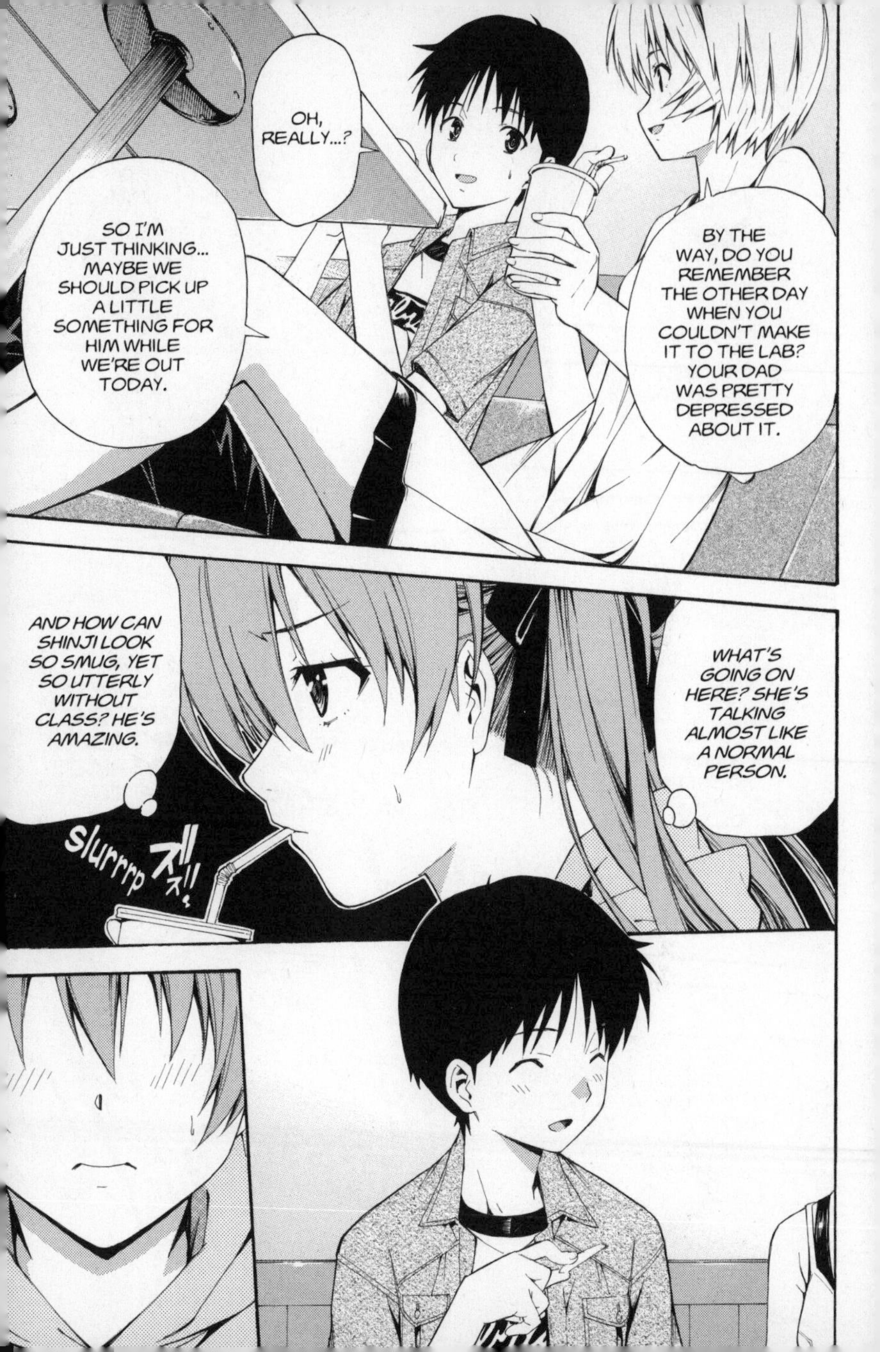
BY THE WAY, DO YOU REMEMBER THE OTHER DAY WHEN YOU COULDN'T MAKE IT TO THE LAB? YOUR DAD WAS PRETTY DEPRESSED ABOUT IT.
OH, REALLY...?
SO I'M JUST THINKING... MAYBE WE SHOULD PICK UP A LITTLE SOMETHING FOR HIM WHILE WE'RE OUT TODAY.
WHAT'S GOING ON HERE? SHE'S TALKING ALMOST LIKE A NORMAL PERSON.
AND HOW CAN SHINJI LOOK SO SMUG, YET SO UTTERLY WITHOUT CLASS? HE'S AMAZING.
slurrrp

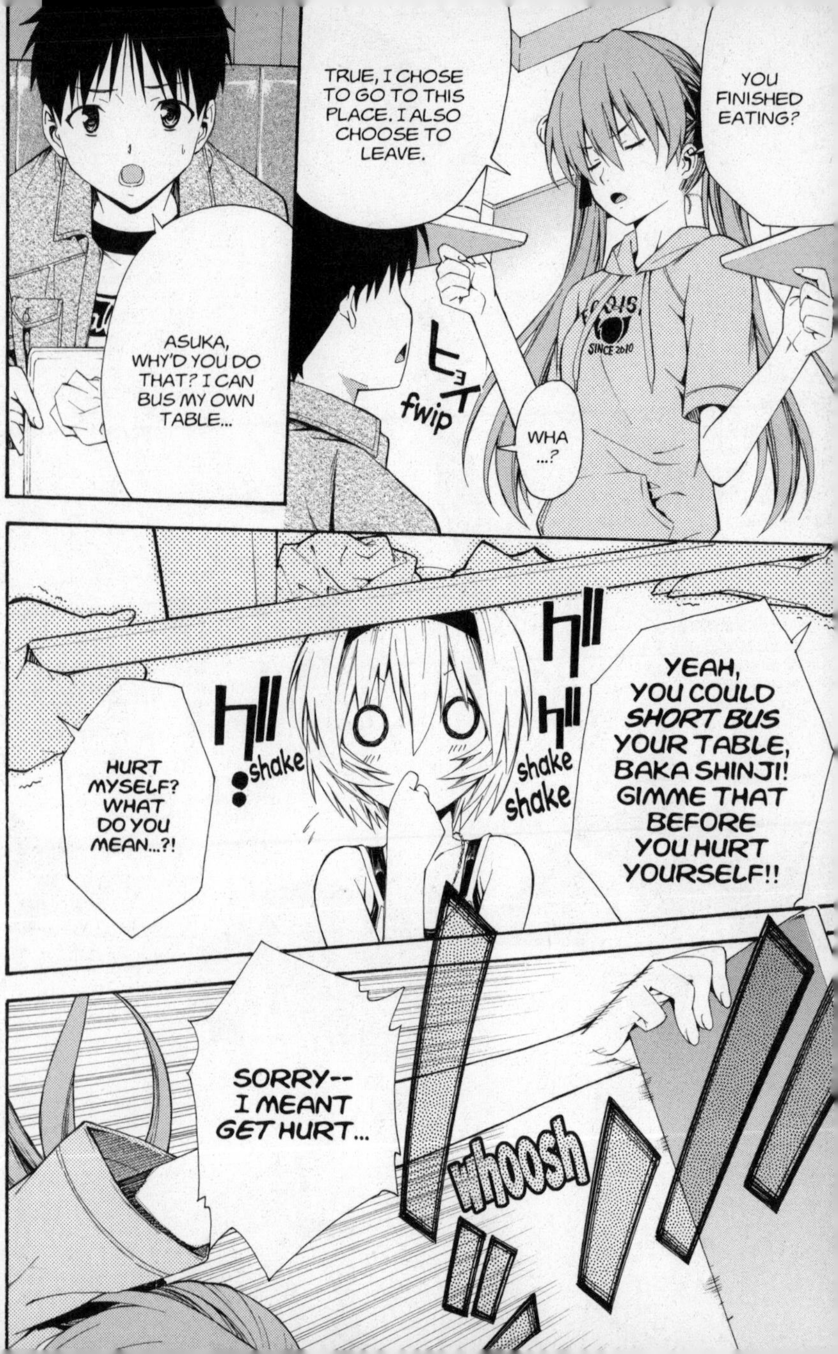
YOU FINISHED EATING?
TRUE, I CHOSE TO GO TO THIS PLACE. I ALSO CHOOSE TO LEAVE.
fwip
WHA ...?
ASUKA, WHY'D YOU DO THAT? I CAN BUS MY OWN TABLE...
YEAH, YOU COULD *SHORT BUS* YOUR TABLE, BAKA SHINJI! GIMME THAT BEFORE YOU HURT YOURSELF!!
shake shake
shake
HURT MYSELF? WHAT DO YOU MEAN...?!
whoosh
SORRY-- I MEANT *GET* HURT...

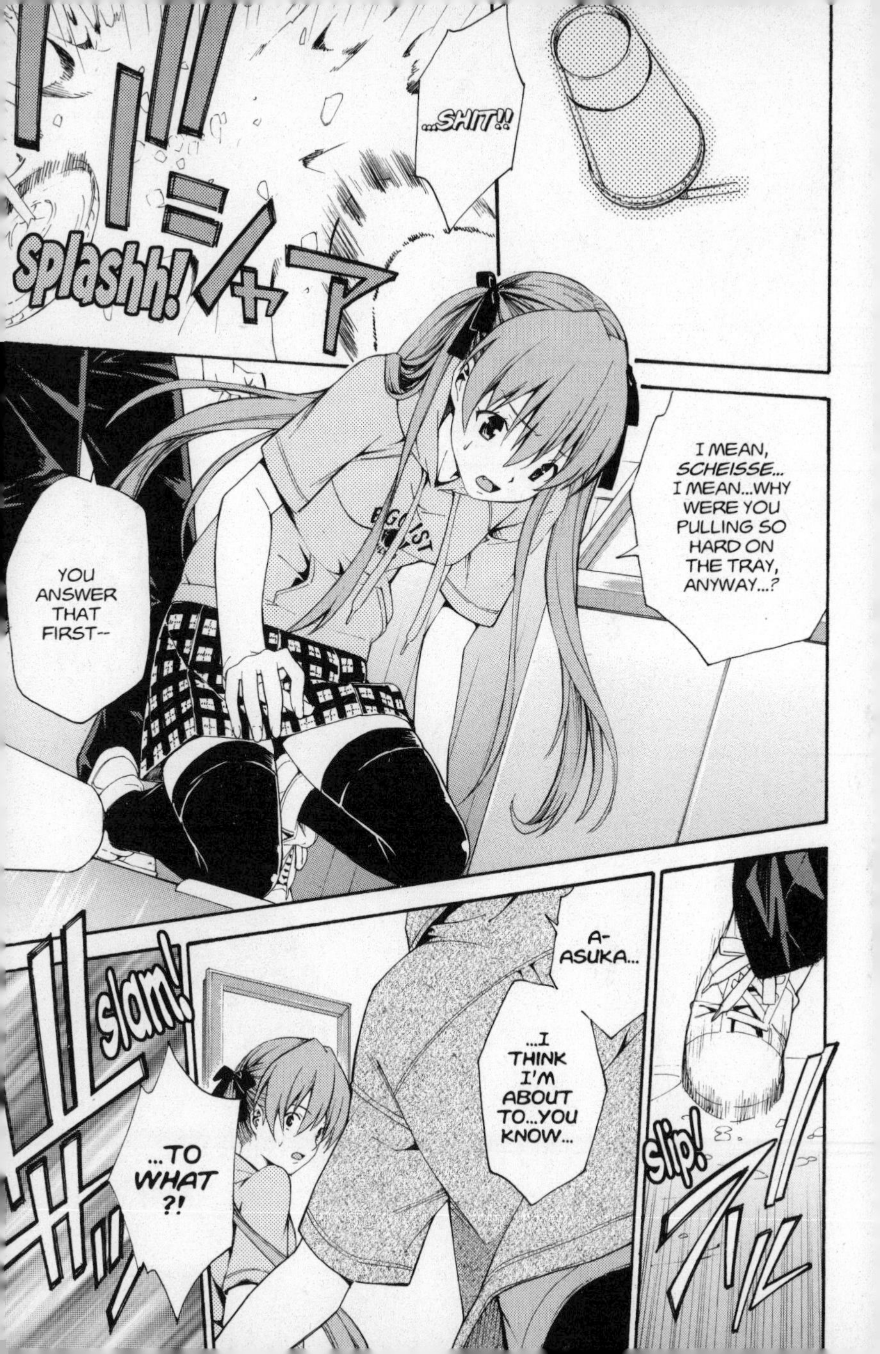
...SHIT!!
splashh!
I MEAN, SCHEISSE... I MEAN...WHY WERE YOU PULLING SO HARD ON THE TRAY, ANYWAY...?
YOU ANSWER THAT FIRST--
slip!
A-ASUKA...
...I THINK I'M ABOUT TO...YOU KNOW...
...TO WHAT?!
slam!

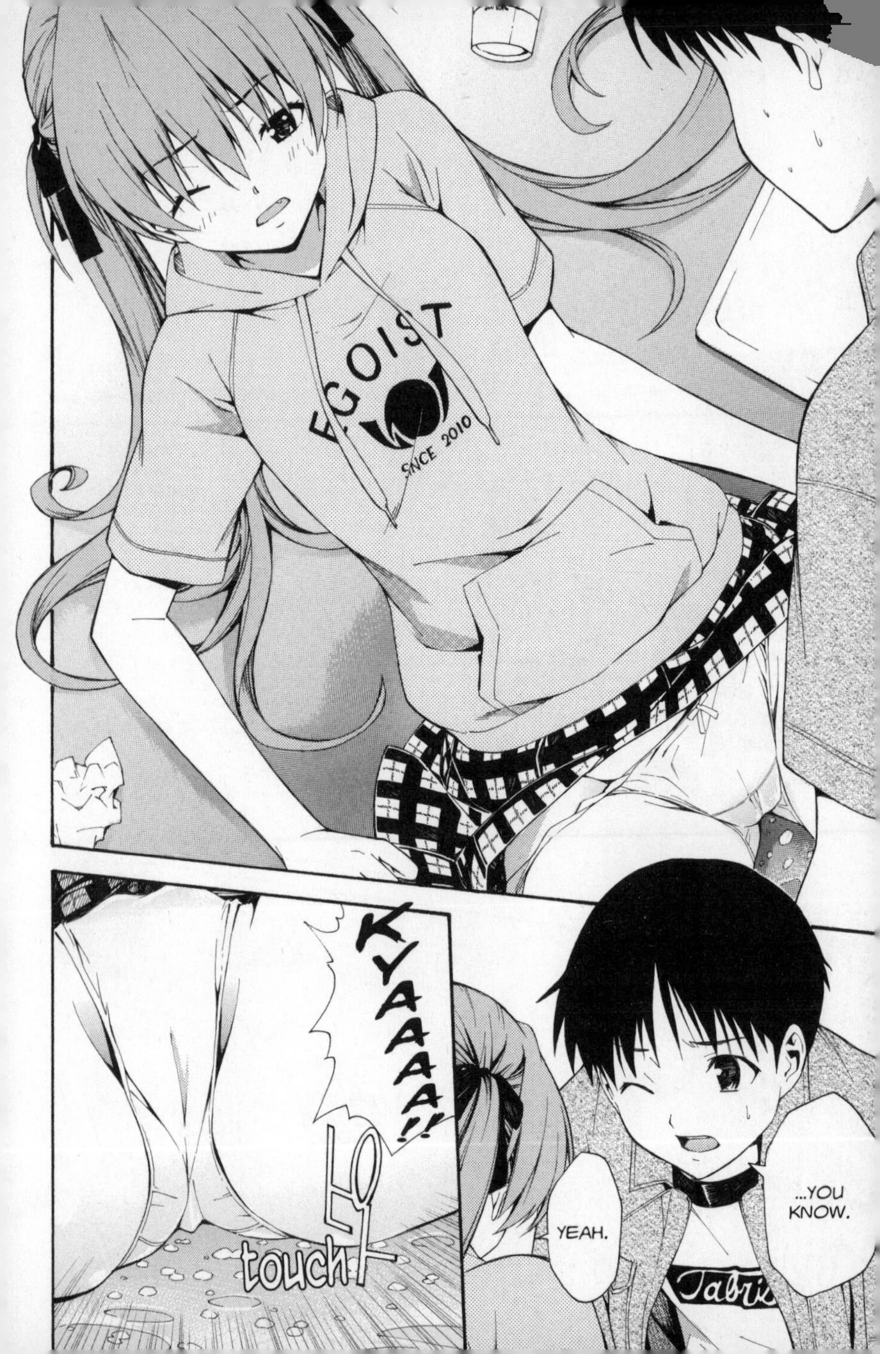
EGOIST
SINCE 2010
...YOU KNOW.
YEAH.
KYAAAAA!!
touch

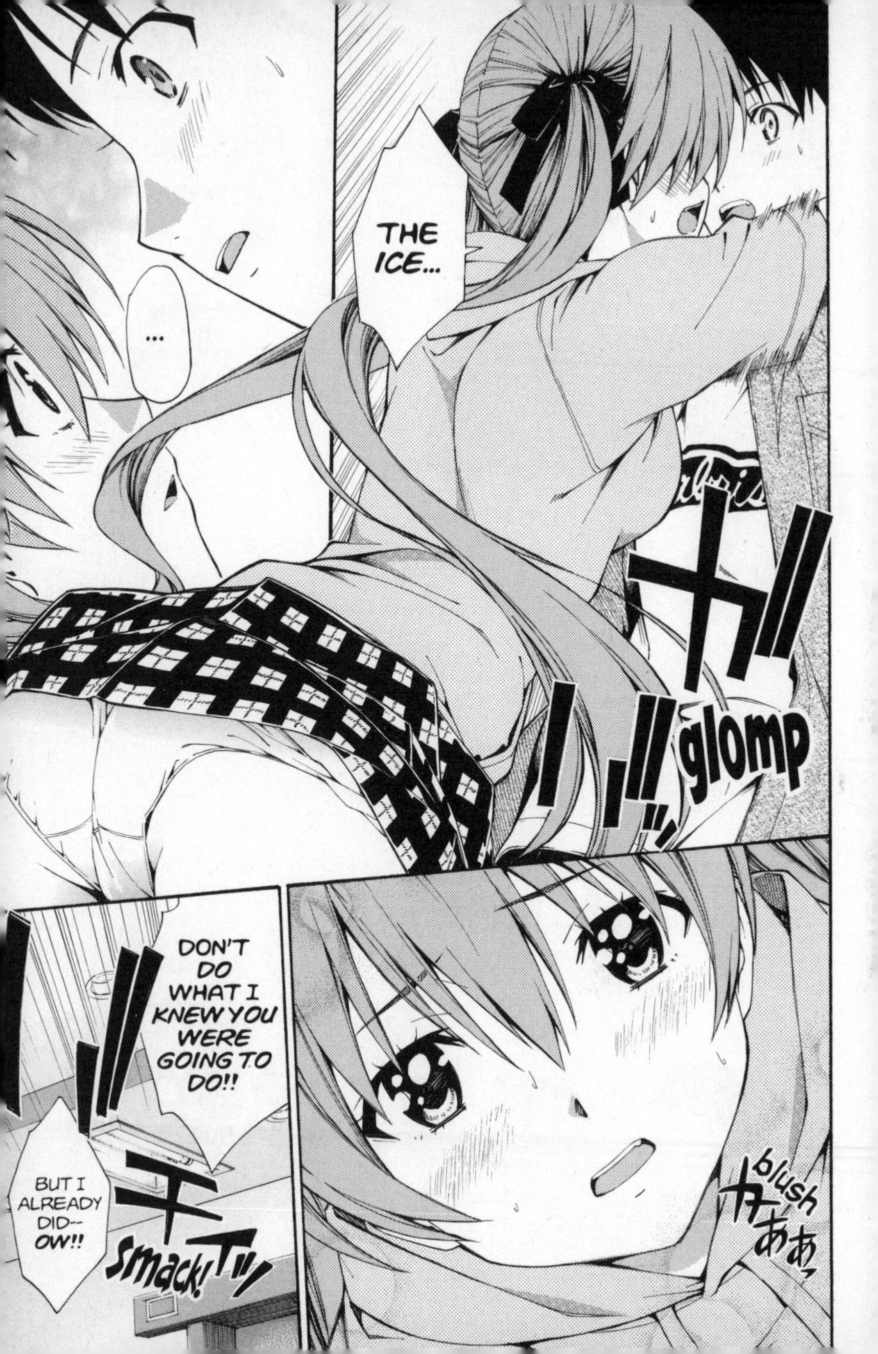
THE ICE...
glomp
...
blush
DON'T DO WHAT I KNEW YOU WERE GOING TO DO!!
BUT I ALREADY DID-- OW!!
smack!

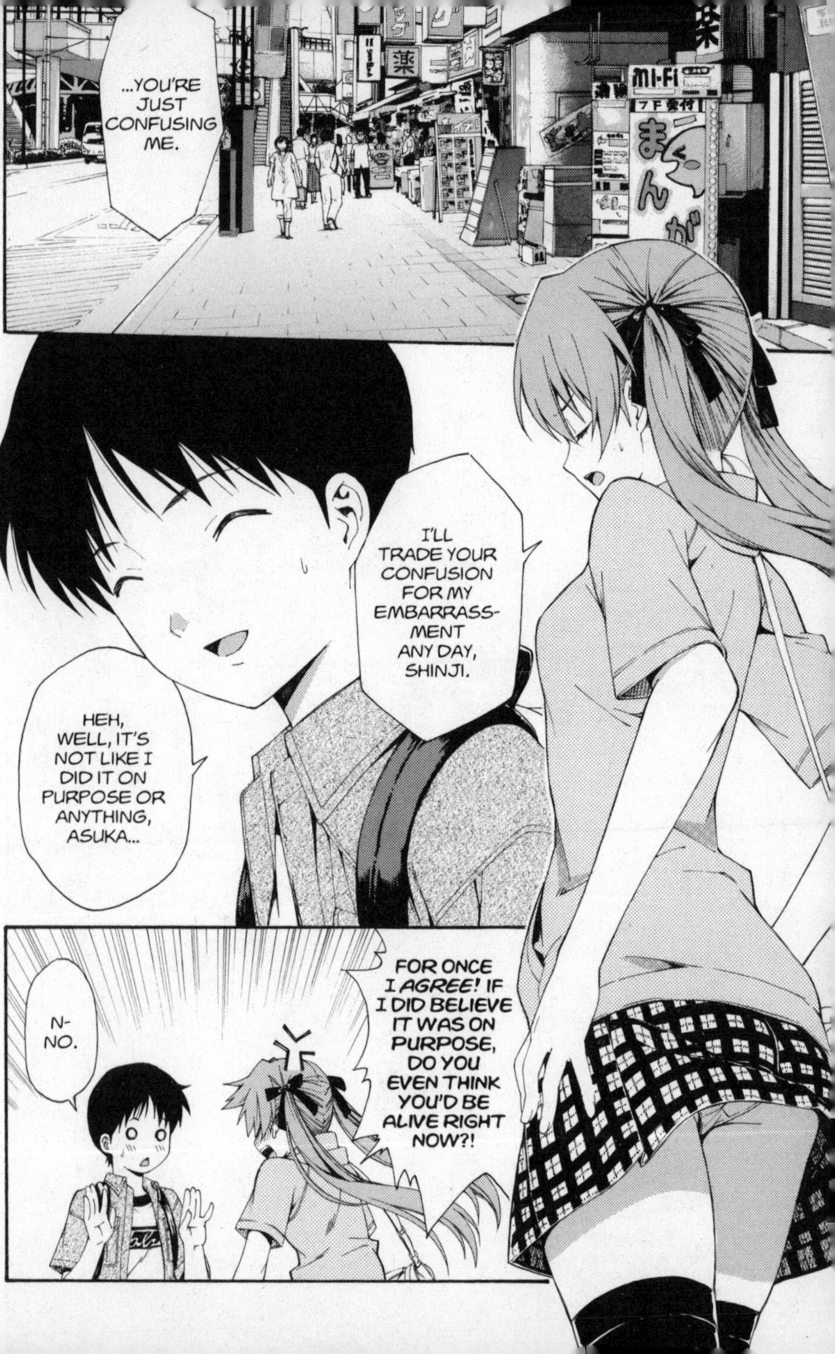
...YOU'RE JUST CONFUSING ME.
I'LL TRADE YOUR CONFUSION FOR MY EMBARRASS-MENT ANY DAY, SHINJI.
HEH, WELL, IT'S NOT LIKE I DID IT ON PURPOSE OR ANYTHING, ASUKA...
FOR ONCE I *AGREE!* IF I DID BELIEVE IT WAS ON PURPOSE, DO YOU EVEN THINK YOU'D BE ALIVE RIGHT NOW?!
N-NO.

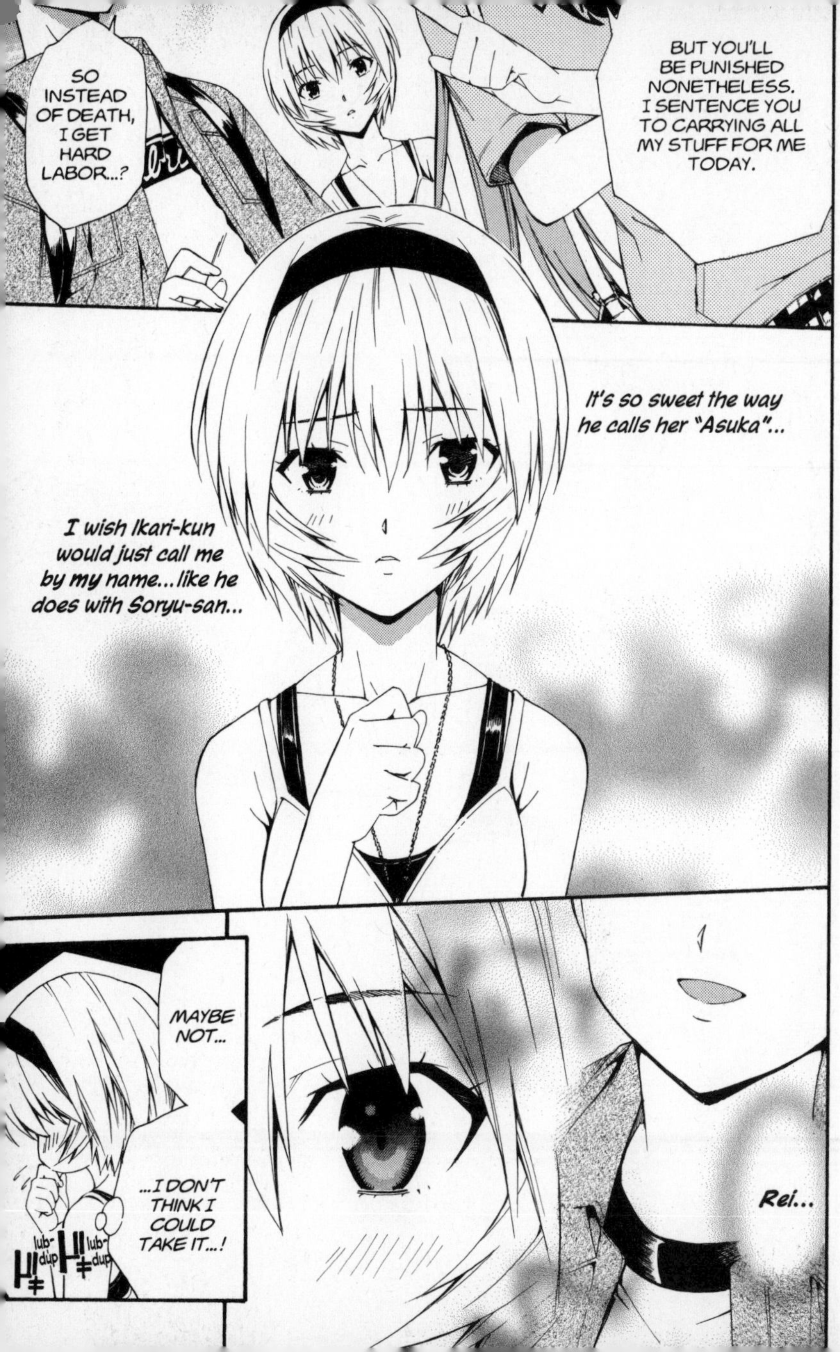
BUT YOU'LL BE PUNISHED NONETHELESS. I SENTENCE YOU TO CARRYING ALL MY STUFF FOR ME TODAY.
SO INSTEAD OF DEATH, I GET HARD LABOR...?
It's so sweet the way he calls her "Asuka"...
I wish Ikari-kun would just call me by my name...like he does with Soryu-san...
Rei...
MAYBE NOT...
...I DON'T THINK I COULD TAKE IT...!
lub-dup
lub-dup

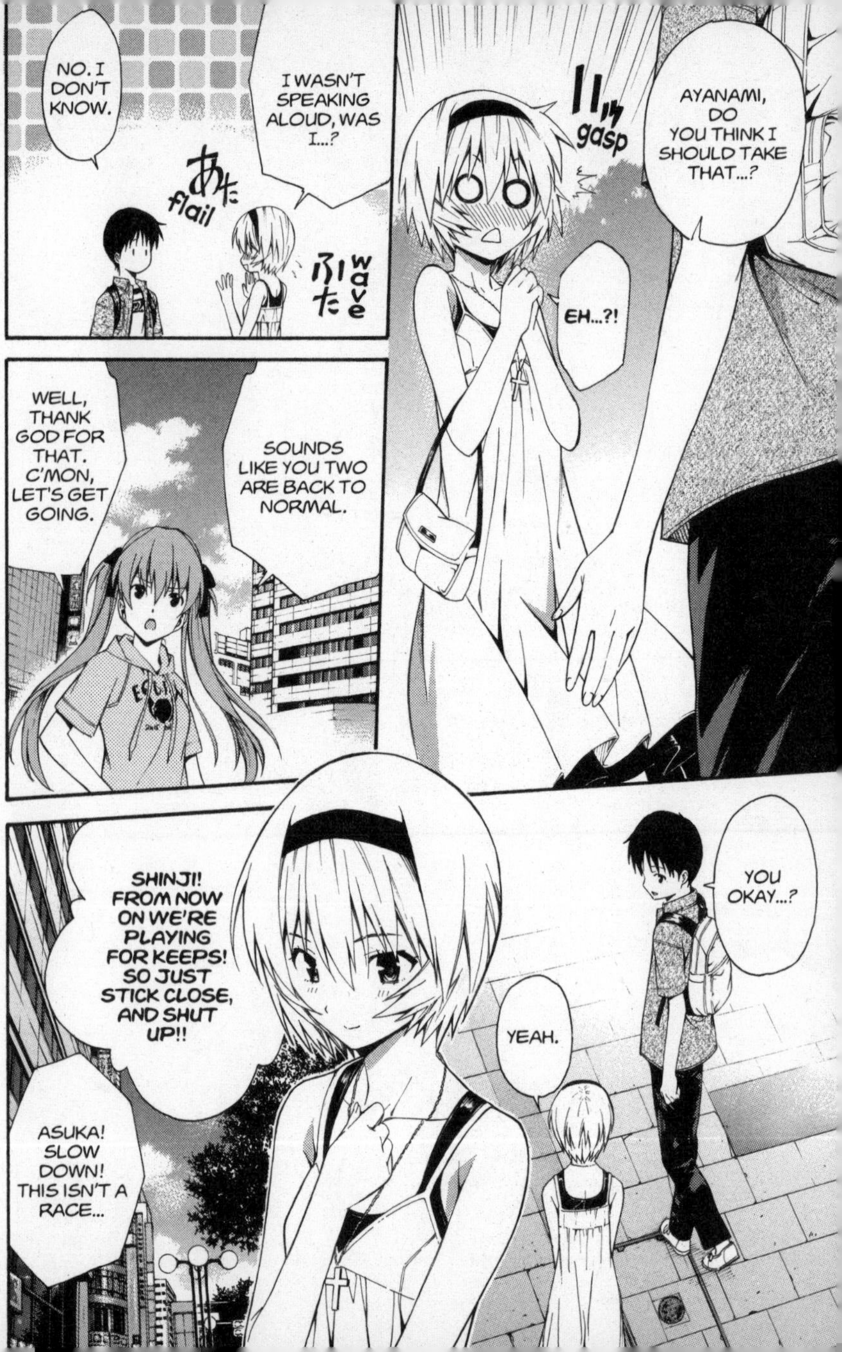
AYANAMI, DO YOU THINK I SHOULD TAKE THAT...?
ハッ gasp
EH...?!
I WASN'T SPEAKING ALOUD, WAS I...?
NO. I DON'T KNOW.
あた flail
ふた wave
SOUNDS LIKE YOU TWO ARE BACK TO NORMAL.
WELL, THANK GOD FOR THAT. C'MON, LET'S GET GOING.
YOU OKAY...?
YEAH.
SHINJI! FROM NOW ON WE'RE PLAYING FOR KEEPS! SO JUST STICK CLOSE, AND SHUT UP!!
ASUKA! SLOW DOWN! THIS ISN'T A RACE...

the shinji ikari raising project

glance

NEON GENESIS
EVANGELION
THE SHINJI IKARI RAISING PROJECT

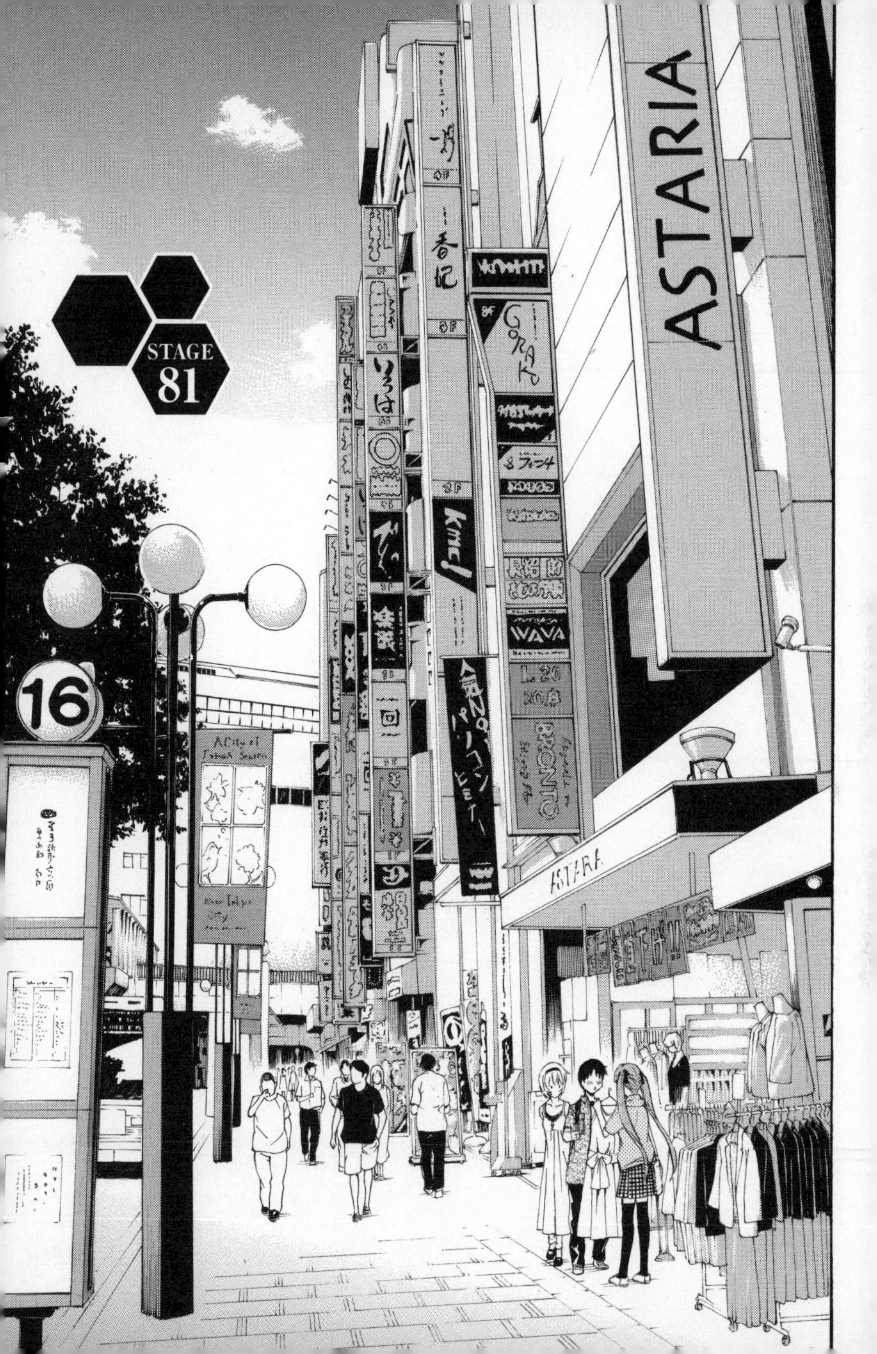
STAGE
81
ASTARIA
GORAKU
WAVA
PRONTO
16
A City of Future Search
New Tokyo City
ASTARIA

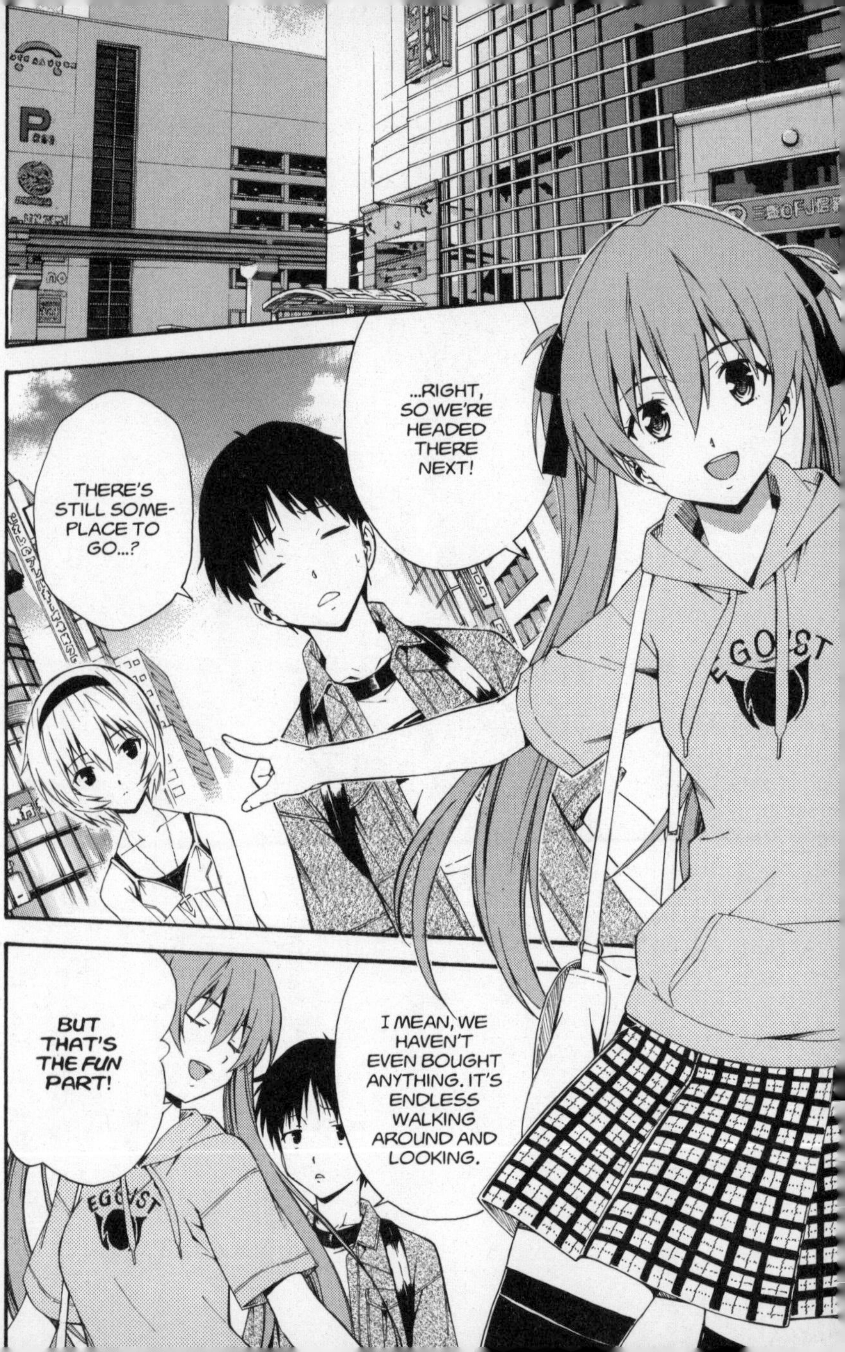
...RIGHT, SO WE'RE HEADED THERE NEXT!
THERE'S STILL SOME-PLACE TO GO...?
I MEAN, WE HAVEN'T EVEN BOUGHT ANYTHING. IT'S ENDLESS WALKING AROUND AND LOOKING.
BUT THAT'S THE *FUN* PART!

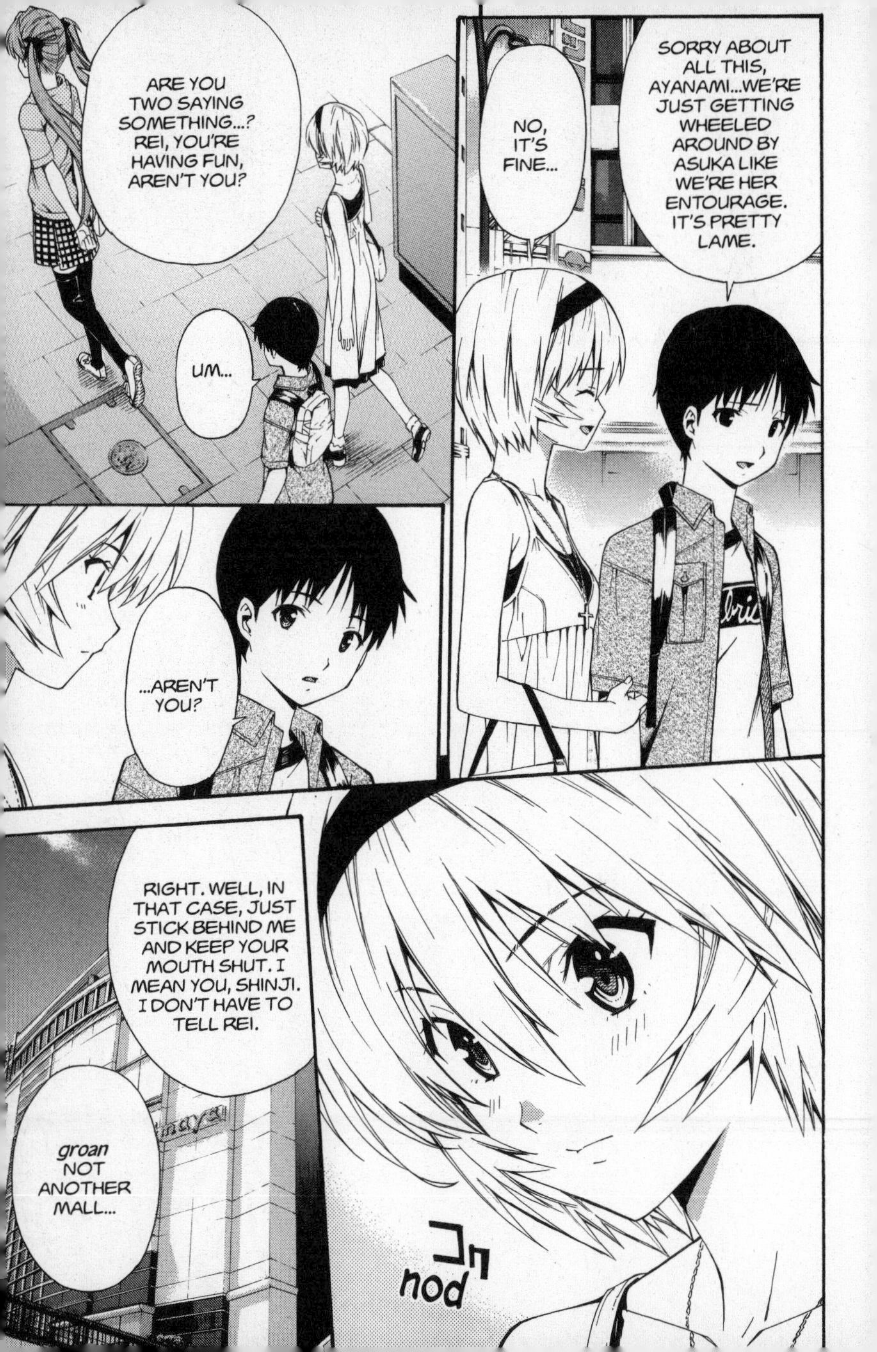
SORRY ABOUT ALL THIS, AYANAMI...WE'RE JUST GETTING WHEELED AROUND BY ASUKA LIKE WE'RE HER ENTOURAGE. IT'S PRETTY LAME.
NO, IT'S FINE...
ARE YOU TWO SAYING SOMETHING...? REI, YOU'RE HAVING FUN, AREN'T YOU?
UM...
...AREN'T YOU?
nod
RIGHT. WELL, IN THAT CASE, JUST STICK BEHIND ME AND KEEP YOUR MOUTH SHUT. I MEAN YOU, SHINJI. I DON'T HAVE TO TELL REI.
groan NOT ANOTHER MALL...

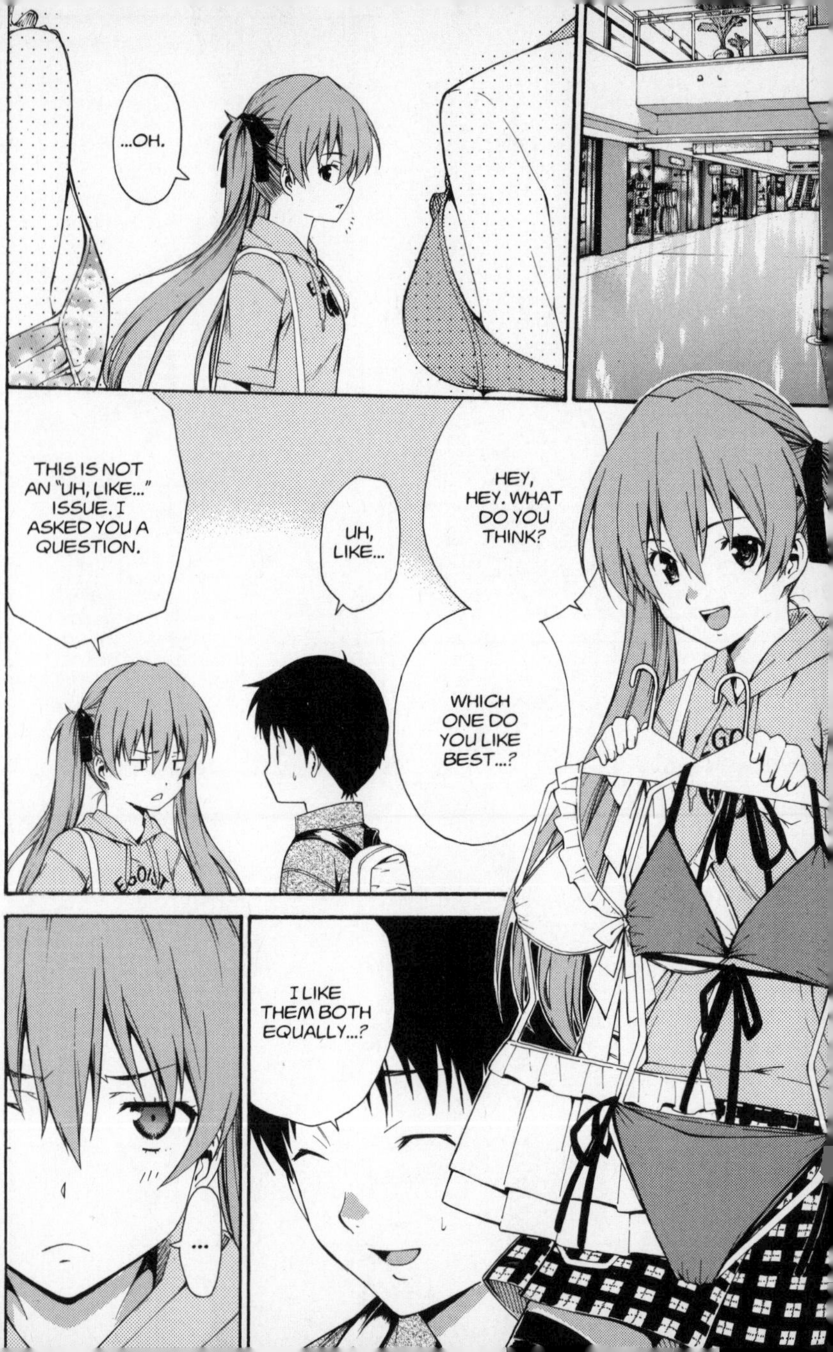

...OH.
HEY, HEY. WHAT DO YOU THINK?
WHICH ONE DO YOU LIKE BEST...?
UH, LIKE...
THIS IS NOT AN "UH, LIKE..." ISSUE. I ASKED YOU A QUESTION.
I LIKE THEM BOTH EQUALLY...?
...

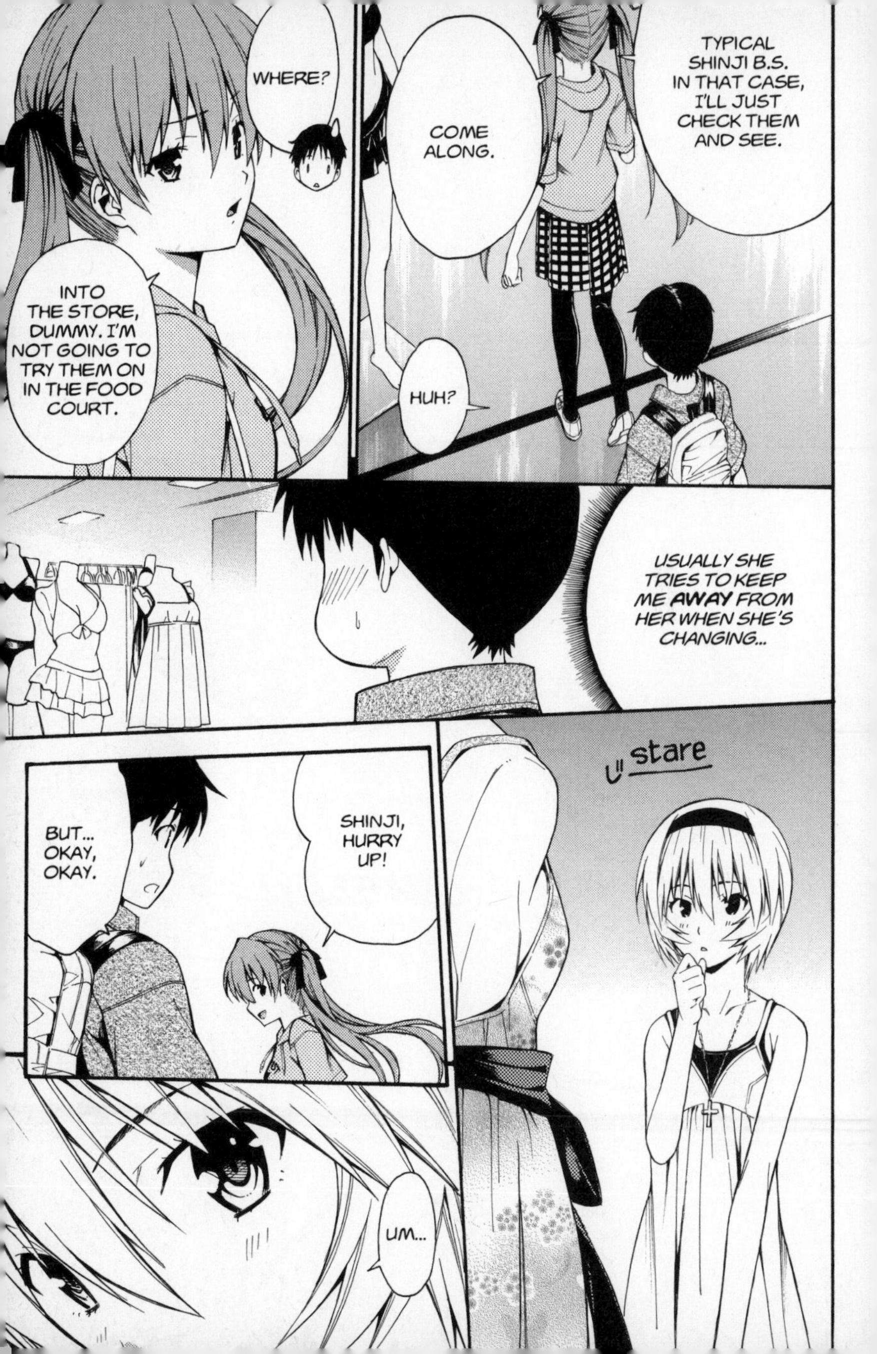
TYPICAL SHINJI B.S. IN THAT CASE, I'LL JUST CHECK THEM AND SEE.
COME ALONG.
HUH?
WHERE?
INTO THE STORE, DUMMY. I'M NOT GOING TO TRY THEM ON IN THE FOOD COURT.
USUALLY SHE TRIES TO KEEP ME **AWAY** FROM HER WHEN SHE'S CHANGING...
stare
SHINJI, HURRY UP!
BUT... OKAY, OKAY.
UM...

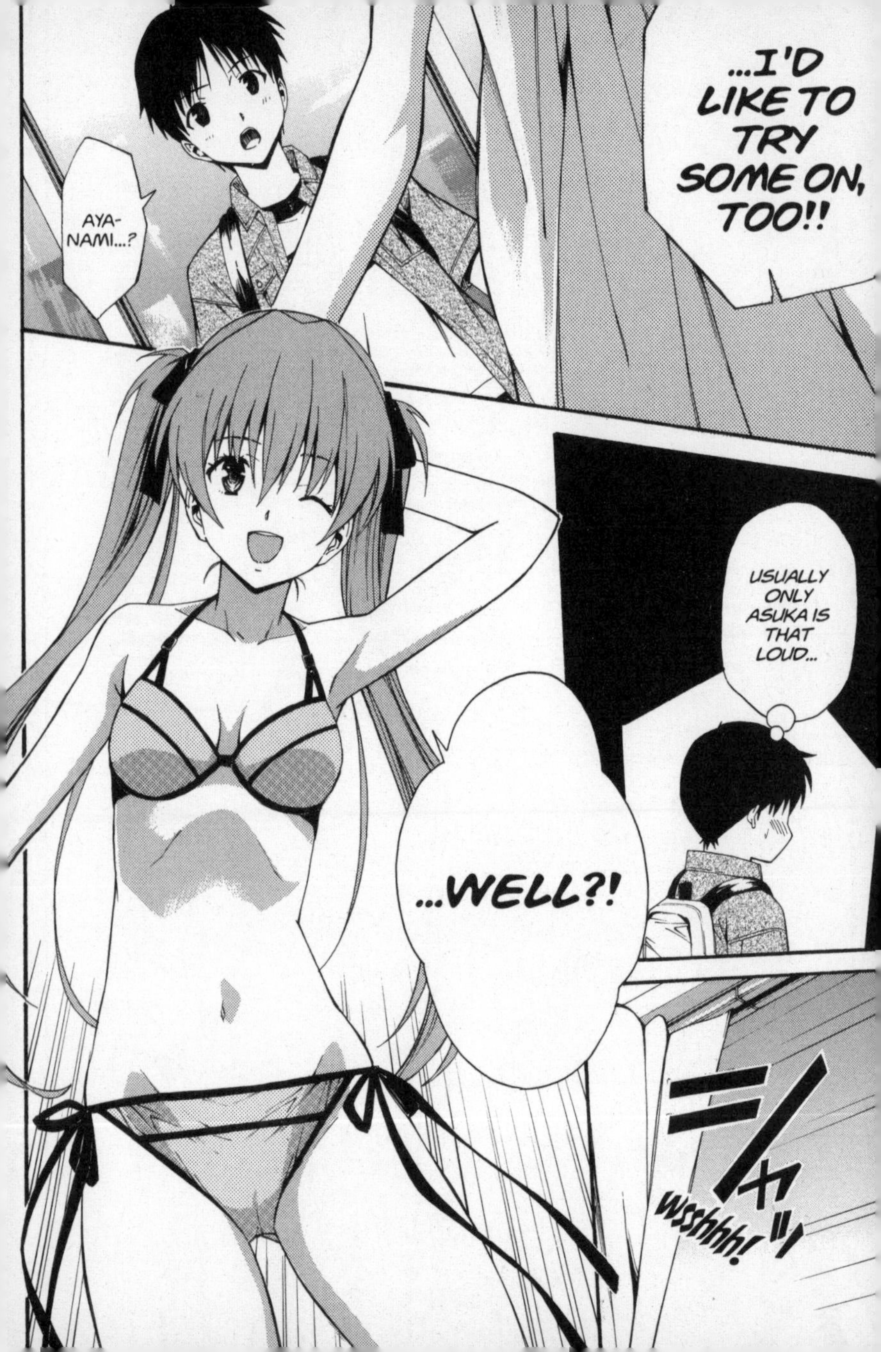
...I'D LIKE TO TRY SOME ON, TOO!!
AYA-NAMI...?
USUALLY ONLY ASUKA IS THAT LOUD...
wsshhh!
...WELL?!

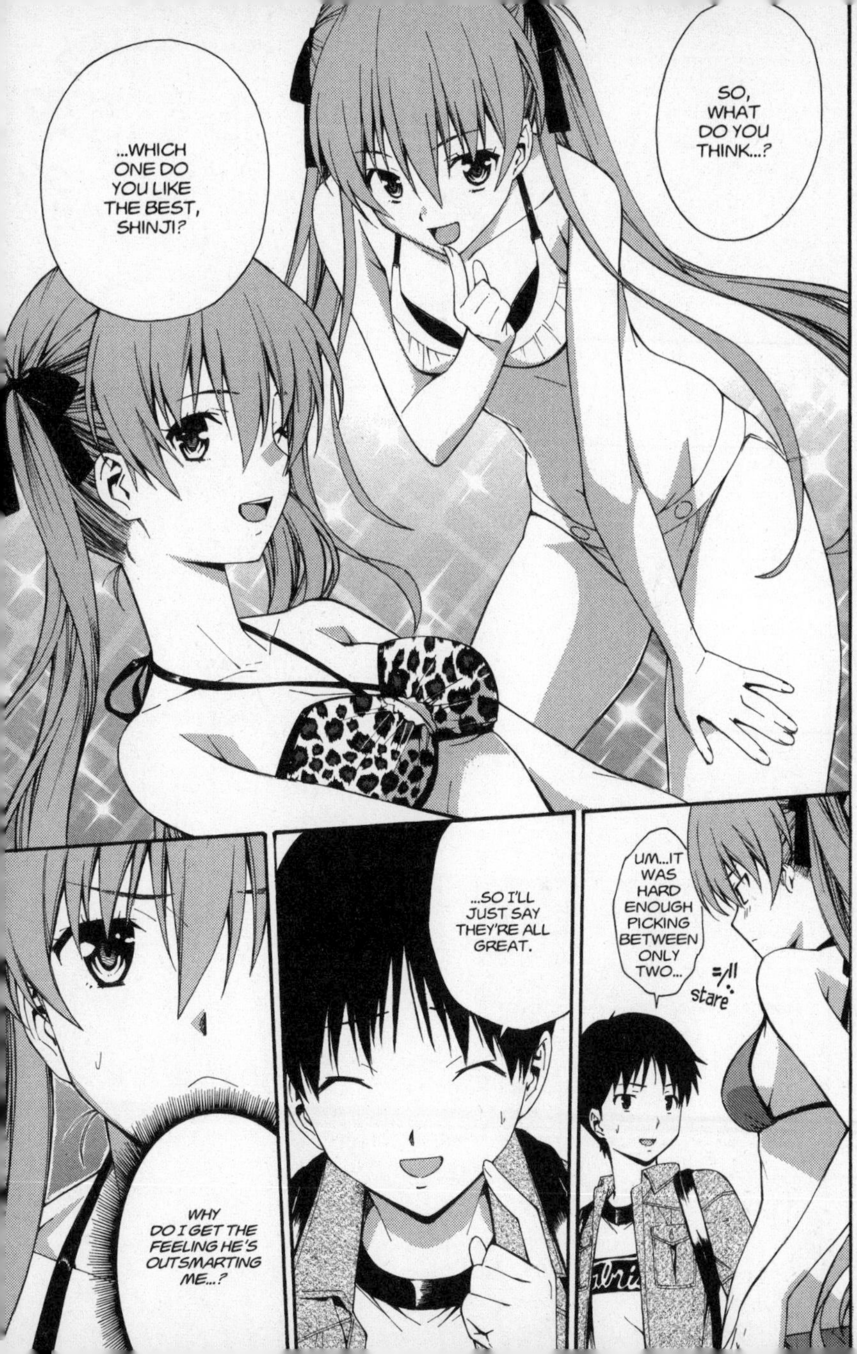
SO, WHAT DO YOU THINK...?
...WHICH ONE DO YOU LIKE THE BEST, SHINJI?
UM...IT WAS HARD ENOUGH PICKING BETWEEN ONLY TWO...
stare
...SO I'LL JUST SAY THEY'RE ALL GREAT.
WHY DO I GET THE FEELING HE'S OUTSMARTING ME...?

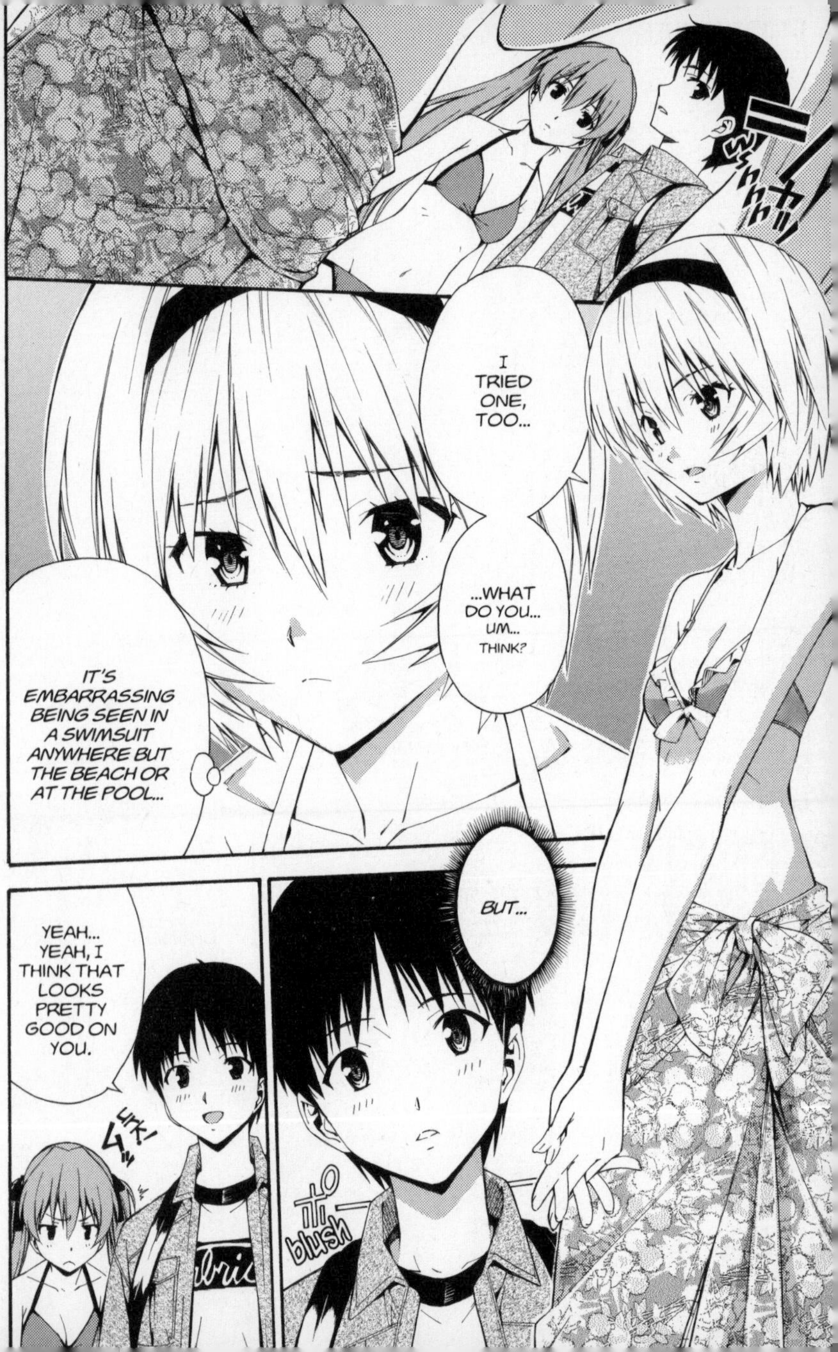
I TRIED ONE, TOO...
...WHAT DO YOU... UM... THINK?
IT'S EMBARRASSING BEING SEEN IN A SWIMSUIT ANYWHERE BUT THE BEACH OR AT THE POOL...
BUT...
blush
YEAH... YEAH, I THINK THAT LOOKS PRETTY GOOD ON YOU.
URK!

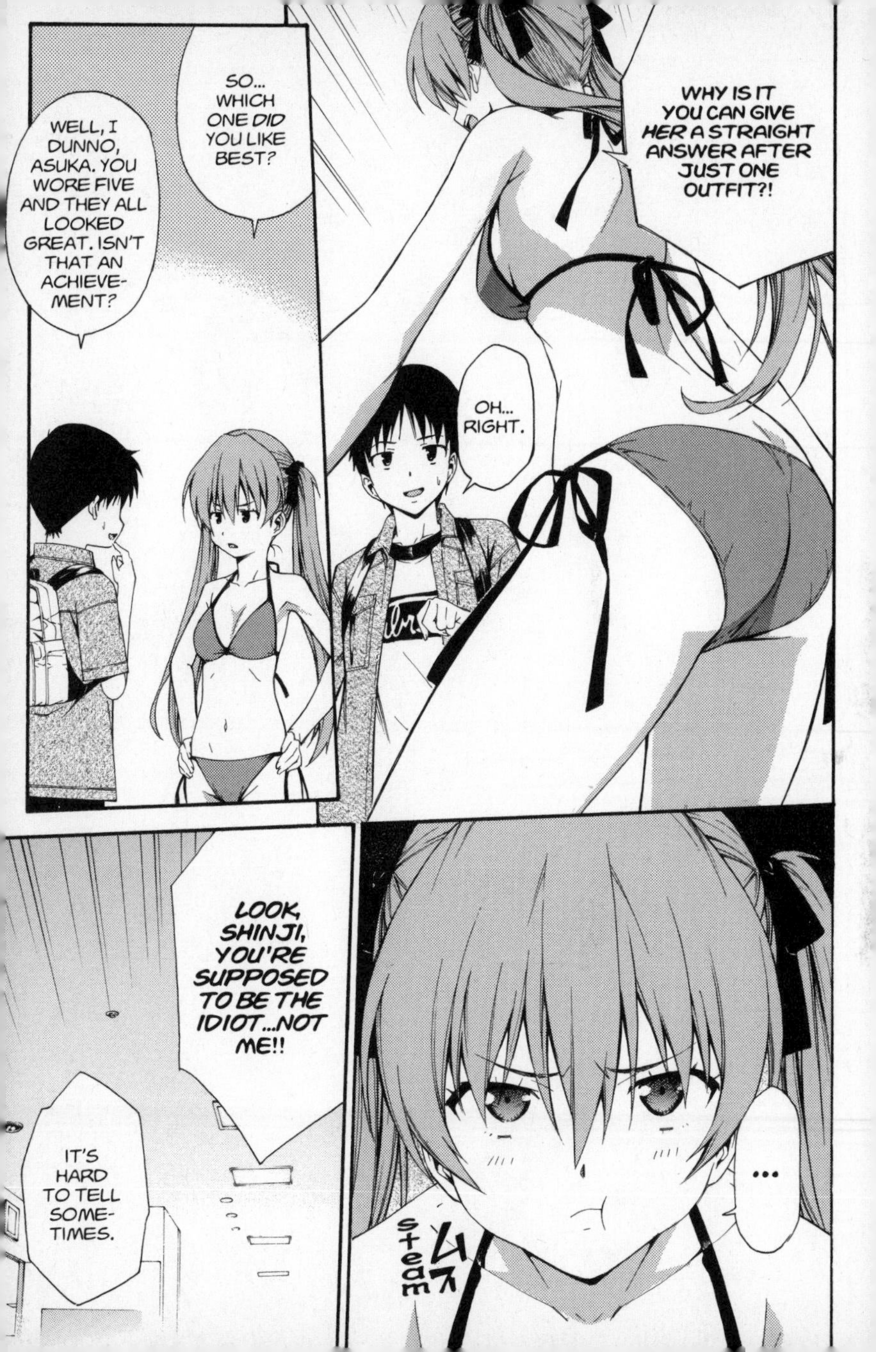
WHY IS IT YOU CAN GIVE *HER* A STRAIGHT ANSWER AFTER JUST ONE OUTFIT?!
OH... RIGHT.
SO... WHICH ONE *DID* YOU LIKE BEST?
WELL, I DUNNO, ASUKA. YOU WORE FIVE AND THEY ALL LOOKED GREAT. ISN'T THAT AN ACHIEVE-MENT?
...
steam
LOOK, SHINJI, YOU'RE SUPPOSED TO BE THE IDIOT...NOT ME!!
IT'S HARD TO TELL SOME-TIMES.

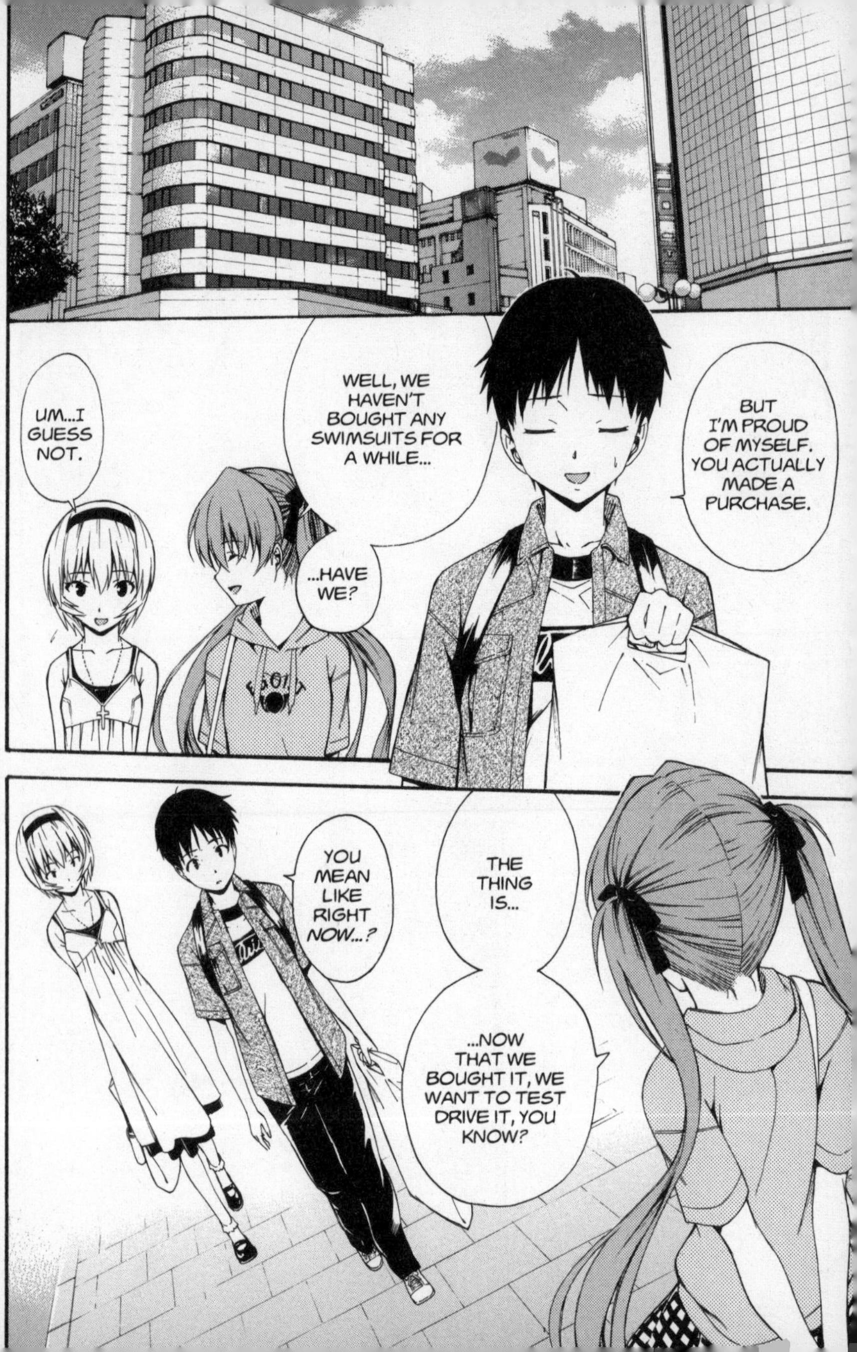
BUT I'M PROUD OF MYSELF. YOU ACTUALLY MADE A PURCHASE.
WELL, WE HAVEN'T BOUGHT ANY SWIMSUITS FOR A WHILE...
...HAVE WE?
UM...I GUESS NOT.
THE THING IS...
...NOW THAT WE BOUGHT IT, WE WANT TO TEST DRIVE IT, YOU KNOW?
YOU MEAN LIKE RIGHT *NOW...?*

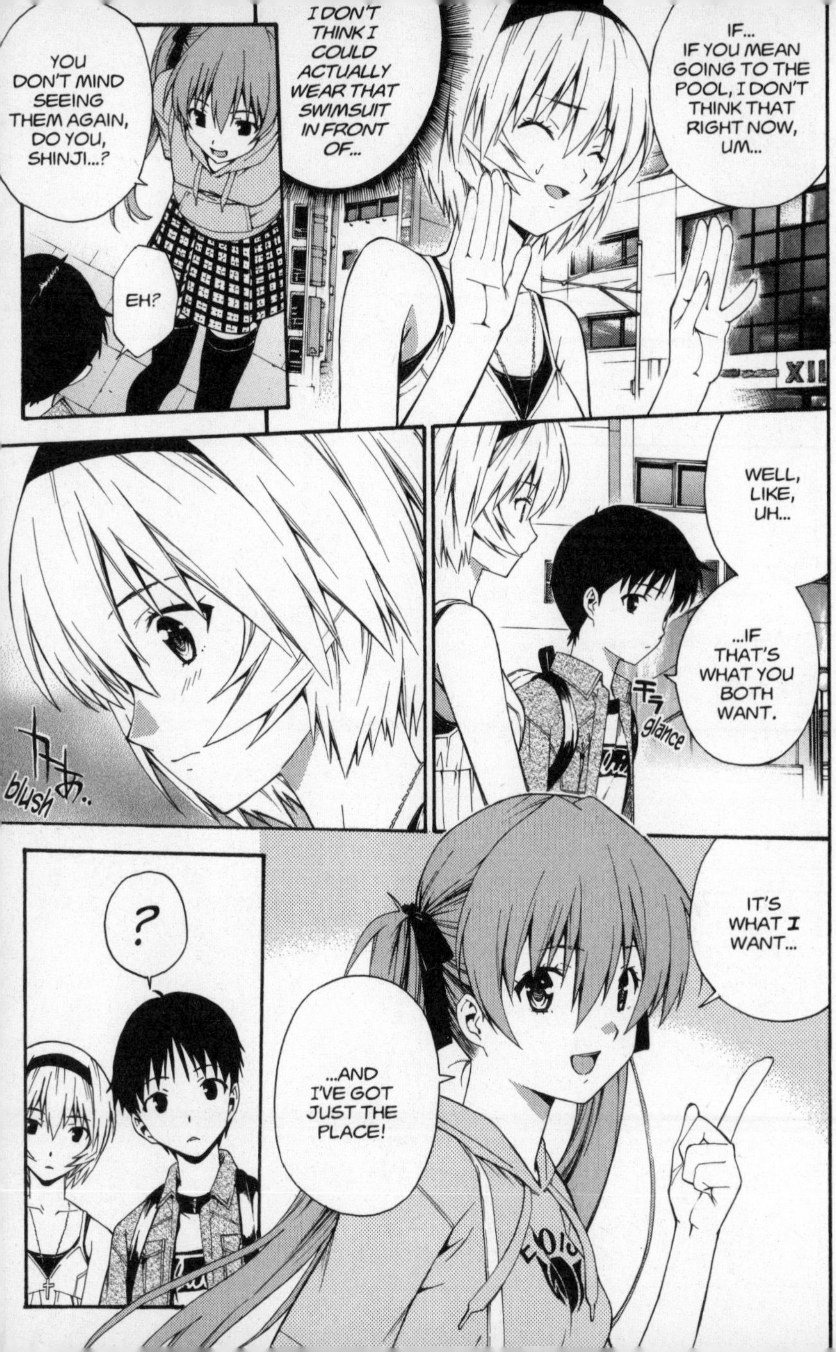
IF... IF YOU MEAN GOING TO THE POOL, I DON'T THINK THAT RIGHT NOW, UM...
I DON'T THINK I COULD ACTUALLY WEAR THAT SWIMSUIT IN FRONT OF...
YOU DON'T MIND SEEING THEM AGAIN, DO YOU, SHINJI...?
EH?
WELL, LIKE, UH...
...IF THAT'S WHAT YOU BOTH WANT.
glance
blush
IT'S WHAT I WANT...
...AND I'VE GOT JUST THE PLACE!
?

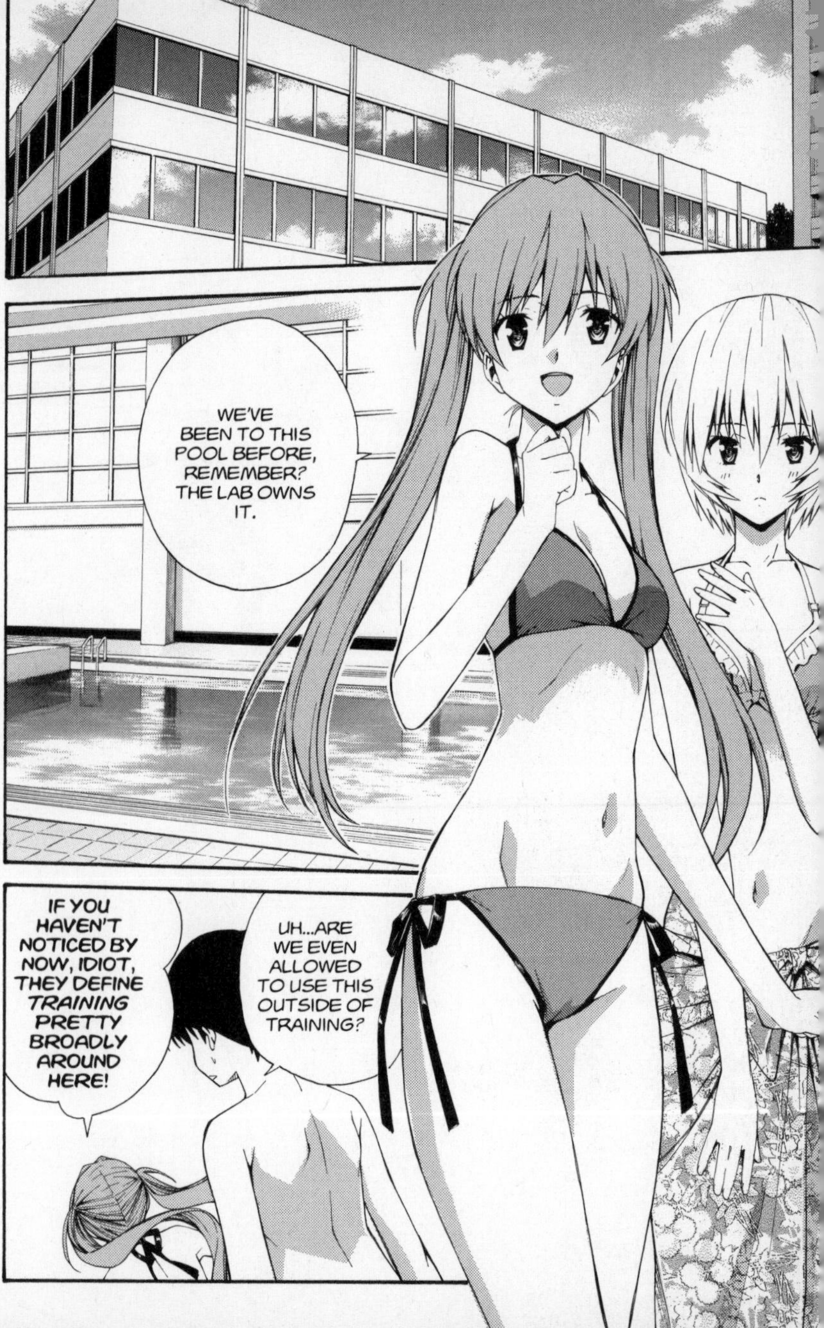
WE'VE BEEN TO THIS POOL BEFORE, REMEMBER? THE LAB OWNS IT.
UH...ARE WE EVEN ALLOWED TO USE THIS OUTSIDE OF TRAINING?
IF YOU HAVEN'T NOTICED BY NOW, IDIOT, THEY DEFINE *TRAINING* PRETTY BROADLY AROUND HERE!

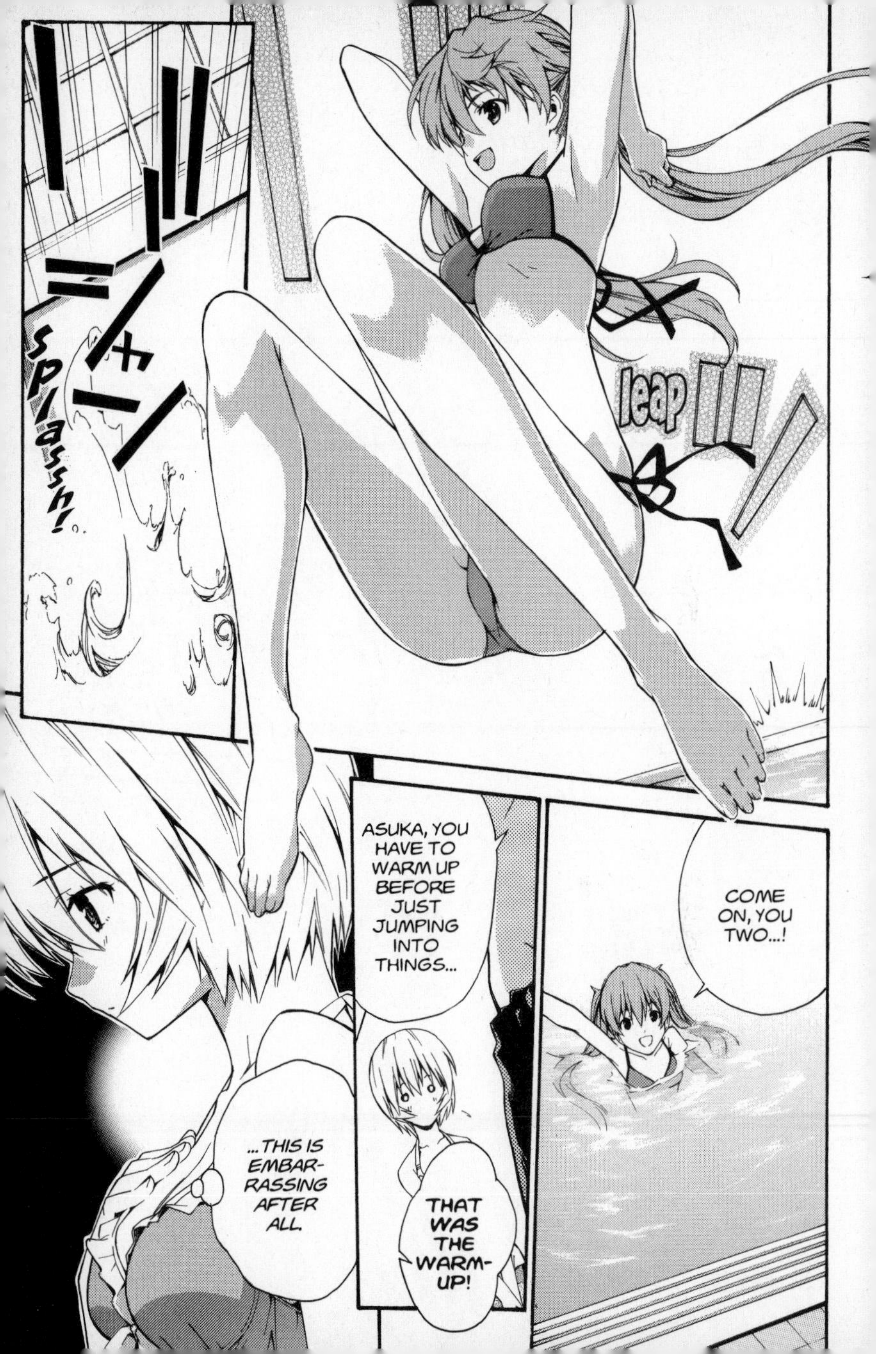
leap!!
splassh!
COME ON, YOU TWO...!
ASUKA, YOU HAVE TO WARM UP BEFORE JUST JUMPING INTO THINGS...
THAT WAS THE WARM-UP!
...THIS IS EMBARRASSING AFTER ALL.

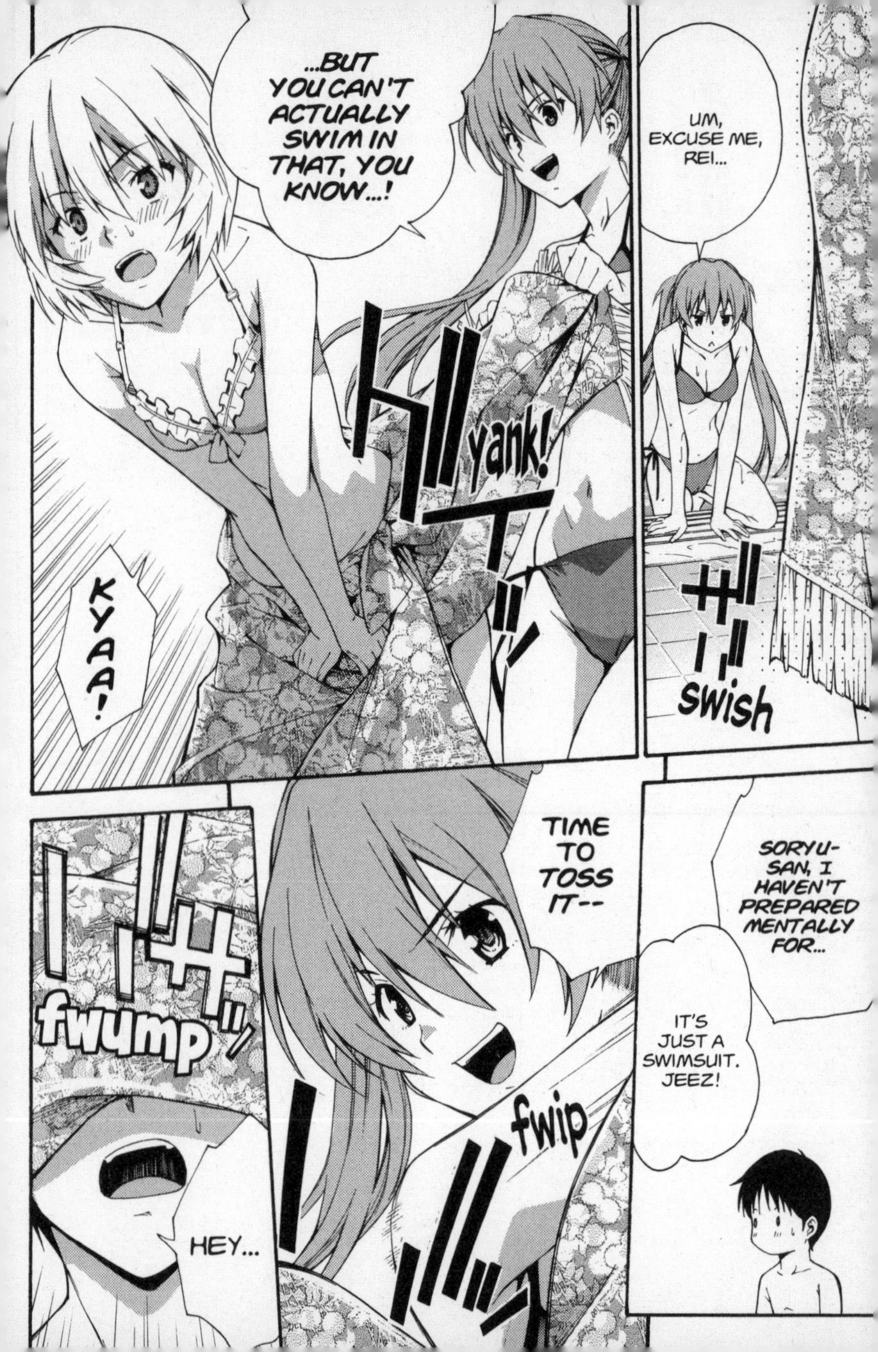
UM, EXCUSE ME, REI...
swish
...BUT YOU CAN'T ACTUALLY SWIM IN THAT, YOU KNOW...!
yank!
KYAA!
SORYU-SAN, I HAVEN'T PREPARED MENTALLY FOR...
IT'S JUST A SWIMSUIT. JEEZ!
TIME TO TOSS IT--
fwip
fwump
HEY...

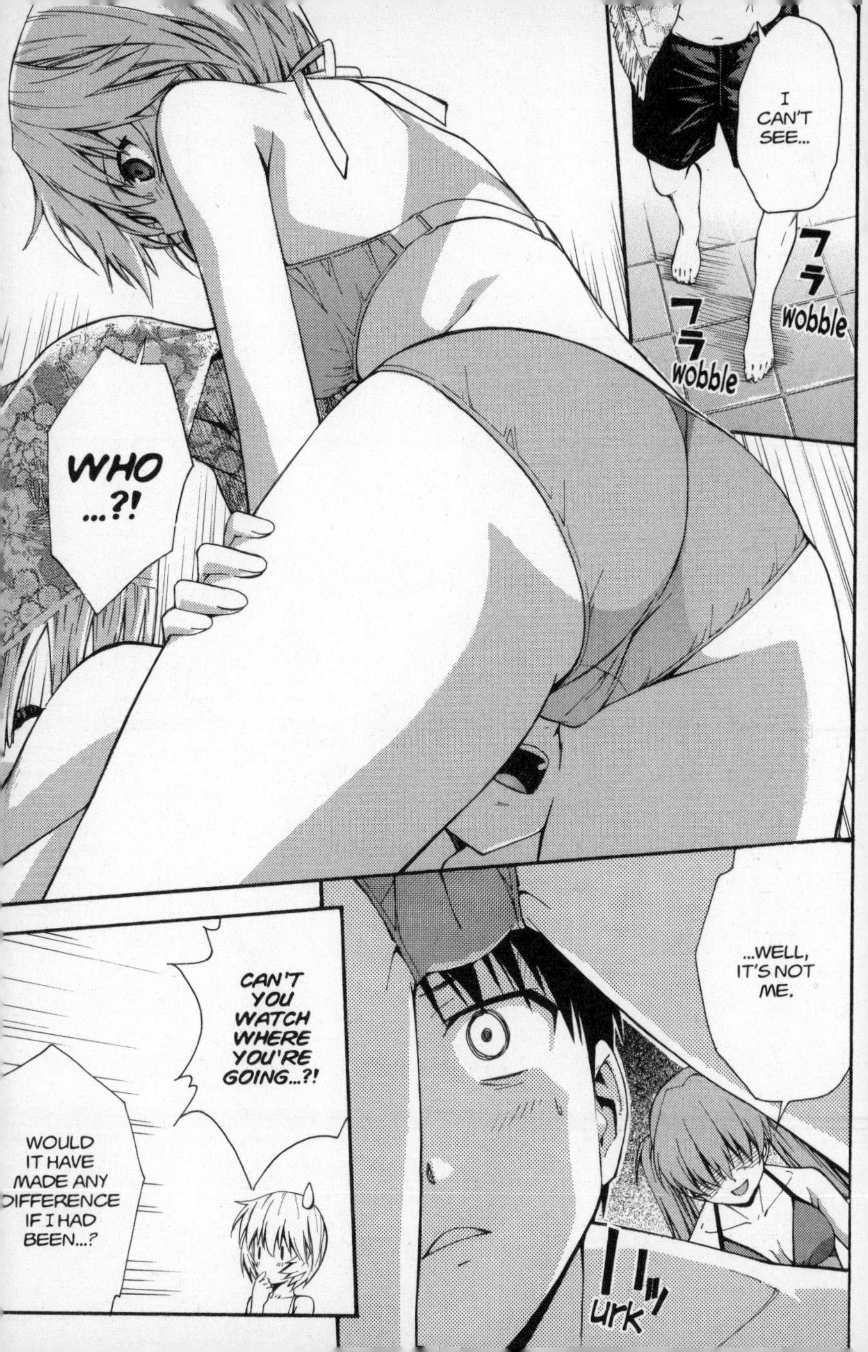
I CAN'T SEE...
フラ wobble
フラ wobble
WHO ...?!
...WELL, IT'S NOT ME.
urk
CAN'T YOU WATCH WHERE YOU'RE GOING...?!
WOULD IT HAVE MADE ANY DIFFERENCE IF I HAD BEEN...?

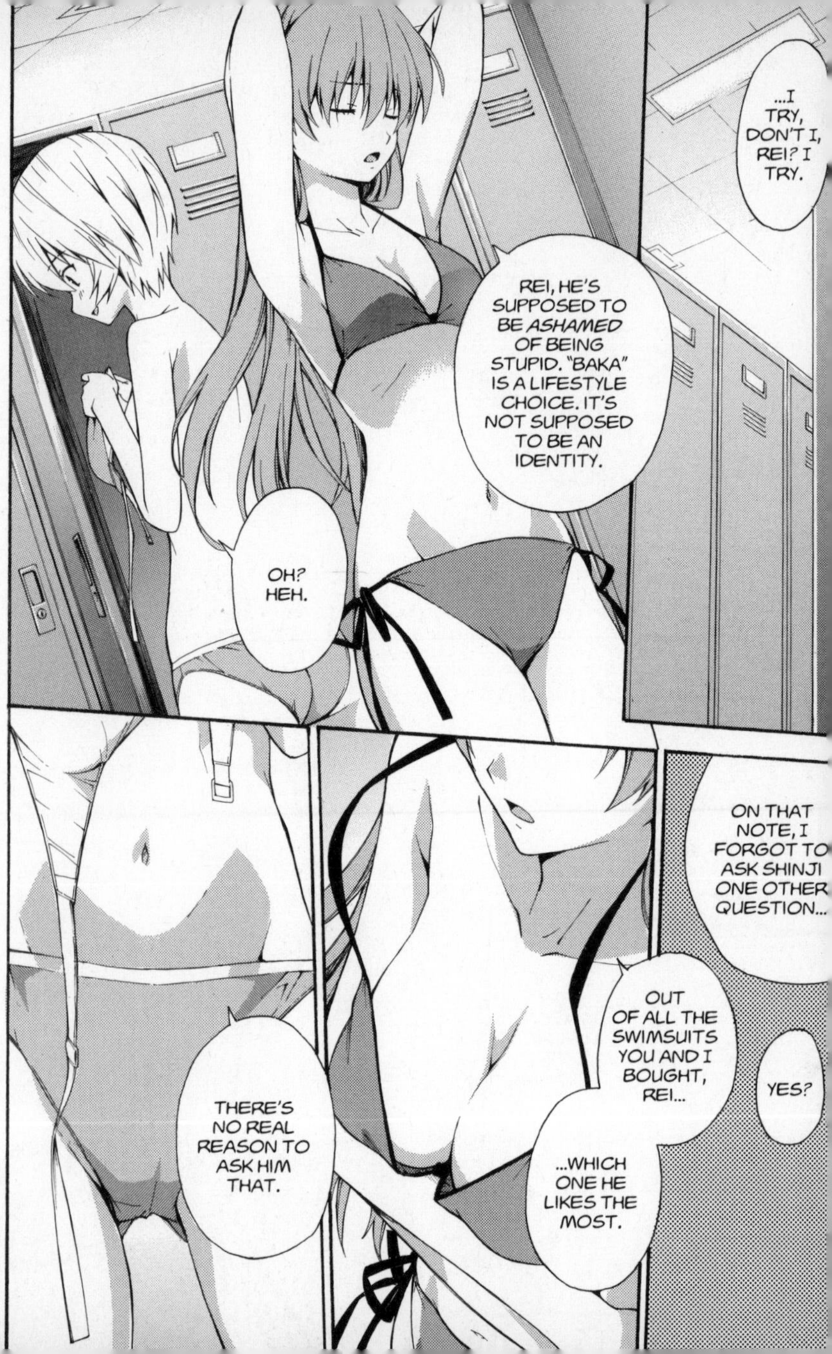
...I TRY, DON'T I, REI? I TRY.
REI, HE'S SUPPOSED TO BE ASHAMED OF BEING STUPID. "BAKA" IS A LIFESTYLE CHOICE. IT'S NOT SUPPOSED TO BE AN IDENTITY.
OH? HEH.
ON THAT NOTE, I FORGOT TO ASK SHINJI ONE OTHER QUESTION...
YES?
OUT OF ALL THE SWIMSUITS YOU AND I BOUGHT, REI...
...WHICH ONE HE LIKES THE MOST.
THERE'S NO REAL REASON TO ASK HIM THAT.

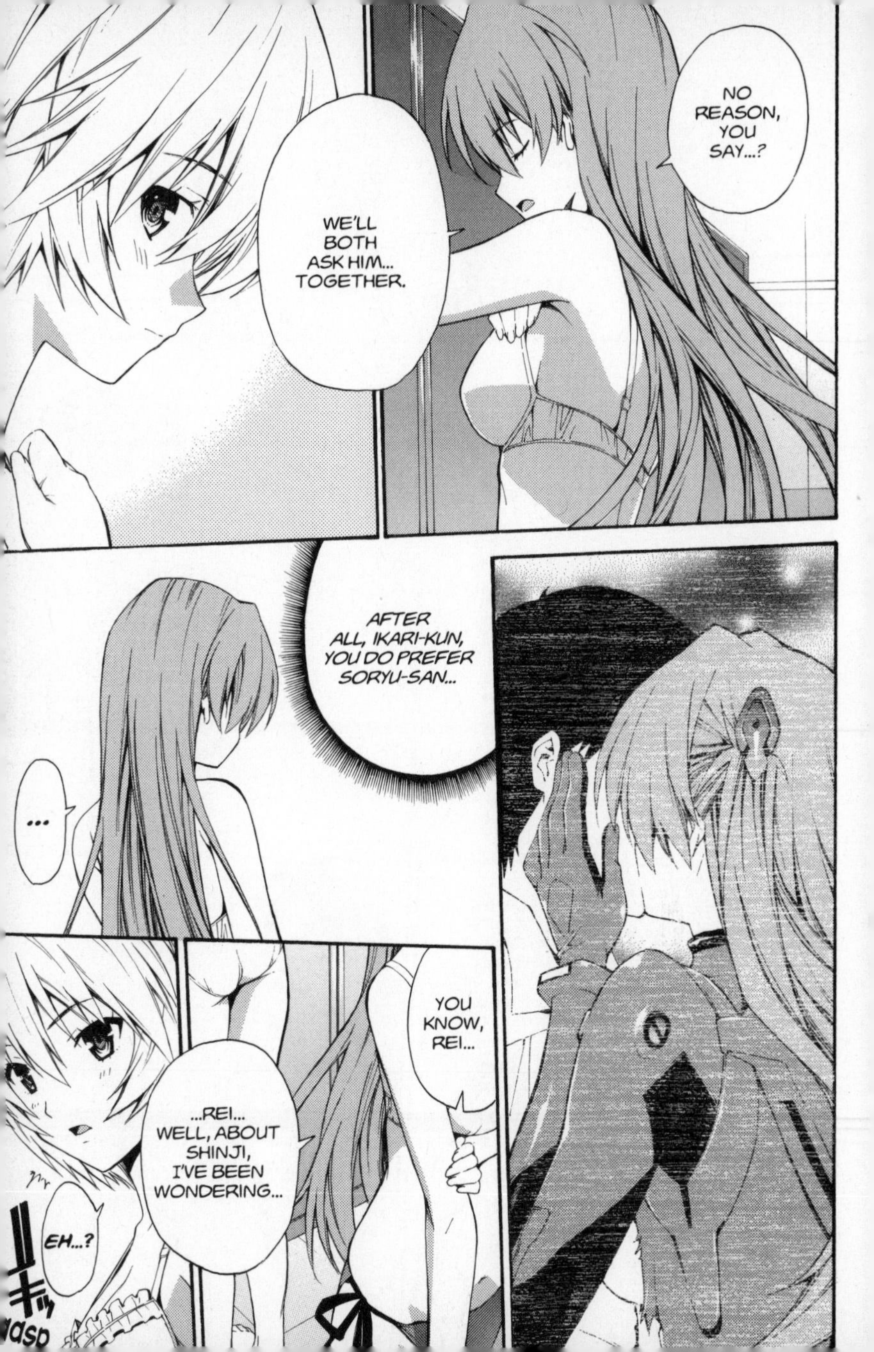
NO REASON, YOU SAY...?
WE'LL BOTH ASK HIM... TOGETHER.
AFTER ALL, IKARI-KUN, YOU DO PREFER SORYU-SAN...
...
YOU KNOW, REI...
...REI... WELL, ABOUT SHINJI, I'VE BEEN WONDERING...
EH...?
gasp

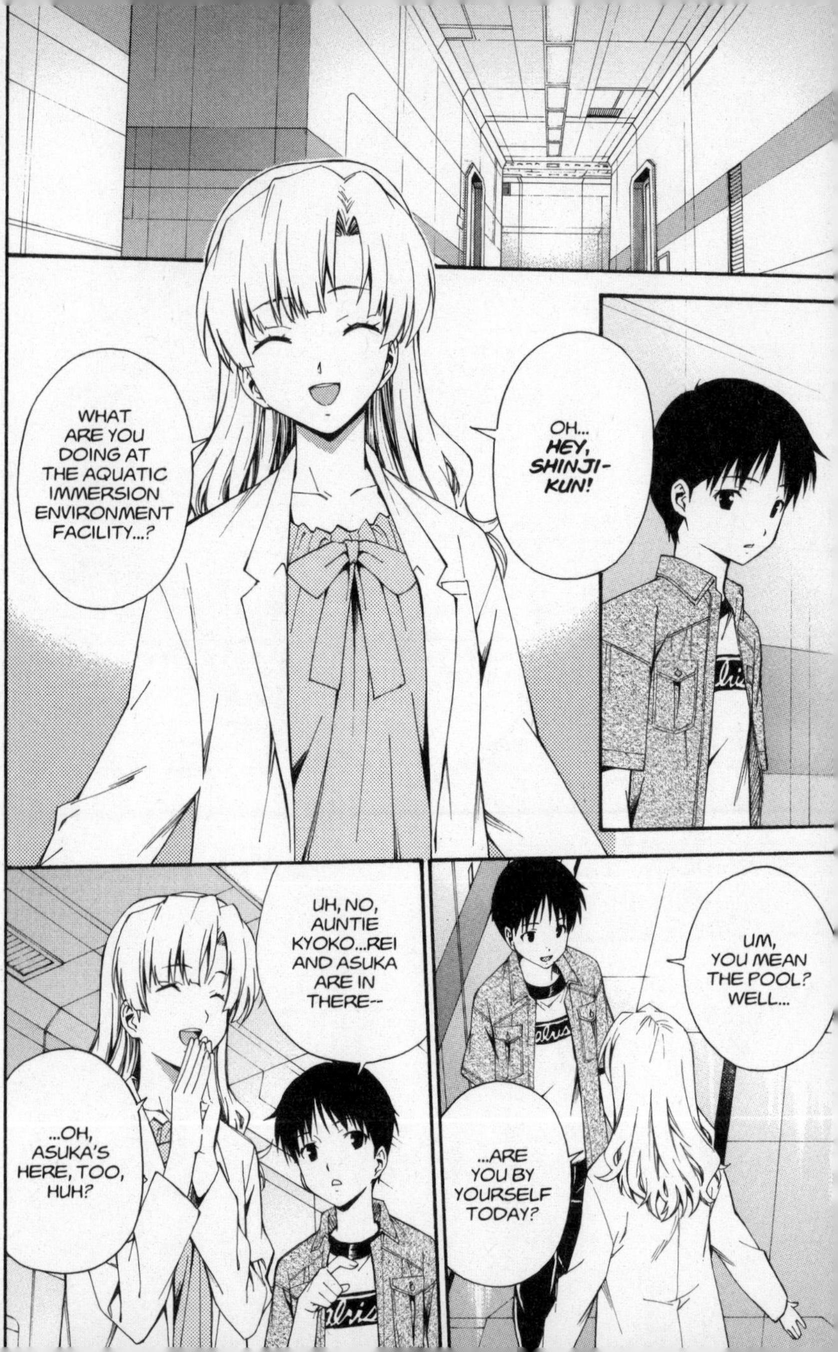
OH... **HEY, SHINJI-KUN!**
WHAT ARE YOU DOING AT THE AQUATIC IMMERSION ENVIRONMENT FACILITY...?
UM, YOU MEAN THE POOL? WELL...
...ARE YOU BY YOURSELF TODAY?
UH, NO, AUNTIE KYOKO...REI AND ASUKA ARE IN THERE--
...OH, ASUKA'S HERE, TOO, HUH?

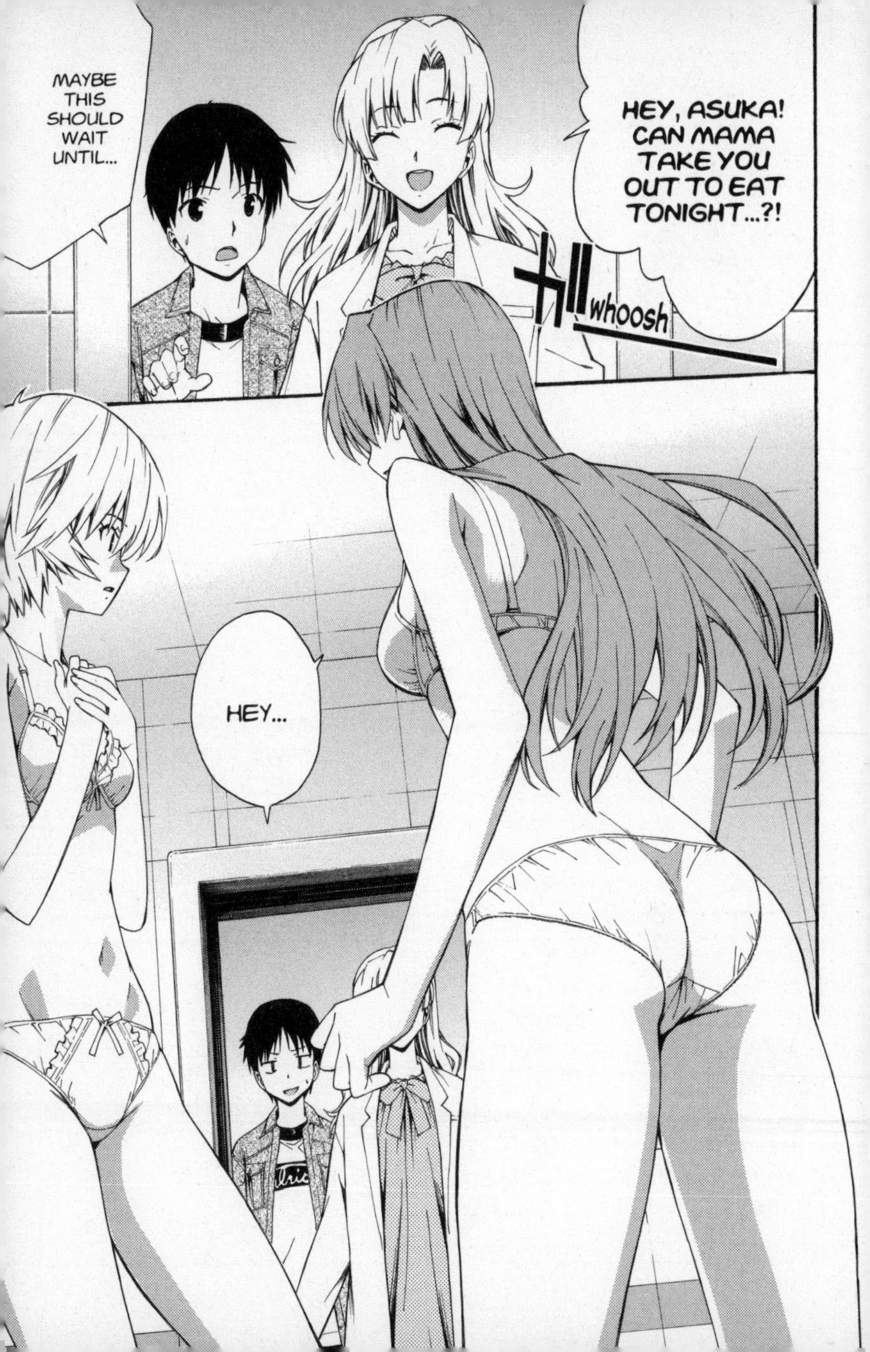
HEY, ASUKA! CAN MAMA TAKE YOU OUT TO EAT TONIGHT...?!
whoosh
MAYBE THIS SHOULD WAIT UNTIL...
HEY...

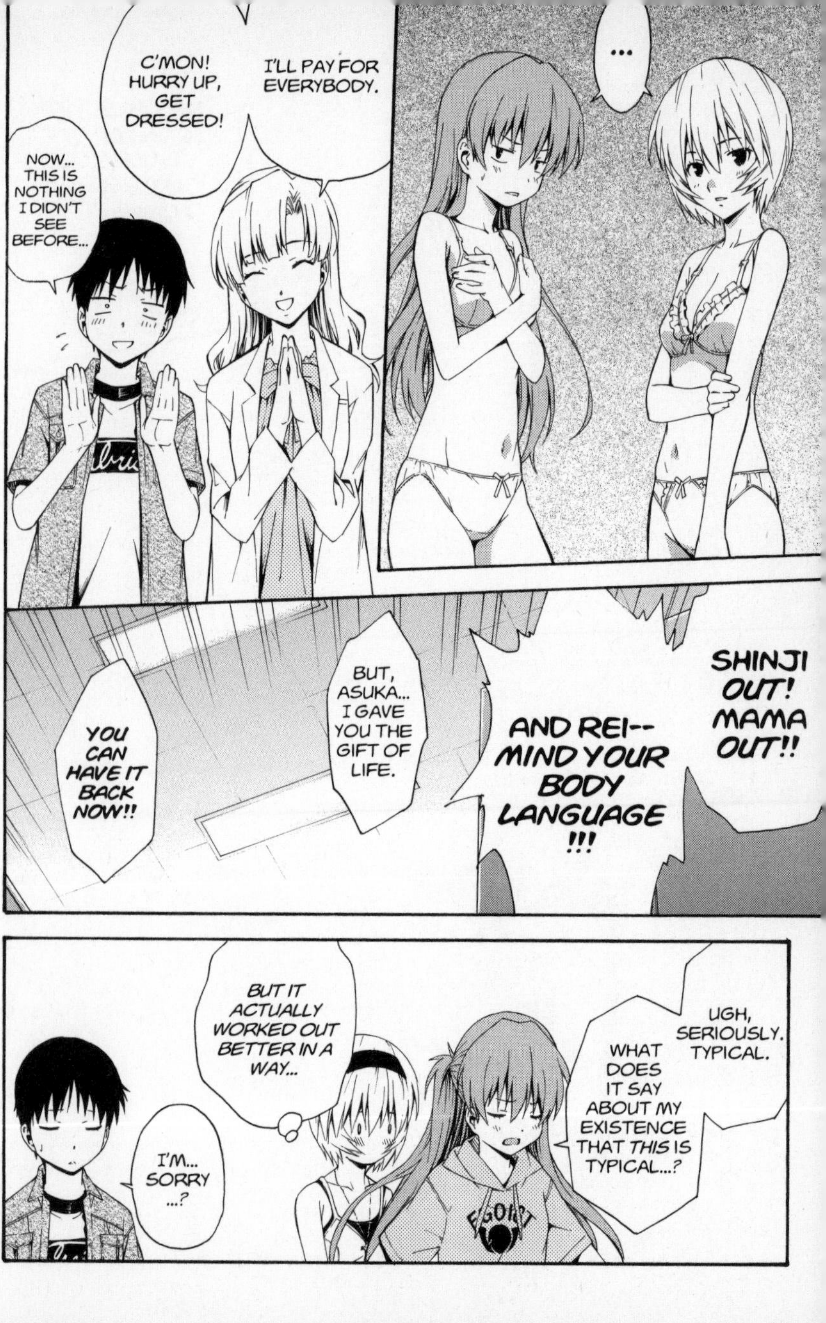
...
I'LL PAY FOR EVERYBODY.
C'MON! HURRY UP, GET DRESSED!
NOW... THIS IS NOTHING I DIDN'T SEE BEFORE...
SHINJI OUT! MAMA OUT!!
AND REI-- MIND YOUR BODY LANGUAGE!!!
BUT, ASUKA... I GAVE YOU THE GIFT OF LIFE.
YOU CAN HAVE IT BACK NOW!!
UGH, SERIOUSLY. TYPICAL.
WHAT DOES IT SAY ABOUT MY EXISTENCE THAT THIS IS TYPICAL...?
BUT IT ACTUALLY WORKED OUT BETTER IN A WAY...
I'M... SORRY ...?

υ" stare

the shinji ikari raising project

NEON GENESIS
EVANGELION
THE SHINJI IKARI RAISING PROJECT

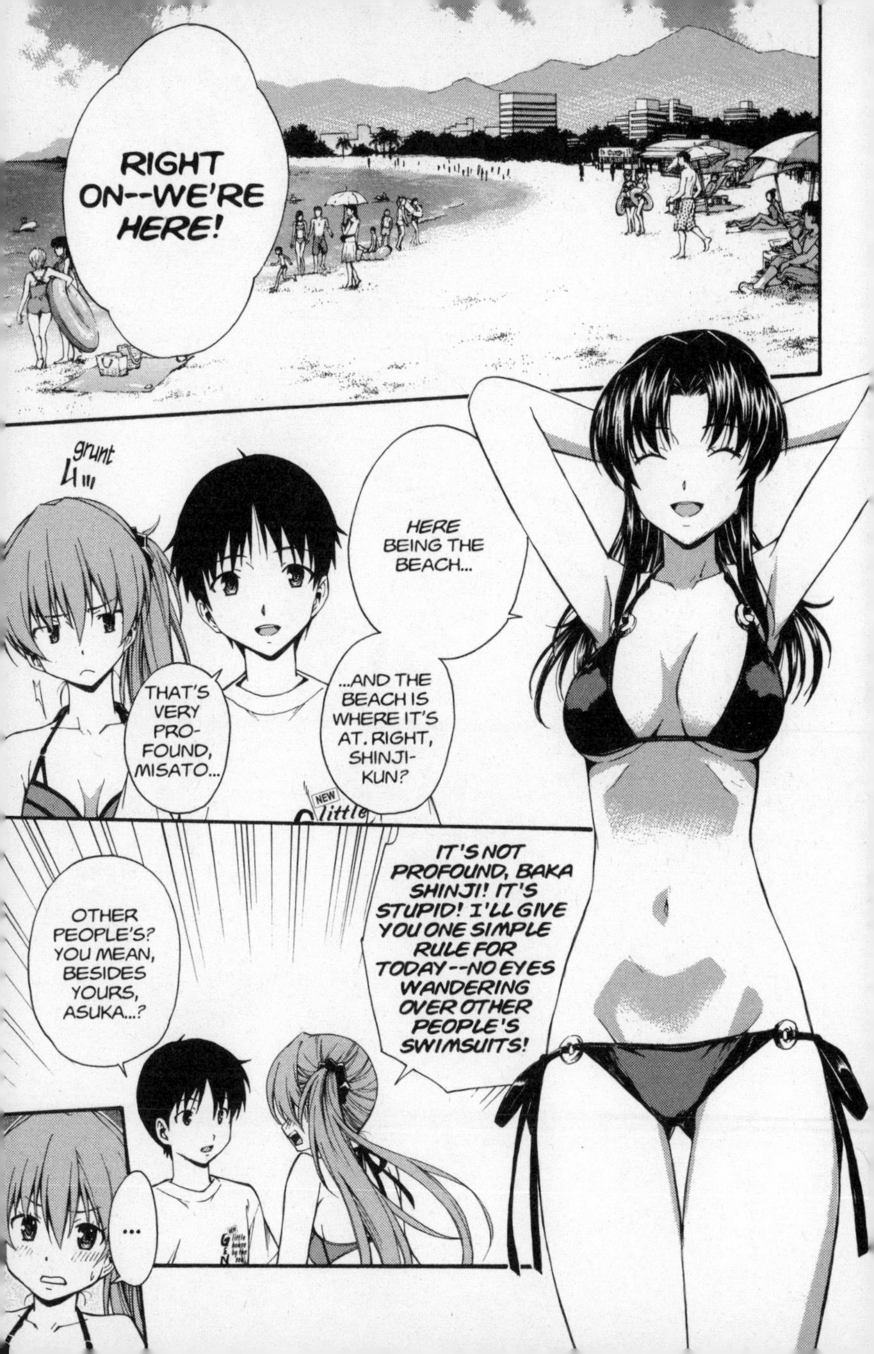
RIGHT ON--WE'RE HERE!
HERE BEING THE BEACH...
...AND THE BEACH IS WHERE IT'S AT. RIGHT, SHINJI-KUN?
grunt
THAT'S VERY PRO-FOUND, MISATO...
IT'S NOT PROFOUND, BAKA SHINJI! IT'S STUPID! I'LL GIVE YOU ONE SIMPLE RULE FOR TODAY--NO EYES WANDERING OVER OTHER PEOPLE'S SWIMSUITS!
OTHER PEOPLE'S? YOU MEAN, BESIDES YOURS, ASUKA...?
...

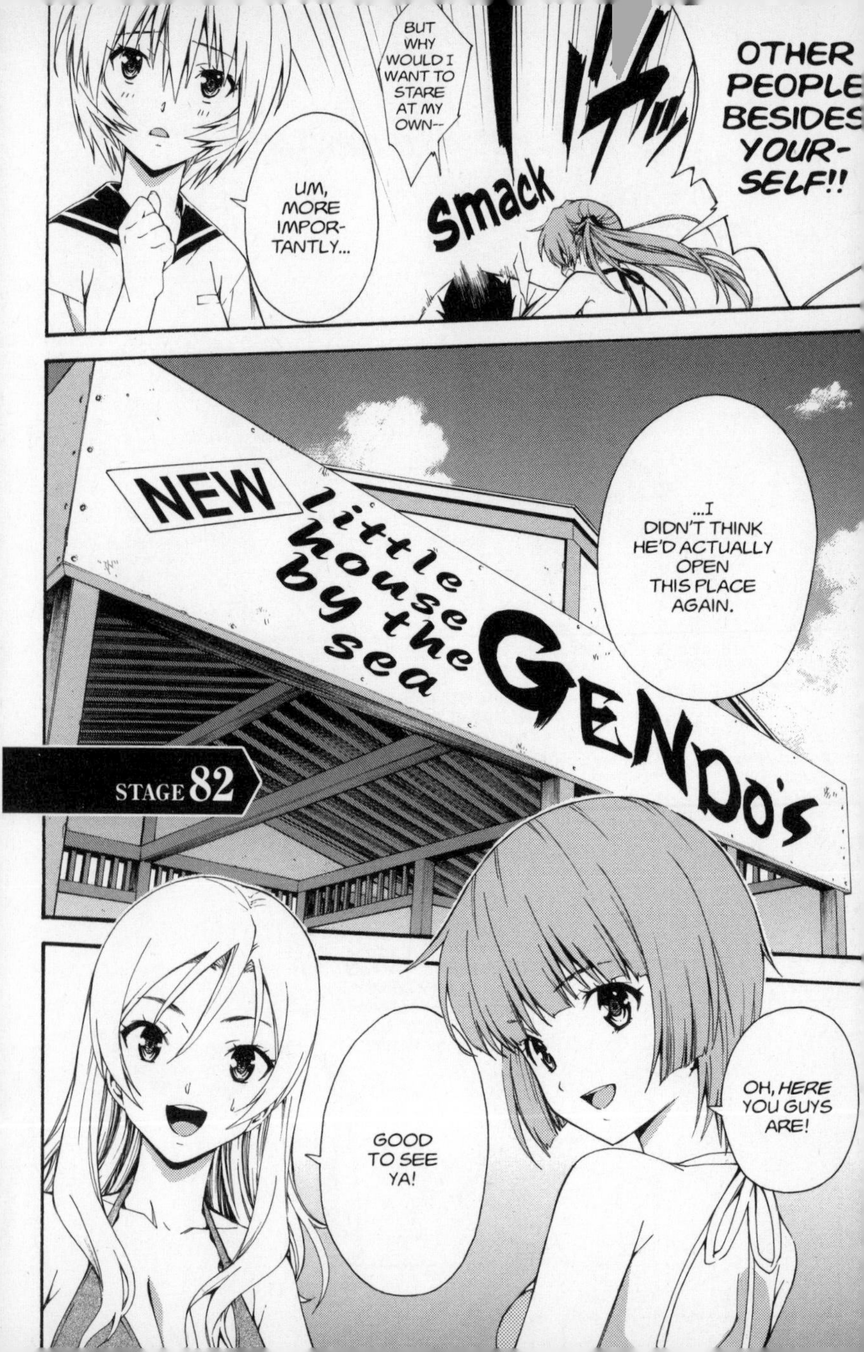
BUT WHY WOULD I WANT TO STARE AT MY OWN--
Smack
OTHER PEOPLE BESIDES YOURSELF!!
UM, MORE IMPORTANTLY...
NEW
GENDO'S little house by the sea
STAGE 82
...I DIDN'T THINK HE'D ACTUALLY OPEN THIS PLACE AGAIN.
OH, HERE YOU GUYS ARE!
GOOD TO SEE YA!

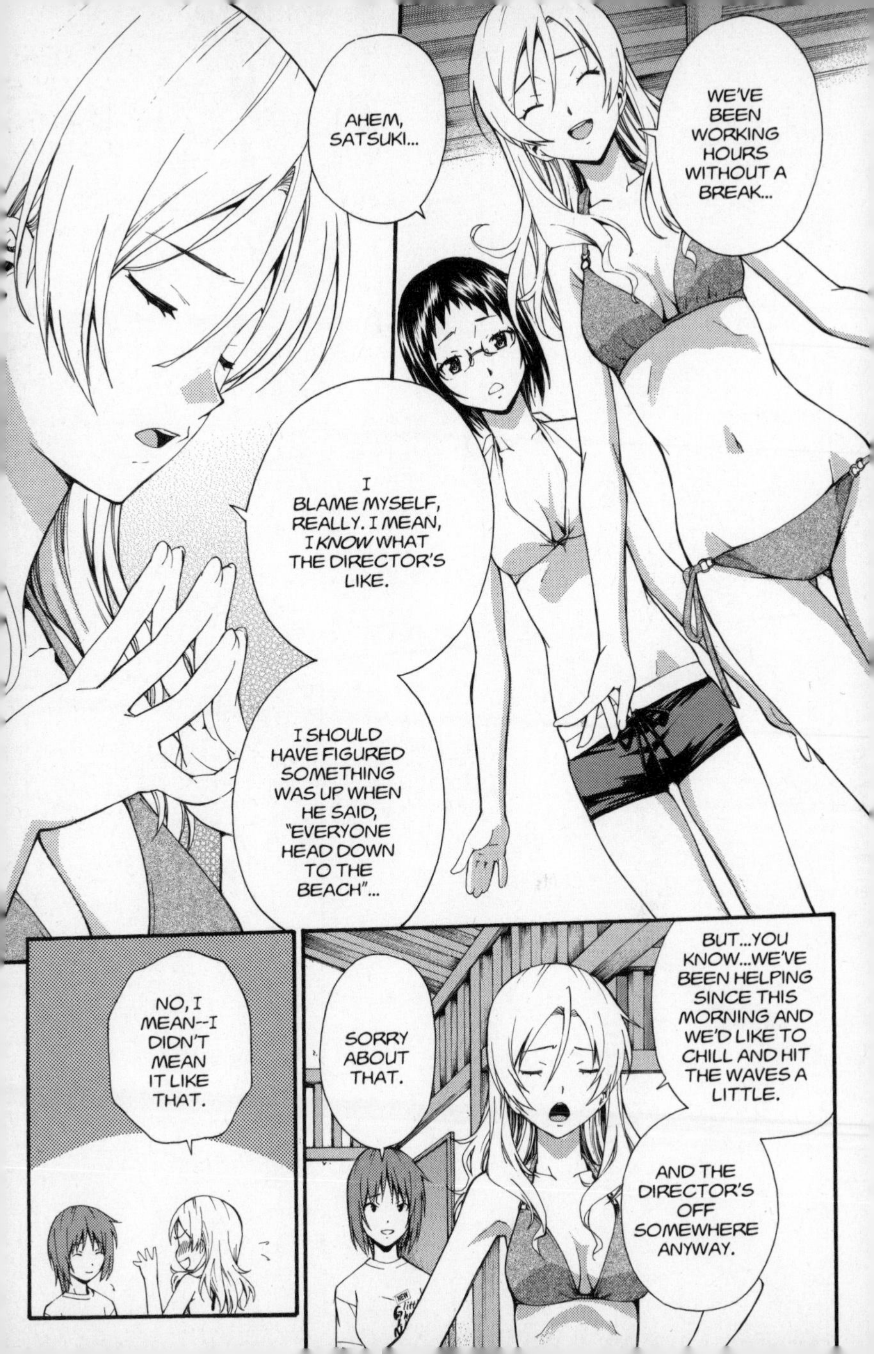
WE'VE BEEN WORKING HOURS WITHOUT A BREAK...
AHEM, SATSUKI...
I BLAME MYSELF, REALLY. I MEAN, I *KNOW* WHAT THE DIRECTOR'S LIKE.
I SHOULD HAVE FIGURED SOMETHING WAS UP WHEN HE SAID, "EVERYONE HEAD DOWN TO THE BEACH"...
BUT...YOU KNOW...WE'VE BEEN HELPING SINCE THIS MORNING AND WE'D LIKE TO CHILL AND HIT THE WAVES A LITTLE.
AND THE DIRECTOR'S OFF SOMEWHERE ANYWAY.
SORRY ABOUT THAT.
NO, I MEAN--I DIDN'T MEAN IT LIKE THAT.

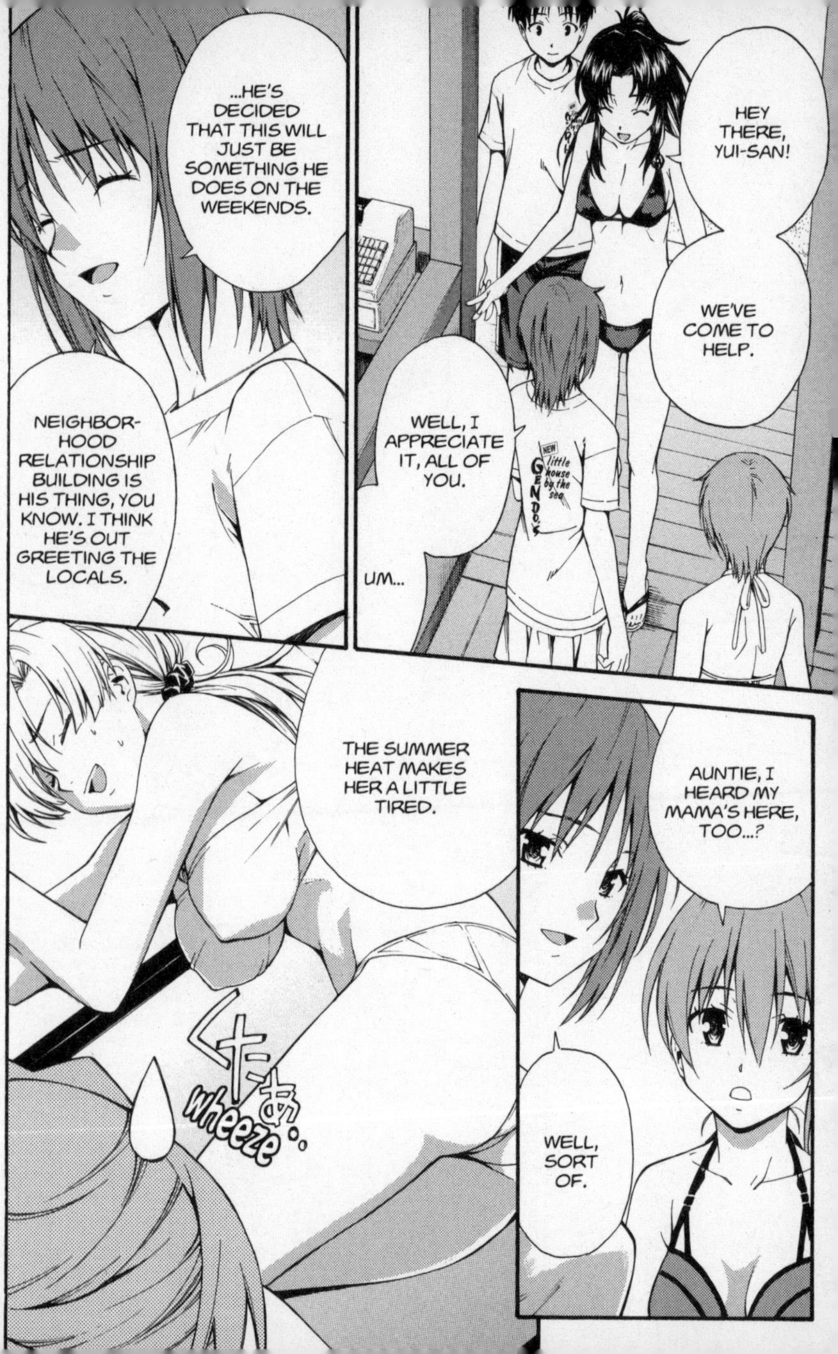
HEY THERE, YUI-SAN!
WE'VE COME TO HELP.
WELL, I APPRECIATE IT, ALL OF YOU.
UM...
...HE'S DECIDED THAT THIS WILL JUST BE SOMETHING HE DOES ON THE WEEKENDS.
NEIGHBOR-HOOD RELATIONSHIP BUILDING IS HIS THING, YOU KNOW. I THINK HE'S OUT GREETING THE LOCALS.
AUNTIE, I HEARD MY MAMA'S HERE, TOO...?
WELL, SORT OF.
THE SUMMER HEAT MAKES HER A LITTLE TIRED.
くたーあ。。
wheeze

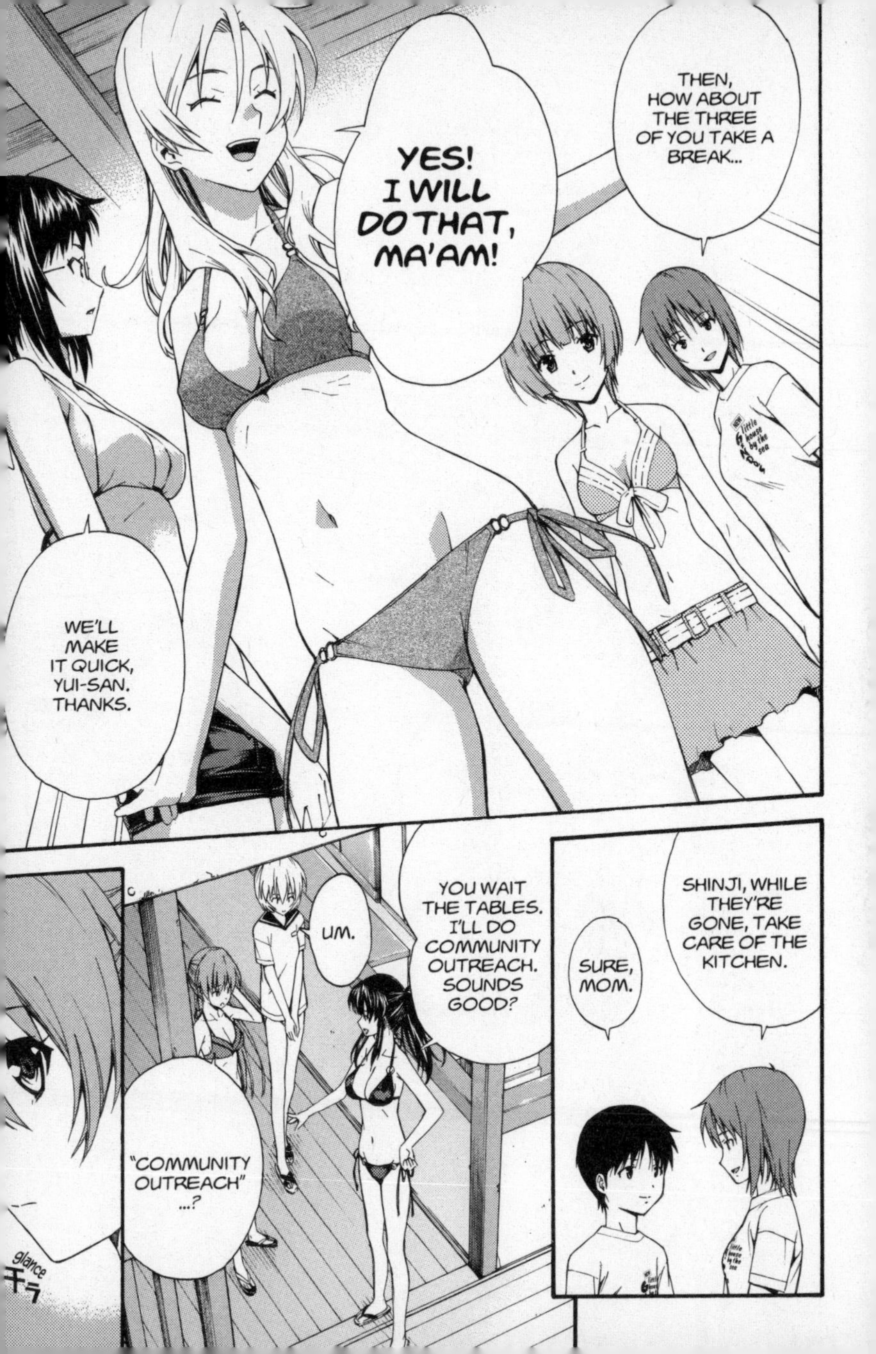
THEN, HOW ABOUT THE THREE OF YOU TAKE A BREAK...
YES! I WILL DO THAT, MA'AM!
WE'LL MAKE IT QUICK, YUI-SAN. THANKS.
SHINJI, WHILE THEY'RE GONE, TAKE CARE OF THE KITCHEN.
SURE, MOM.
YOU WAIT THE TABLES. I'LL DO COMMUNITY OUTREACH. SOUNDS GOOD?
UM.
"COMMUNITY OUTREACH" ...?
glance
チラ

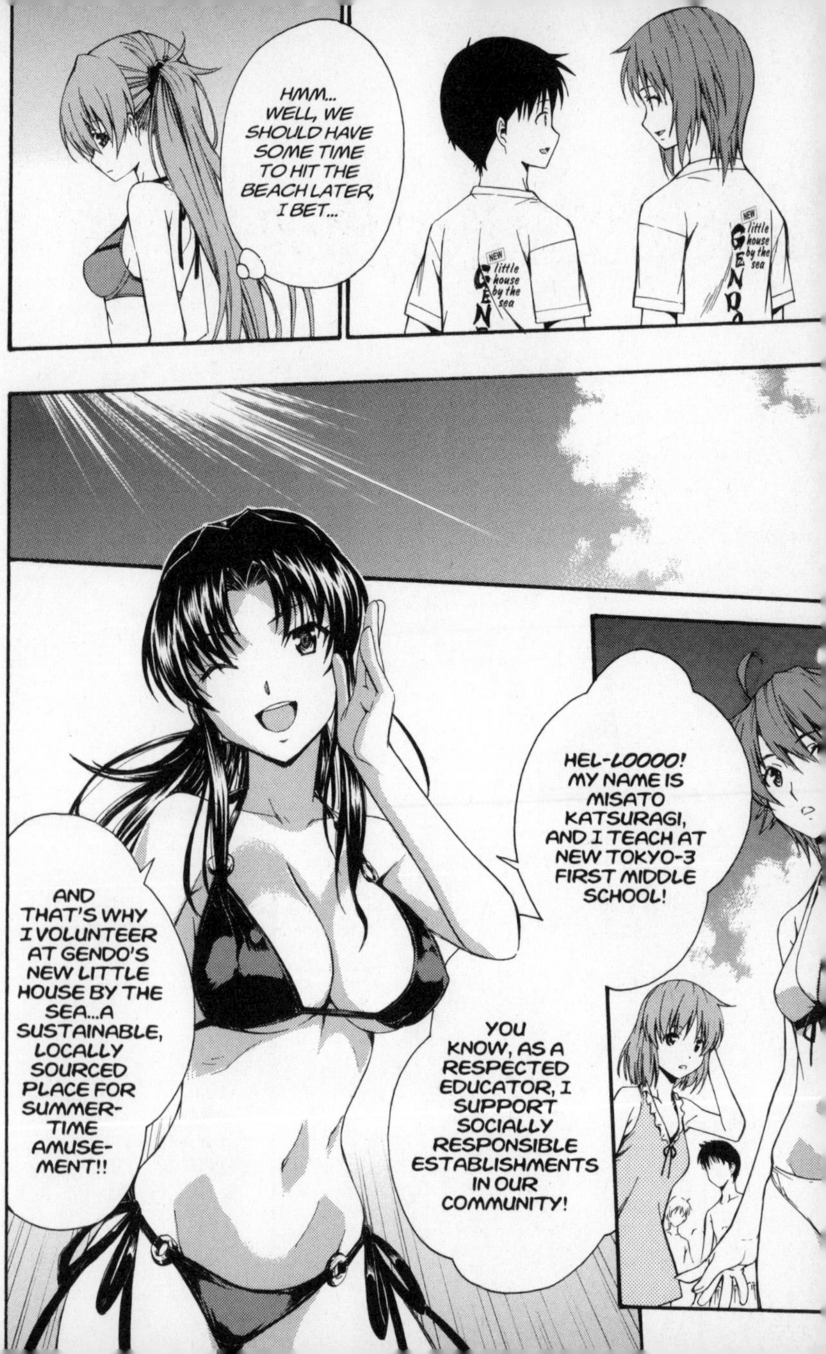
NEW
little house by the sea
HMM... WELL, WE SHOULD HAVE SOME TIME TO HIT THE BEACH LATER, I BET...
HEL-LOOOO! MY NAME IS MISATO KATSURAGI, AND I TEACH AT NEW TOKYO-3 FIRST MIDDLE SCHOOL!
YOU KNOW, AS A RESPECTED EDUCATOR, I SUPPORT SOCIALLY RESPONSIBLE ESTABLISHMENTS IN OUR COMMUNITY!
AND THAT'S WHY I VOLUNTEER AT GENDO'S NEW LITTLE HOUSE BY THE SEA...A SUSTAINABLE, LOCALLY SOURCED PLACE FOR SUMMER-TIME AMUSE-MENT!!

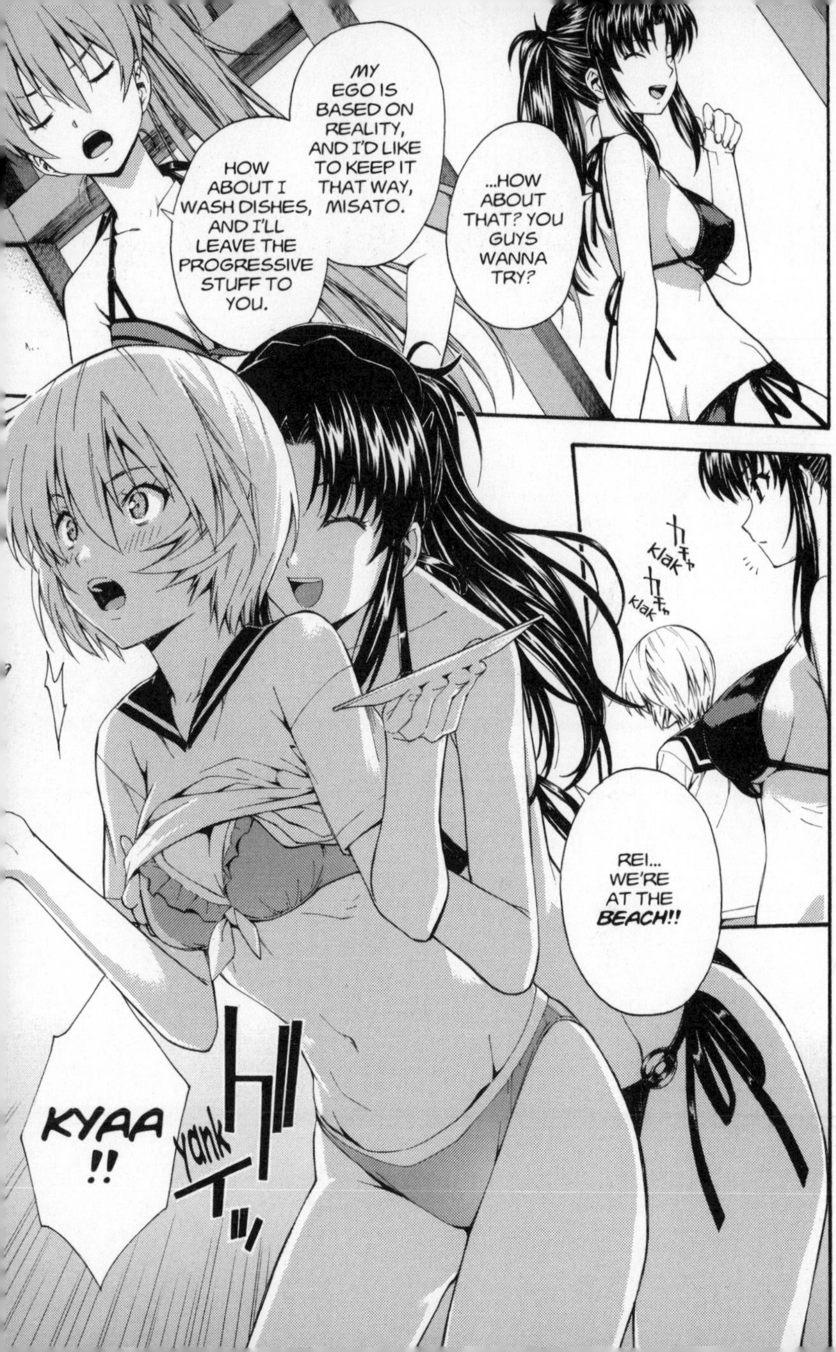
...HOW ABOUT THAT? YOU GUYS WANNA TRY?
MY EGO IS BASED ON REALITY, AND I'D LIKE TO KEEP IT THAT WAY, MISATO.
HOW ABOUT I WASH DISHES, AND I'LL LEAVE THE PROGRESSIVE STUFF TO YOU.
カチャ klak
カチャ klak
REI... WE'RE AT THE *BEACH*!!
yank
KYAA!!

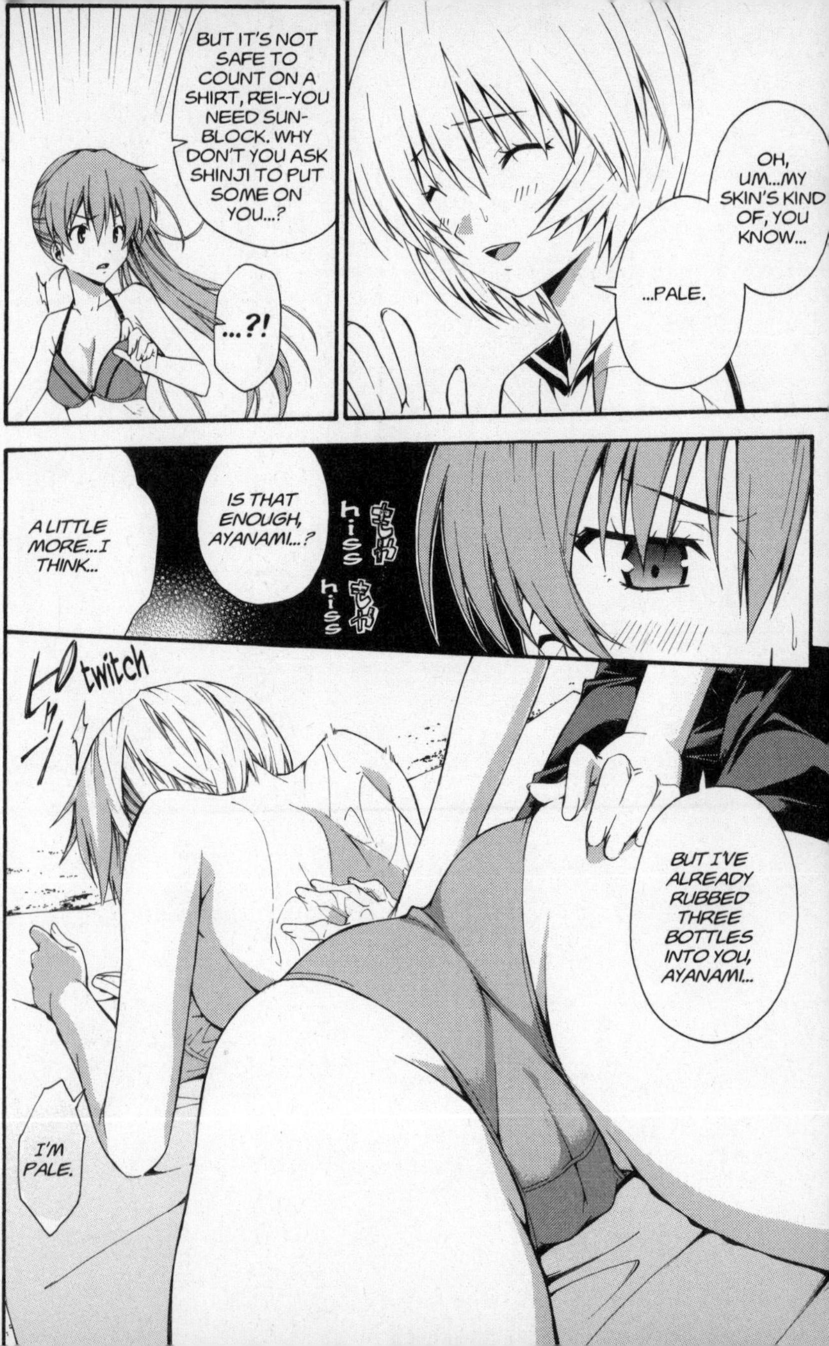
OH, UM...MY SKIN'S KIND OF, YOU KNOW...
...PALE.
BUT IT'S NOT SAFE TO COUNT ON A SHIRT, REI--YOU NEED SUN-BLOCK. WHY DON'T YOU ASK SHINJI TO PUT SOME ON YOU...?
...?!
hiss
hiss
IS THAT ENOUGH, AYANAMI...?
A LITTLE MORE...I THINK...
BUT I'VE ALREADY RUBBED THREE BOTTLES INTO YOU, AYANAMI...
twitch
I'M PALE.

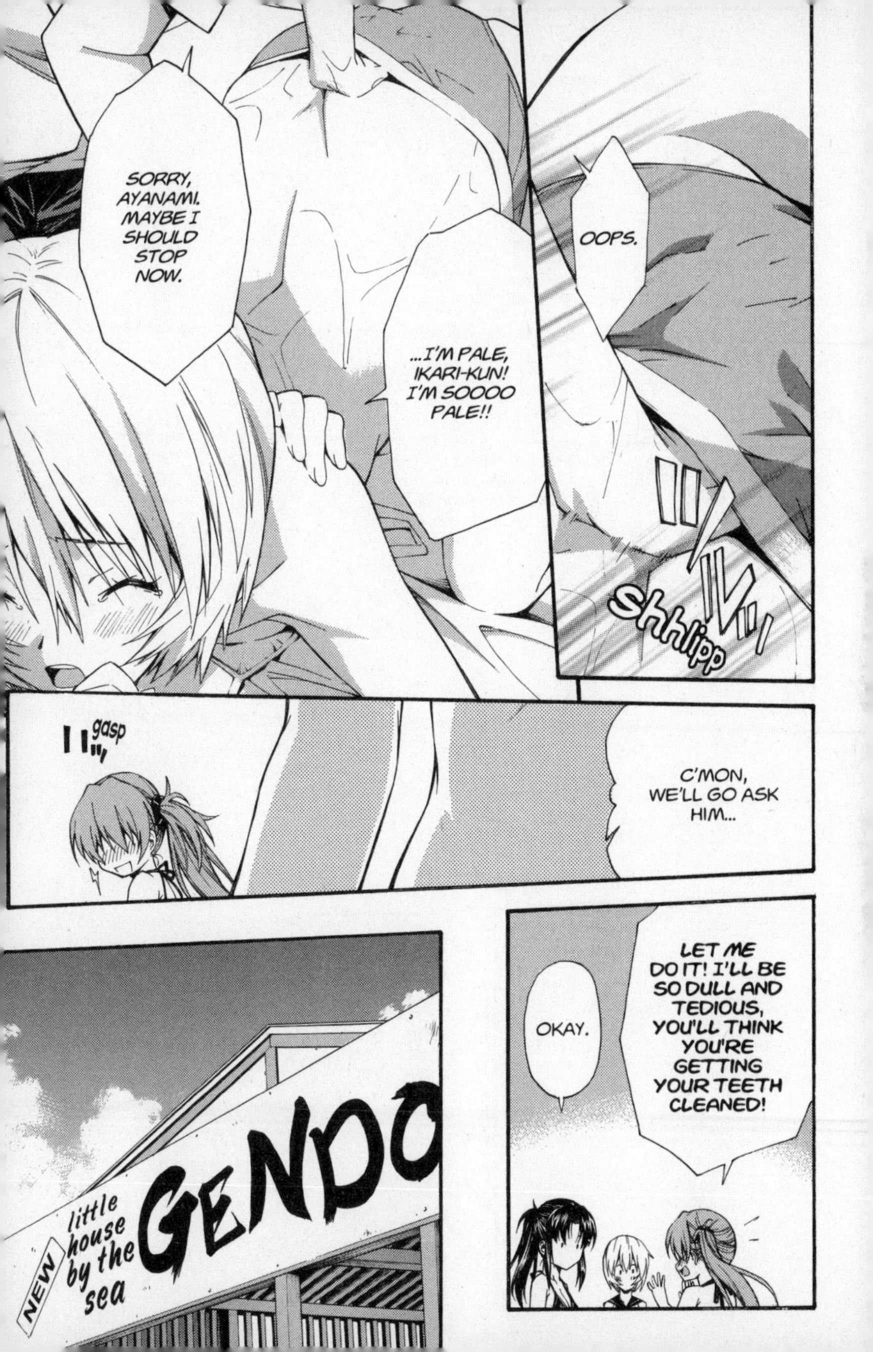
OOPS.
shhlipp
SORRY, AYANAMI. MAYBE I SHOULD STOP NOW.
...I'M PALE, IKARI-KUN! I'M SOOOO PALE!!
C'MON, WE'LL GO ASK HIM...
gasp
LET ME DO IT! I'LL BE SO DULL AND TEDIOUS, YOU'LL THINK YOU'RE GETTING YOUR TEETH CLEANED!
OKAY.
NEW
little house by the sea
GENDO

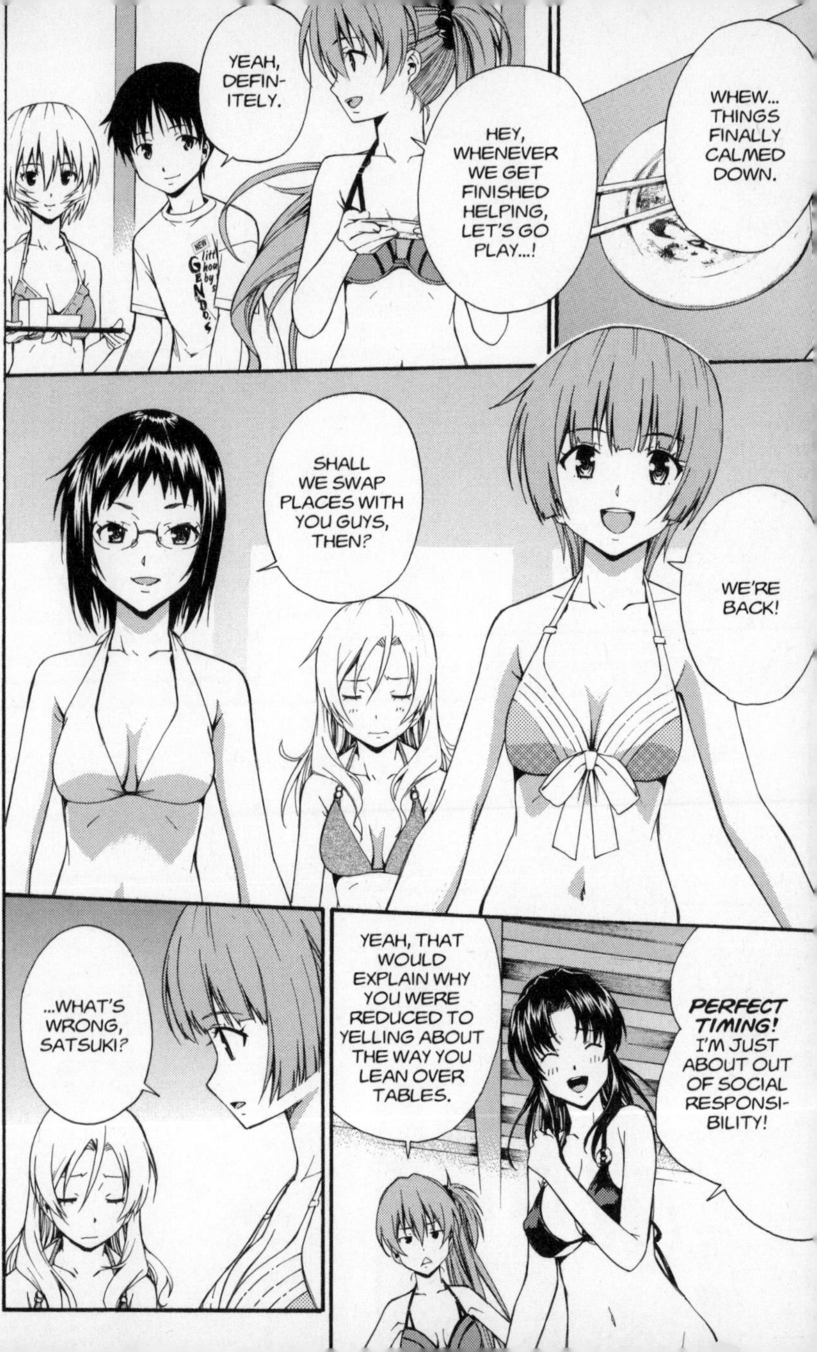
WHEW... THINGS FINALLY CALMED DOWN.
HEY, WHENEVER WE GET FINISHED HELPING, LET'S GO PLAY...!
YEAH, DEFINITELY.
WE'RE BACK!
SHALL WE SWAP PLACES WITH YOU GUYS, THEN?
PERFECT TIMING! I'M JUST ABOUT OUT OF SOCIAL RESPONSIBILITY!
YEAH, THAT WOULD EXPLAIN WHY YOU WERE REDUCED TO YELLING ABOUT THE WAY YOU LEAN OVER TABLES.
...WHAT'S WRONG, SATSUKI?

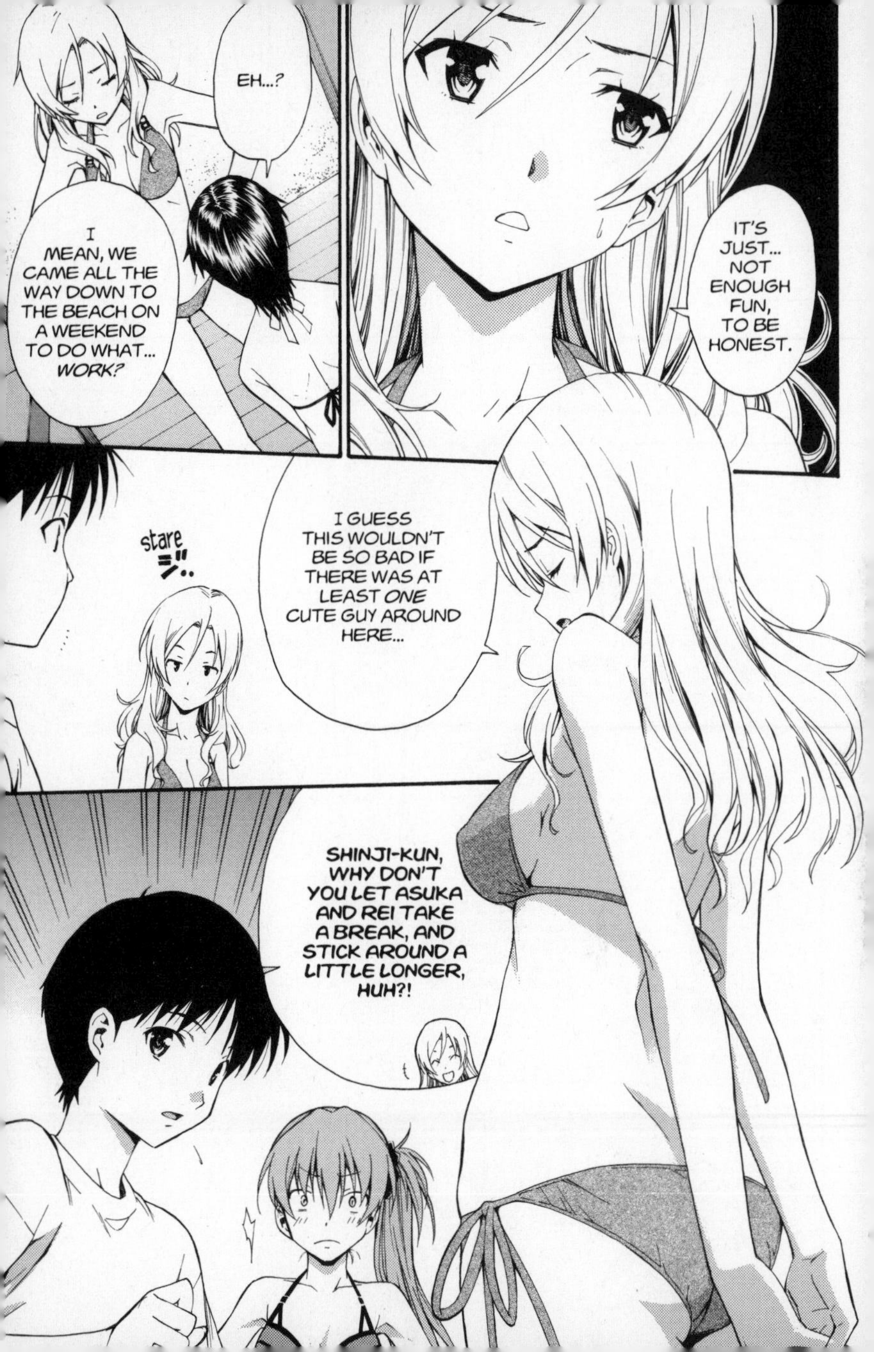
IT'S JUST... NOT ENOUGH FUN, TO BE HONEST.
EH...?
I MEAN, WE CAME ALL THE WAY DOWN TO THE BEACH ON A WEEKEND TO DO WHAT... *WORK?*
I GUESS THIS WOULDN'T BE SO BAD IF THERE WAS AT LEAST *ONE* CUTE GUY AROUND HERE...
stare
SHINJI-KUN, WHY DON'T YOU LET ASUKA AND REI TAKE A BREAK, AND STICK AROUND A LITTLE LONGER, HUH?!

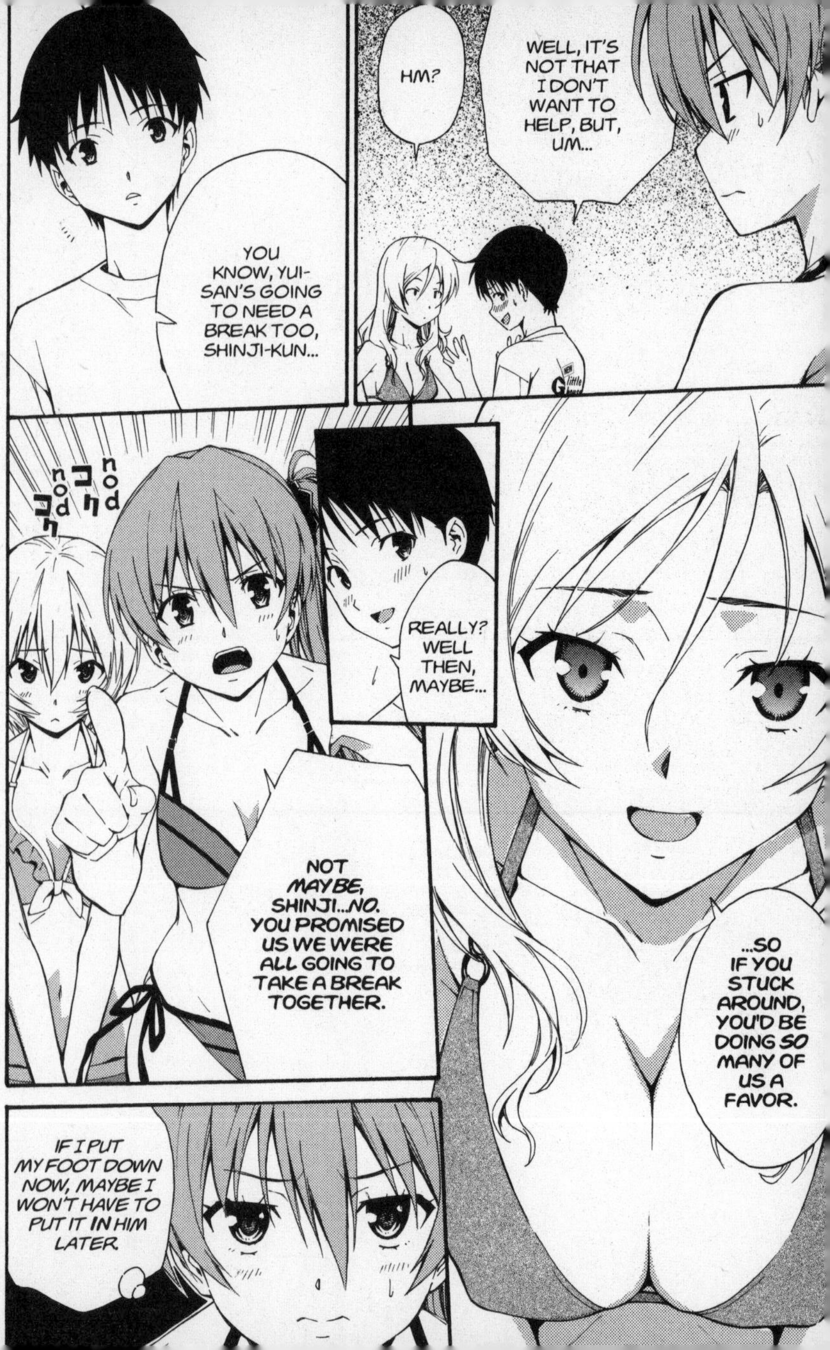

WELL, IT'S NOT THAT I DON'T WANT TO HELP, BUT, UM...
HM?
YOU KNOW, YUI-SAN'S GOING TO NEED A BREAK TOO, SHINJI-KUN...
...SO IF YOU STUCK AROUND, YOU'D BE DOING SO MANY OF US A FAVOR.
REALLY? WELL THEN, MAYBE...
nod nod
NOT *MAYBE*, SHINJI...*NO*. YOU PROMISED US WE WERE ALL GOING TO TAKE A BREAK TOGETHER.
IF I PUT MY FOOT DOWN NOW, MAYBE I WON'T HAVE TO PUT IT IN HIM LATER.

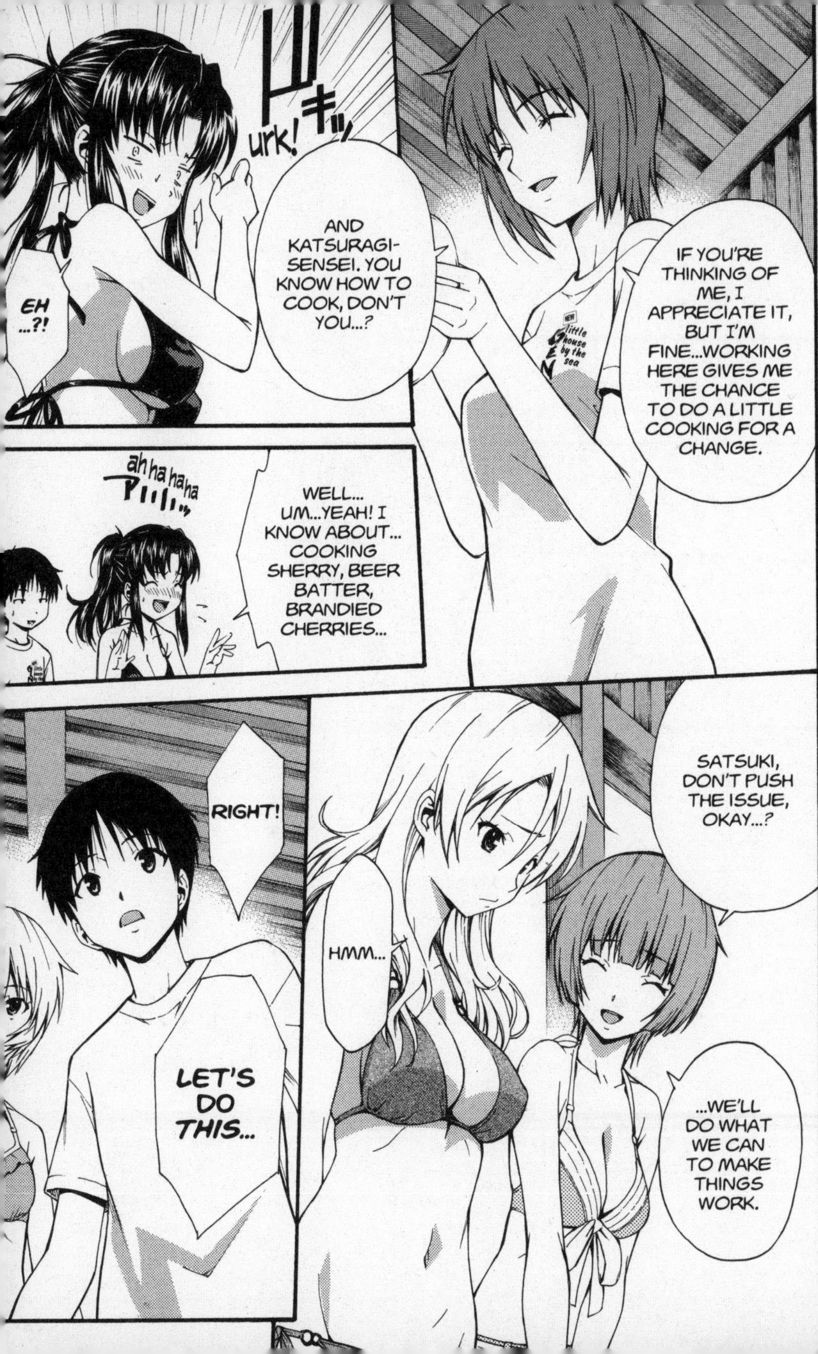
IF YOU'RE THINKING OF ME, I APPRECIATE IT, BUT I'M FINE...WORKING HERE GIVES ME THE CHANCE TO DO A LITTLE COOKING FOR A CHANGE.
NEW little house by the sea
AND KATSURAGI-SENSEI. YOU KNOW HOW TO COOK, DON'T YOU...?
ギッ
urk!
EH ...?!
WELL... UM...YEAH! I KNOW ABOUT... COOKING SHERRY, BEER BATTER, BRANDIED CHERRIES...
アハハハ
ah ha ha ha
SATSUKI, DON'T PUSH THE ISSUE, OKAY...?
HMM...
...WE'LL DO WHAT WE CAN TO MAKE THINGS WORK.
RIGHT!
LET'S DO THIS...

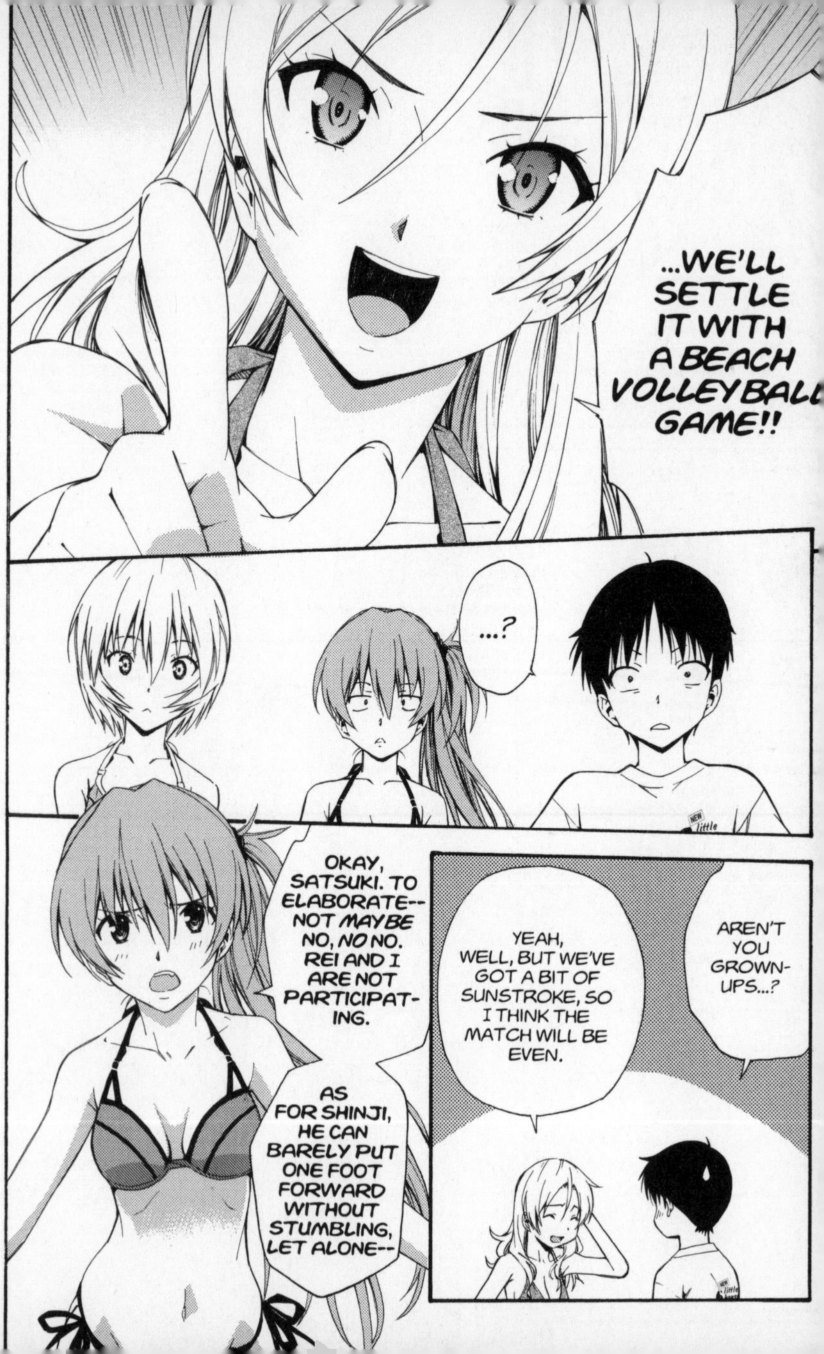
...WE'LL SETTLE IT WITH A *BEACH VOLLEYBALL GAME!!*
...?
AREN'T YOU GROWN-UPS...?
YEAH, WELL, BUT WE'VE GOT A BIT OF SUNSTROKE, SO I THINK THE MATCH WILL BE EVEN.
OKAY, SATSUKI. TO ELABORATE--NOT *MAYBE* NO, *NO* NO. REI AND I ARE NOT PARTICIPATING.
AS FOR SHINJI, HE CAN BARELY PUT ONE FOOT FORWARD WITHOUT STUMBLING, LET ALONE--

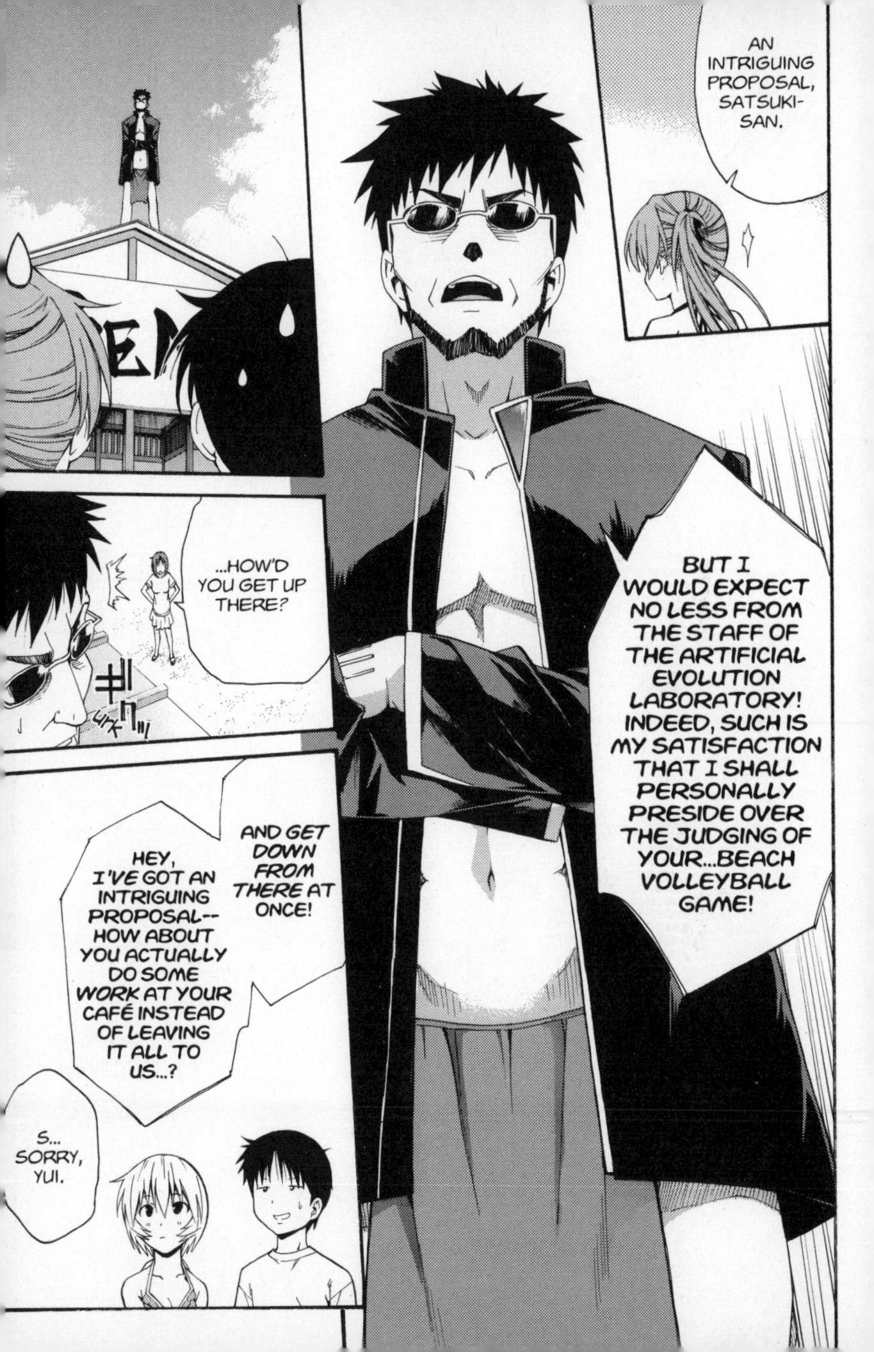
AN INTRIGUING PROPOSAL, SATSUKI-SAN.
BUT I WOULD EXPECT NO LESS FROM THE STAFF OF THE ARTIFICIAL EVOLUTION LABORATORY! INDEED, SUCH IS MY SATISFACTION THAT I SHALL PERSONALLY PRESIDE OVER THE JUDGING OF YOUR...BEACH VOLLEYBALL GAME!
...HOW'D YOU GET UP THERE?
urk
HEY, I'VE GOT AN INTRIGUING PROPOSAL-- HOW ABOUT YOU ACTUALLY DO SOME WORK AT YOUR CAFÉ INSTEAD OF LEAVING IT ALL TO US...?
AND GET DOWN FROM THERE AT ONCE!
S... SORRY, YUI.

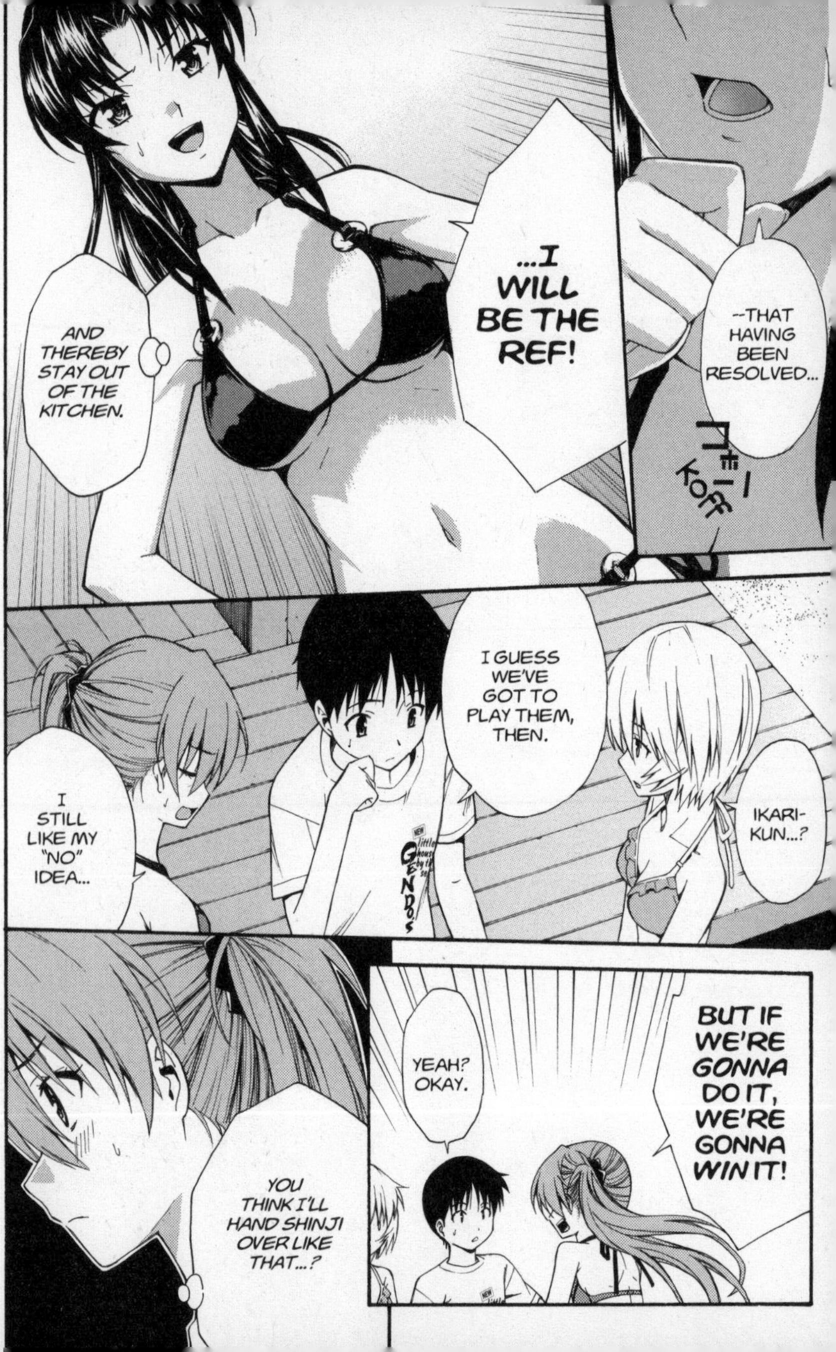
--THAT HAVING BEEN RESOLVED...
KOFF
...I WILL BE THE REF!
AND THEREBY STAY OUT OF THE KITCHEN.
IKARI-KUN...?
I GUESS WE'VE GOT TO PLAY THEM, THEN.
I STILL LIKE MY "NO" IDEA...
BUT IF WE'RE GONNA DO IT, WE'RE GONNA WIN IT!
YEAH? OKAY.
YOU THINK I'LL HAND SHINJI OVER LIKE THAT...?

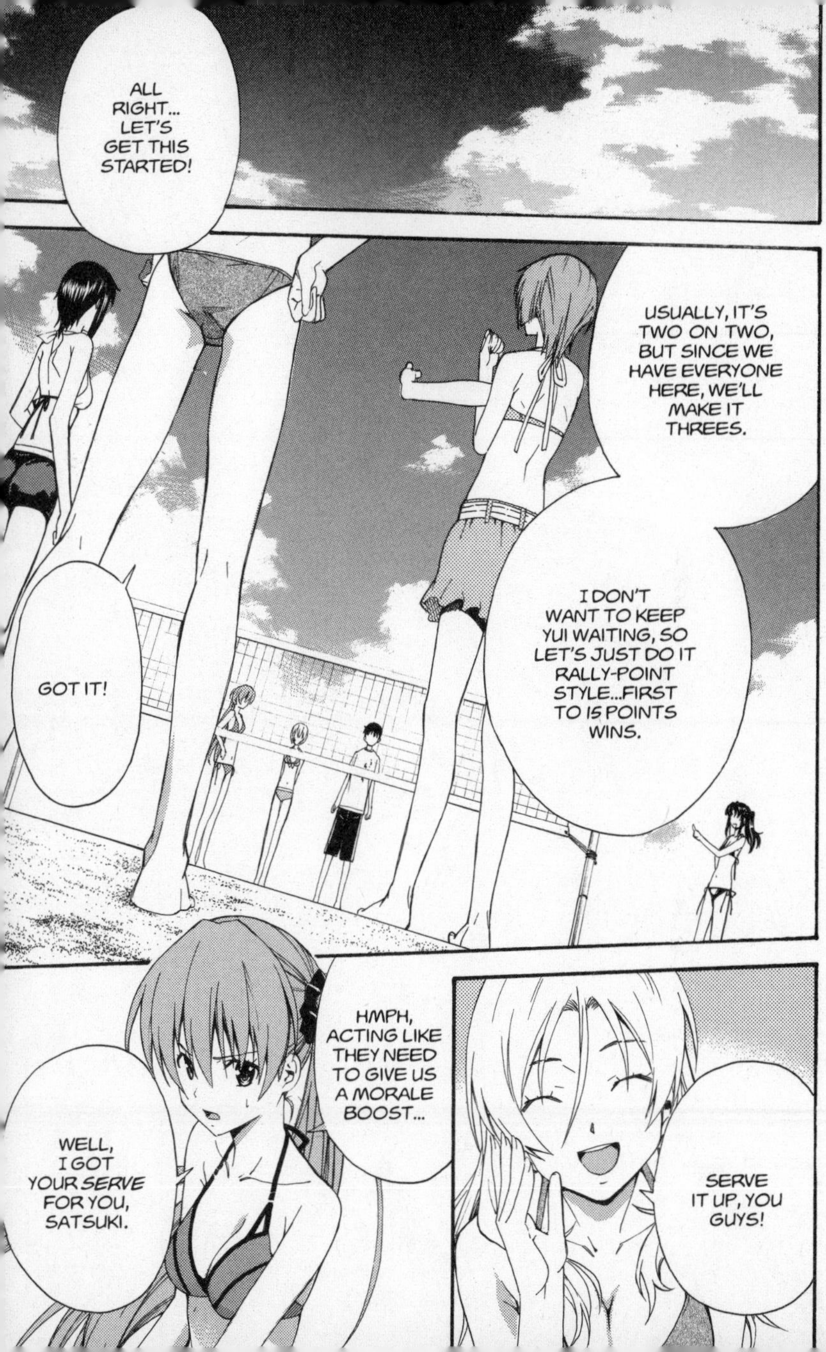
ALL RIGHT... LET'S GET THIS STARTED!
USUALLY, IT'S TWO ON TWO, BUT SINCE WE HAVE EVERYONE HERE, WE'LL MAKE IT THREES.
I DON'T WANT TO KEEP YUI WAITING, SO LET'S JUST DO IT RALLY-POINT STYLE...FIRST TO 15 POINTS WINS.
GOT IT!
SERVE IT UP, YOU GUYS!
HMPH, ACTING LIKE THEY NEED TO GIVE US A MORALE BOOST...
WELL, I GOT YOUR *SERVE* FOR YOU, SATSUKI.

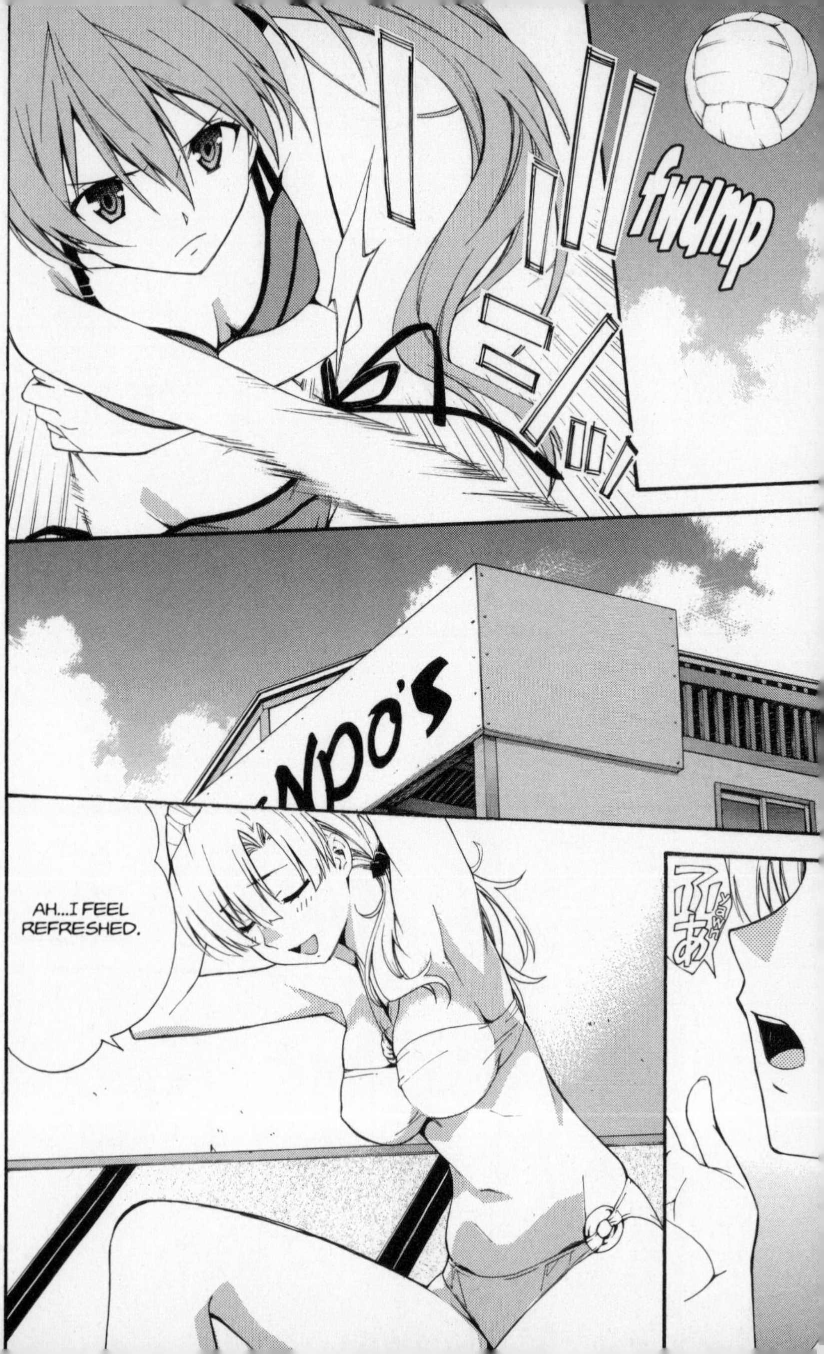
fwump
NDO'S
ふあ
yawn
AH...I FEEL REFRESHED.

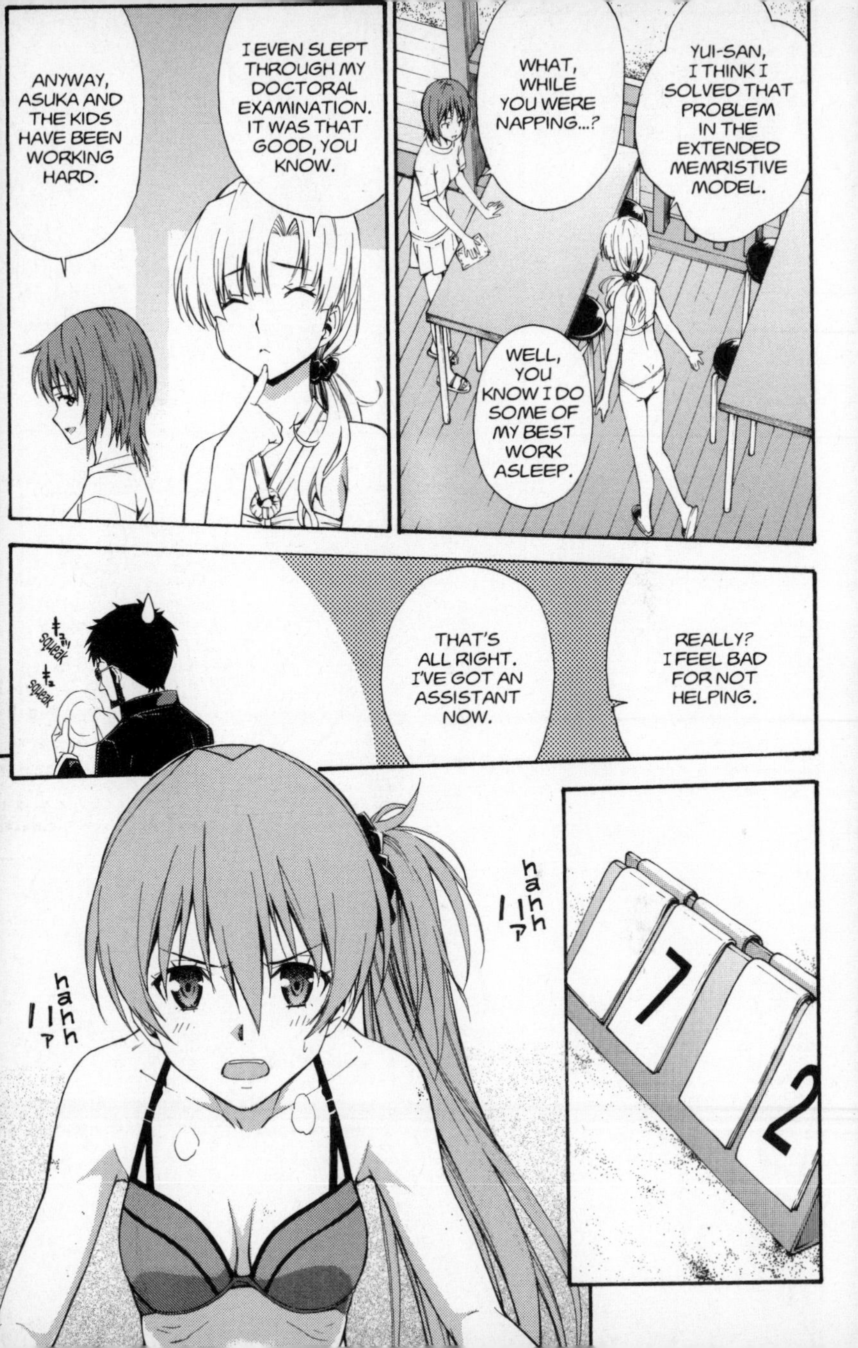
YUI-SAN, I THINK I SOLVED THAT PROBLEM IN THE EXTENDED MEMRISTIVE MODEL.
WHAT, WHILE YOU WERE NAPPING...?
WELL, YOU KNOW I DO SOME OF MY BEST WORK ASLEEP.
I EVEN SLEPT THROUGH MY DOCTORAL EXAMINATION. IT WAS THAT GOOD, YOU KNOW.
ANYWAY, ASUKA AND THE KIDS HAVE BEEN WORKING HARD.
REALLY? I FEEL BAD FOR NOT HELPING.
THAT'S ALL RIGHT. I'VE GOT AN ASSISTANT NOW.
squeak
squeak
7
2
hahn
hahn

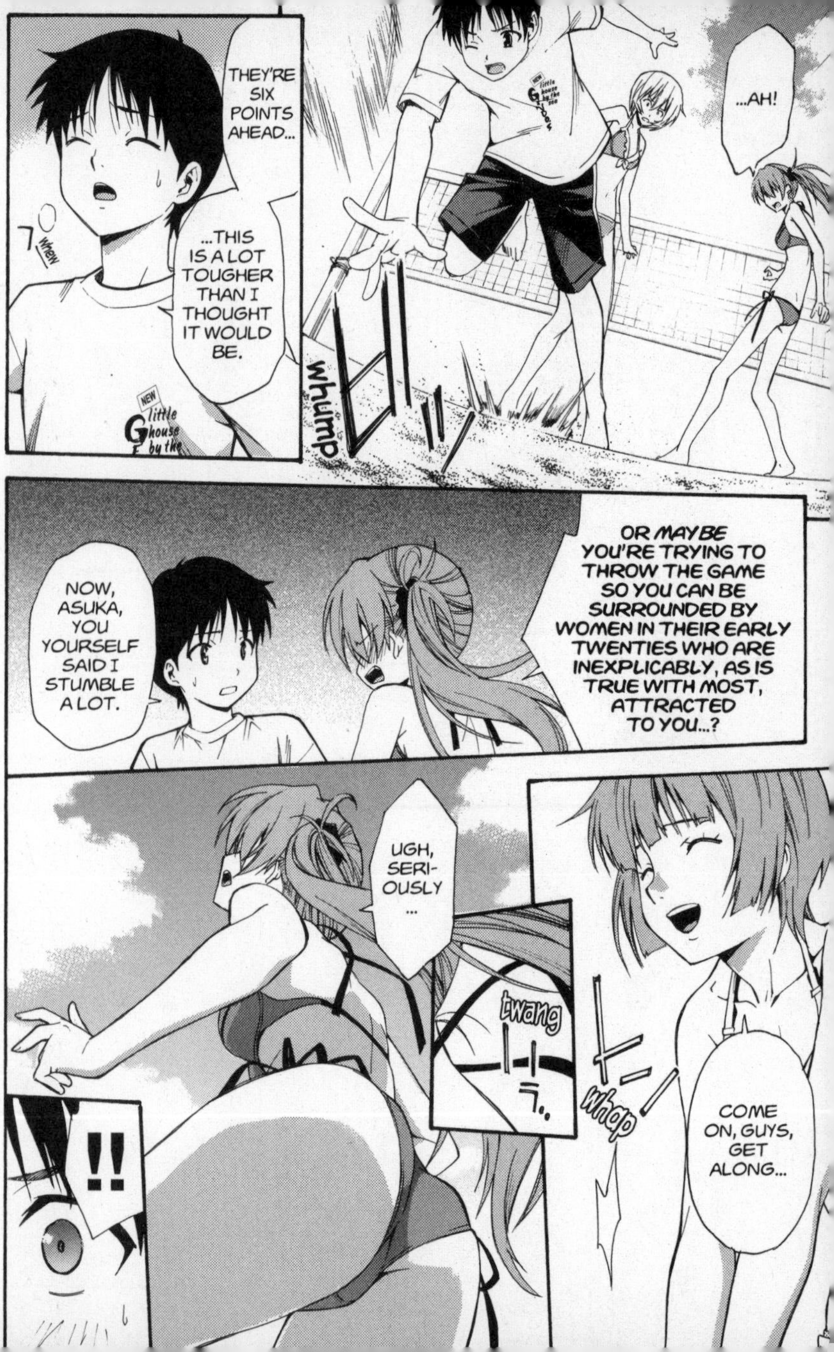
...AH!
whump
THEY'RE SIX POINTS AHEAD...
...THIS IS A LOT TOUGHER THAN I THOUGHT IT WOULD BE.
whew
OR *MAYBE* YOU'RE TRYING TO THROW THE GAME SO YOU CAN BE SURROUNDED BY WOMEN IN THEIR EARLY TWENTIES WHO ARE INEXPLICABLY, AS IS TRUE WITH MOST, ATTRACTED TO YOU...?
NOW, ASUKA, YOU YOURSELF SAID I STUMBLE A LOT.
COME ON, GUYS, GET ALONG...
whap
UGH, SERIOUSLY...
twang
!!

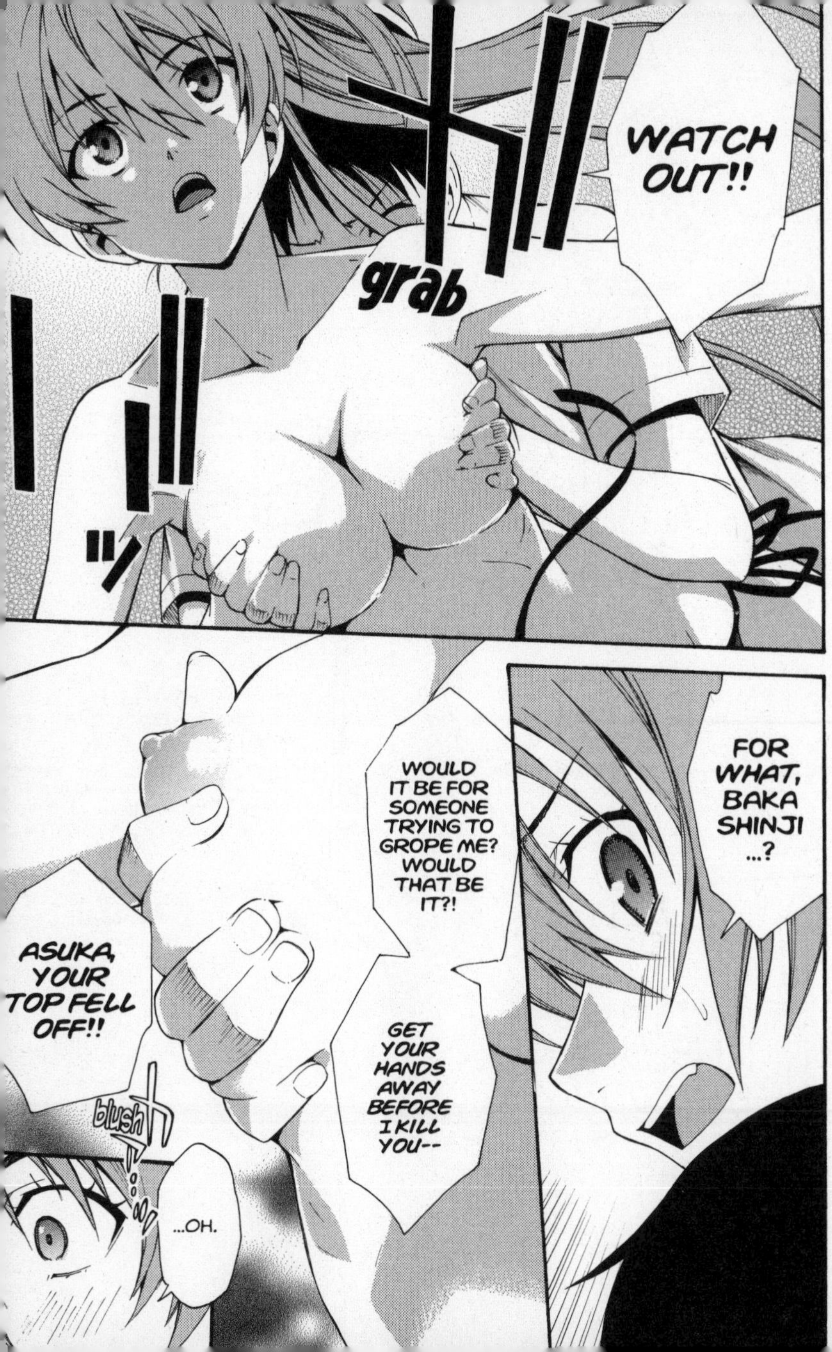
WATCH OUT!!
grab
FOR WHAT, BAKA SHINJI ...?
WOULD IT BE FOR SOMEONE TRYING TO GROPE ME? WOULD THAT BE IT?!
GET YOUR HANDS AWAY BEFORE I KILL YOU--
ASUKA, YOUR TOP FELL OFF!!
blush
...OH.

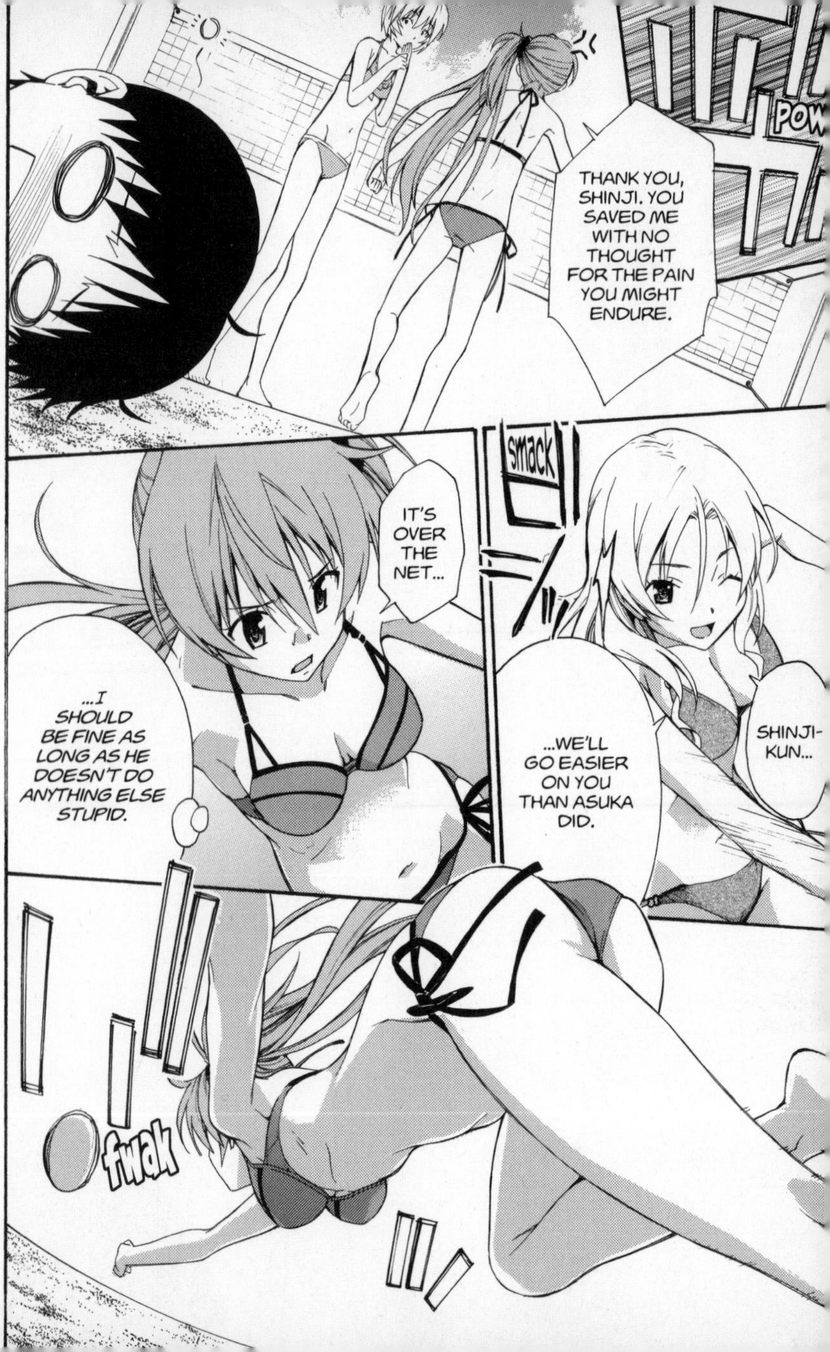
POW
THANK YOU, SHINJI. YOU SAVED ME WITH NO THOUGHT FOR THE PAIN YOU MIGHT ENDURE.
smack
SHINJI-KUN...
...WE'LL GO EASIER ON YOU THAN ASUKA DID.
IT'S OVER THE NET...
...I SHOULD BE FINE AS LONG AS HE DOESN'T DO ANYTHING ELSE STUPID.
fwak

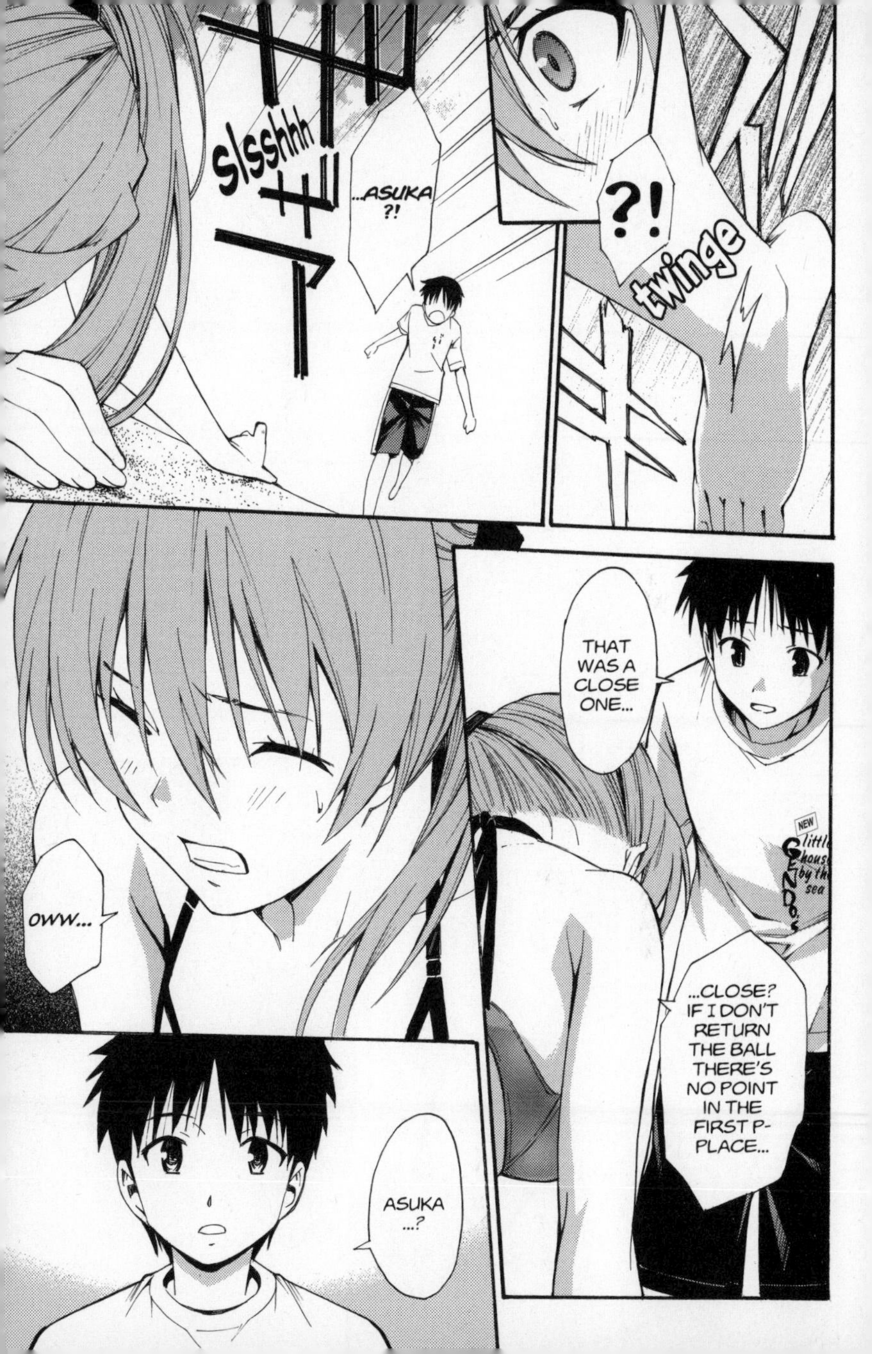
?!
twinge
slsshhh
...ASUKA ?!
THAT WAS A CLOSE ONE...
...CLOSE? IF I DON'T RETURN THE BALL THERE'S NO POINT IN THE FIRST P-PLACE...
OWW...
ASUKA ...?

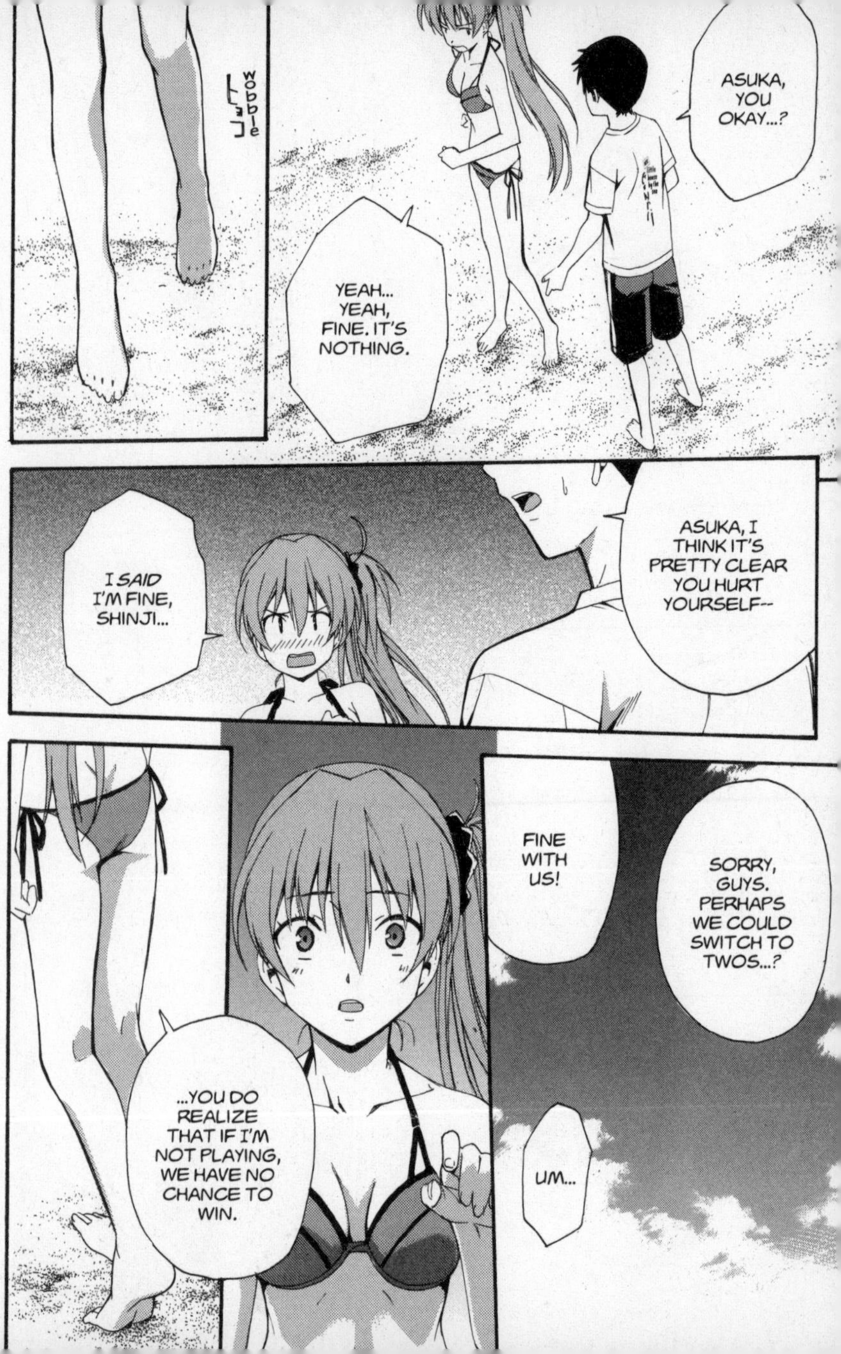
ASUKA, YOU OKAY...?
YEAH... YEAH, FINE. IT'S NOTHING.
wobble
ASUKA, I THINK IT'S PRETTY CLEAR YOU HURT YOURSELF--
I SAID I'M FINE, SHINJI...
SORRY, GUYS. PERHAPS WE COULD SWITCH TO TWOS...?
FINE WITH US!
UM...
...YOU DO REALIZE THAT IF I'M NOT PLAYING, WE HAVE NO CHANCE TO WIN.

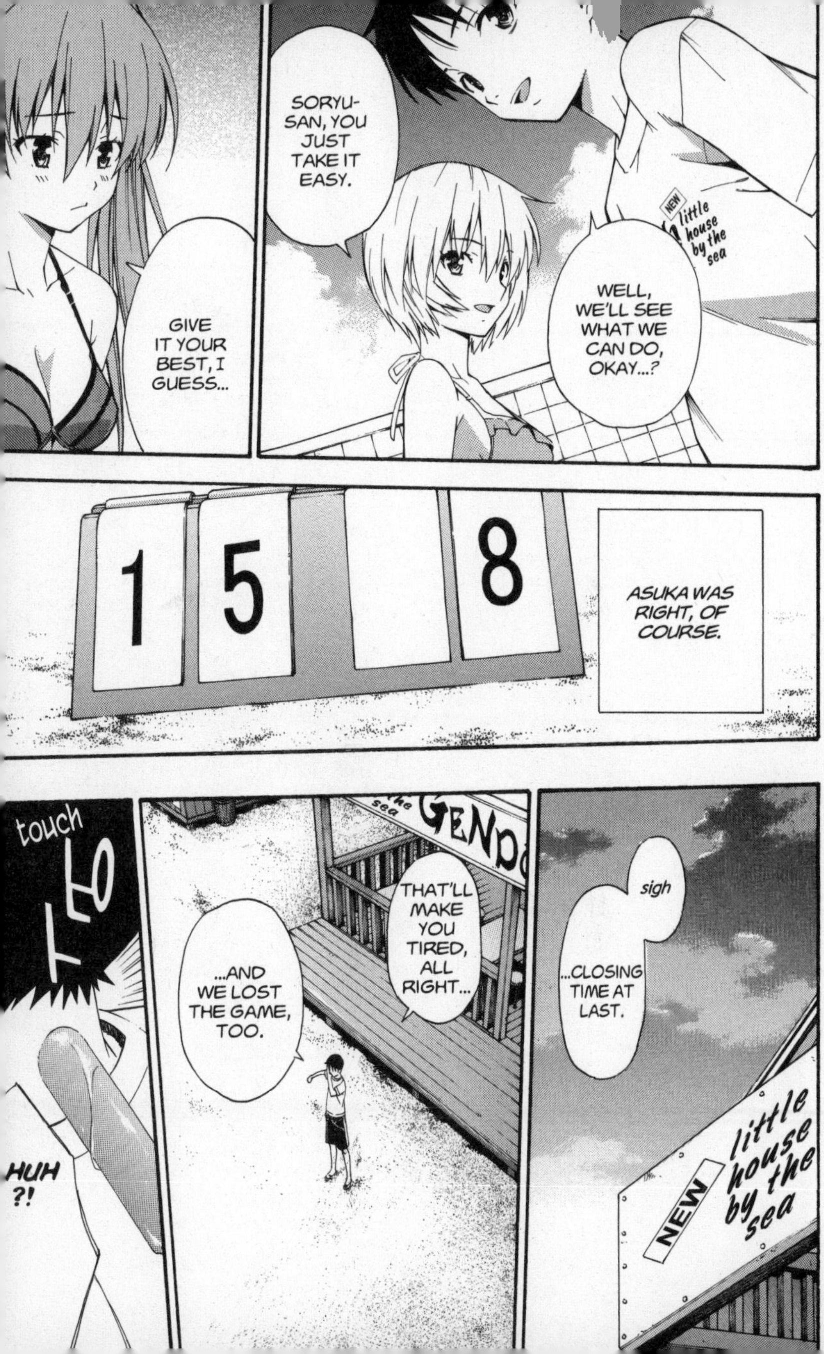
NEW little house by the sea
SORYU-SAN, YOU JUST TAKE IT EASY.
WELL, WE'LL SEE WHAT WE CAN DO, OKAY...?
GIVE IT YOUR BEST, I GUESS...
ASUKA WAS RIGHT, OF COURSE.
15
8
NEW little house by the sea
sigh
...CLOSING TIME AT LAST.
THAT'LL MAKE YOU TIRED, ALL RIGHT...
...AND WE LOST THE GAME, TOO.
touch
HUH ?!

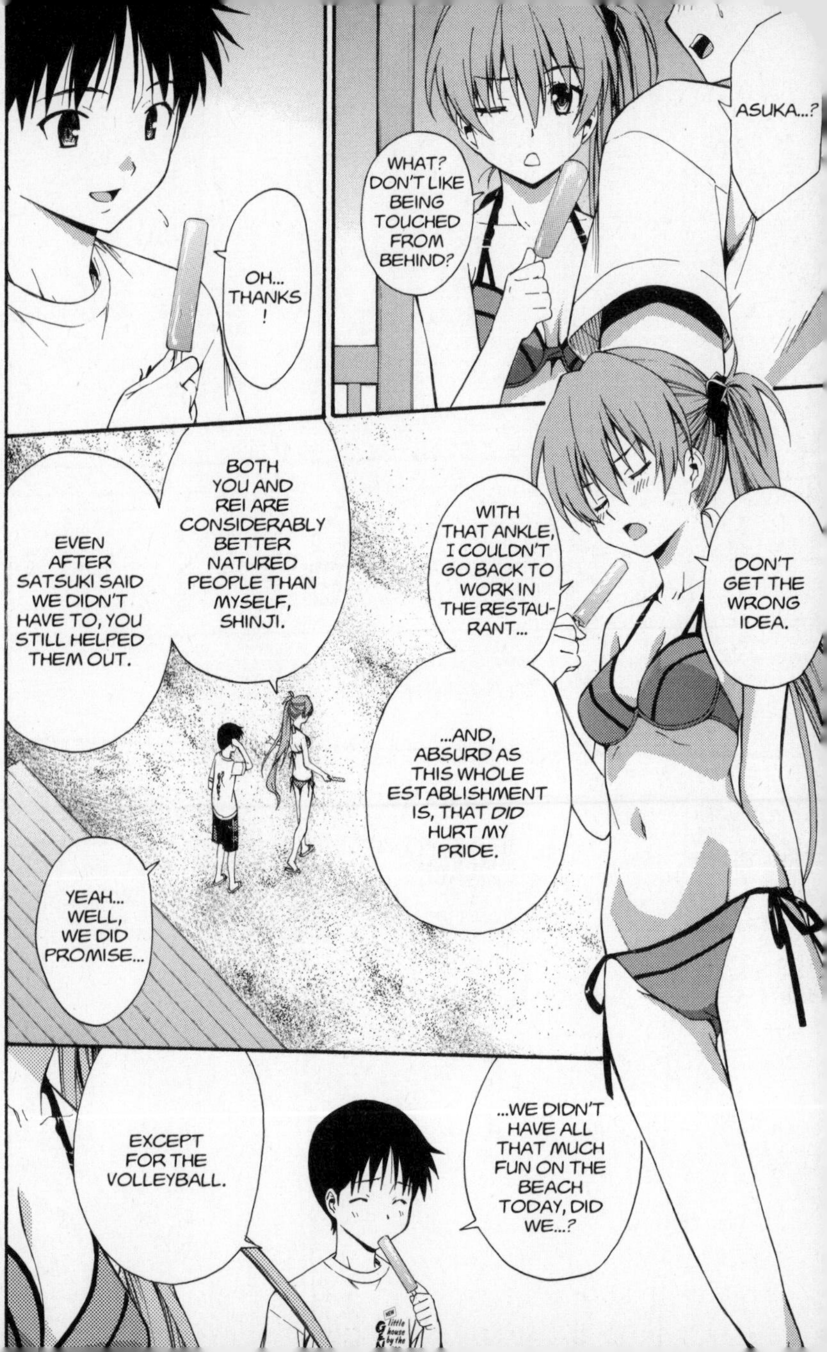
ASUKA...?
WHAT? DON'T LIKE BEING TOUCHED FROM BEHIND?
OH... THANKS!
DON'T GET THE WRONG IDEA.
WITH THAT ANKLE, I COULDN'T GO BACK TO WORK IN THE RESTAURANT...
...AND, ABSURD AS THIS WHOLE ESTABLISHMENT IS, THAT *DID* HURT MY PRIDE.
BOTH YOU AND REI ARE CONSIDERABLY BETTER NATURED PEOPLE THAN MYSELF, SHINJI.
EVEN AFTER SATSUKI SAID WE DIDN'T HAVE TO, YOU STILL HELPED THEM OUT.
YEAH... WELL, WE DID PROMISE...
...WE DIDN'T HAVE ALL THAT MUCH FUN ON THE BEACH TODAY, DID WE...?
EXCEPT FOR THE VOLLEYBALL.

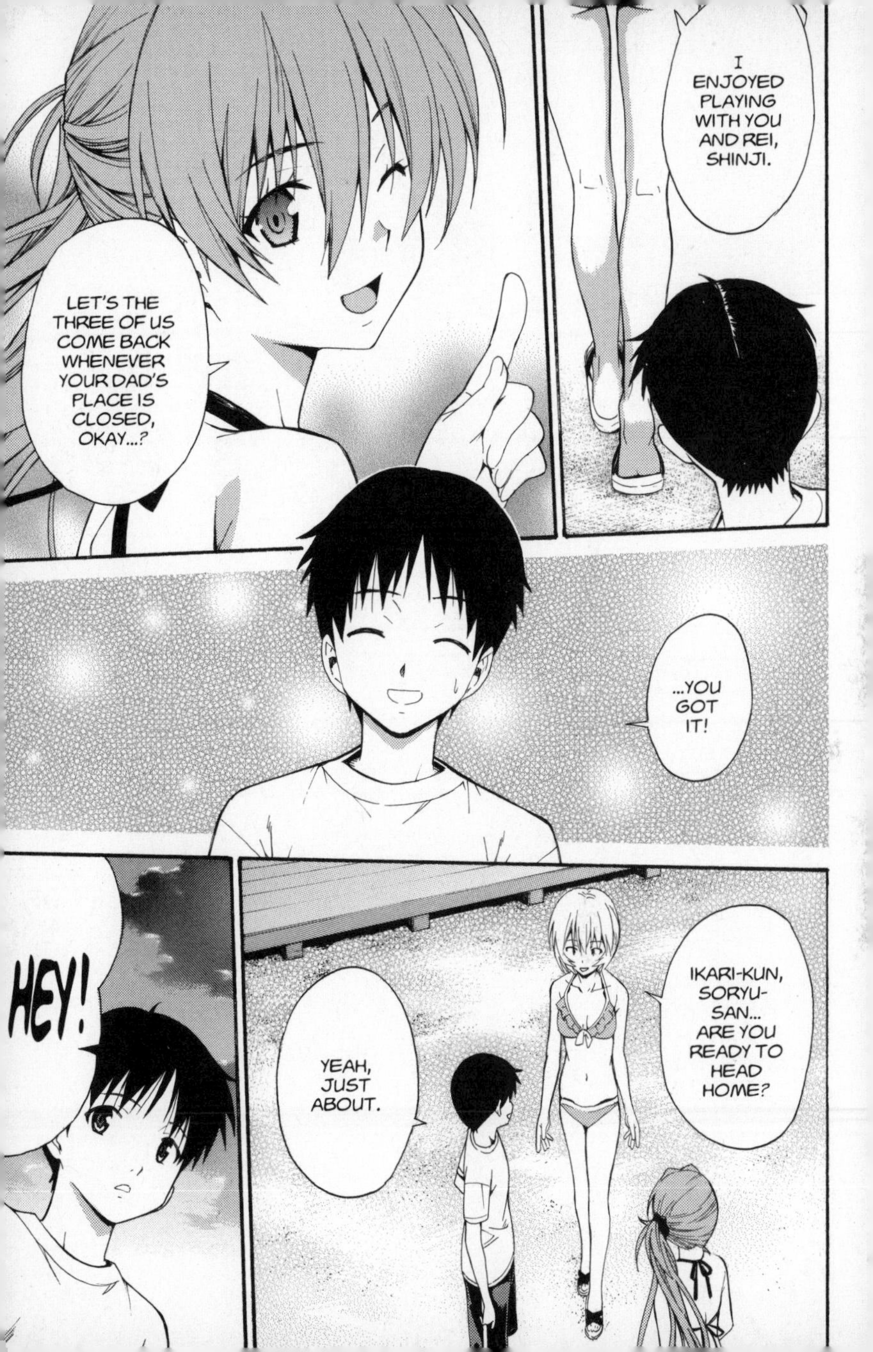
I ENJOYED PLAYING WITH YOU AND REI, SHINJI.
LET'S THE THREE OF US COME BACK WHENEVER YOUR DAD'S PLACE IS CLOSED, OKAY...?
...YOU GOT IT!
IKARI-KUN, SORYU-SAN... ARE YOU READY TO HEAD HOME?
YEAH, JUST ABOUT.
HEY!

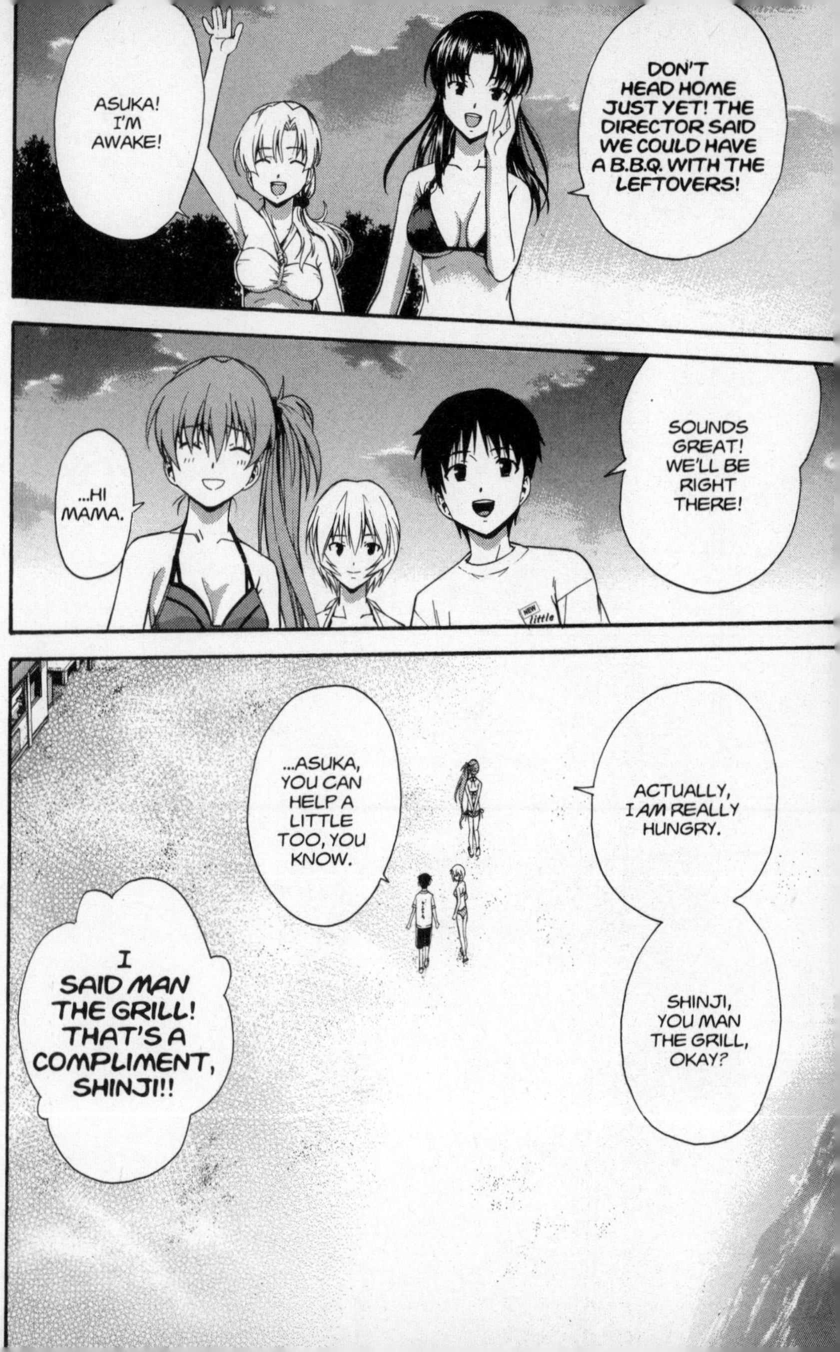
DON'T HEAD HOME JUST YET! THE DIRECTOR SAID WE COULD HAVE A B.B.Q. WITH THE LEFTOVERS!
ASUKA! I'M AWAKE!
SOUNDS GREAT! WE'LL BE RIGHT THERE!
...HI MAMA.
ACTUALLY, I *AM* REALLY HUNGRY.
SHINJI, YOU MAN THE GRILL, OKAY?
...ASUKA, YOU CAN HELP A LITTLE TOO, YOU KNOW.
I SAID *MAN* THE GRILL! THAT'S A COMPLIMENT, SHINJI!!

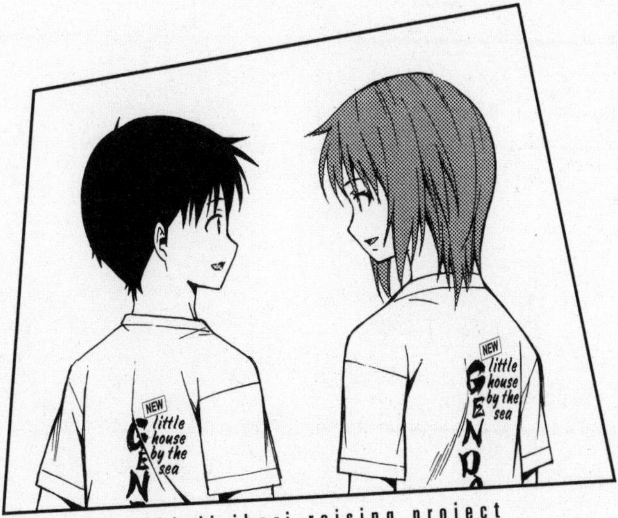
NEW
little house by the sea
NEW
little house by the sea

the shinji ikari raising project

NEON GENESIS EVANGELION
THE SHINJI IKARI RAISING PROJECT

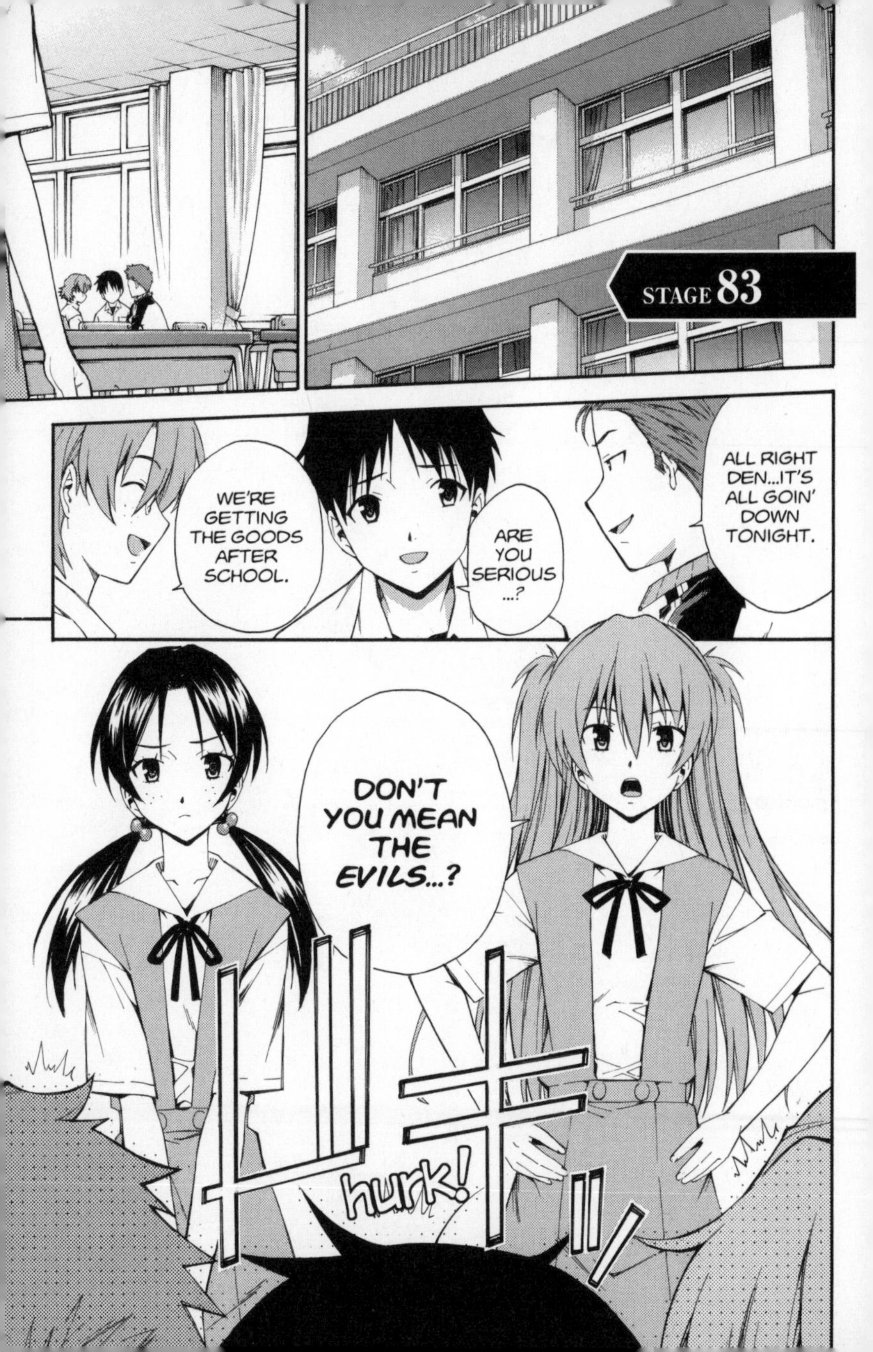
STAGE 83
ALL RIGHT DEN...IT'S ALL GOIN' DOWN TONIGHT.
ARE YOU SERIOUS ...?
WE'RE GETTING THE GOODS AFTER SCHOOL.
DON'T YOU MEAN THE EVILS...?
hurk!

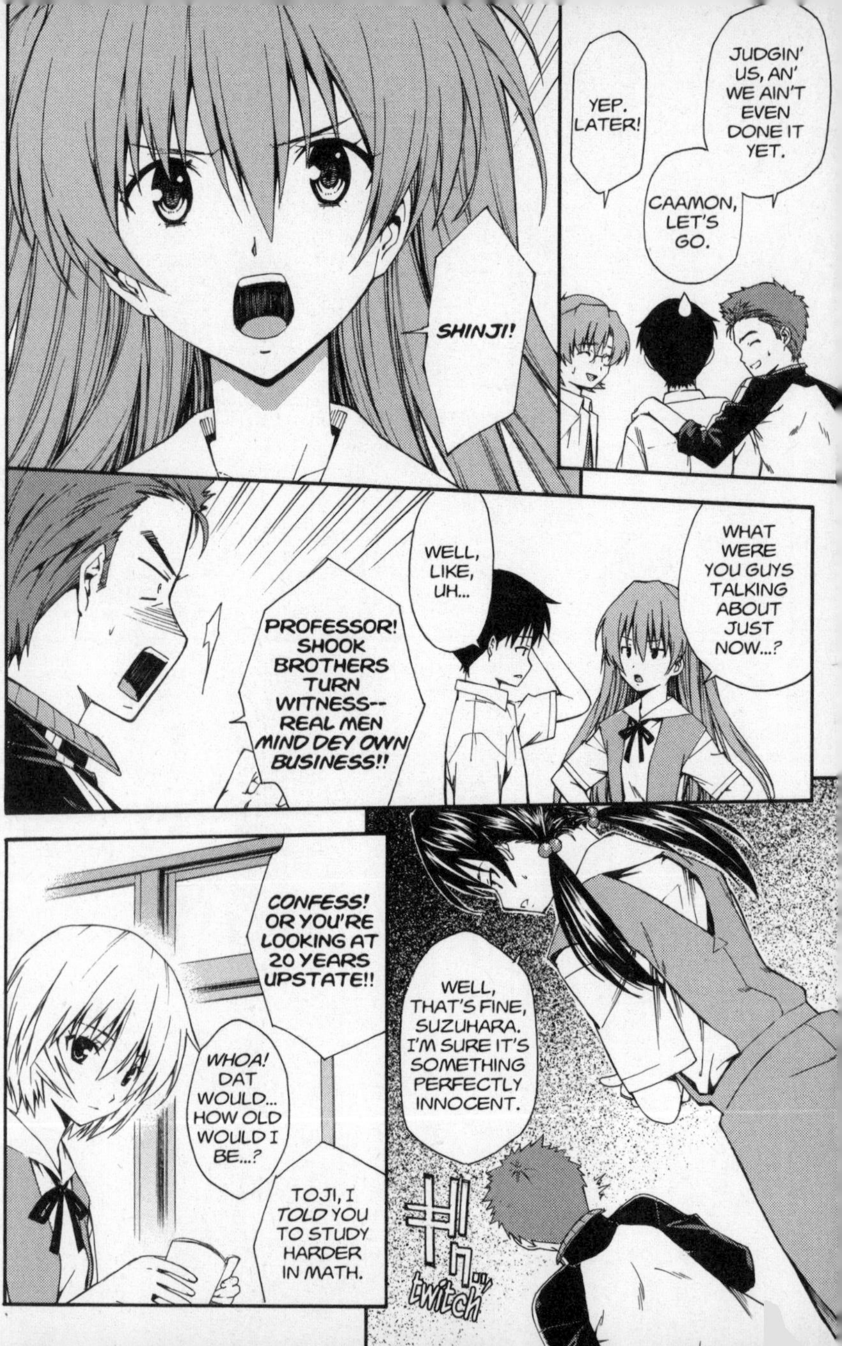
JUDGIN' US, AN' WE AIN'T EVEN DONE IT YET.
CAAMON, LET'S GO.
YEP. LATER!
SHINJI!
WHAT WERE YOU GUYS TALKING ABOUT JUST NOW...?
WELL, LIKE, UH...
PROFESSOR! SHOOK BROTHERS TURN WITNESS-- REAL MEN MIND DEY OWN BUSINESS!!
WELL, THAT'S FINE, SUZUHARA. I'M SURE IT'S SOMETHING PERFECTLY INNOCENT.
twitch
CONFESS! OR YOU'RE LOOKING AT 20 YEARS UPSTATE!!
WHOA! DAT WOULD... HOW OLD WOULD I BE...?
TOJI, I TOLD YOU TO STUDY HARDER IN MATH.

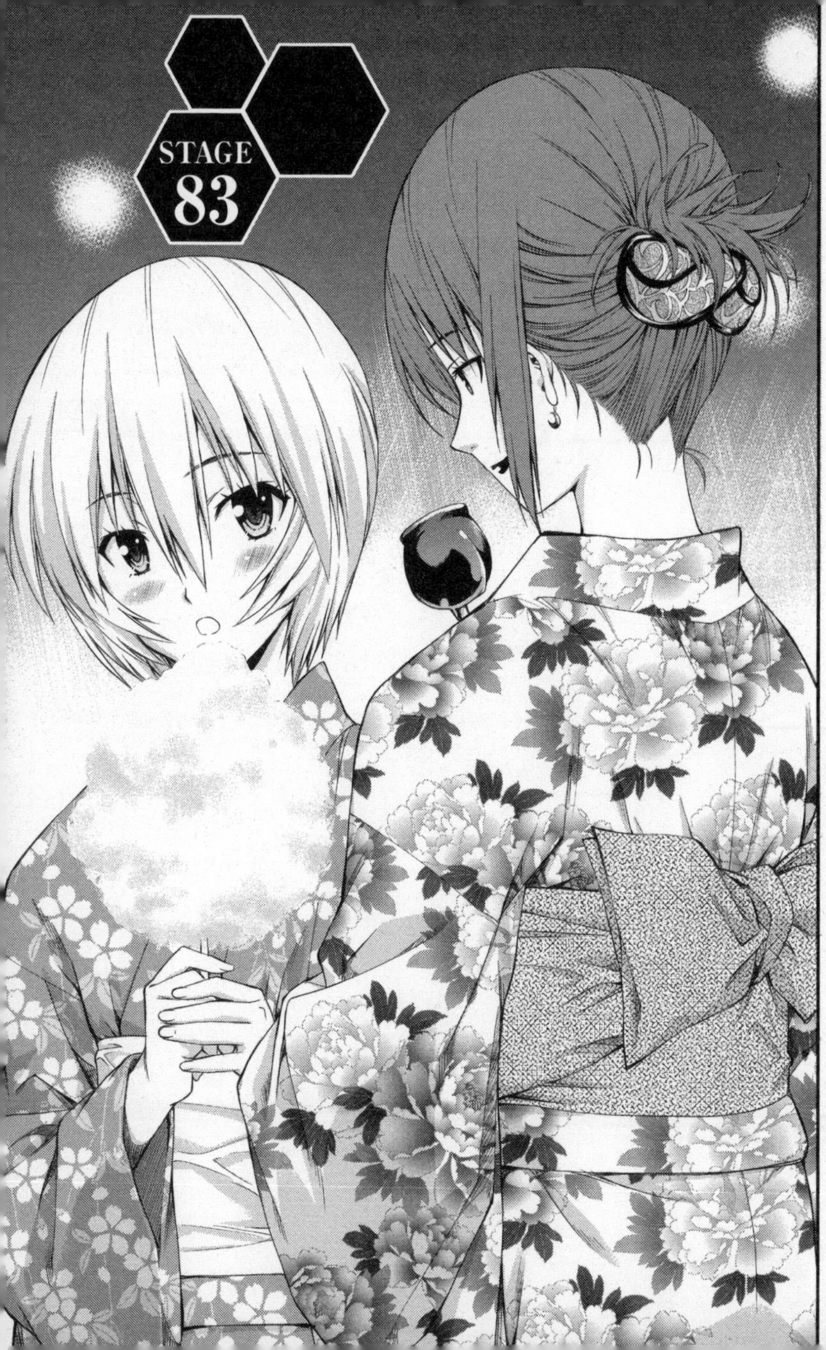
STAGE
83

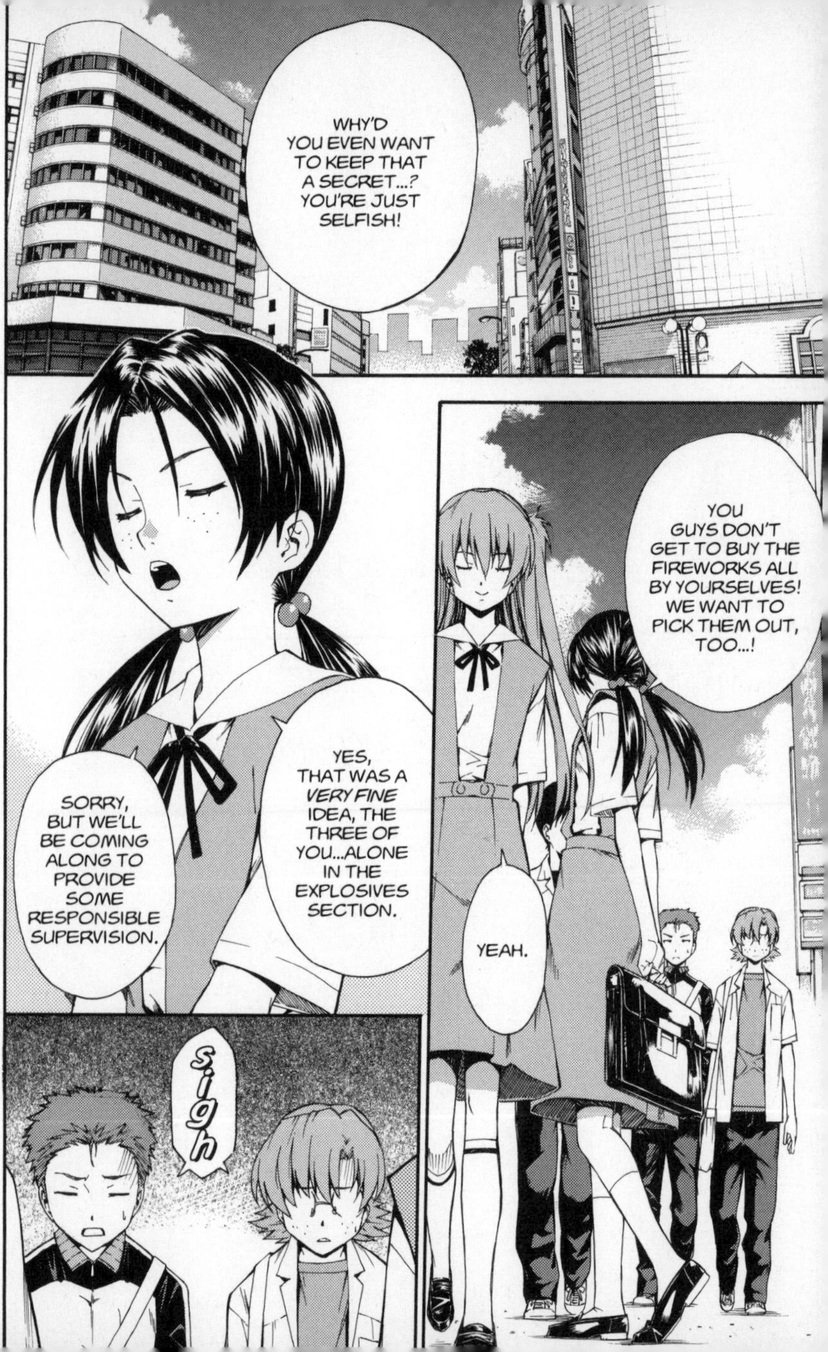
WHY'D YOU EVEN WANT TO KEEP THAT A SECRET...? YOU'RE JUST SELFISH!
YOU GUYS DON'T GET TO BUY THE FIREWORKS ALL BY YOURSELVES! WE WANT TO PICK THEM OUT, TOO...!
YEAH.
YES, THAT WAS A *VERY FINE* IDEA, THE THREE OF YOU...ALONE IN THE EXPLOSIVES SECTION.
SORRY, BUT WE'LL BE COMING ALONG TO PROVIDE SOME RESPONSIBLE SUPERVISION.
Sigh

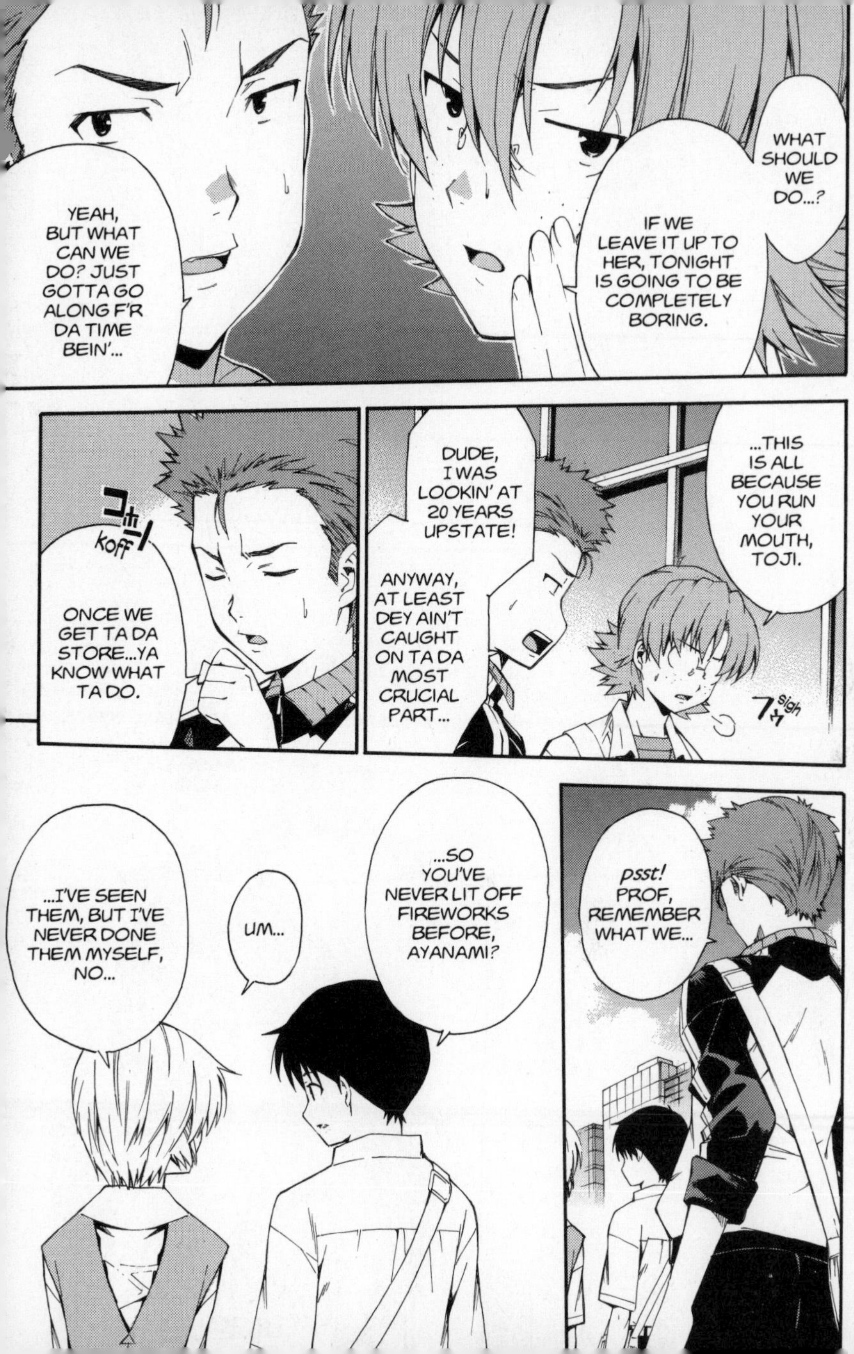
WHAT SHOULD WE DO...?
IF WE LEAVE IT UP TO HER, TONIGHT IS GOING TO BE COMPLETELY BORING.
YEAH, BUT WHAT CAN WE DO? JUST GOTTA GO ALONG F'R DA TIME BEIN'...
...THIS IS ALL BECAUSE YOU RUN YOUR MOUTH, TOJI.
DUDE, I WAS LOOKIN' AT 20 YEARS UPSTATE!
ANYWAY, AT LEAST DEY AIN'T CAUGHT ON TA DA MOST CRUCIAL PART...
sigh
koff
ONCE WE GET TA DA STORE...YA KNOW WHAT TA DO.
psst! PROF, REMEMBER WHAT WE...
...SO YOU'VE NEVER LIT OFF FIREWORKS BEFORE, AYANAMI?
UM...
...I'VE SEEN THEM, BUT I'VE NEVER DONE THEM MYSELF, NO...

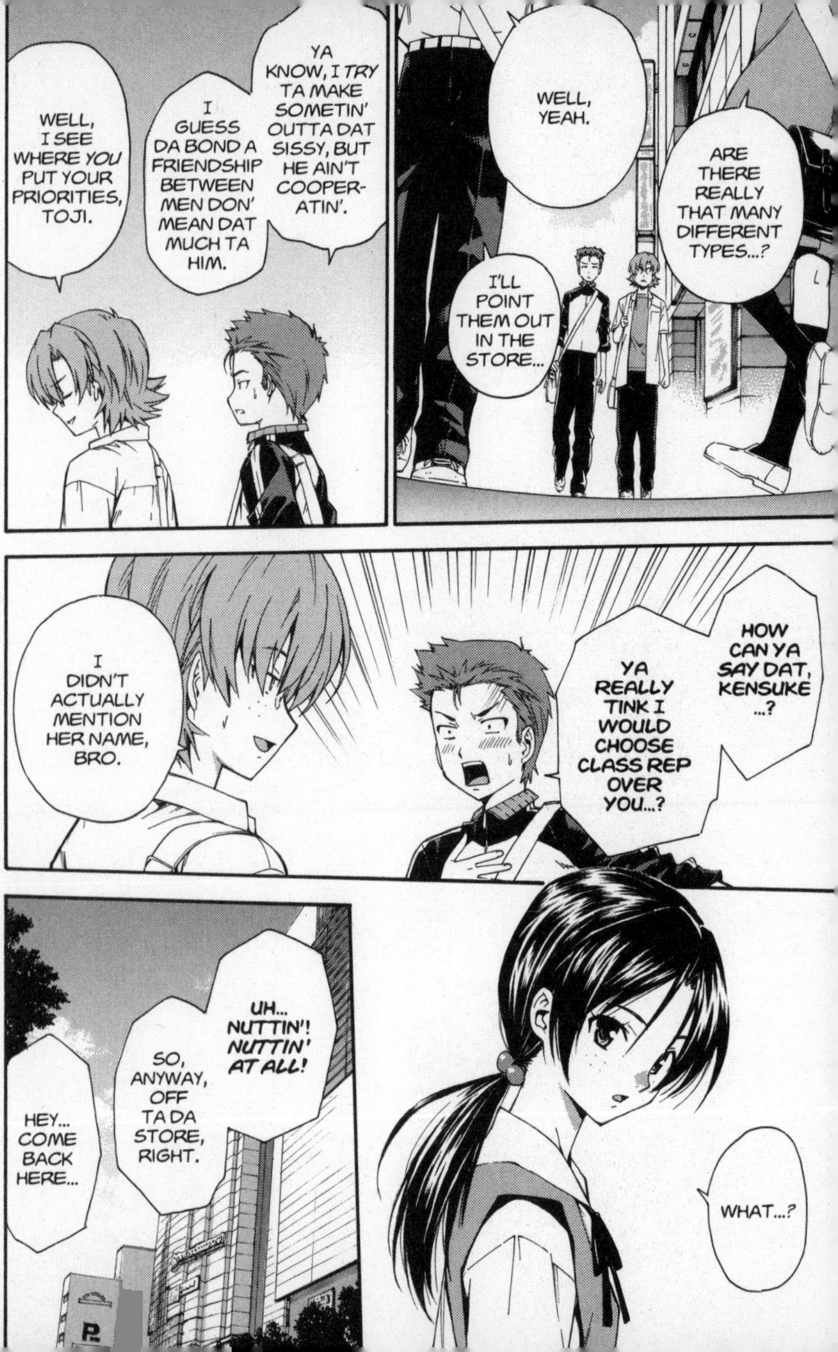
ARE THERE REALLY THAT MANY DIFFERENT TYPES...?
WELL, YEAH.
I'LL POINT THEM OUT IN THE STORE...
YA KNOW, I *TRY* TA MAKE SOMETIN' OUTTA DAT SISSY, BUT HE AIN'T COOPER-ATIN'.
I GUESS DA BOND A FRIENDSHIP BETWEEN MEN DON' MEAN DAT MUCH TA HIM.
WELL, I SEE WHERE *YOU* PUT YOUR PRIORITIES, TOJI.
HOW CAN YA SAY DAT, KENSUKE ...?
YA REALLY TINK I WOULD CHOOSE CLASS REP OVER YOU...?
I DIDN'T ACTUALLY MENTION HER NAME, BRO.
WHAT...?
UH... NUTTIN'! *NUTTIN' AT ALL!*
SO, ANYWAY, OFF TA DA STORE, RIGHT.
HEY... COME BACK HERE...

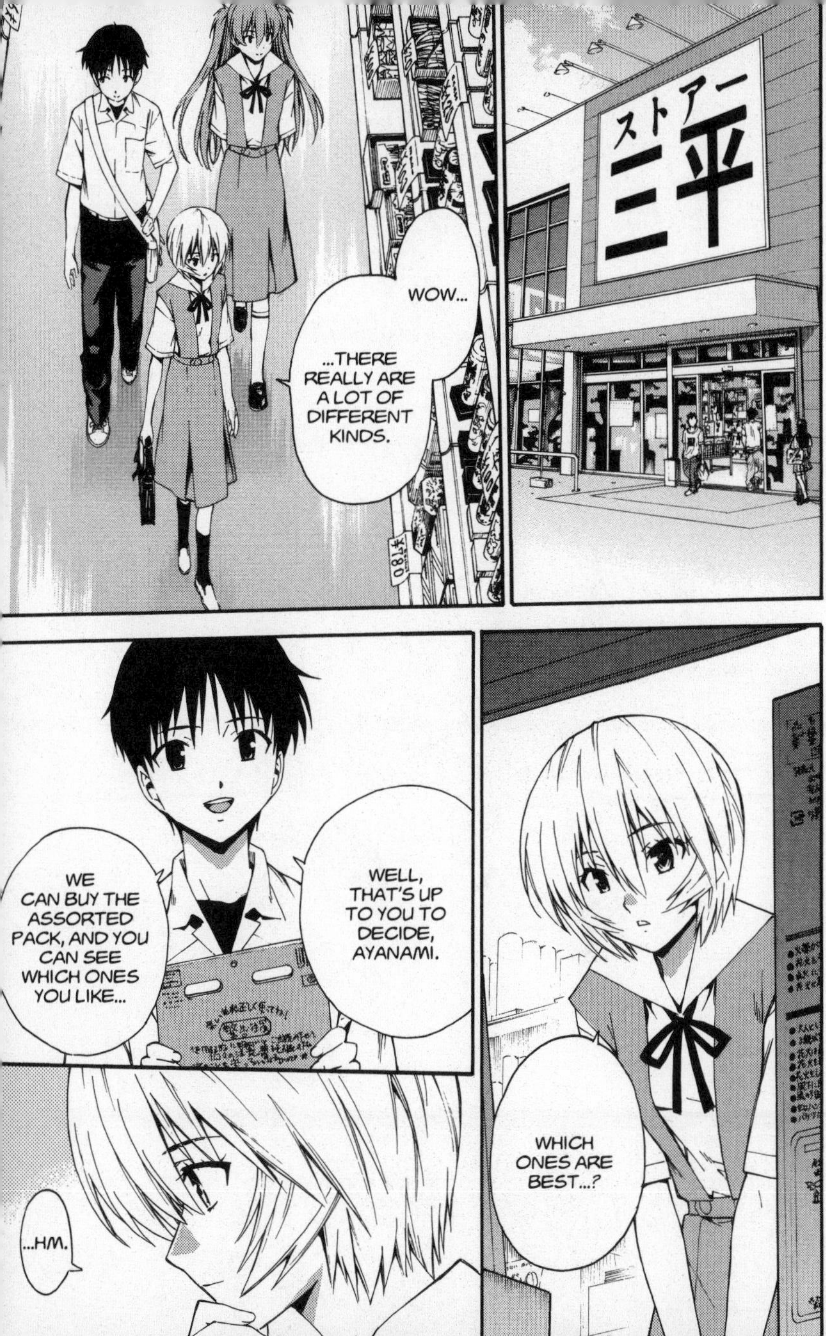
ストアー
三平
¥180
WOW...
...THERE REALLY ARE A LOT OF DIFFERENT KINDS.
WHICH ONES ARE BEST...?
WELL, THAT'S UP TO YOU TO DECIDE, AYANAMI.
WE CAN BUY THE ASSORTED PACK, AND YOU CAN SEE WHICH ONES YOU LIKE...
...HM.

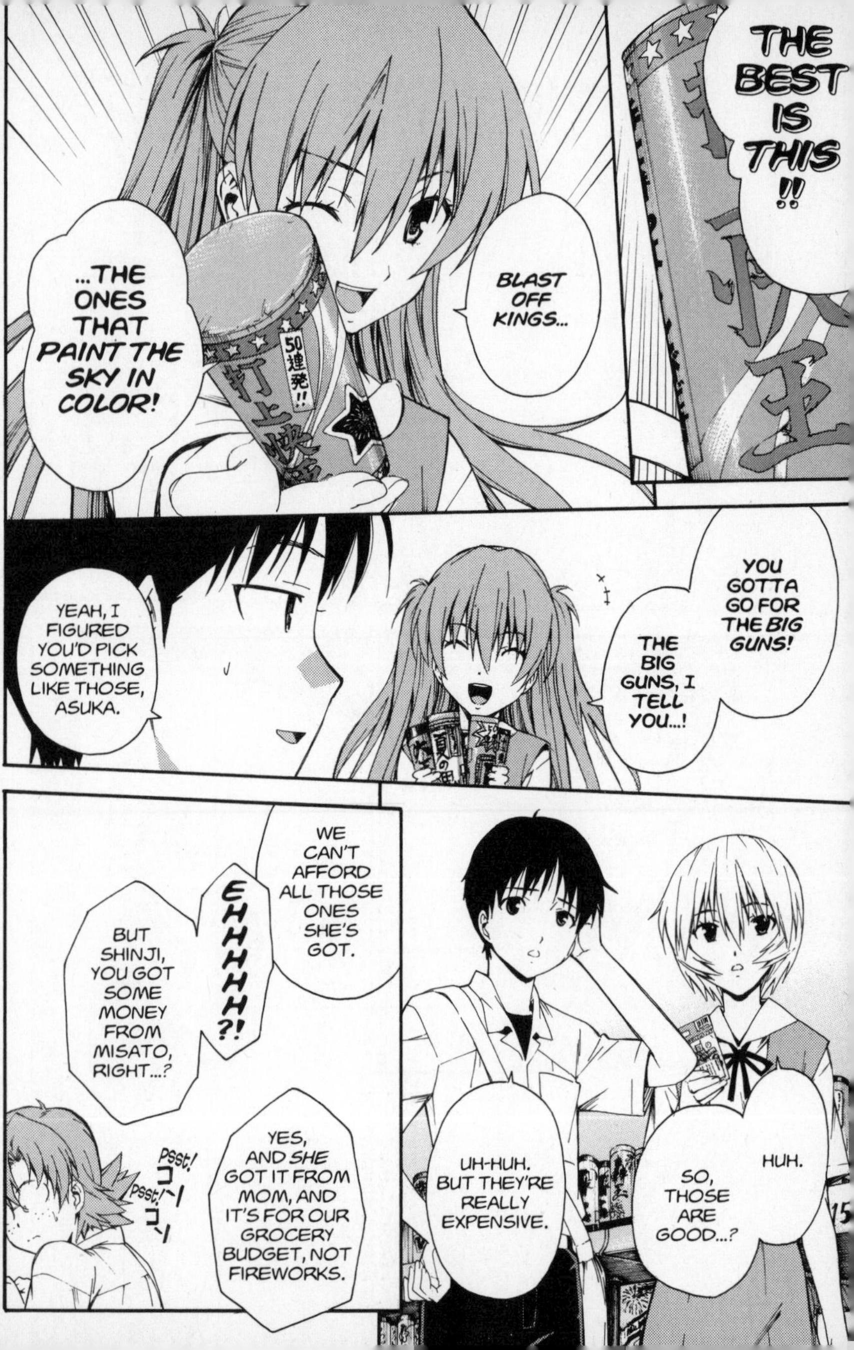
THE BEST IS THIS!!
BLAST OFF KINGS...
...THE ONES THAT PAINT THE SKY IN COLOR!
50連発!!
YOU GOTTA GO FOR THE BIG GUNS!
THE BIG GUNS, I TELL YOU...!
YEAH, I FIGURED YOU'D PICK SOMETHING LIKE THOSE, ASUKA.
HUH.
SO, THOSE ARE GOOD...?
UH-HUH. BUT THEY'RE REALLY EXPENSIVE.
WE CAN'T AFFORD ALL THOSE ONES SHE'S GOT.
EHHHHHH?!
BUT SHINJI, YOU GOT SOME MONEY FROM MISATO, RIGHT...?
YES, AND SHE GOT IT FROM MOM, AND IT'S FOR OUR GROCERY BUDGET, NOT FIREWORKS.
Psst! Psst!

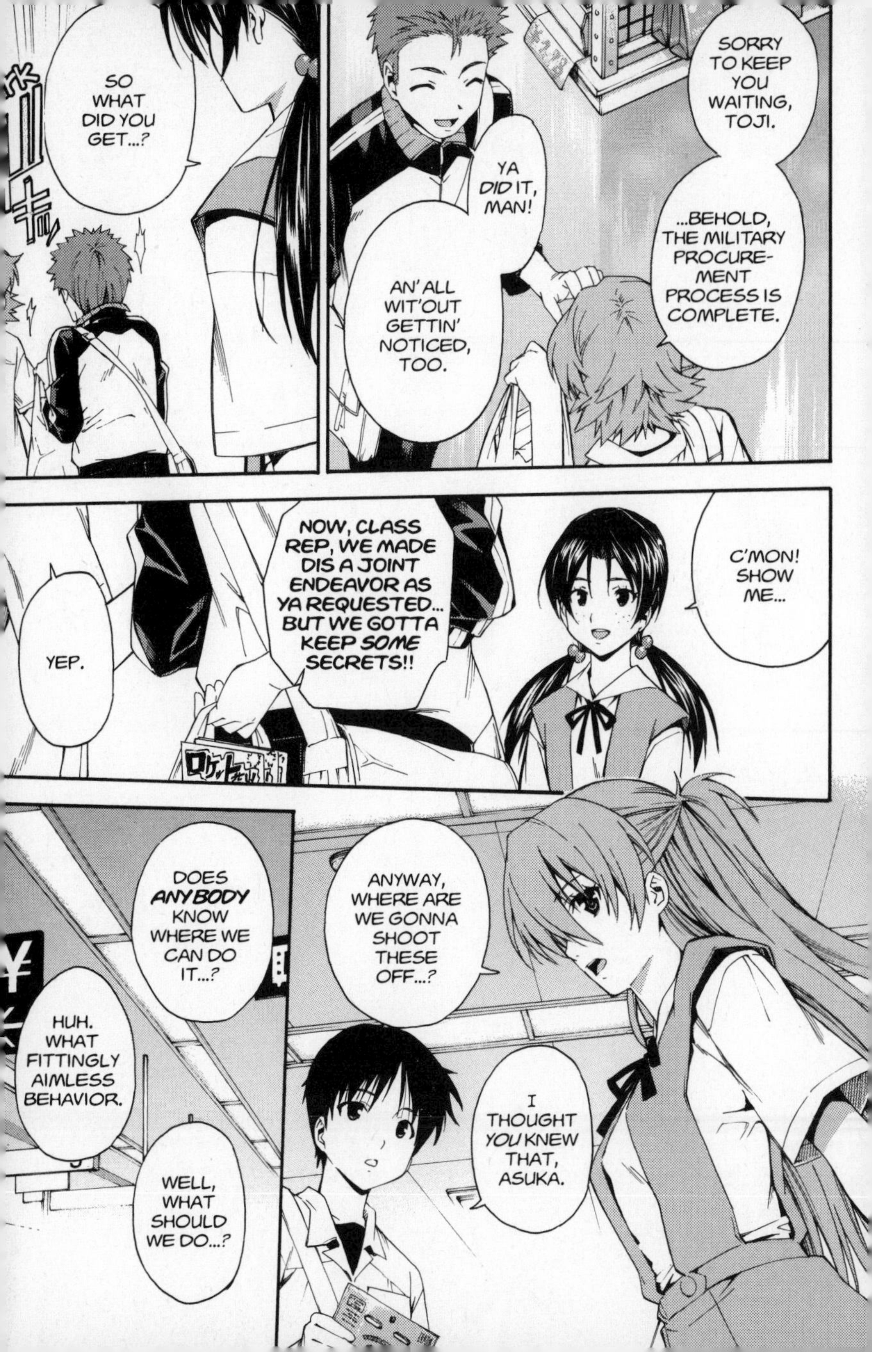
SORRY TO KEEP YOU WAITING, TOJI.
...BEHOLD, THE MILITARY PROCURE-MENT PROCESS IS COMPLETE.
YA DID IT, MAN!
AN' ALL WIT'OUT GETTIN' NOTICED, TOO.
SO WHAT DID YOU GET...?
C'MON! SHOW ME...
NOW, CLASS REP, WE MADE DIS A JOINT ENDEAVOR AS YA REQUESTED... BUT WE GOTTA KEEP SOME SECRETS!!
YEP.
ANYWAY, WHERE ARE WE GONNA SHOOT THESE OFF...?
DOES ANYBODY KNOW WHERE WE CAN DO IT...?
I THOUGHT YOU KNEW THAT, ASUKA.
HUH. WHAT FITTINGLY AIMLESS BEHAVIOR.
WELL, WHAT SHOULD WE DO...?

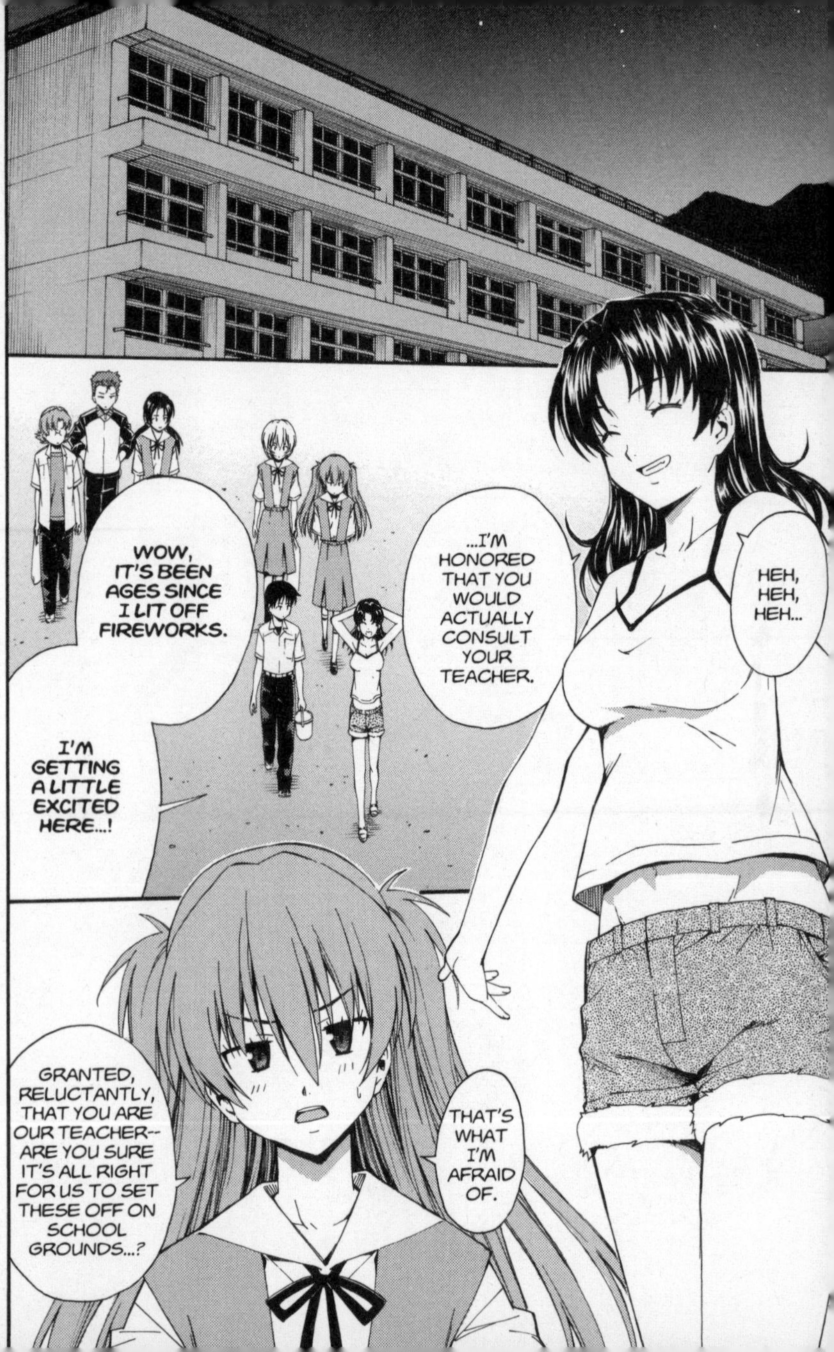
HEH, HEH, HEH...
...I'M HONORED THAT YOU WOULD ACTUALLY CONSULT YOUR TEACHER.
WOW, IT'S BEEN AGES SINCE I LIT OFF FIREWORKS.
I'M GETTING A LITTLE EXCITED HERE...!
THAT'S WHAT I'M AFRAID OF.
GRANTED, RELUCTANTLY, THAT YOU ARE OUR TEACHER-- ARE YOU SURE IT'S ALL RIGHT FOR US TO SET THESE OFF ON SCHOOL GROUNDS...?

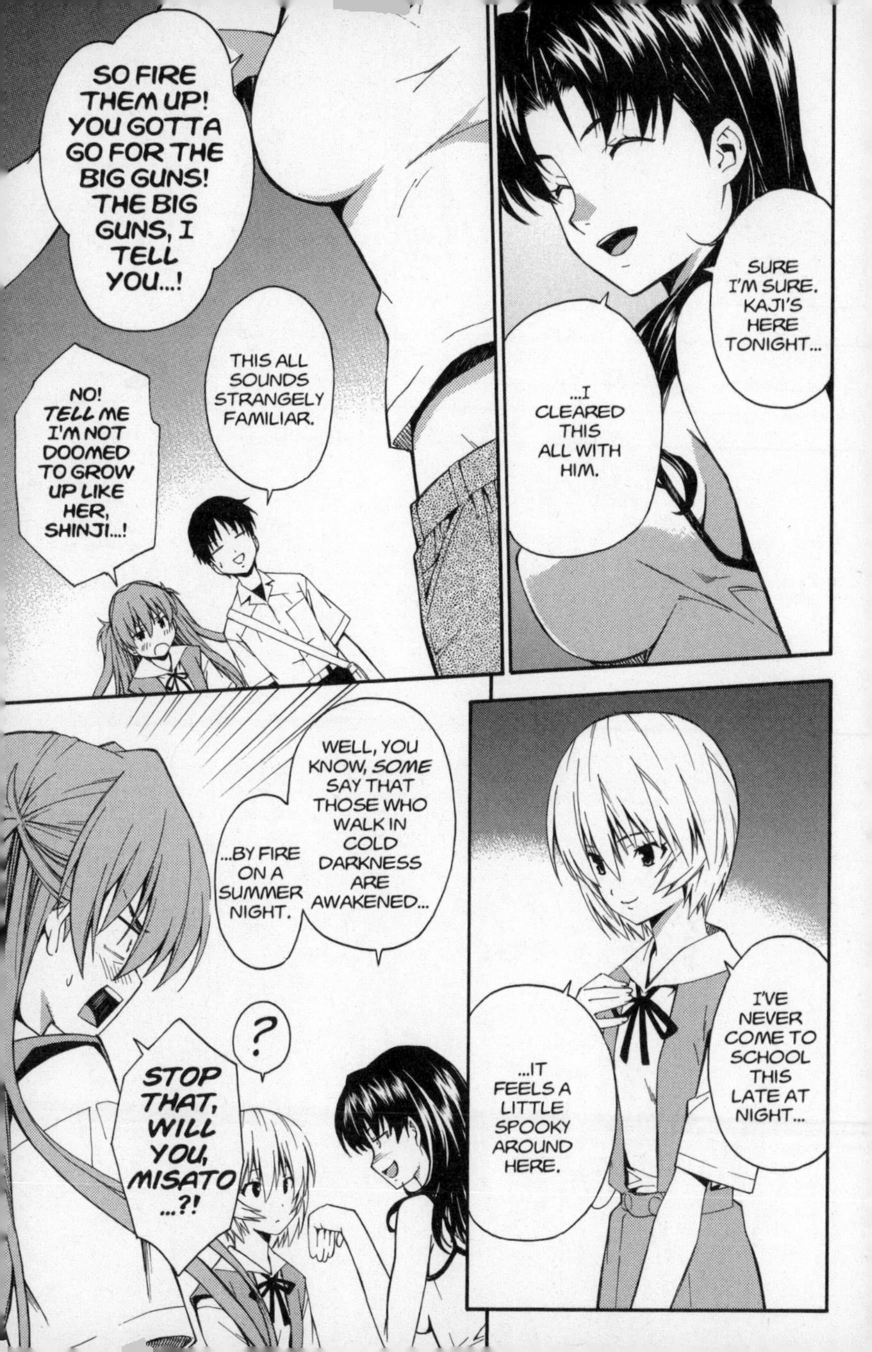
SURE I'M SURE. KAJI'S HERE TONIGHT...
...I CLEARED THIS ALL WITH HIM.
SO FIRE THEM UP! YOU GOTTA GO FOR THE BIG GUNS! THE BIG GUNS, I TELL YOU...!
THIS ALL SOUNDS STRANGELY FAMILIAR.
NO! *TELL ME* I'M NOT DOOMED TO GROW UP LIKE HER, SHINJI...!
I'VE NEVER COME TO SCHOOL THIS LATE AT NIGHT...
...IT FEELS A LITTLE SPOOKY AROUND HERE.
WELL, YOU KNOW, *SOME* SAY THAT THOSE WHO WALK IN COLD DARKNESS ARE AWAKENED...
...BY FIRE ON A SUMMER NIGHT.
?
STOP THAT, WILL YOU, MISATO...?!

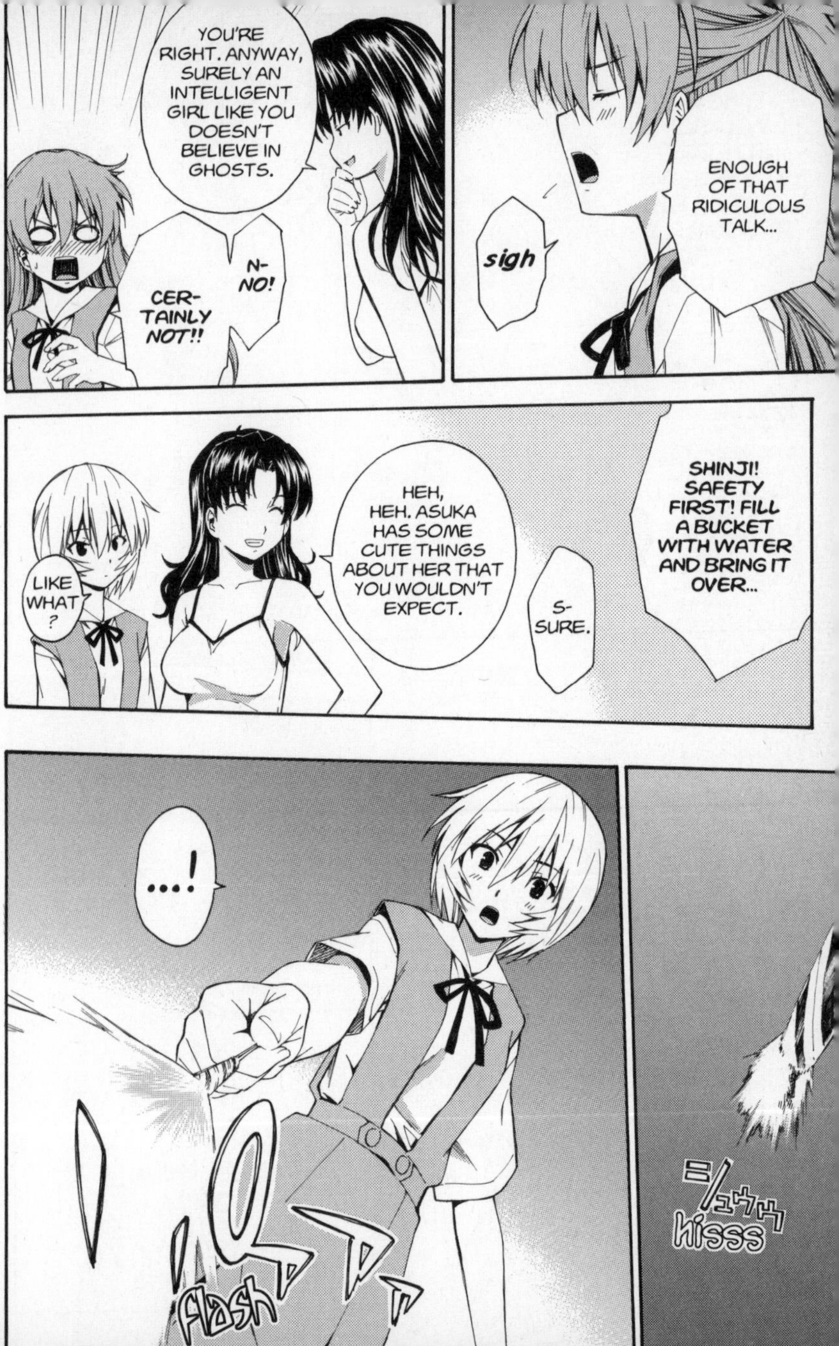
ENOUGH OF THAT RIDICULOUS TALK...
sigh
YOU'RE RIGHT. ANYWAY, SURELY AN INTELLIGENT GIRL LIKE YOU DOESN'T BELIEVE IN GHOSTS.
N-NO!
CER-TAINLY NOT!!
SHINJI! SAFETY FIRST! FILL A BUCKET WITH WATER AND BRING IT OVER...
S-SURE.
HEH, HEH. ASUKA HAS SOME CUTE THINGS ABOUT HER THAT YOU WOULDN'T EXPECT.
LIKE WHAT?
hisss
...!
flash

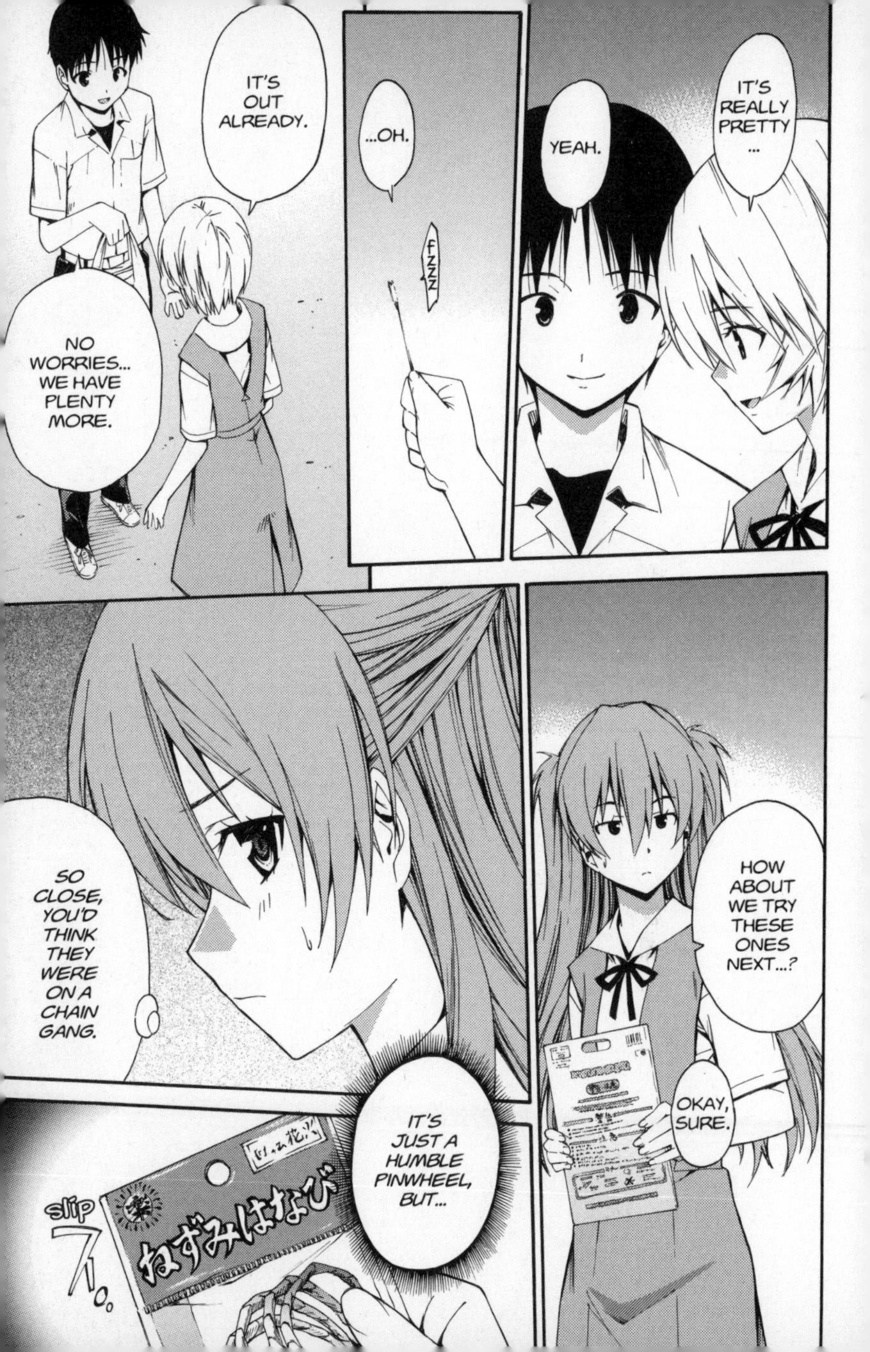
IT'S REALLY PRETTY ...
YEAH.
...OH.
FZZZ
IT'S OUT ALREADY.
NO WORRIES... WE HAVE PLENTY MORE.
HOW ABOUT WE TRY THESE ONES NEXT...?
OKAY, SURE.
SO CLOSE, YOU'D THINK THEY WERE ON A CHAIN GANG.
IT'S JUST A HUMBLE PINWHEEL, BUT...
ねずみはなび
slip

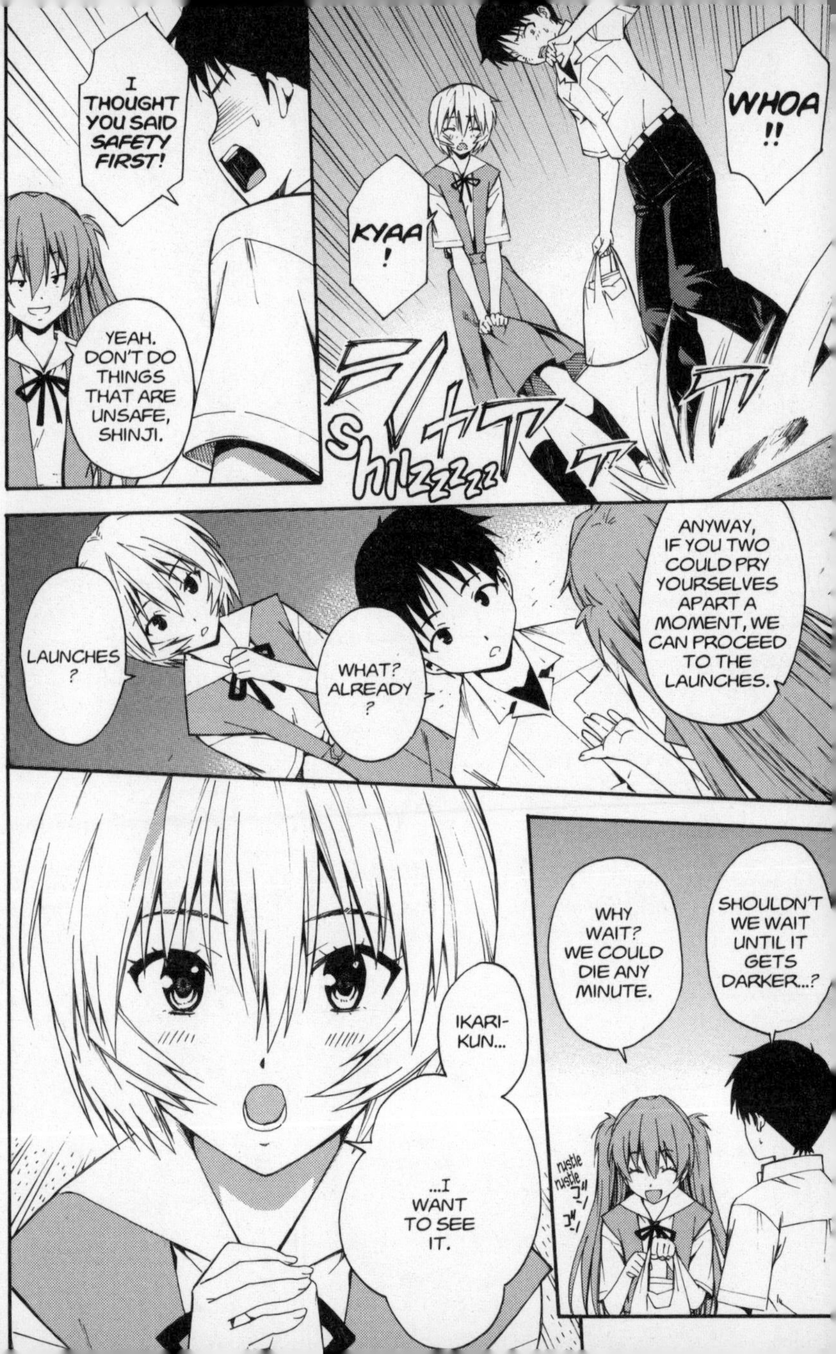
WHOA !!
KYAA !
shizzzzzz
I THOUGHT YOU SAID SAFETY FIRST!
YEAH. DON'T DO THINGS THAT ARE UNSAFE, SHINJI.
ANYWAY, IF YOU TWO COULD PRY YOURSELVES APART A MOMENT, WE CAN PROCEED TO THE LAUNCHES.
WHAT? ALREADY ?
LAUNCHES ?
SHOULDN'T WE WAIT UNTIL IT GETS DARKER...?
WHY WAIT? WE COULD DIE ANY MINUTE.
rustle rustle
IKARI-KUN...
...I WANT TO SEE IT.

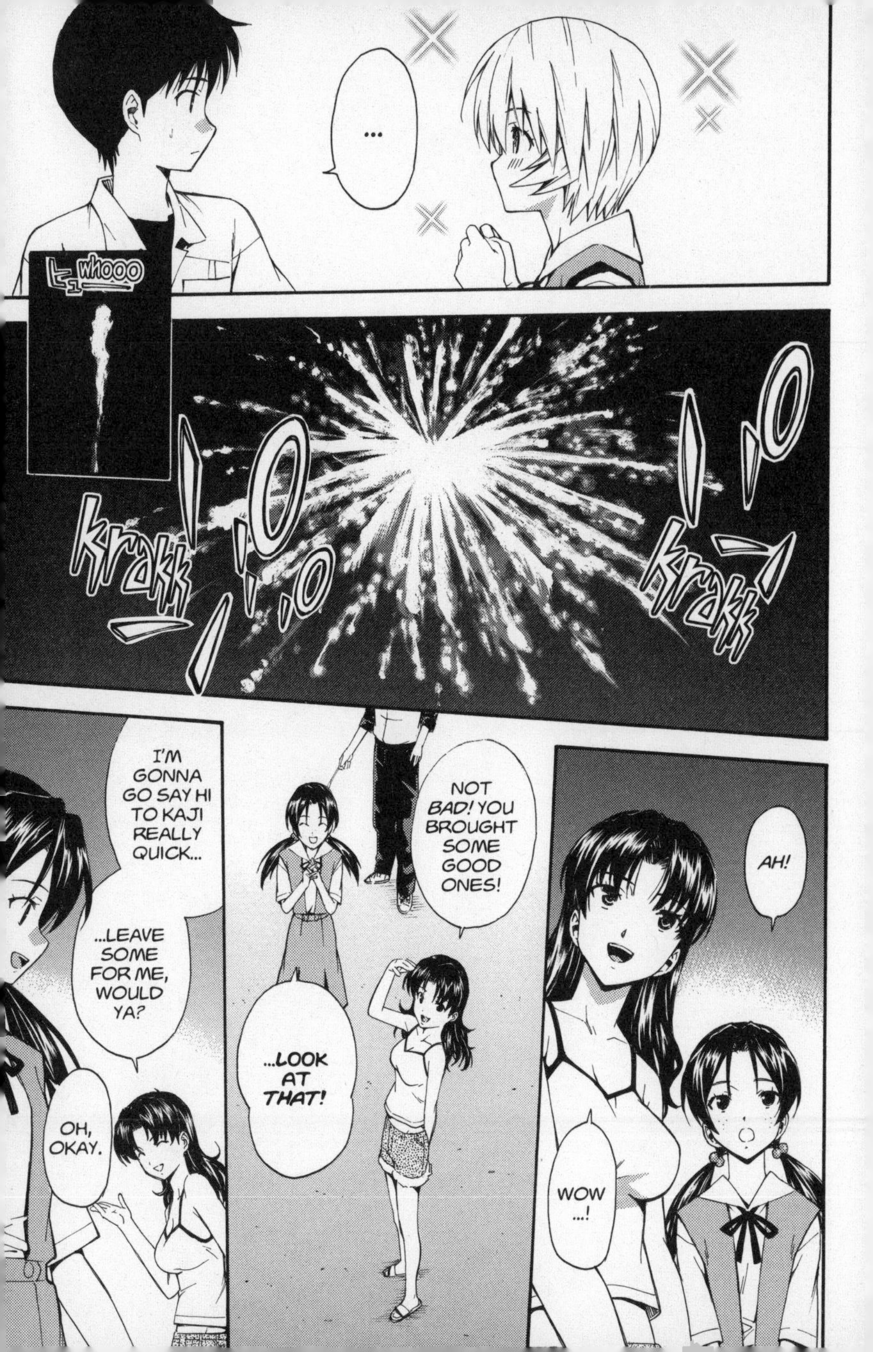
...
whooo
krakk
krakk
AH!
WOW ...!
NOT BAD! YOU BROUGHT SOME GOOD ONES!
...LOOK AT THAT!
I'M GONNA GO SAY HI TO KAJI REALLY QUICK...
...LEAVE SOME FOR ME, WOULD YA?
OH, OKAY.

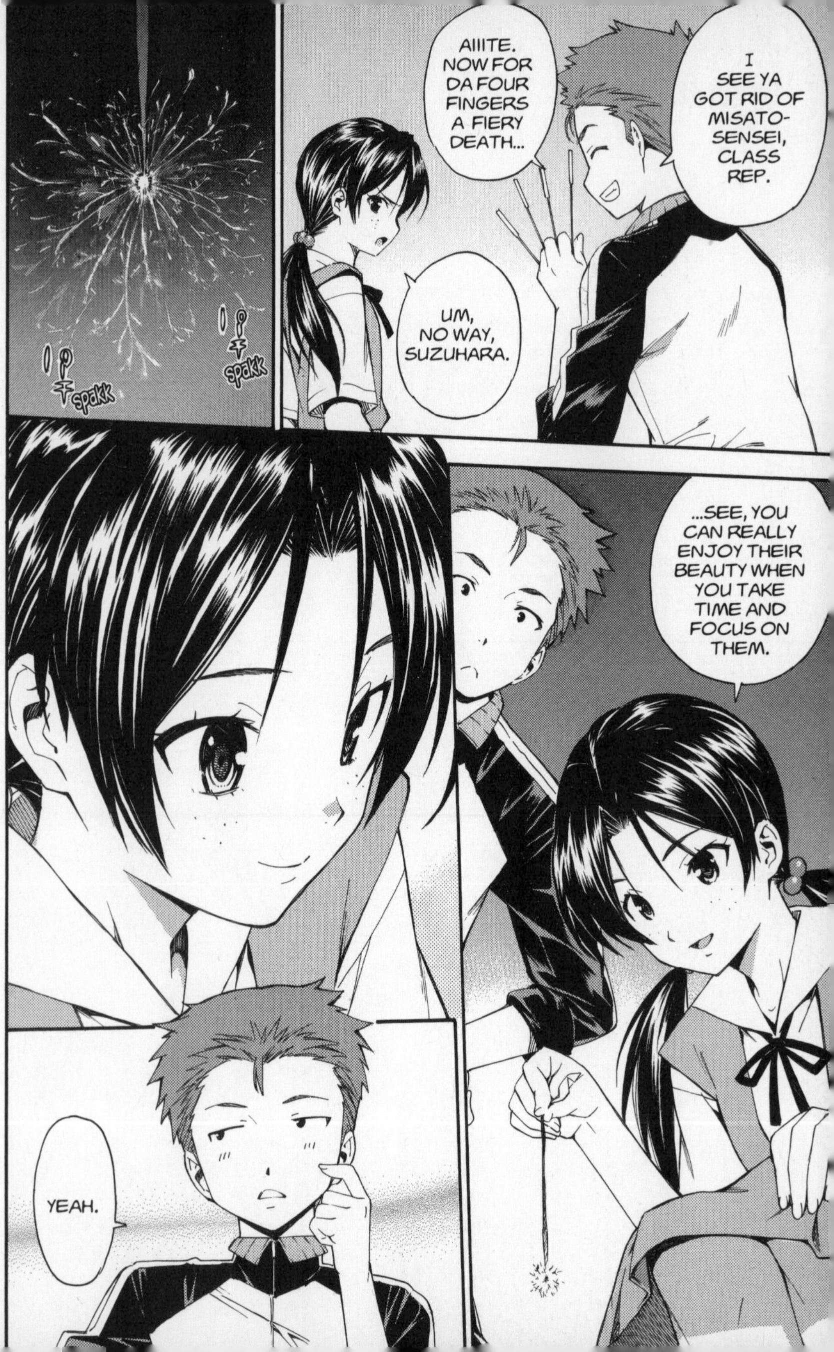
I SEE YA GOT RID OF MISATO-SENSEI, CLASS REP.
AIIITE. NOW FOR DA FOUR FINGERS A FIERY DEATH...
UM, NO WAY, SUZUHARA.
spakk
spakk
...SEE, YOU CAN REALLY ENJOY THEIR BEAUTY WHEN YOU TAKE TIME AND FOCUS ON THEM.
YEAH.

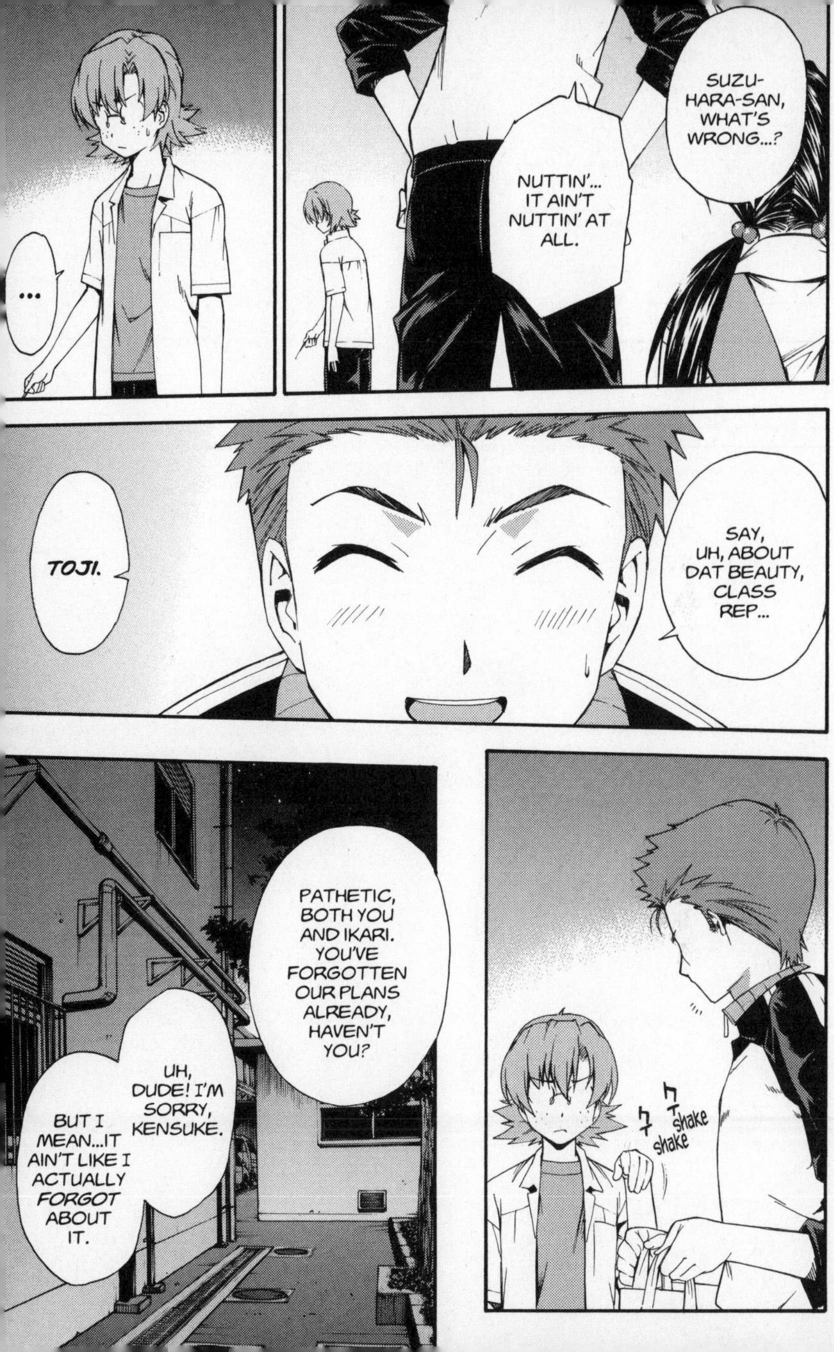
SUZU-HARA-SAN, WHAT'S WRONG...?
NUTTIN'... IT AIN'T NUTTIN' AT ALL.
...
SAY, UH, ABOUT DAT BEAUTY, CLASS REP...
TOJI.
shake shake
PATHETIC, BOTH YOU AND IKARI. YOU'VE FORGOTTEN OUR PLANS ALREADY, HAVEN'T YOU?
UH, DUDE! I'M SORRY, KENSUKE.
BUT I MEAN...IT AIN'T LIKE I ACTUALLY *FORGOT* ABOUT IT.

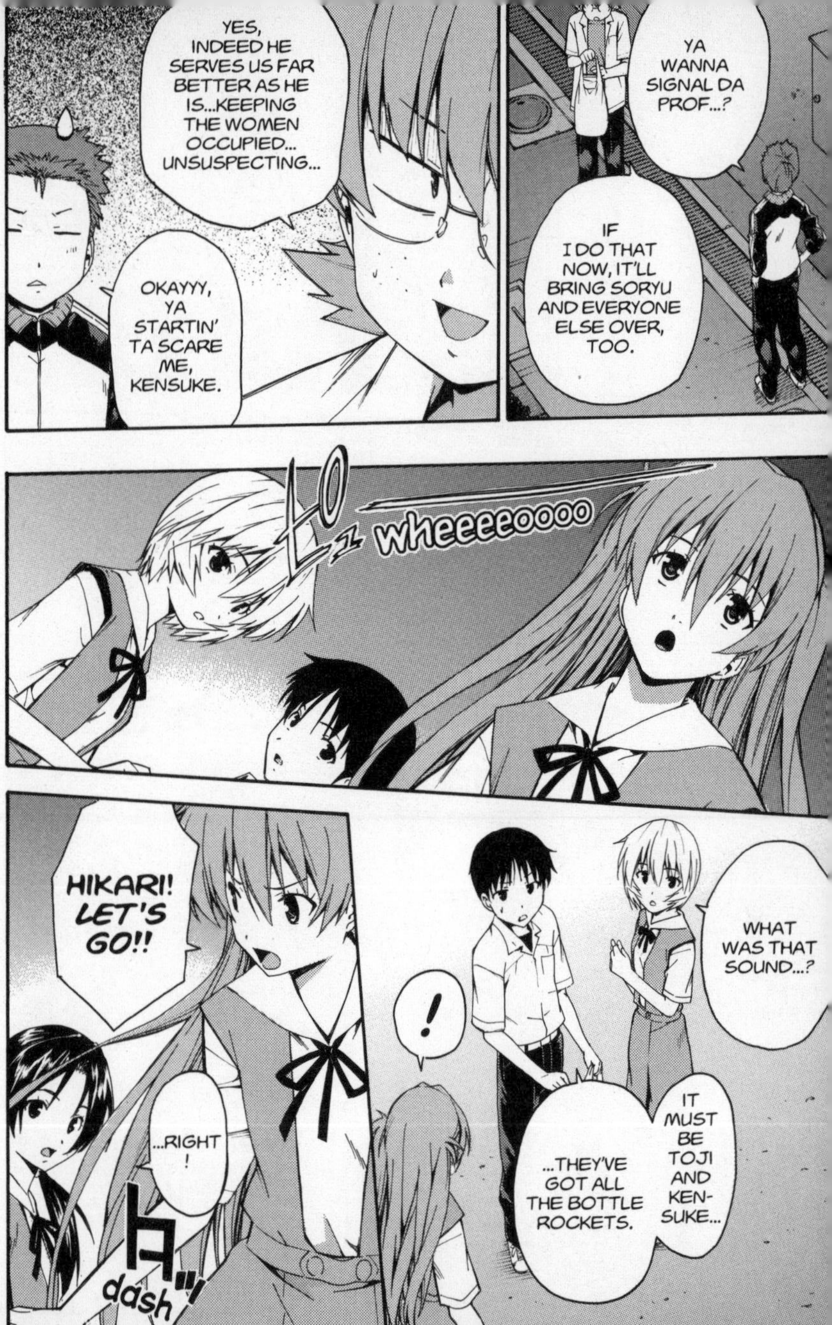
YA WANNA SIGNAL DA PROF...?
IF I DO THAT NOW, IT'LL BRING SORYU AND EVERYONE ELSE OVER, TOO.
YES, INDEED HE SERVES US FAR BETTER AS HE IS...KEEPING THE WOMEN OCCUPIED... UNSUSPECTING...
OKAYYY, YA STARTIN' TA SCARE ME, KENSUKE.
wheeeeoooo
WHAT WAS THAT SOUND...?
IT MUST BE TOJI AND KEN-SUKE...
...THEY'VE GOT ALL THE BOTTLE ROCKETS.
!
HIKARI! LET'S GO!!
...RIGHT!
dash

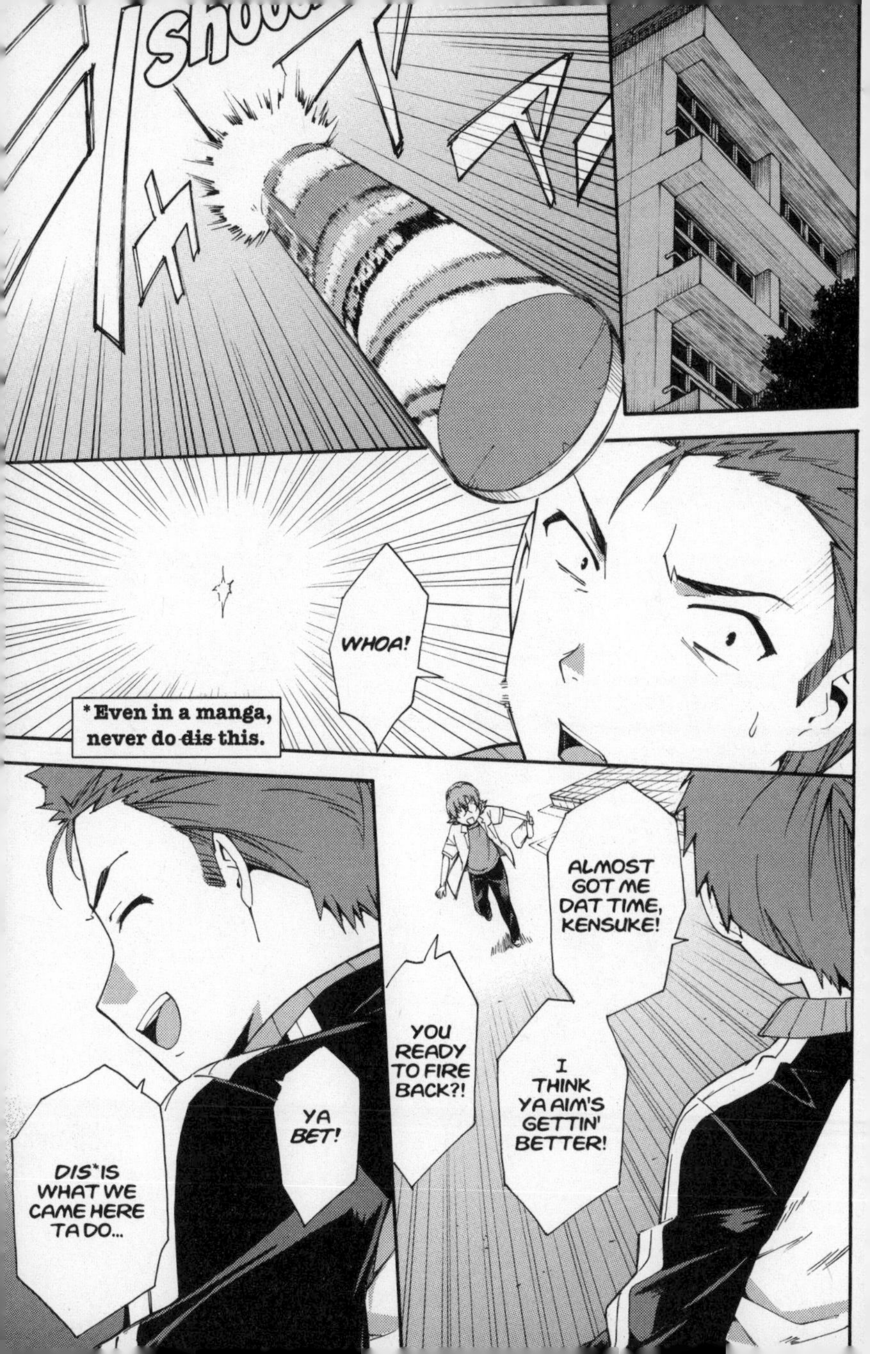
Shoo
WHOA!
* Even in a manga, never do ~~dis~~ this.
ALMOST GOT ME DAT TIME, KENSUKE!
I THINK YA AIM'S GETTIN' BETTER!
YOU READY TO FIRE BACK?!
YA BET!
DIS* IS WHAT WE CAME HERE TA DO...

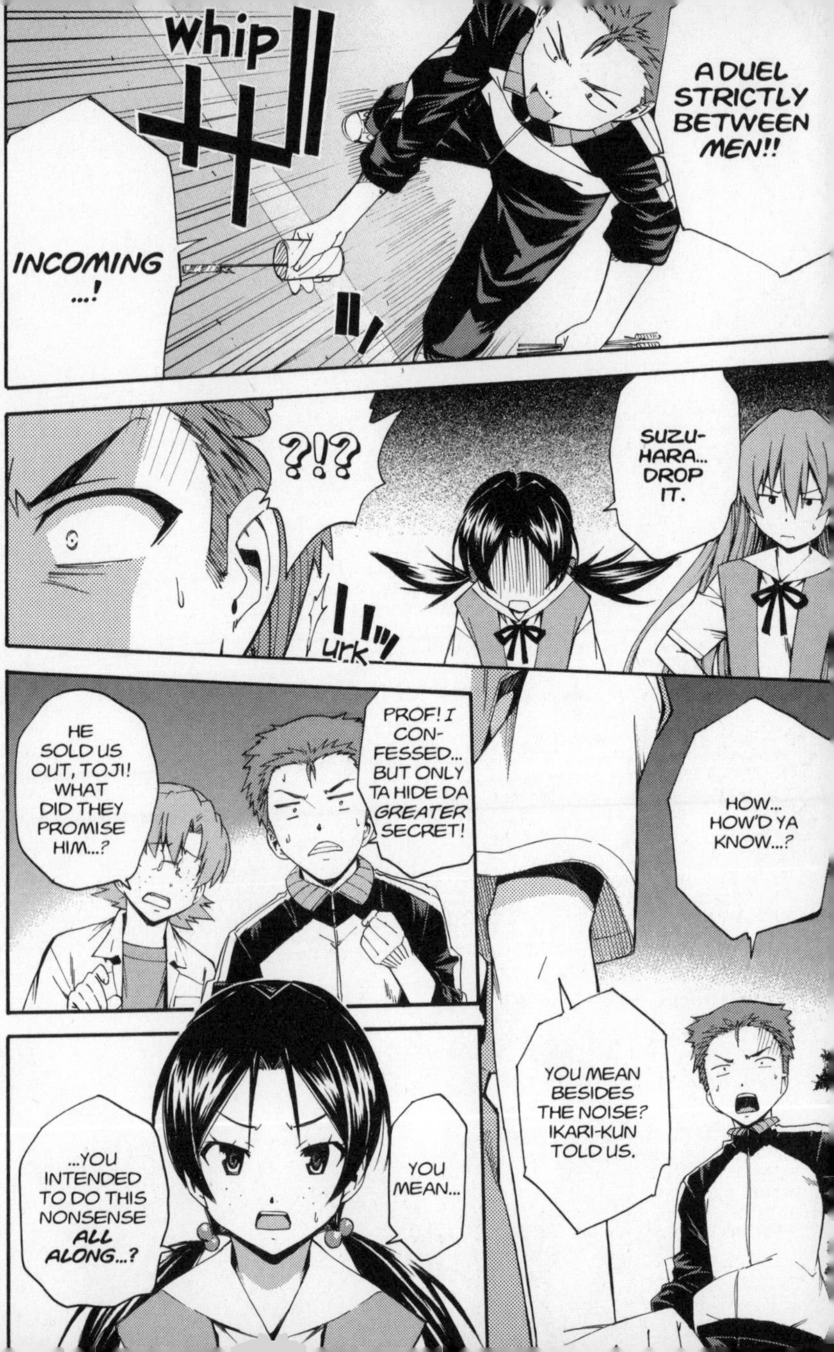
A DUEL STRICTLY BETWEEN MEN!!
whip
INCOMING ...!
SUZU-HARA... DROP IT.
?!?
urk
HOW... HOW'D YA KNOW...?
YOU MEAN BESIDES THE NOISE? IKARI-KUN TOLD US.
PROF! I CON-FESSED... BUT ONLY TA HIDE DA GREATER SECRET!
HE SOLD US OUT, TOJI! WHAT DID THEY PROMISE HIM...?
YOU MEAN...
...YOU INTENDED TO DO THIS NONSENSE ALL ALONG...?

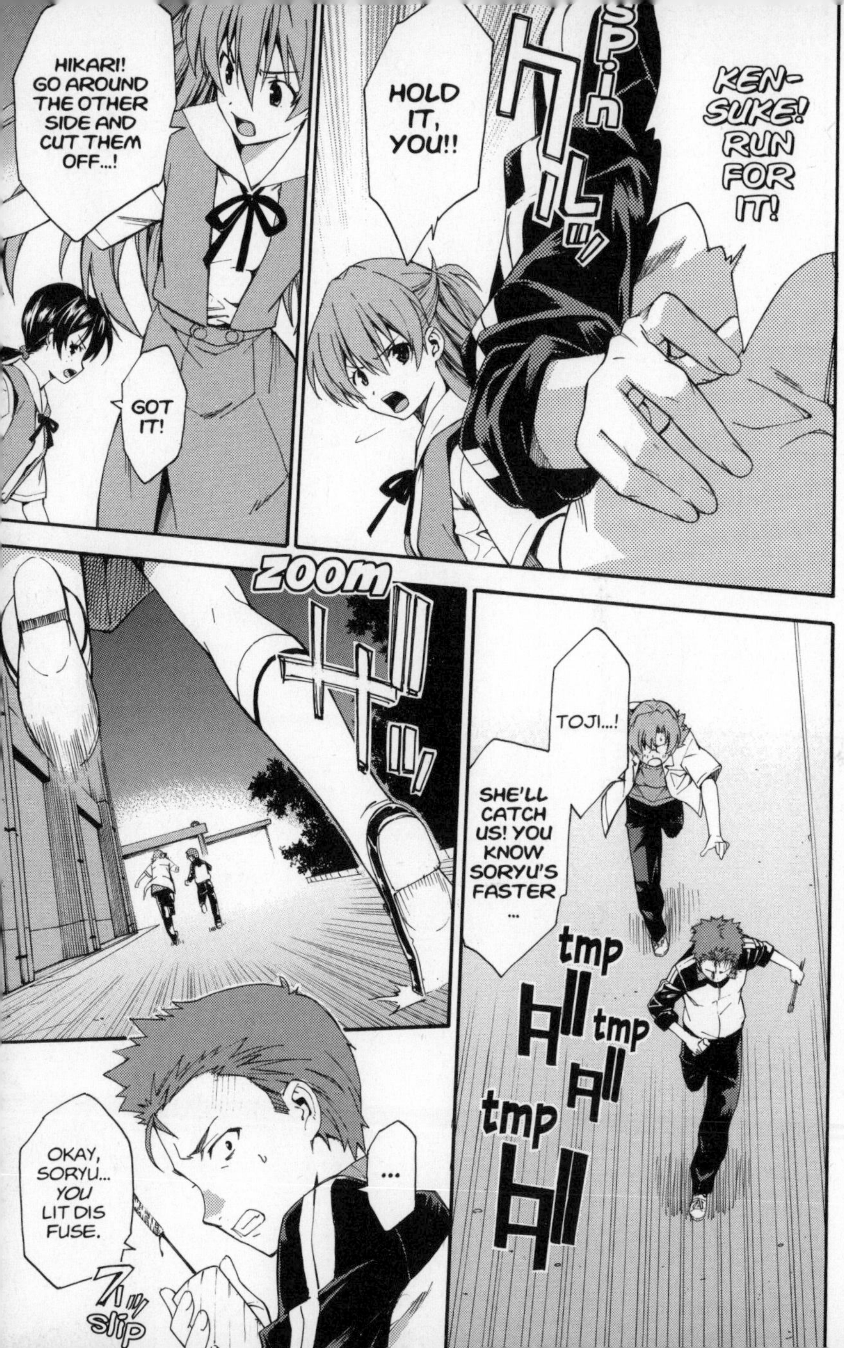
KEN-SUKE! RUN FOR IT!
spin
HOLD IT, YOU!!
HIKARI! GO AROUND THE OTHER SIDE AND CUT THEM OFF...!
GOT IT!
TOJI...!
SHE'LL CATCH US! YOU KNOW SORYU'S FASTER ...
tmp
tmp
tmp
zoom
...
OKAY, SORYU... YOU LIT DIS FUSE.
slip

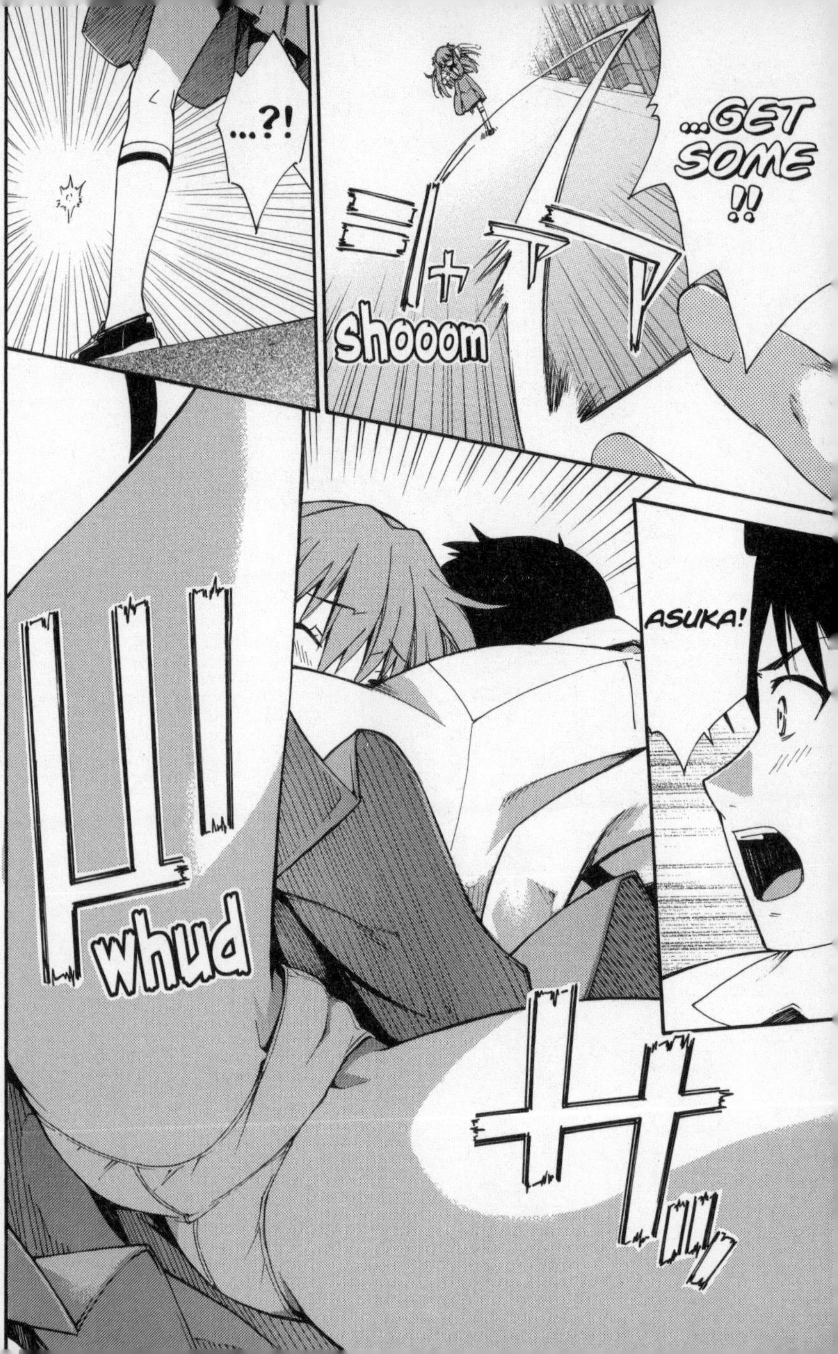

...GET SOME!!
shooom
...?!
ASUKA!
whud

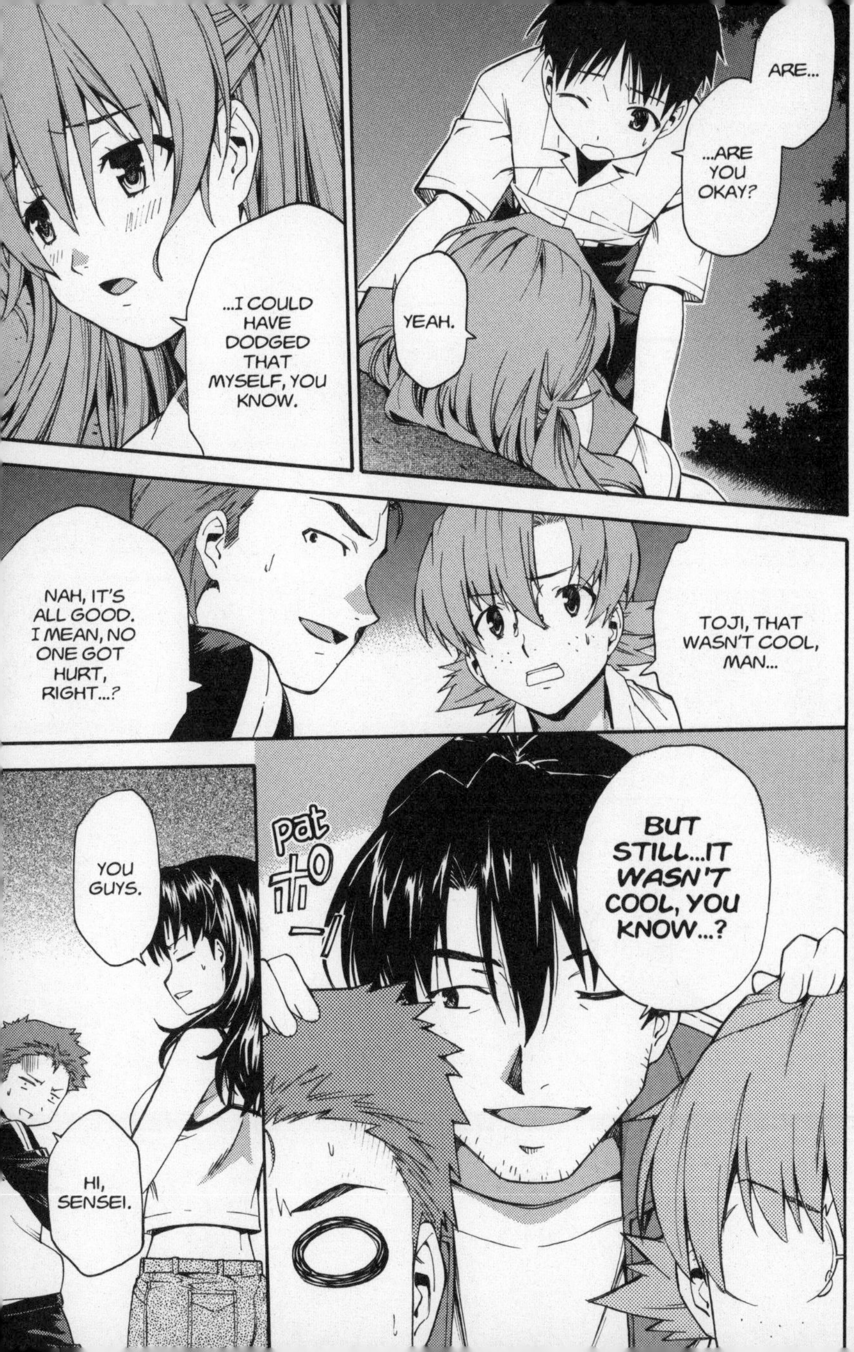
ARE...
...ARE YOU OKAY?
YEAH.
...I COULD HAVE DODGED THAT MYSELF, YOU KNOW.
TOJI, THAT WASN'T COOL, MAN...
NAH, IT'S ALL GOOD. I MEAN, NO ONE GOT HURT, RIGHT...?
BUT STILL...IT WASN'T COOL, YOU KNOW...?
pat
YOU GUYS.
HI, SENSEI.

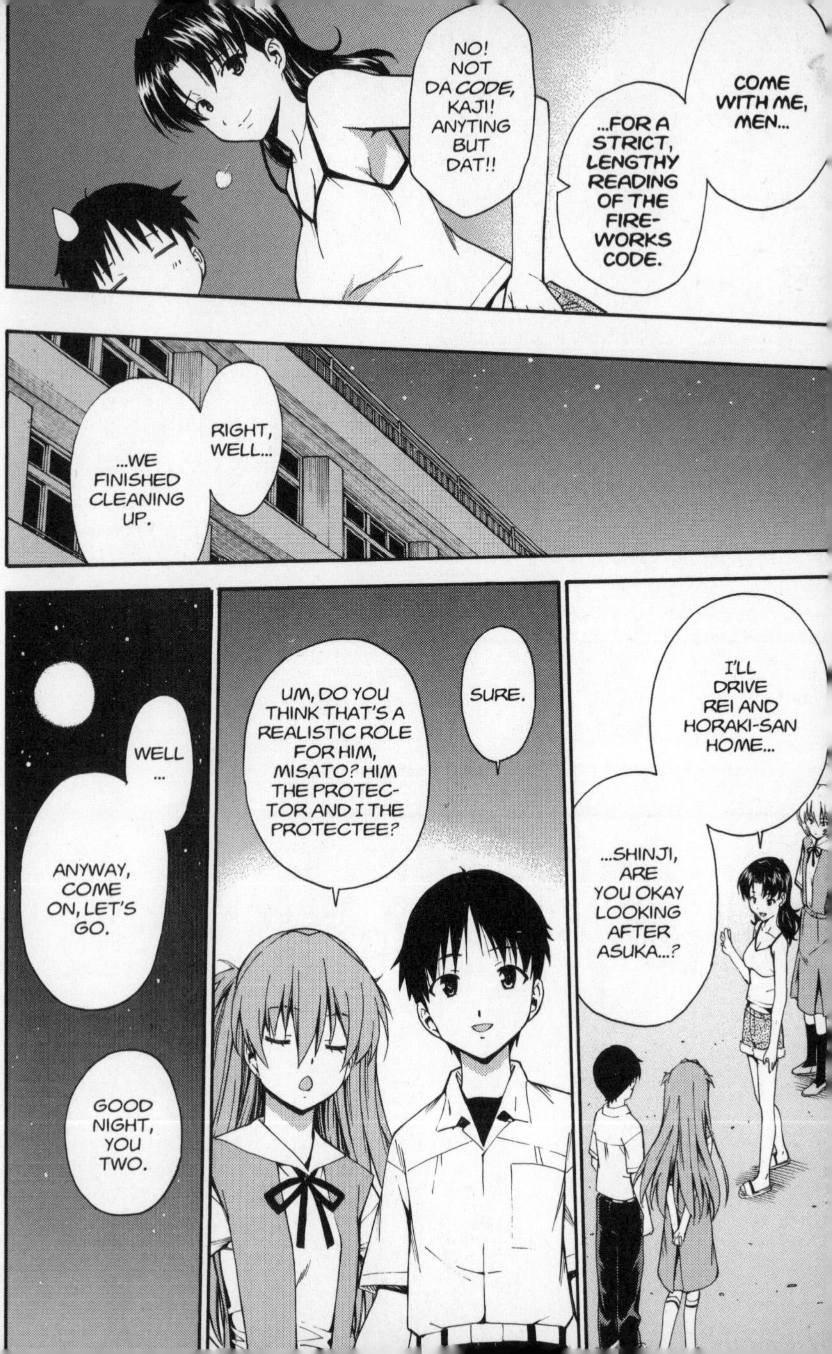
COME WITH ME, MEN...
...FOR A STRICT, LENGTHY READING OF THE FIRE-WORKS CODE.
NO! NOT DA CODE, KAJI! ANYTING BUT DAT!!
RIGHT, WELL...
...WE FINISHED CLEANING UP.
I'LL DRIVE REI AND HORAKI-SAN HOME...
...SHINJI, ARE YOU OKAY LOOKING AFTER ASUKA...?
SURE.
UM, DO YOU THINK THAT'S A REALISTIC ROLE FOR HIM, MISATO? HIM THE PROTECTOR AND I THE PROTECTEE?
WELL ...
ANYWAY, COME ON, LET'S GO.
GOOD NIGHT, YOU TWO.

flik チカ
flik チカ
THE STREET-LIGHTS AREN'T THAT BRIGHT, ARE THEY...?
THOSE WHO WALK IN COLD DARKNESS ARE AWAKENED...
GREAT... HAD TO REMEMBER THAT.
ASUKA ...?
WHAT ...?
whoosh- カ
KYAA !!

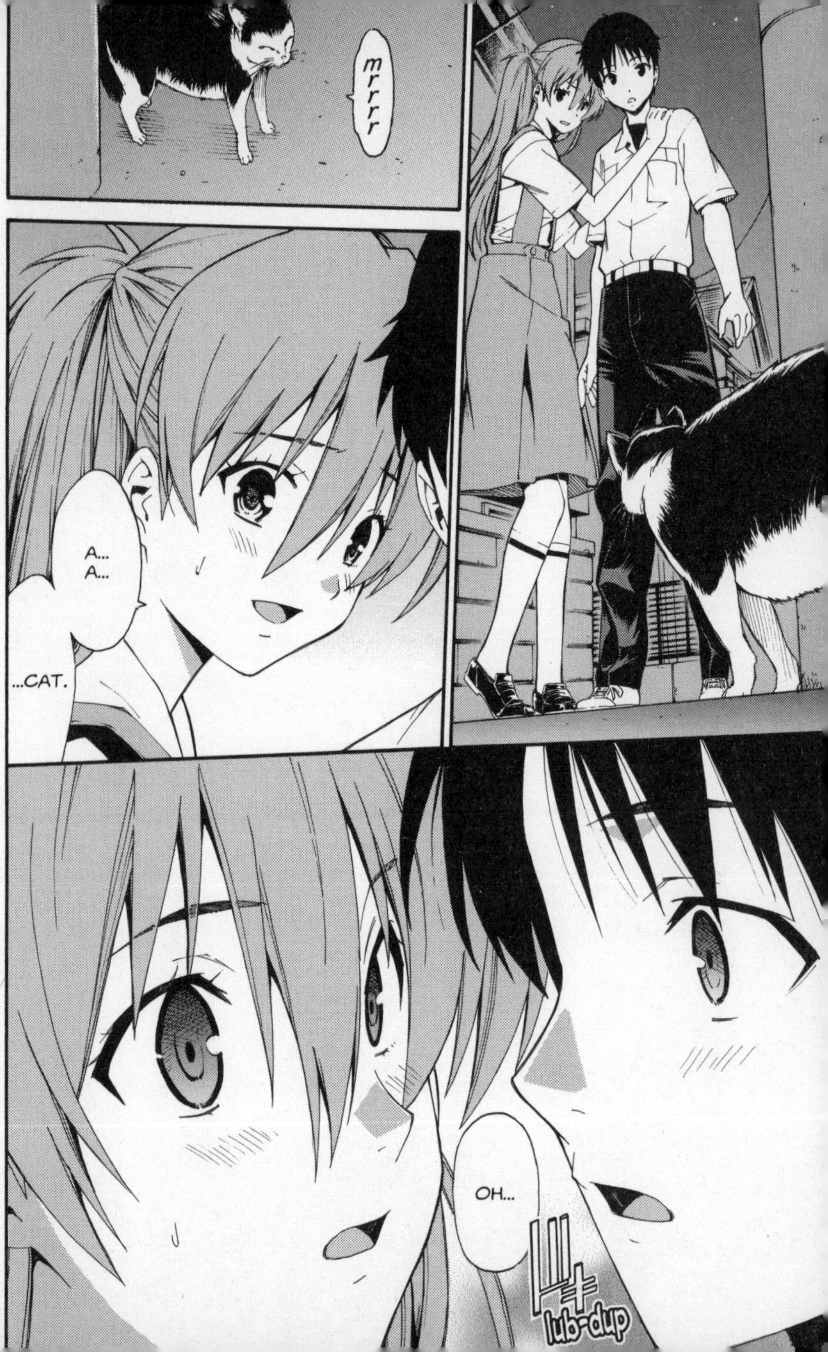
mrrrr
A... A...
...CAT.
OH...
lub-dup

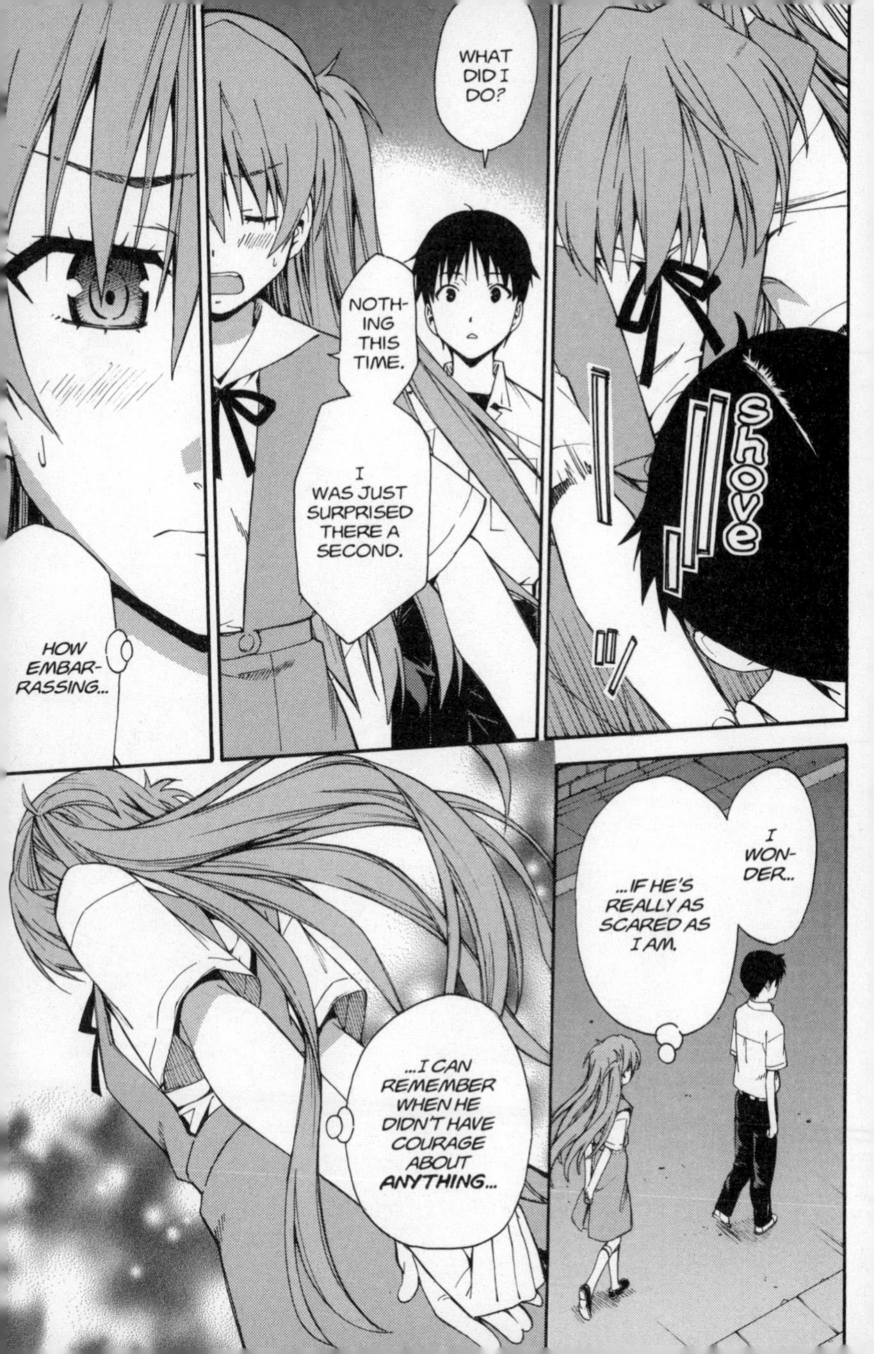
SHOVE
WHAT DID I DO?
NOTHING THIS TIME.
I WAS JUST SURPRISED THERE A SECOND.
HOW EMBARRASSING...
I WONDER...
...IF HE'S REALLY AS SCARED AS I AM.
...I CAN REMEMBER WHEN HE DIDN'T HAVE COURAGE ABOUT ANYTHING...

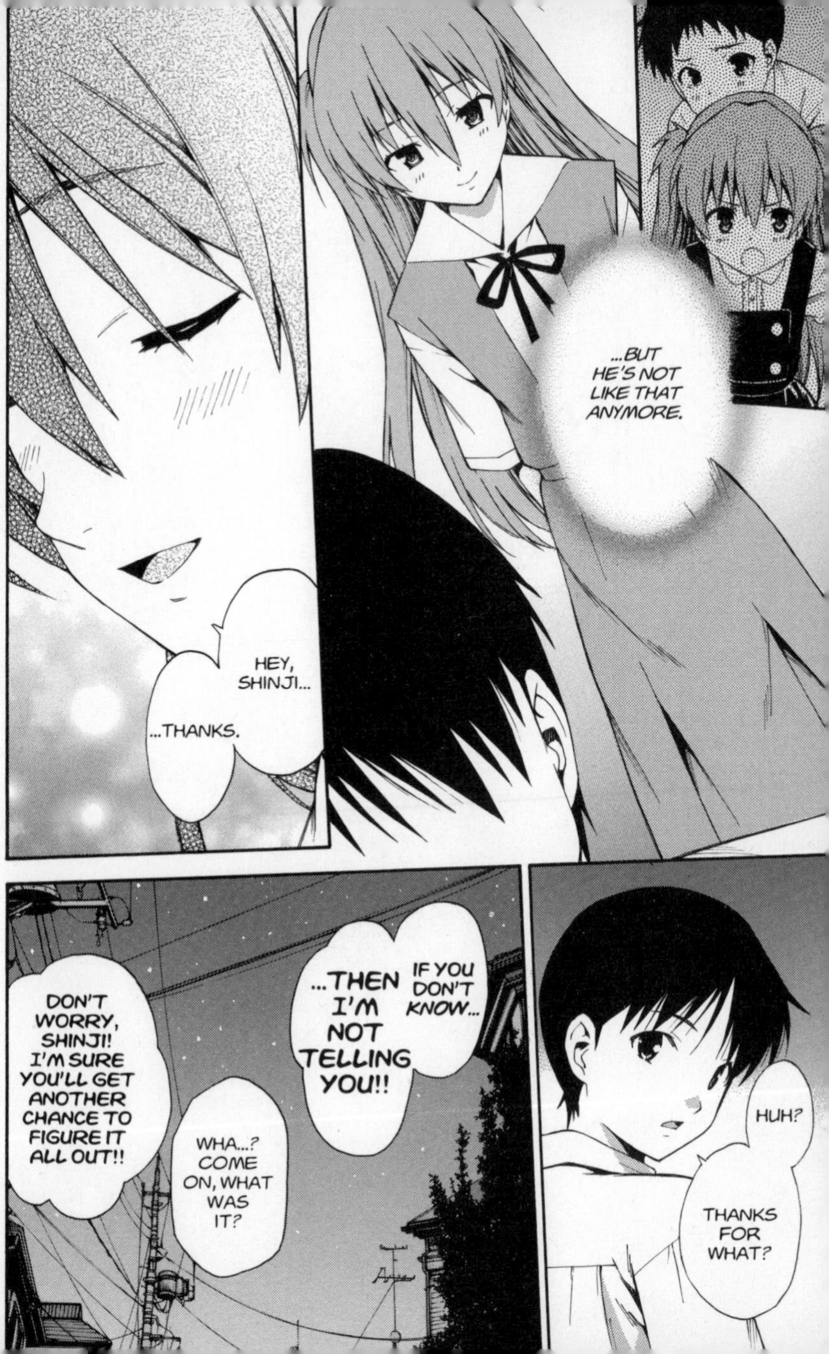
...BUT HE'S NOT LIKE THAT ANYMORE.
HEY, SHINJI...
...THANKS.
HUH?
THANKS FOR WHAT?
IF YOU DON'T KNOW...
...THEN I'M NOT TELLING YOU!!
WHA...? COME ON, WHAT WAS IT?
DON'T WORRY, SHINJI! I'M SURE YOU'LL GET ANOTHER CHANCE TO FIGURE IT ALL OUT!!

the shinji ikari raising project

NEON GENESIS EVANGELION
THE SHINJI IKARI RAISING PROJECT

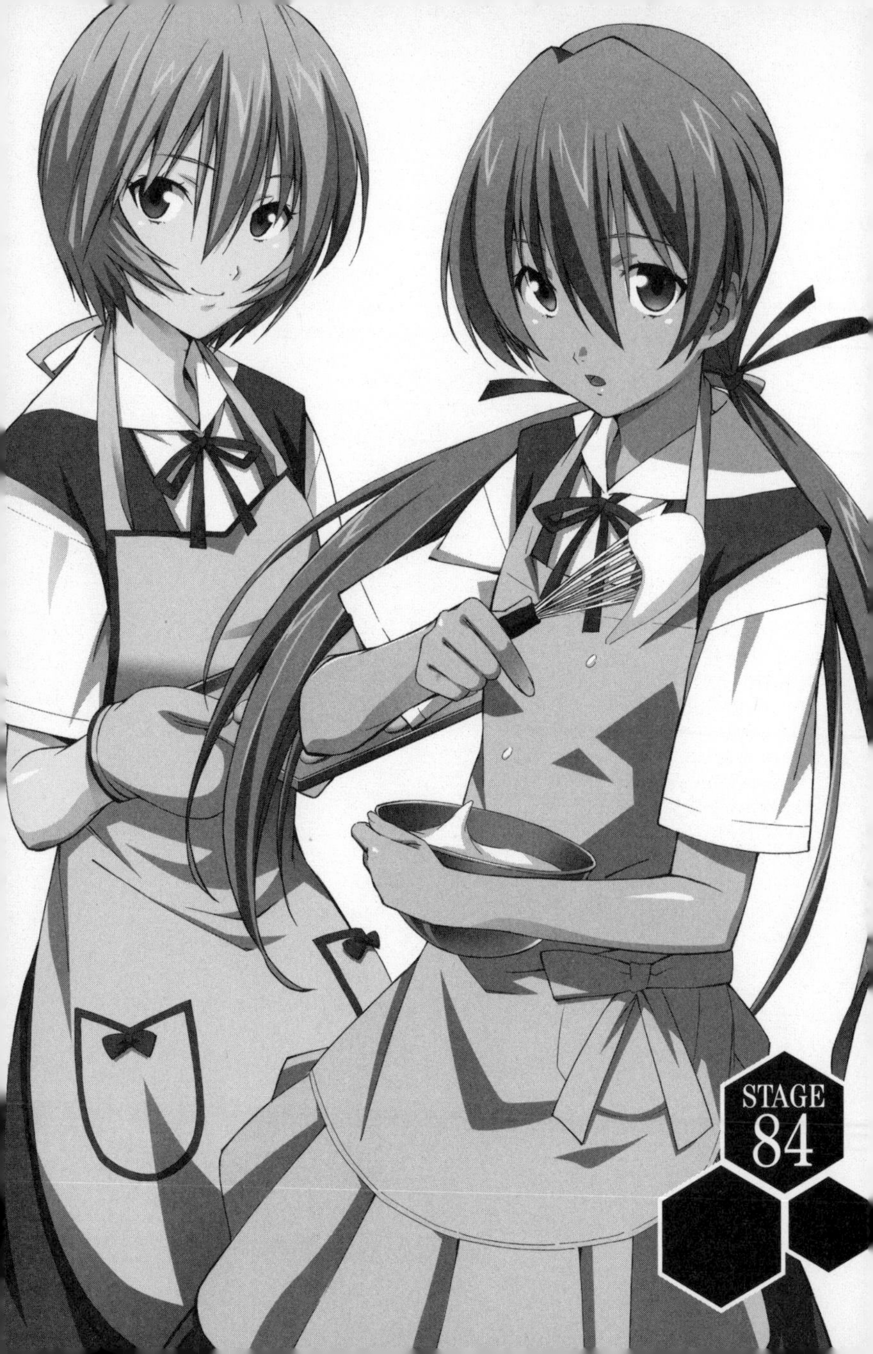
STAGE
84

NEON GENESIS
EVANGELION
THE SHINJI IKARI RAISING PROJECT

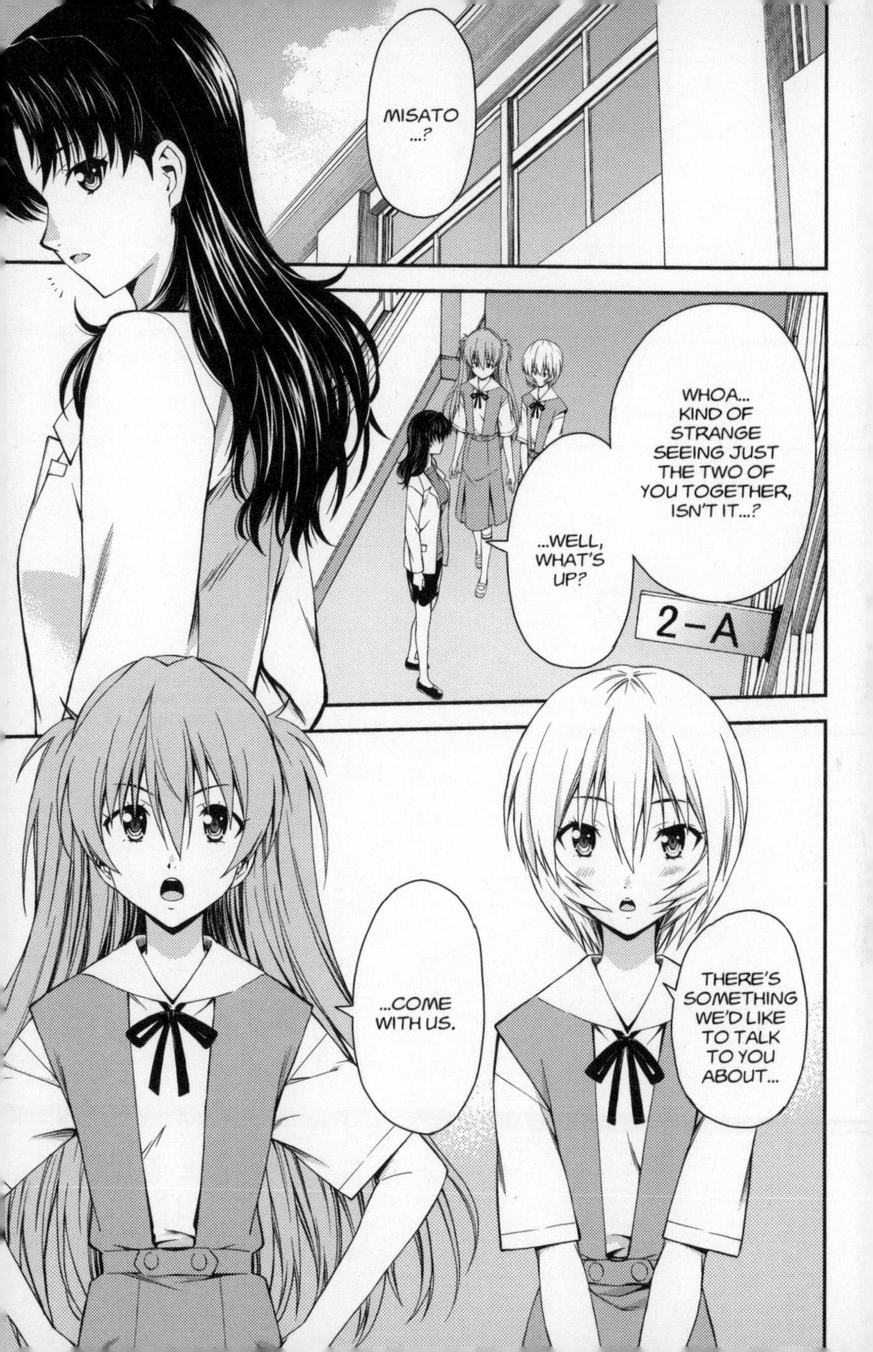
MISATO ...?
WHOA... KIND OF STRANGE SEEING JUST THE TWO OF YOU TOGETHER, ISN'T IT...?
...WELL, WHAT'S UP?
2-A
THERE'S SOMETHING WE'D LIKE TO TALK TO YOU ABOUT...
...COME WITH US.

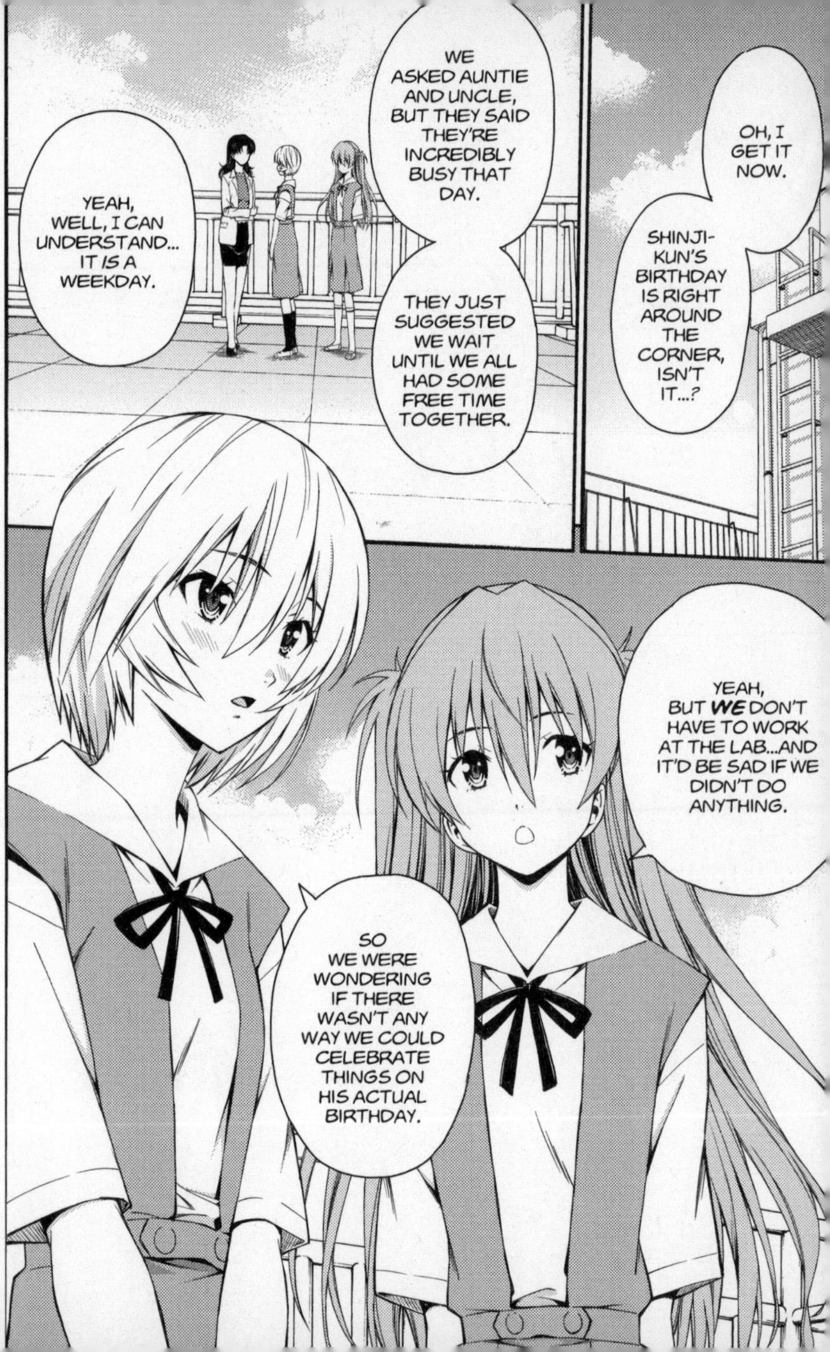
OH, I GET IT NOW.
SHINJI-KUN'S BIRTHDAY IS RIGHT AROUND THE CORNER, ISN'T IT...?
WE ASKED AUNTIE AND UNCLE, BUT THEY SAID THEY'RE INCREDIBLY BUSY THAT DAY.
THEY JUST SUGGESTED WE WAIT UNTIL WE ALL HAD SOME FREE TIME TOGETHER.
YEAH, WELL, I CAN UNDERSTAND... IT *IS* A WEEKDAY.
YEAH, BUT ***WE*** DON'T HAVE TO WORK AT THE LAB...AND IT'D BE SAD IF WE DIDN'T DO ANYTHING.
SO WE WERE WONDERING IF THERE WASN'T ANY WAY WE COULD CELEBRATE THINGS ON HIS ACTUAL BIRTHDAY.

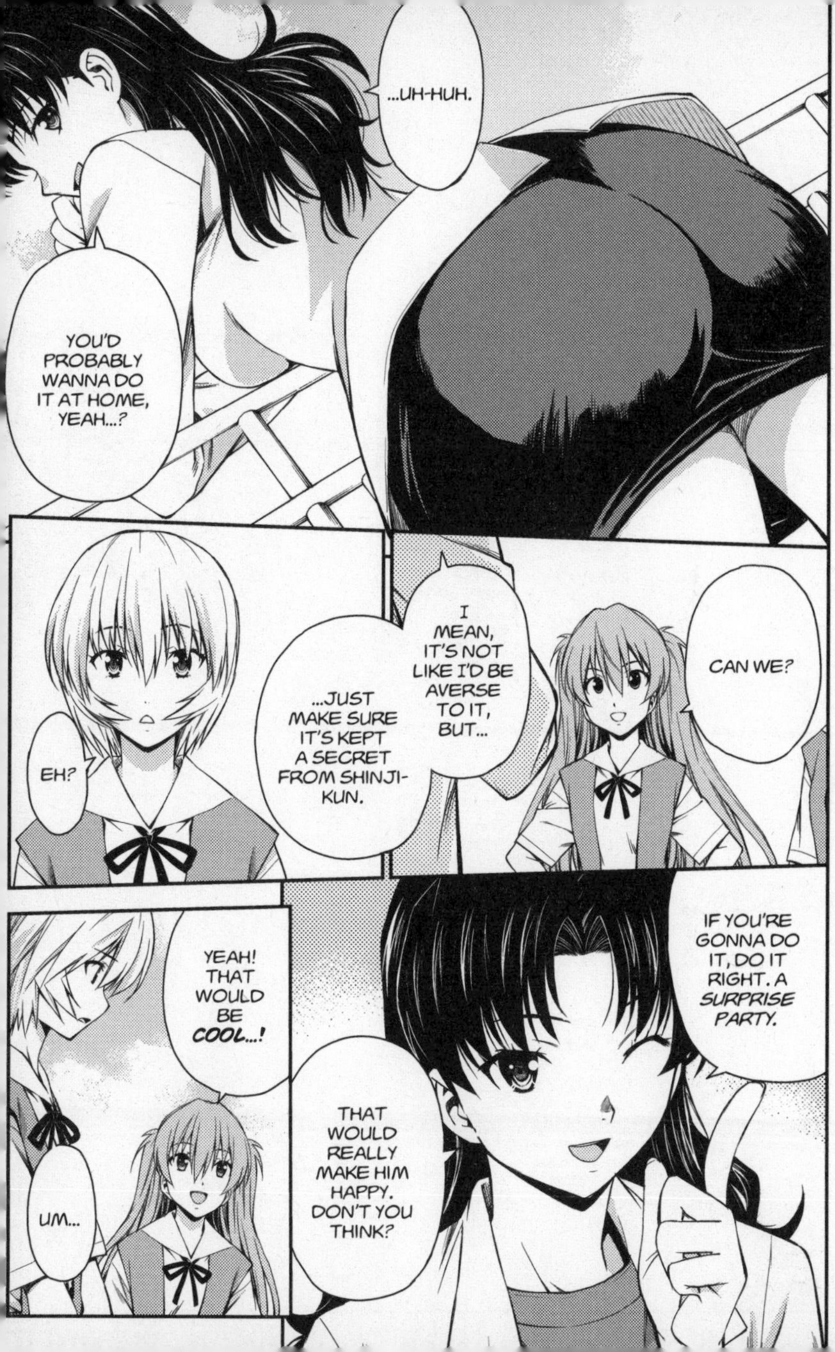
...UH-HUH.
YOU'D PROBABLY WANNA DO IT AT HOME, YEAH...?
CAN WE?
I MEAN, IT'S NOT LIKE I'D BE AVERSE TO IT, BUT...
...JUST MAKE SURE IT'S KEPT A SECRET FROM SHINJI-KUN.
EH?
IF YOU'RE GONNA DO IT, DO IT RIGHT. A *SURPRISE PARTY.*
THAT WOULD REALLY MAKE HIM HAPPY. DON'T YOU THINK?
YEAH! THAT WOULD BE ***COOL...!***
UM...

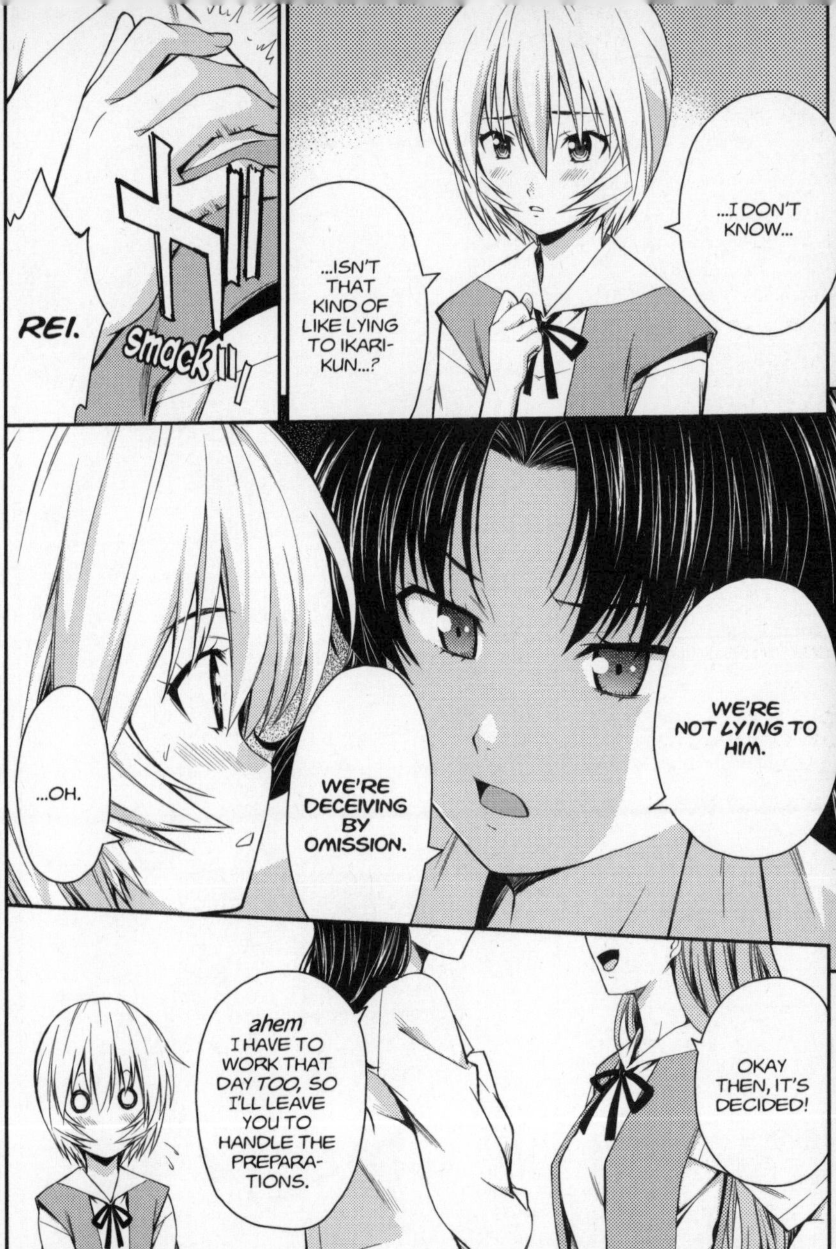
...I DON'T KNOW...
...ISN'T THAT KIND OF LIKE LYING TO IKARI-KUN...?
smack
REI.
WE'RE NOT *LYING* TO HIM.
WE'RE DECEIVING BY OMISSION.
...OH.
OKAY THEN, IT'S DECIDED!
ahem I HAVE TO WORK THAT DAY *TOO*, SO I'LL LEAVE YOU TO HANDLE THE PREPARATIONS.

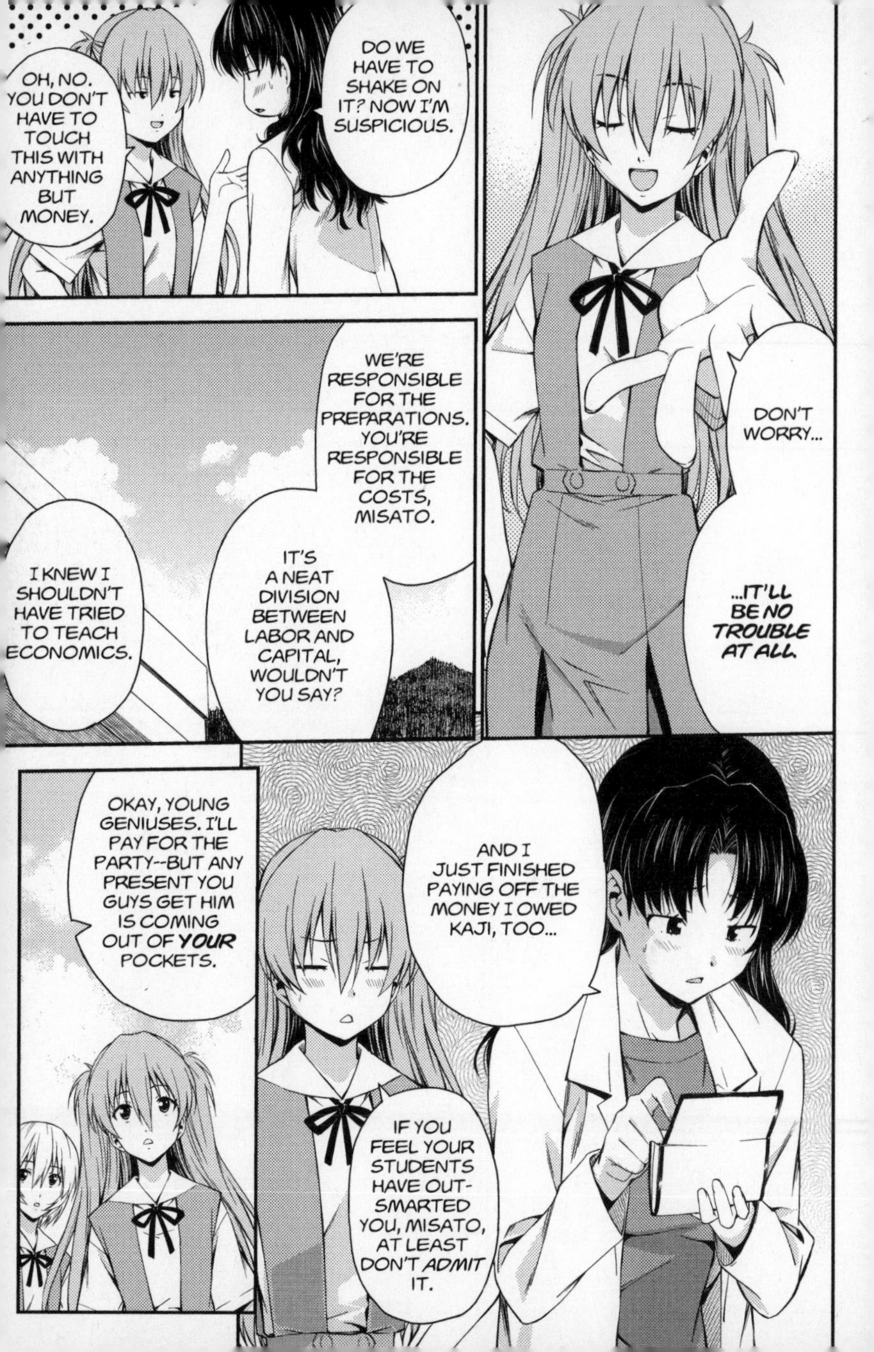
DON'T WORRY...
...IT'LL BE NO TROUBLE AT ALL.
DO WE HAVE TO SHAKE ON IT? NOW I'M SUSPICIOUS.
OH, NO. YOU DON'T HAVE TO TOUCH THIS WITH ANYTHING BUT MONEY.
WE'RE RESPONSIBLE FOR THE PREPARATIONS. YOU'RE RESPONSIBLE FOR THE COSTS, MISATO.
IT'S A NEAT DIVISION BETWEEN LABOR AND CAPITAL, WOULDN'T YOU SAY?
I KNEW I SHOULDN'T HAVE TRIED TO TEACH ECONOMICS.
AND I JUST FINISHED PAYING OFF THE MONEY I OWED KAJI, TOO...
IF YOU FEEL YOUR STUDENTS HAVE OUT-SMARTED YOU, MISATO, AT LEAST DON'T *ADMIT* IT.
OKAY, YOUNG GENIUSES. I'LL PAY FOR THE PARTY--BUT ANY PRESENT YOU GUYS GET HIM IS COMING OUT OF ***YOUR*** POCKETS.

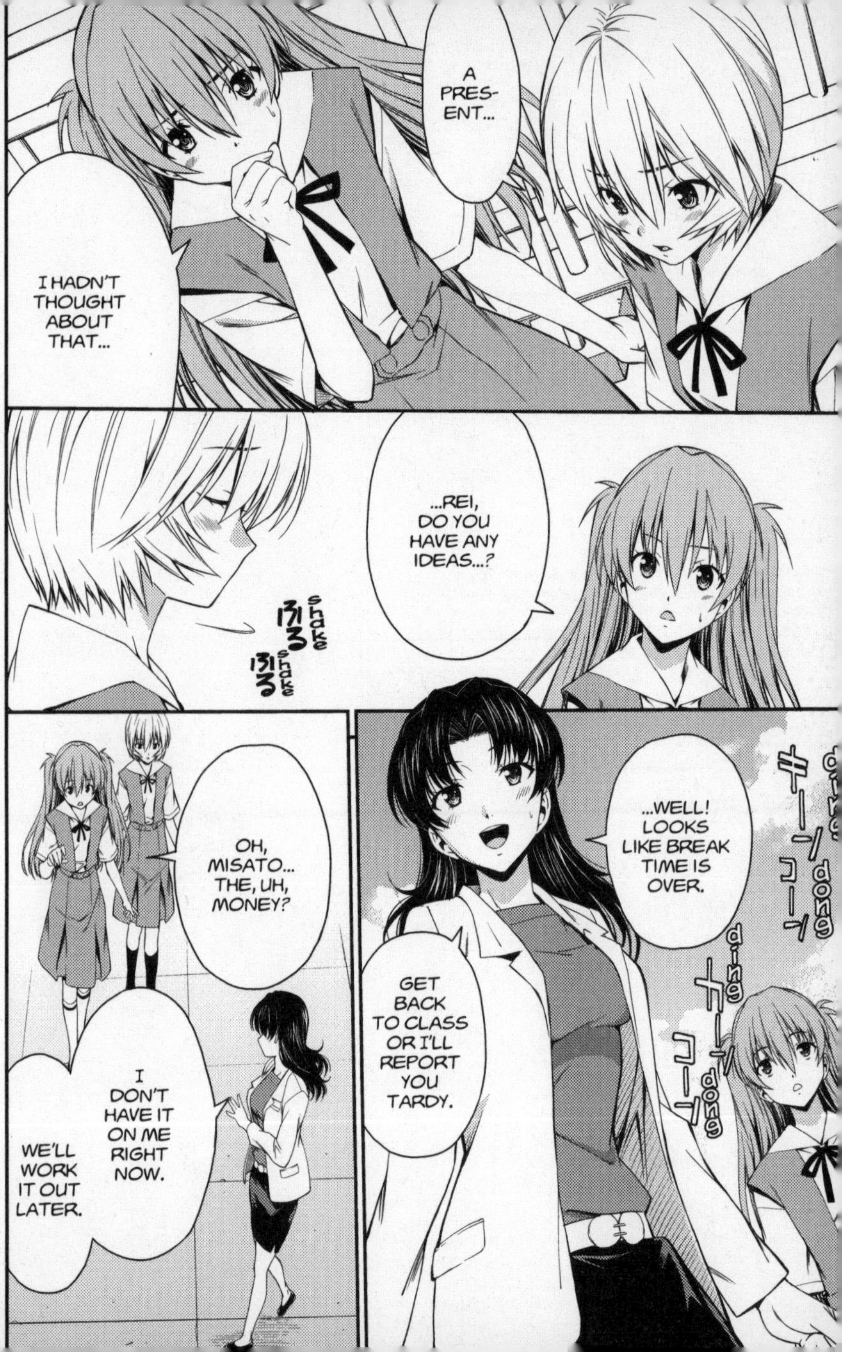
A PRESENT...
I HADN'T THOUGHT ABOUT THAT...
...REI, DO YOU HAVE ANY IDEAS...?
ふるふる shake shake
キーンコーン ding dong
カーンコーン ding dong
...WELL! LOOKS LIKE BREAK TIME IS OVER.
GET BACK TO CLASS OR I'LL REPORT YOU TARDY.
OH, MISATO... THE, UH, MONEY?
I DON'T HAVE IT ON ME RIGHT NOW. WE'LL WORK IT OUT LATER.

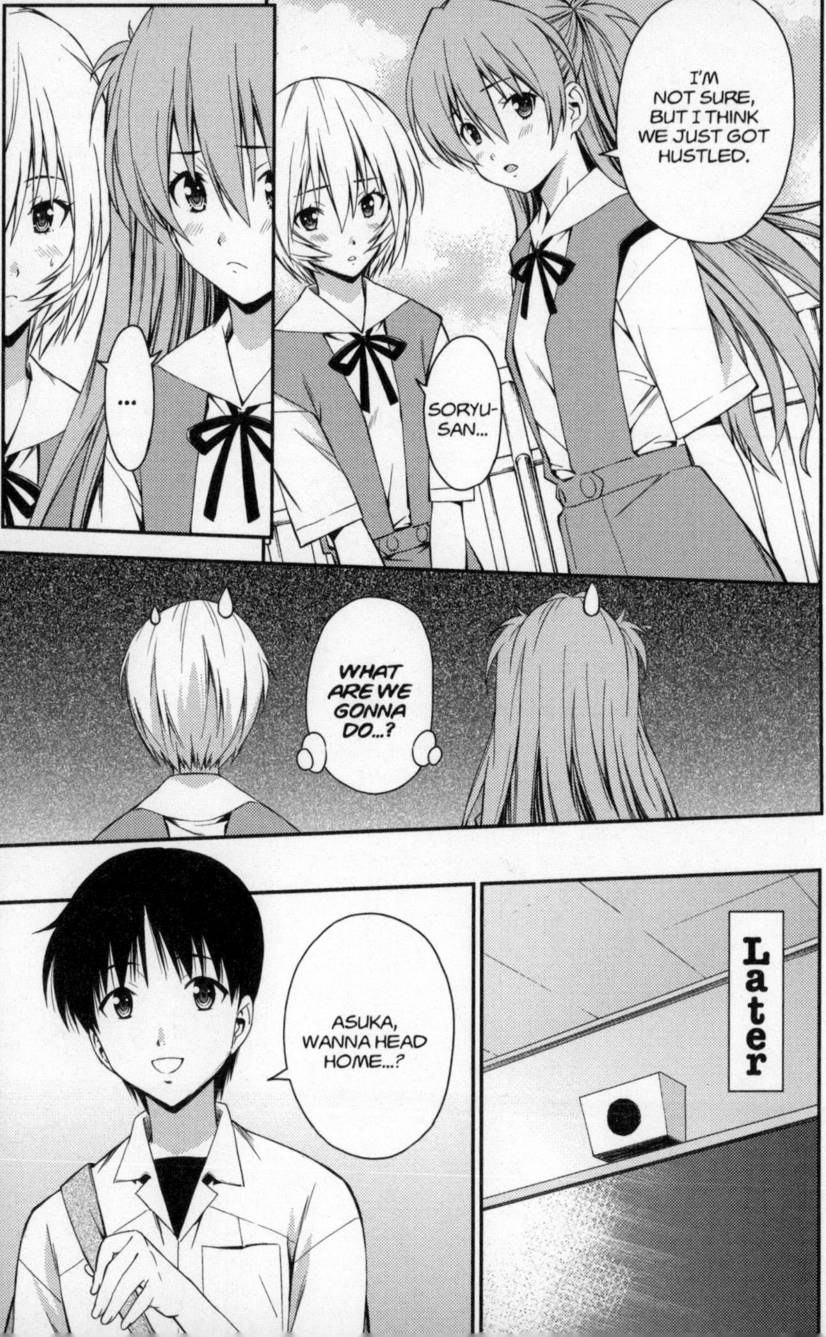
I'M NOT SURE, BUT I THINK WE JUST GOT HUSTLED.
SORYU-SAN...
...
WHAT ARE WE GONNA DO...?
Later
ASUKA, WANNA HEAD HOME...?

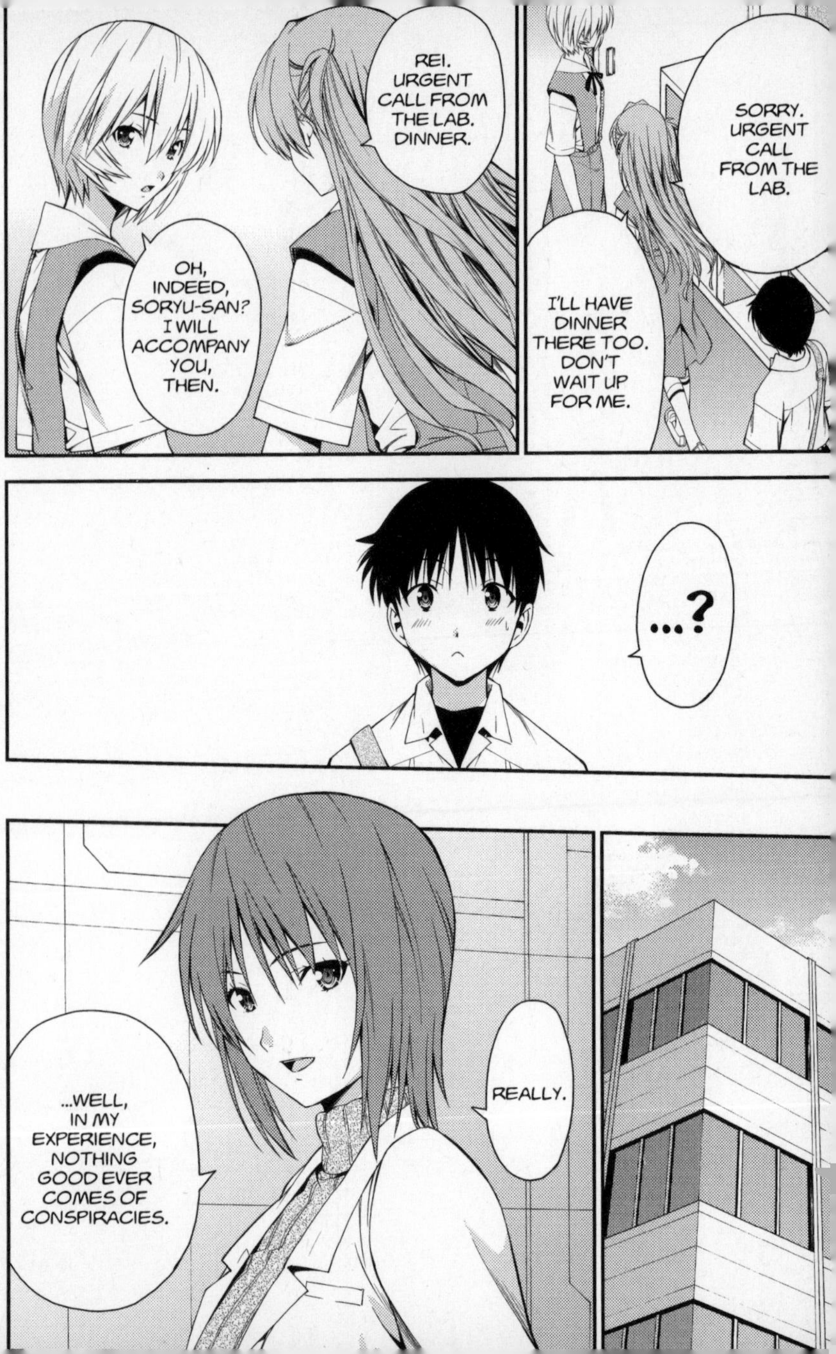
SORRY. URGENT CALL FROM THE LAB.
I'LL HAVE DINNER THERE TOO. DON'T WAIT UP FOR ME.
REI. URGENT CALL FROM THE LAB. DINNER.
OH, INDEED, SORYU-SAN? I WILL ACCOMPANY YOU, THEN.
...?
REALLY.
...WELL, IN MY EXPERIENCE, NOTHING GOOD EVER COMES OF CONSPIRACIES.

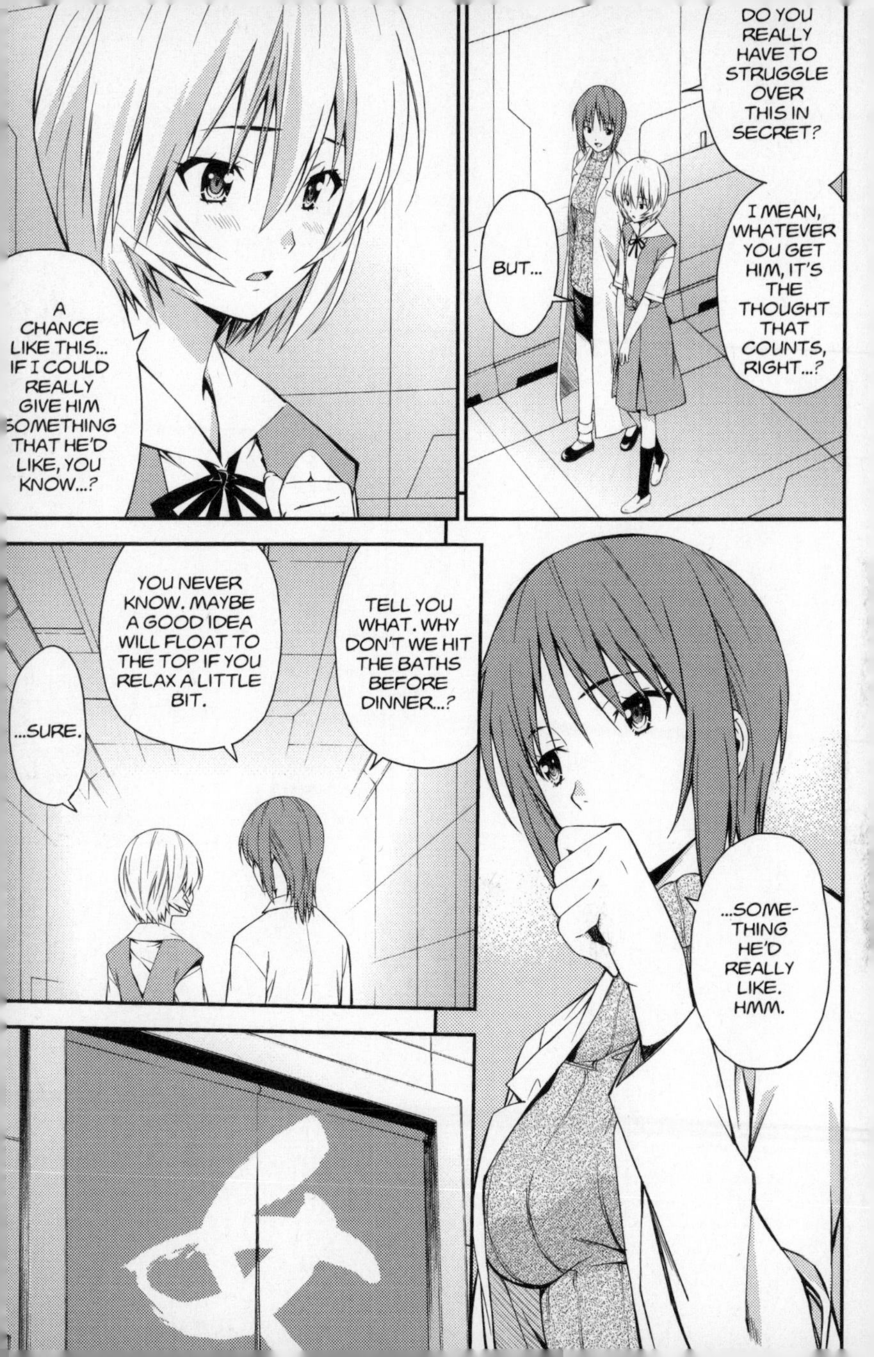
DO YOU REALLY HAVE TO STRUGGLE OVER THIS IN SECRET?
I MEAN, WHATEVER YOU GET HIM, IT'S THE THOUGHT THAT COUNTS, RIGHT...?
BUT...
A CHANCE LIKE THIS... IF I COULD REALLY GIVE HIM SOMETHING THAT HE'D LIKE, YOU KNOW...?
...SOME-THING HE'D REALLY LIKE. HMM.
TELL YOU WHAT. WHY DON'T WE HIT THE BATHS BEFORE DINNER...?
YOU NEVER KNOW. MAYBE A GOOD IDEA WILL FLOAT TO THE TOP IF YOU RELAX A LITTLE BIT.
...SURE.

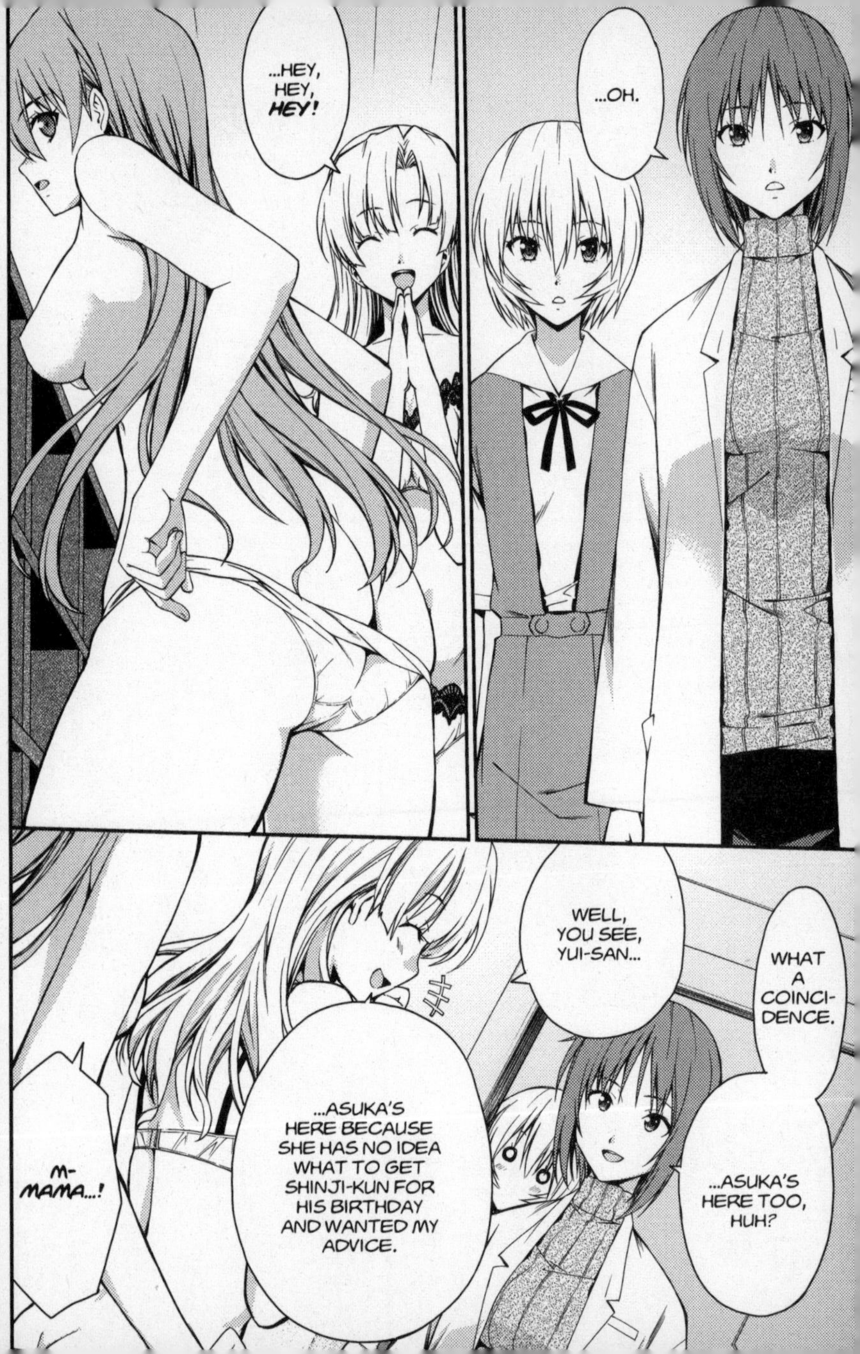
...OH.
...HEY, HEY, HEY!
WHAT A COINCI-DENCE.
...ASUKA'S HERE TOO, HUH?
WELL, YOU SEE, YUI-SAN...
...ASUKA'S HERE BECAUSE SHE HAS NO IDEA WHAT TO GET SHINJI-KUN FOR HIS BIRTHDAY AND WANTED MY ADVICE.
M-MAMA...!

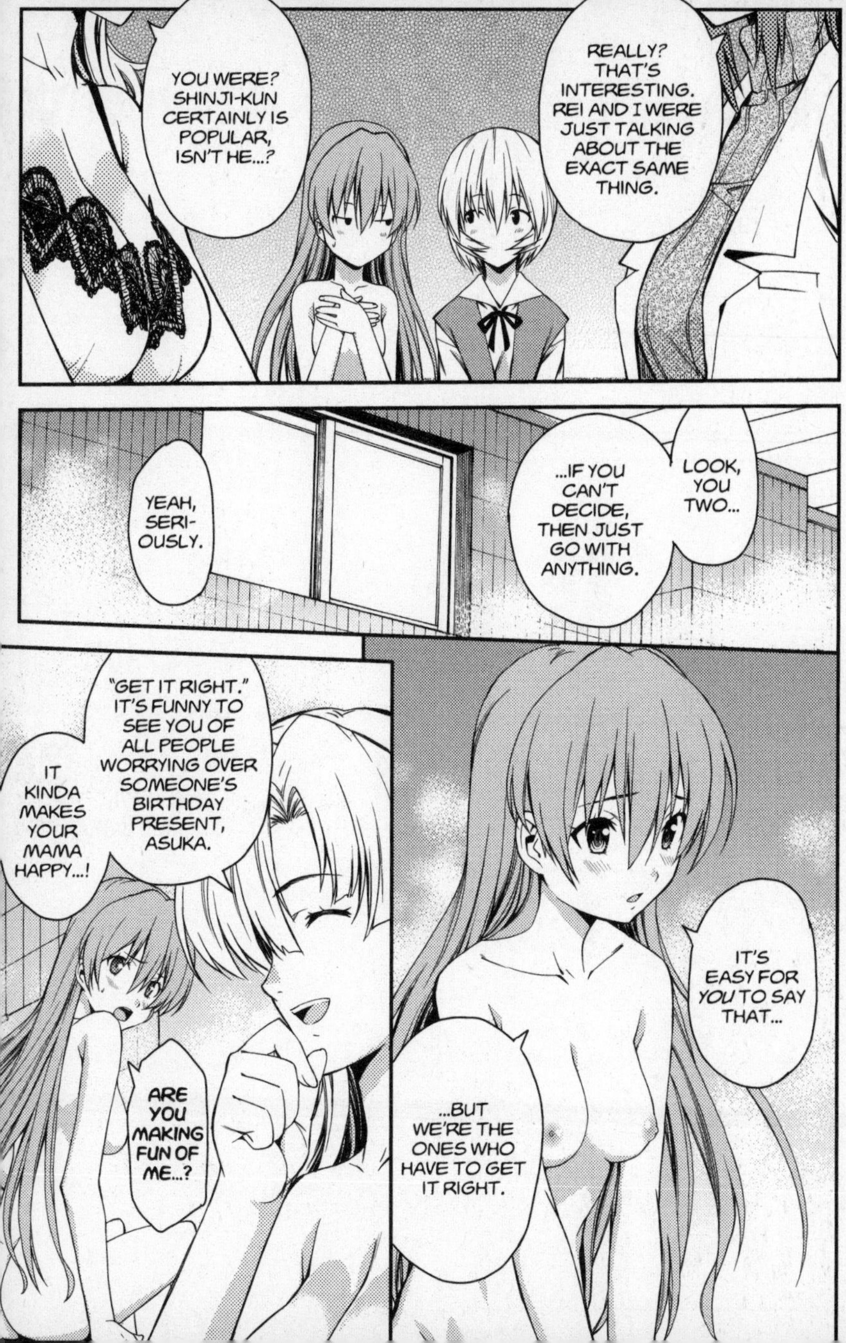
REALLY? THAT'S INTERESTING. REI AND I WERE JUST TALKING ABOUT THE EXACT SAME THING.
YOU WERE? SHINJI-KUN CERTAINLY IS POPULAR, ISN'T HE...?
LOOK, YOU TWO...
...IF YOU CAN'T DECIDE, THEN JUST GO WITH ANYTHING.
YEAH, SERI-OUSLY.
IT'S EASY FOR *YOU* TO SAY THAT...
...BUT WE'RE THE ONES WHO HAVE TO GET IT RIGHT.
"GET IT RIGHT." IT'S FUNNY TO SEE YOU OF ALL PEOPLE WORRYING OVER SOMEONE'S BIRTHDAY PRESENT, ASUKA.
IT KINDA MAKES YOUR MAMA HAPPY...!
ARE YOU MAKING FUN OF ME...?

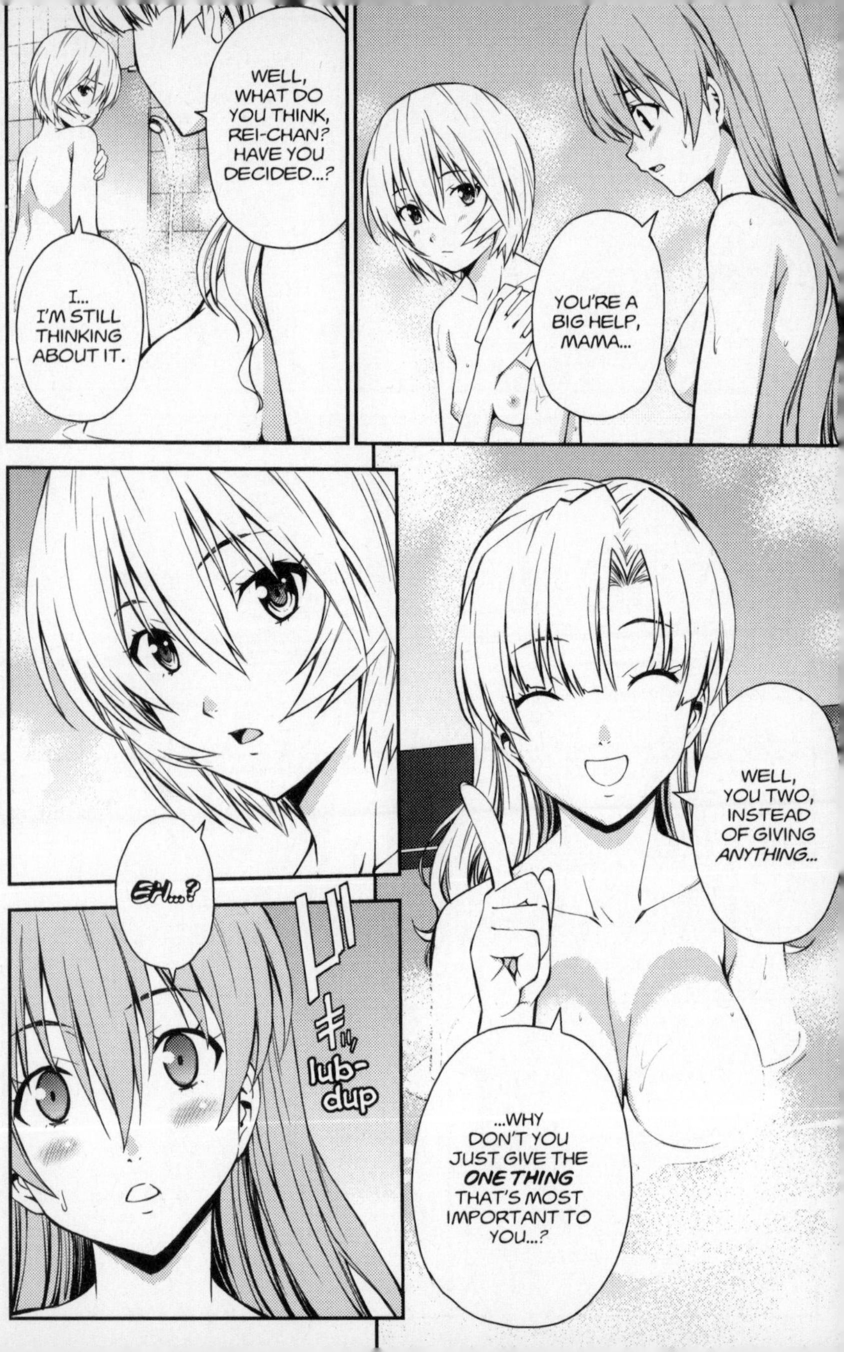
YOU'RE A BIG HELP, MAMA...
WELL, WHAT DO YOU THINK, REI-CHAN? HAVE YOU DECIDED...?
I... I'M STILL THINKING ABOUT IT.
WELL, YOU TWO, INSTEAD OF GIVING ANYTHING...
...WHY DON'T YOU JUST GIVE THE ONE THING THAT'S MOST IMPORTANT TO YOU...?
EH...?
lub-dup

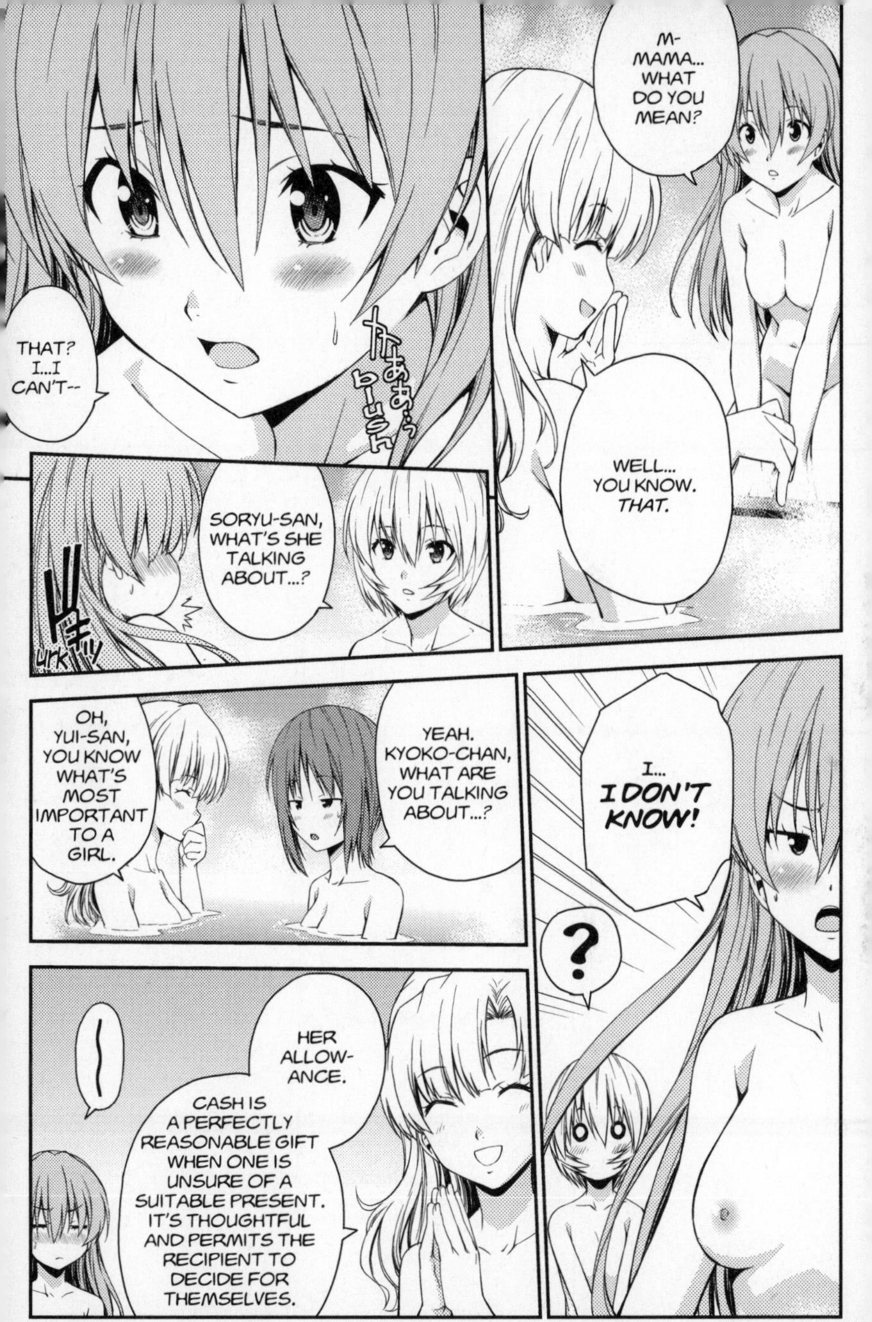
M-MAMA... WHAT DO YOU MEAN?
WELL... YOU KNOW. *THAT.*
THAT? I...I CAN'T--
SORYU-SAN, WHAT'S SHE TALKING ABOUT...?
urk
I... **I DON'T KNOW!**
?
YEAH. KYOKO-CHAN, WHAT ARE YOU TALKING ABOUT...?
OH, YUI-SAN, YOU KNOW WHAT'S MOST IMPORTANT TO A GIRL.
HER ALLOW-ANCE.
CASH IS A PERFECTLY REASONABLE GIFT WHEN ONE IS UNSURE OF A SUITABLE PRESENT. IT'S THOUGHTFUL AND PERMITS THE RECIPIENT TO DECIDE FOR THEMSELVES.

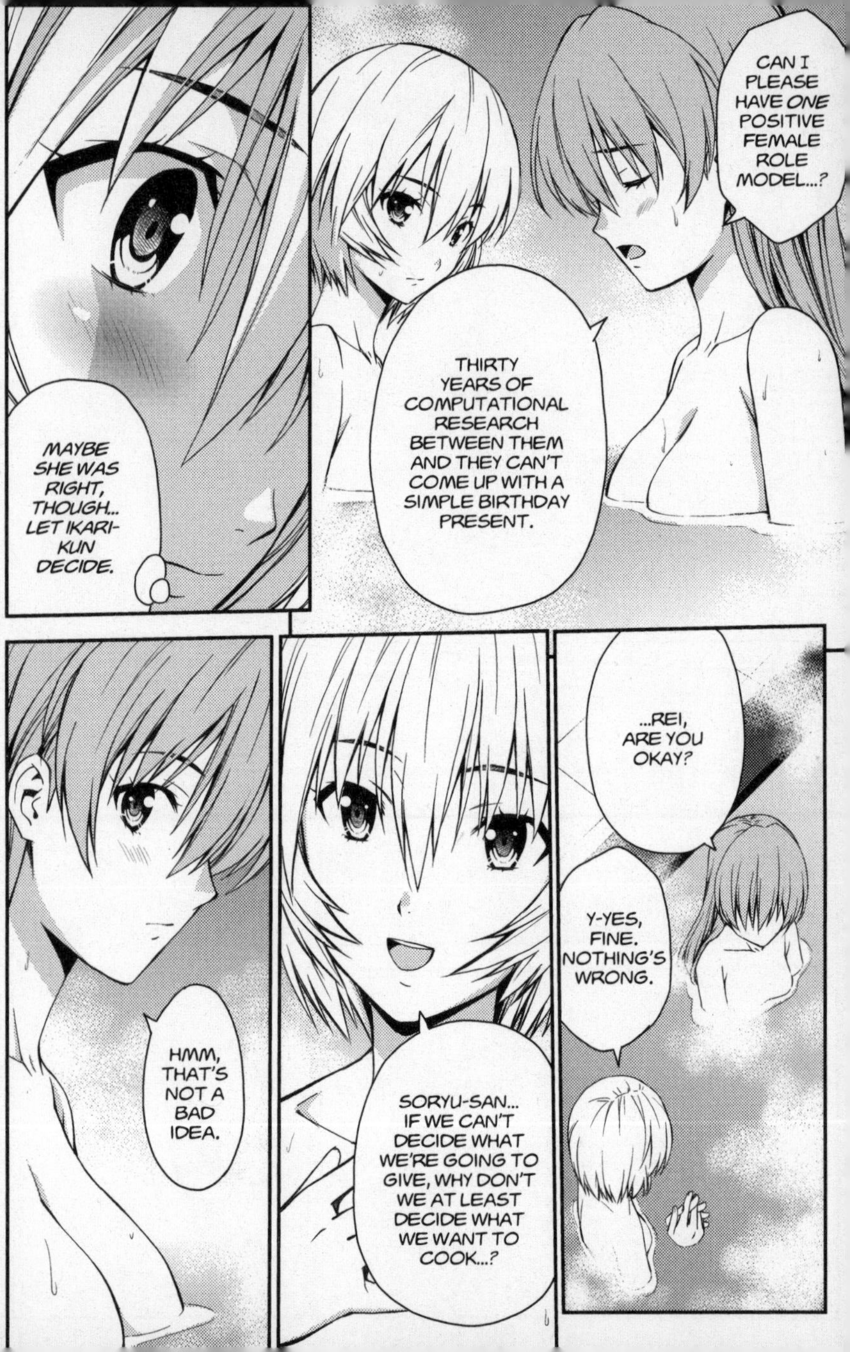
CAN I PLEASE HAVE *ONE* POSITIVE FEMALE ROLE MODEL...?
THIRTY YEARS OF COMPUTATIONAL RESEARCH BETWEEN THEM AND THEY CAN'T COME UP WITH A SIMPLE BIRTHDAY PRESENT.
MAYBE SHE WAS RIGHT, THOUGH... LET IKARI-KUN DECIDE.
...REI, ARE YOU OKAY?
Y-YES, FINE. NOTHING'S WRONG.
SORYU-SAN... IF WE CAN'T DECIDE WHAT WE'RE GOING TO GIVE, WHY DON'T WE AT LEAST DECIDE WHAT WE WANT TO COOK...?
HMM, THAT'S NOT A BAD IDEA.

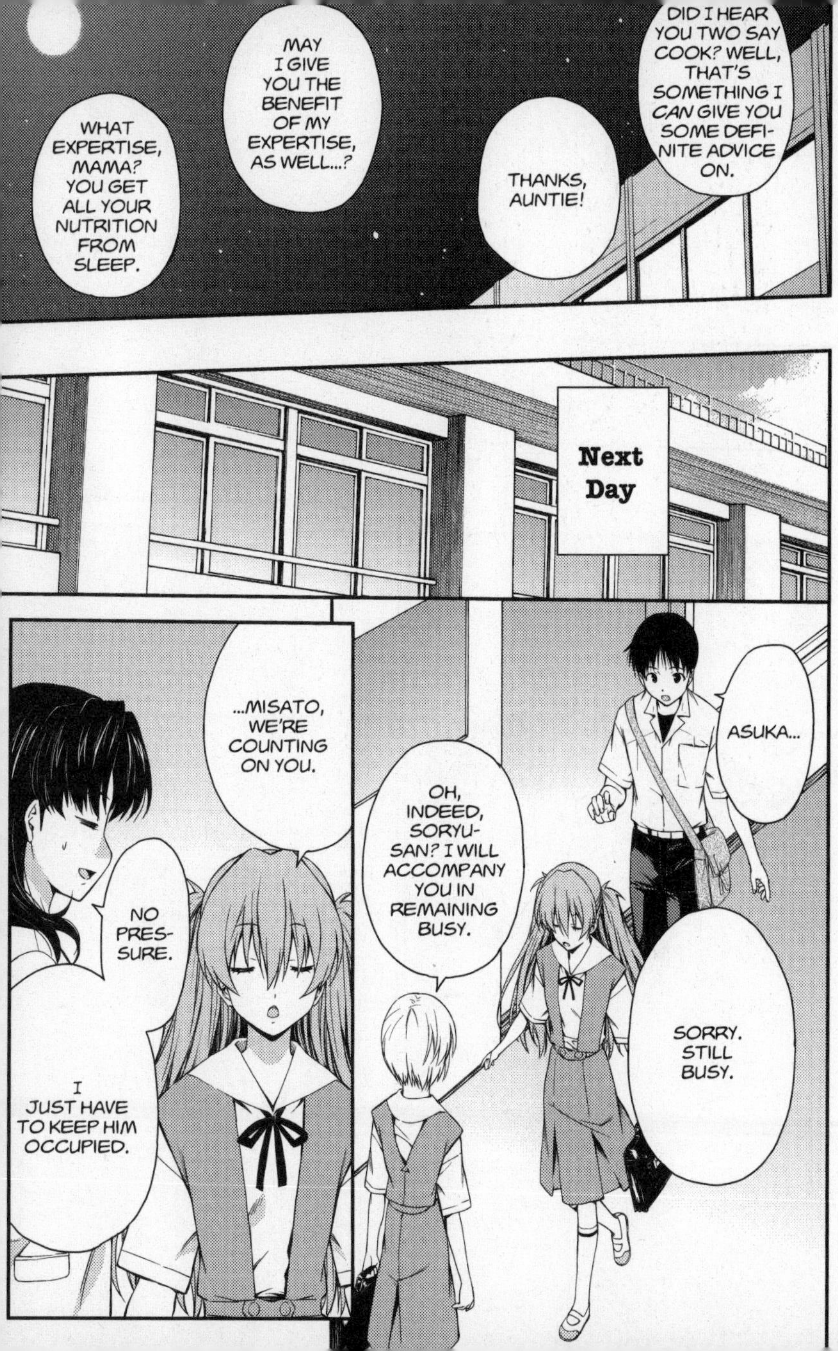

DID I HEAR YOU TWO SAY COOK? WELL, THAT'S SOMETHING I CAN GIVE YOU SOME DEFINITE ADVICE ON.
THANKS, AUNTIE!
MAY I GIVE YOU THE BENEFIT OF MY EXPERTISE, AS WELL...?
WHAT EXPERTISE, MAMA? YOU GET ALL YOUR NUTRITION FROM SLEEP.
Next Day
ASUKA...
SORRY. STILL BUSY.
OH, INDEED, SORYU-SAN? I WILL ACCOMPANY YOU IN REMAINING BUSY.
...MISATO, WE'RE COUNTING ON YOU.
NO PRESSURE.
I JUST HAVE TO KEEP HIM OCCUPIED.

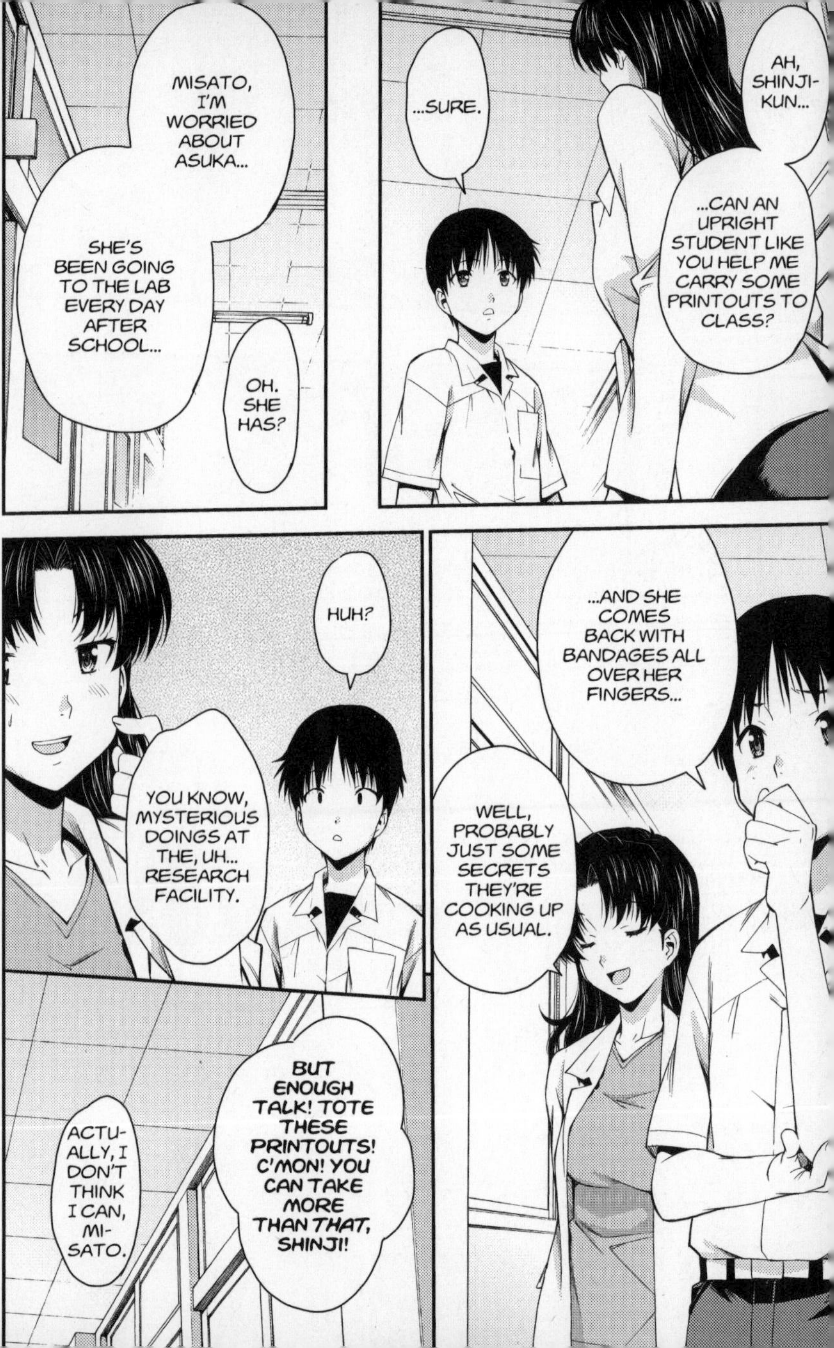
AH, SHINJI-KUN...
...CAN AN UPRIGHT STUDENT LIKE YOU HELP ME CARRY SOME PRINTOUTS TO CLASS?
...SURE.
MISATO, I'M WORRIED ABOUT ASUKA...
SHE'S BEEN GOING TO THE LAB EVERY DAY AFTER SCHOOL...
OH. SHE HAS?
...AND SHE COMES BACK WITH BANDAGES ALL OVER HER FINGERS...
WELL, PROBABLY JUST SOME SECRETS THEY'RE COOKING UP AS USUAL.
HUH?
YOU KNOW, MYSTERIOUS DOINGS AT THE, UH... RESEARCH FACILITY.
BUT ENOUGH TALK! TOTE THESE PRINTOUTS! C'MON! YOU CAN TAKE MORE THAN *THAT*, SHINJI!
ACTUALLY, I DON'T THINK I CAN, MISATO.

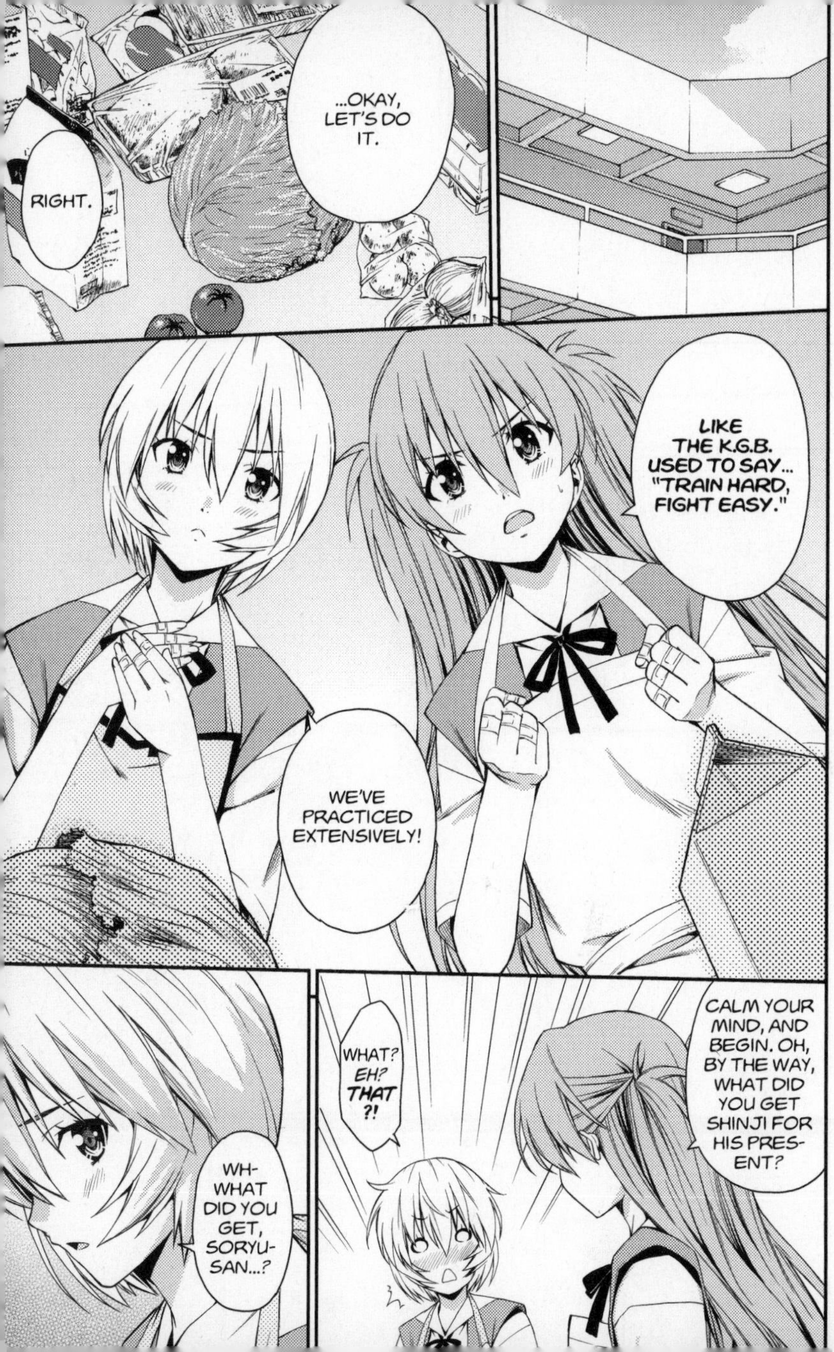
...OKAY, LET'S DO IT.
RIGHT.
LIKE THE K.G.B. USED TO SAY... "TRAIN HARD, FIGHT EASY."
WE'VE PRACTICED EXTENSIVELY!
CALM YOUR MIND, AND BEGIN. OH, BY THE WAY, WHAT DID YOU GET SHINJI FOR HIS PRES-ENT?
WHAT? EH? THAT?!
WH-WHAT DID YOU GET, SORYU-SAN...?

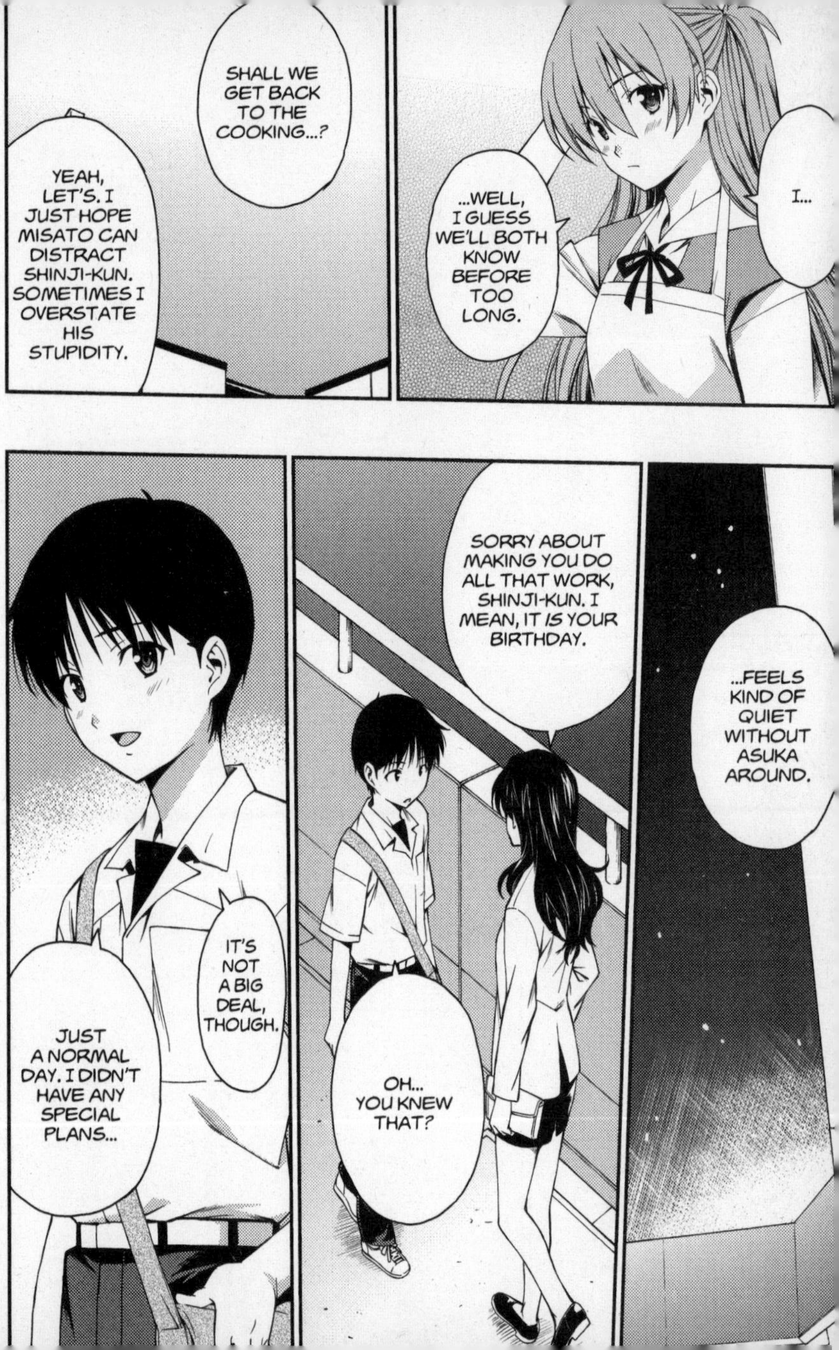
I...
...WELL, I GUESS WE'LL BOTH KNOW BEFORE TOO LONG.
SHALL WE GET BACK TO THE COOKING...?
YEAH, LET'S. I JUST HOPE MISATO CAN DISTRACT SHINJI-KUN. SOMETIMES I OVERSTATE HIS STUPIDITY.
...FEELS KIND OF QUIET WITHOUT ASUKA AROUND.
SORRY ABOUT MAKING YOU DO ALL THAT WORK, SHINJI-KUN. I MEAN, IT *IS* YOUR BIRTHDAY.
OH... YOU KNEW THAT?
IT'S NOT A BIG DEAL, THOUGH.
JUST A NORMAL DAY. I DIDN'T HAVE ANY SPECIAL PLANS...

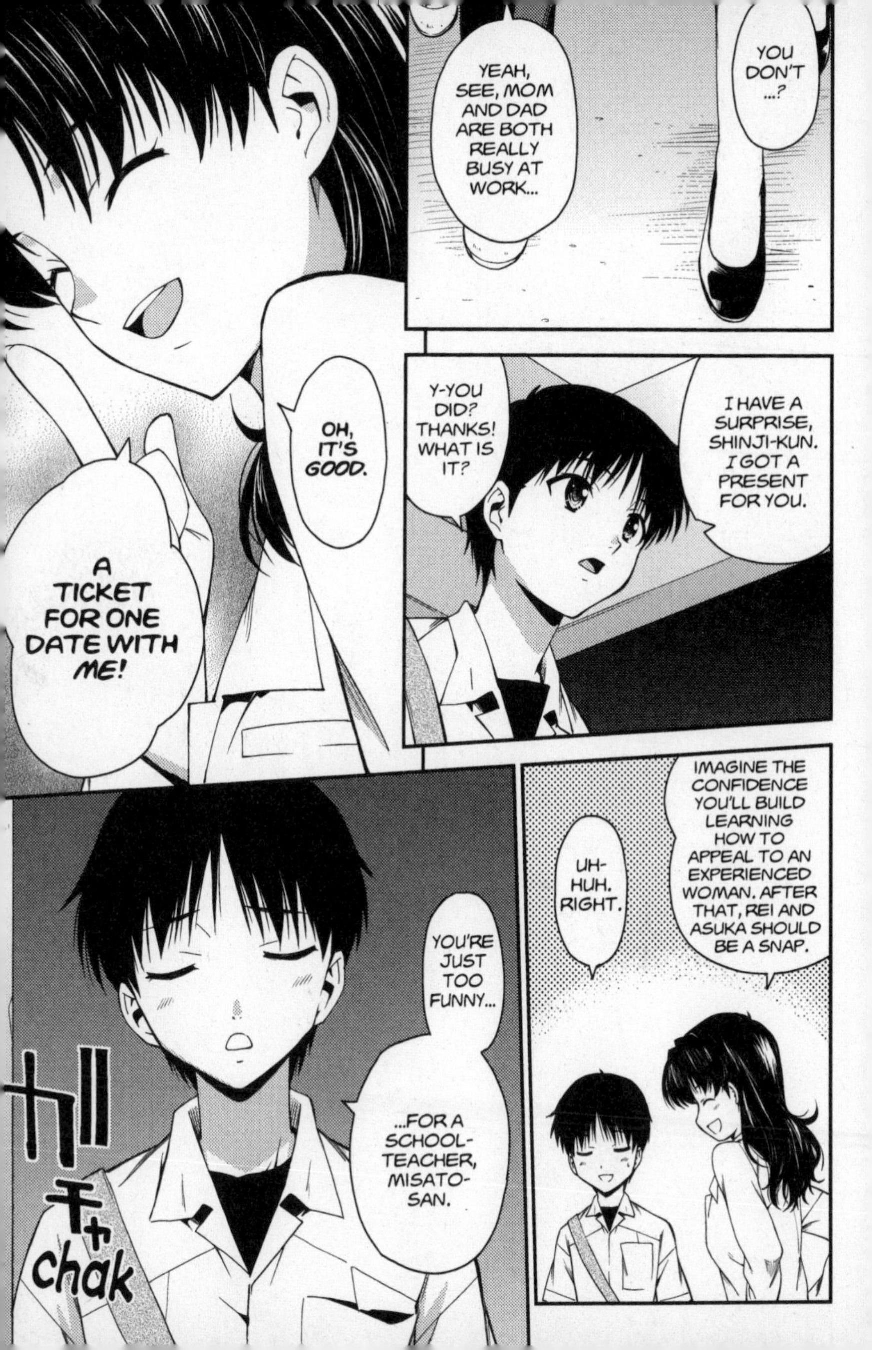
YOU DON'T ...?
YEAH, SEE, MOM AND DAD ARE BOTH REALLY BUSY AT WORK...
I HAVE A SURPRISE, SHINJI-KUN. I GOT A PRESENT FOR YOU.
Y-YOU DID? THANKS! WHAT IS IT?
OH, IT'S GOOD.
A TICKET FOR ONE DATE WITH ME!
IMAGINE THE CONFIDENCE YOU'LL BUILD LEARNING HOW TO APPEAL TO AN EXPERIENCED WOMAN. AFTER THAT, REI AND ASUKA SHOULD BE A SNAP.
UH-HUH. RIGHT.
YOU'RE JUST TOO FUNNY...
...FOR A SCHOOL-TEACHER, MISATO-SAN.
ガチャ
chak

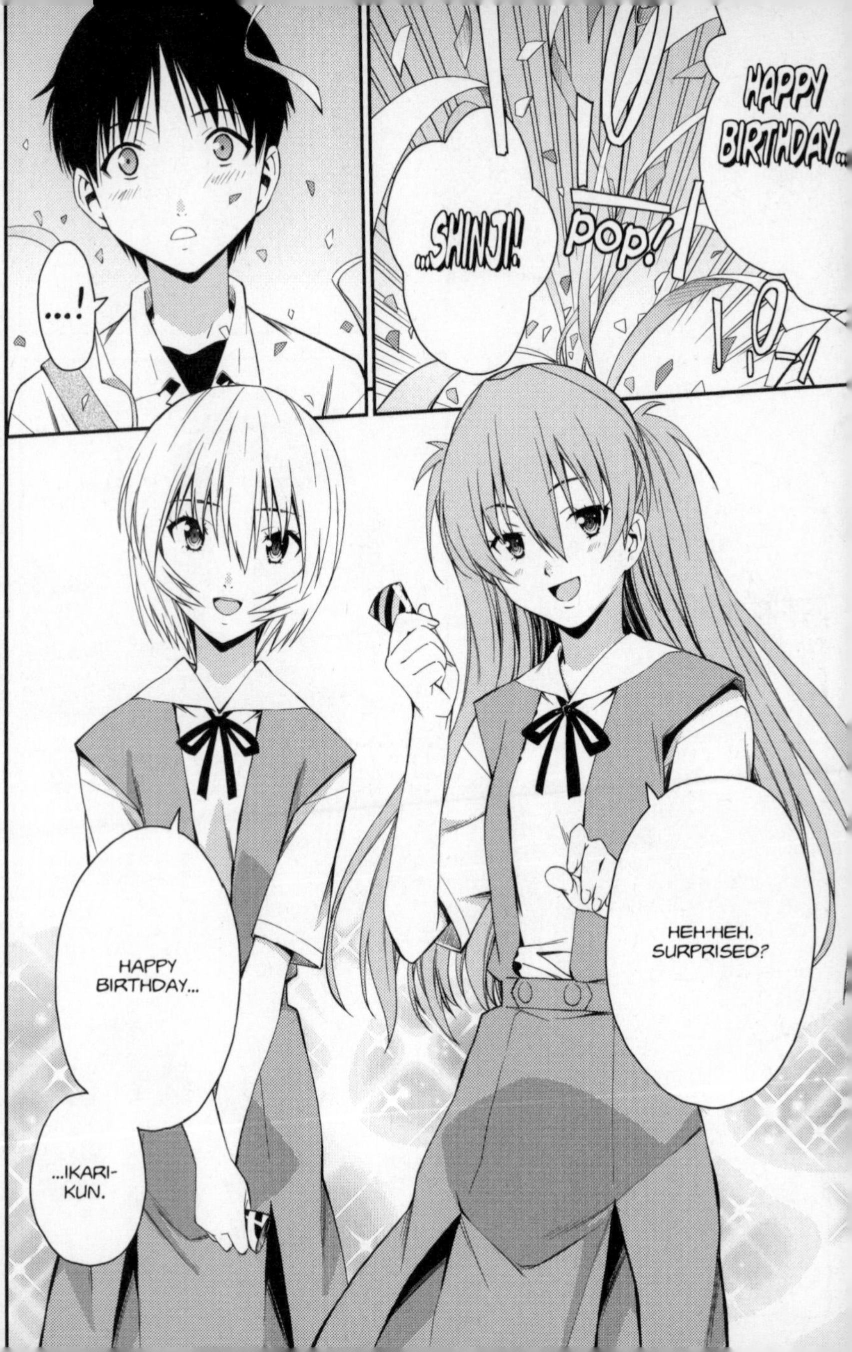
HAPPY BIRTHDAY...
...SHINJI!
pop!
...!
HEH-HEH. SURPRISED?
HAPPY BIRTHDAY...
...IKARI-KUN.

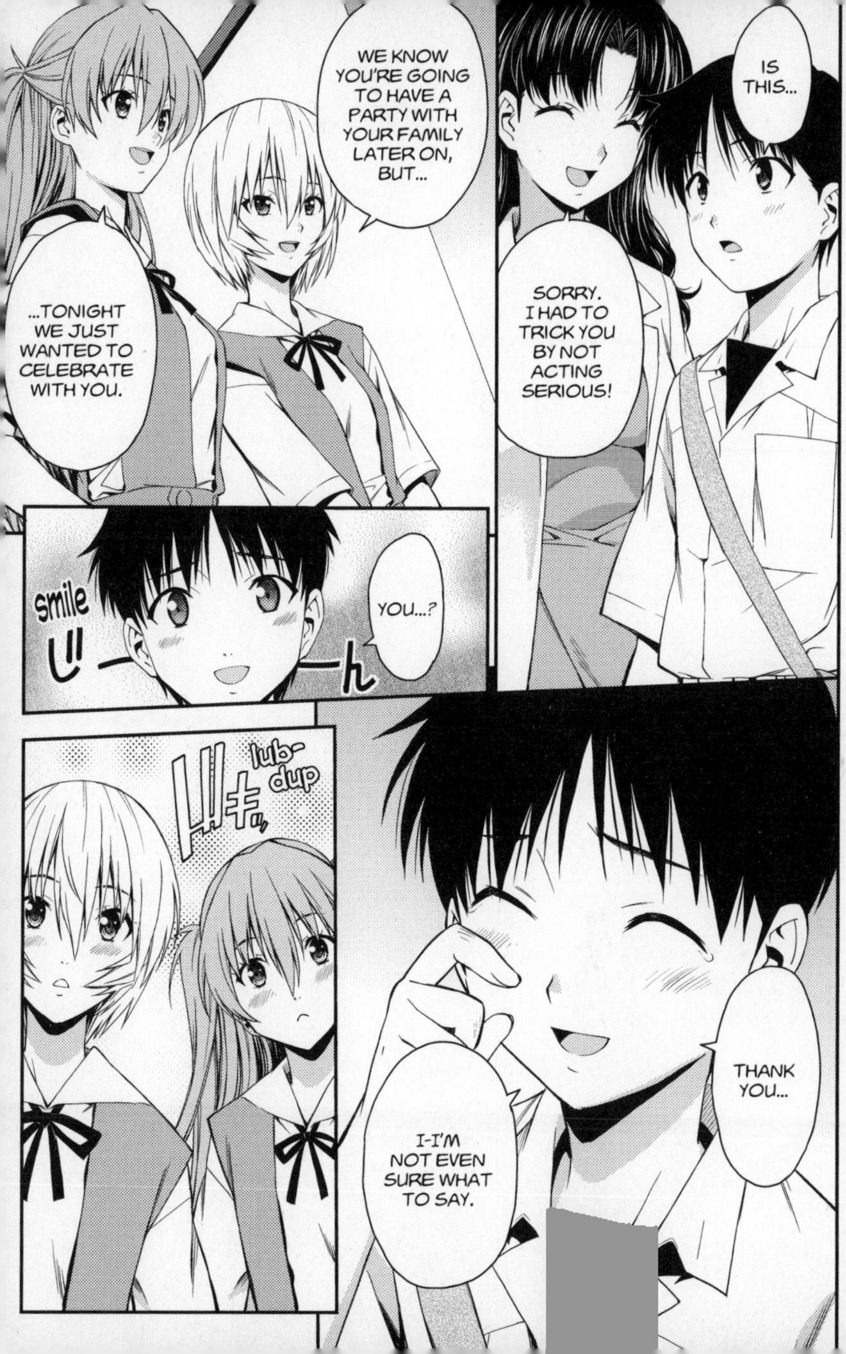
IS THIS...
SORRY. I HAD TO TRICK YOU BY NOT ACTING SERIOUS!
WE KNOW YOU'RE GOING TO HAVE A PARTY WITH YOUR FAMILY LATER ON, BUT...
...TONIGHT WE JUST WANTED TO CELEBRATE WITH YOU.
YOU...?
smile
THANK YOU...
I-I'M NOT EVEN SURE WHAT TO SAY.
lub-dup

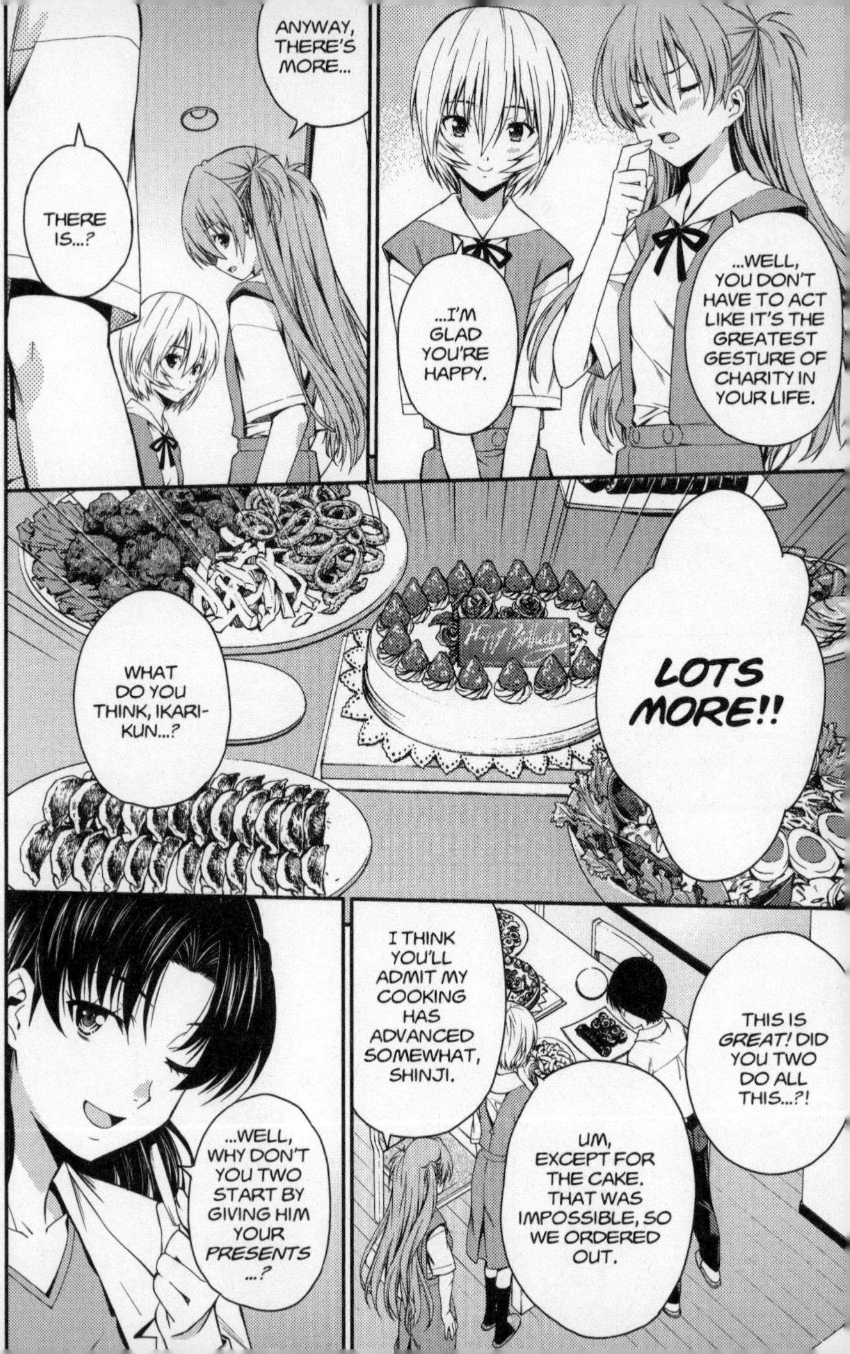
...WELL, YOU DON'T HAVE TO ACT LIKE IT'S THE GREATEST GESTURE OF CHARITY IN YOUR LIFE.
...I'M GLAD YOU'RE HAPPY.
ANYWAY, THERE'S MORE...
THERE IS...?
LOTS MORE!!
WHAT DO YOU THINK, IKARI-KUN...?
THIS IS *GREAT!* DID YOU TWO DO ALL THIS...?!
UM, EXCEPT FOR THE CAKE. THAT WAS IMPOSSIBLE, SO WE ORDERED OUT.
I THINK YOU'LL ADMIT MY COOKING HAS ADVANCED SOMEWHAT, SHINJI.
...WELL, WHY DON'T YOU TWO START BY GIVING HIM YOUR *PRESENTS* ...?

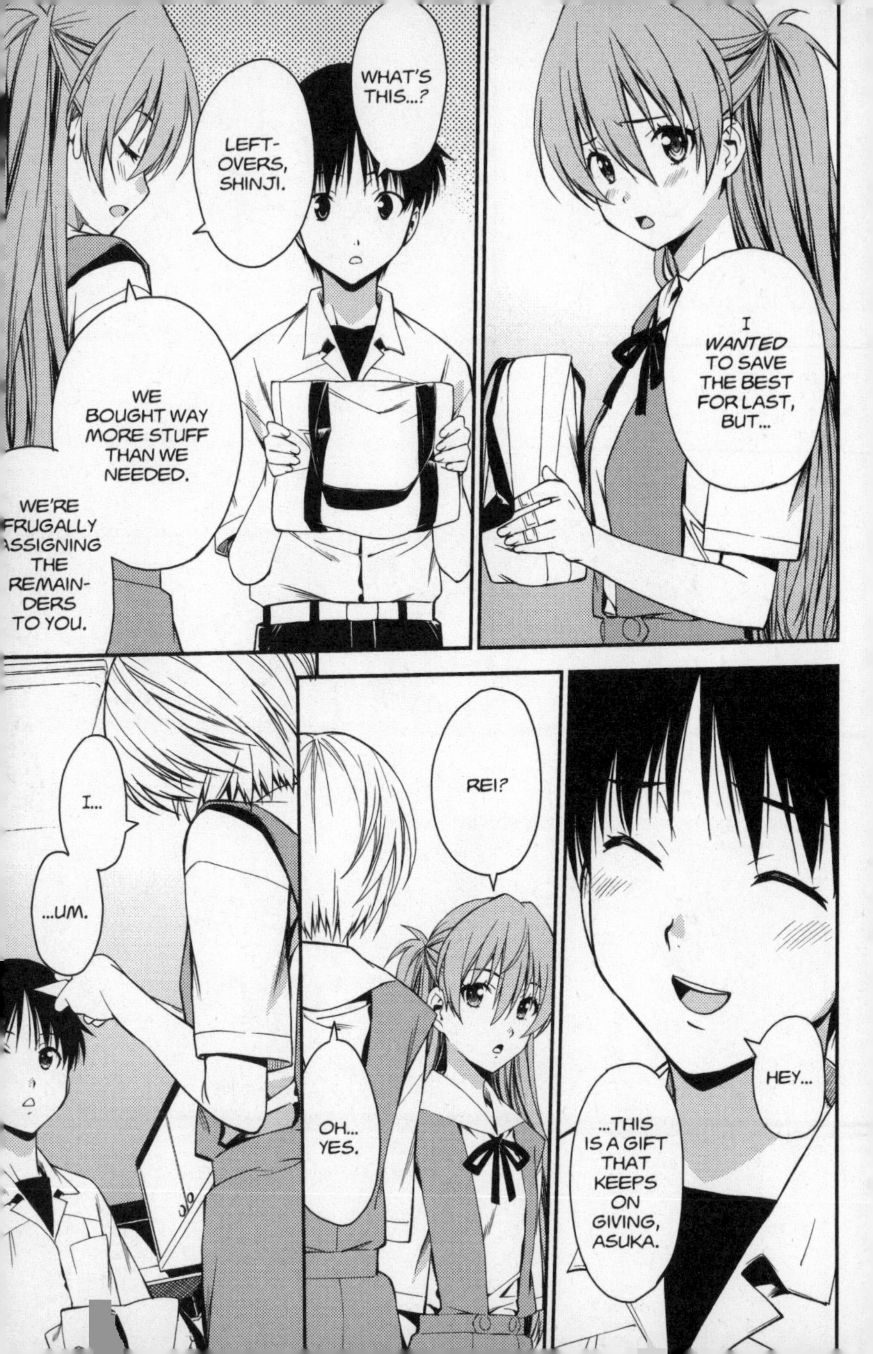
I WANTED TO SAVE THE BEST FOR LAST, BUT...
WHAT'S THIS...?
LEFT-OVERS, SHINJI.
WE BOUGHT WAY MORE STUFF THAN WE NEEDED.
WE'RE FRUGALLY ASSIGNING THE REMAINDERS TO YOU.
HEY...
...THIS IS A GIFT THAT KEEPS ON GIVING, ASUKA.
REI?
OH... YES.
I...
...UM.

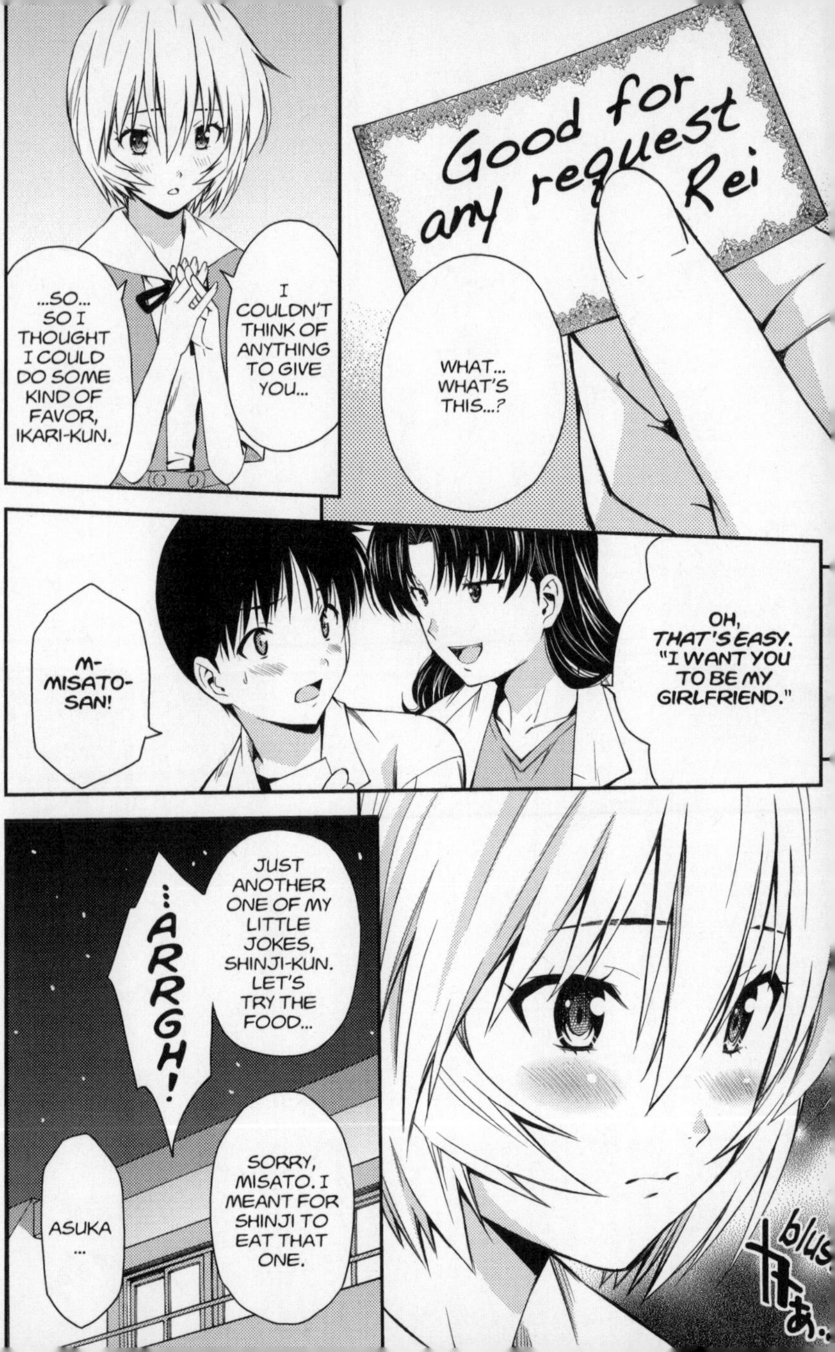
Good for any request Rei
WHAT... WHAT'S THIS...?
I COULDN'T THINK OF ANYTHING TO GIVE YOU...
...SO... SO I THOUGHT I COULD DO SOME KIND OF FAVOR, IKARI-KUN.
OH, THAT'S EASY. "I WANT YOU TO BE MY GIRLFRIEND."
M-MISATO-SAN!
blus
JUST ANOTHER ONE OF MY LITTLE JOKES, SHINJI-KUN. LET'S TRY THE FOOD...
...ARRGH!
SORRY, MISATO. I MEANT FOR SHINJI TO EAT THAT ONE.
ASUKA ...

the shinji ikari raising project

NEON GENESIS EVANGELION

THE SHINJI IKARI RAISING PROJECT

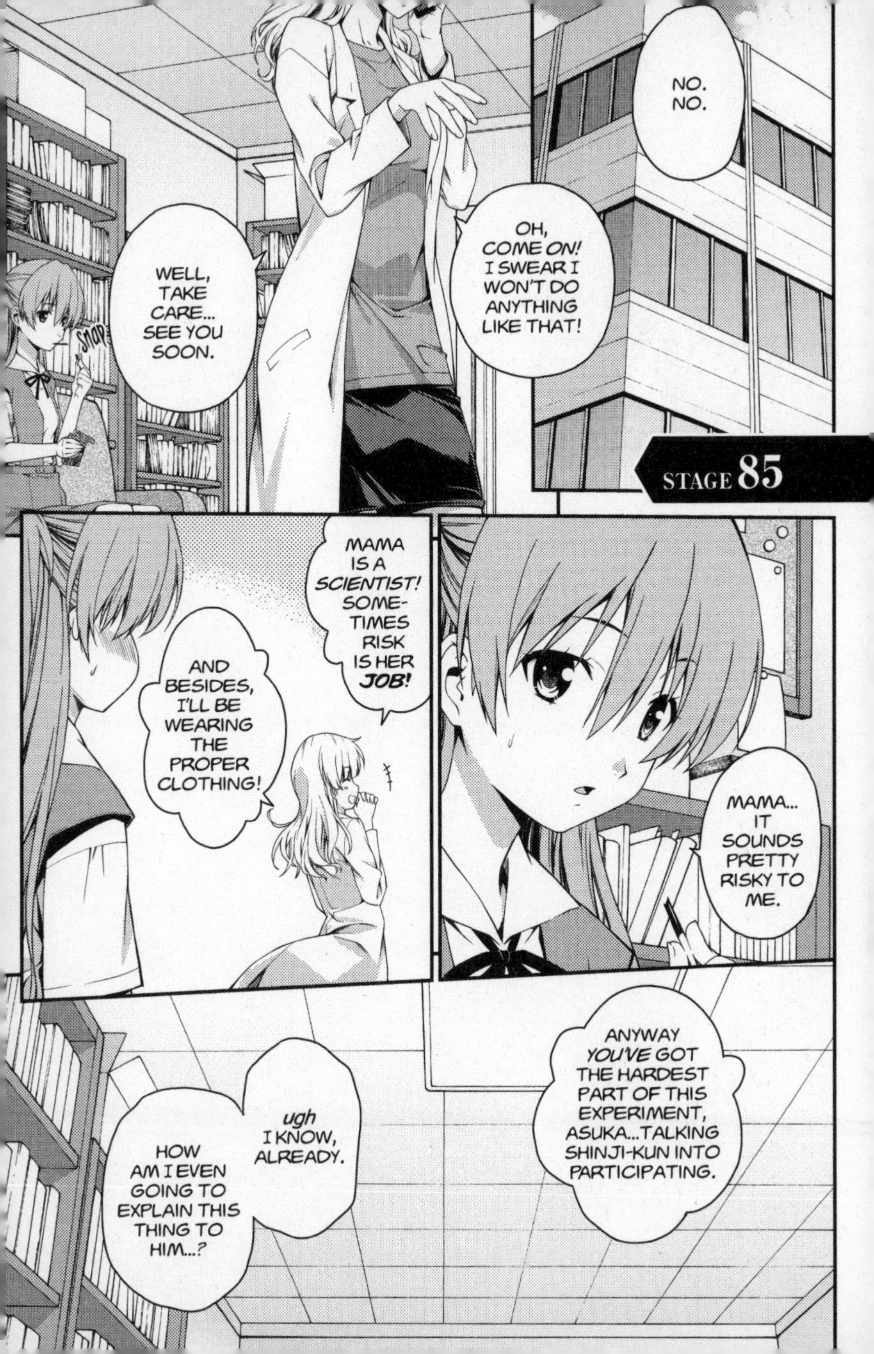
NO. NO.
STAGE 85
OH, COME ON! I SWEAR I WON'T DO ANYTHING LIKE THAT!
WELL, TAKE CARE... SEE YOU SOON.
SNAP
MAMA... IT SOUNDS PRETTY RISKY TO ME.
MAMA IS A SCIENTIST! SOMETIMES RISK IS HER JOB!
AND BESIDES, I'LL BE WEARING THE PROPER CLOTHING!
ANYWAY YOU'VE GOT THE HARDEST PART OF THIS EXPERIMENT, ASUKA...TALKING SHINJI-KUN INTO PARTICIPATING.
ugh I KNOW, ALREADY.
HOW AM I EVEN GOING TO EXPLAIN THIS THING TO HIM...?

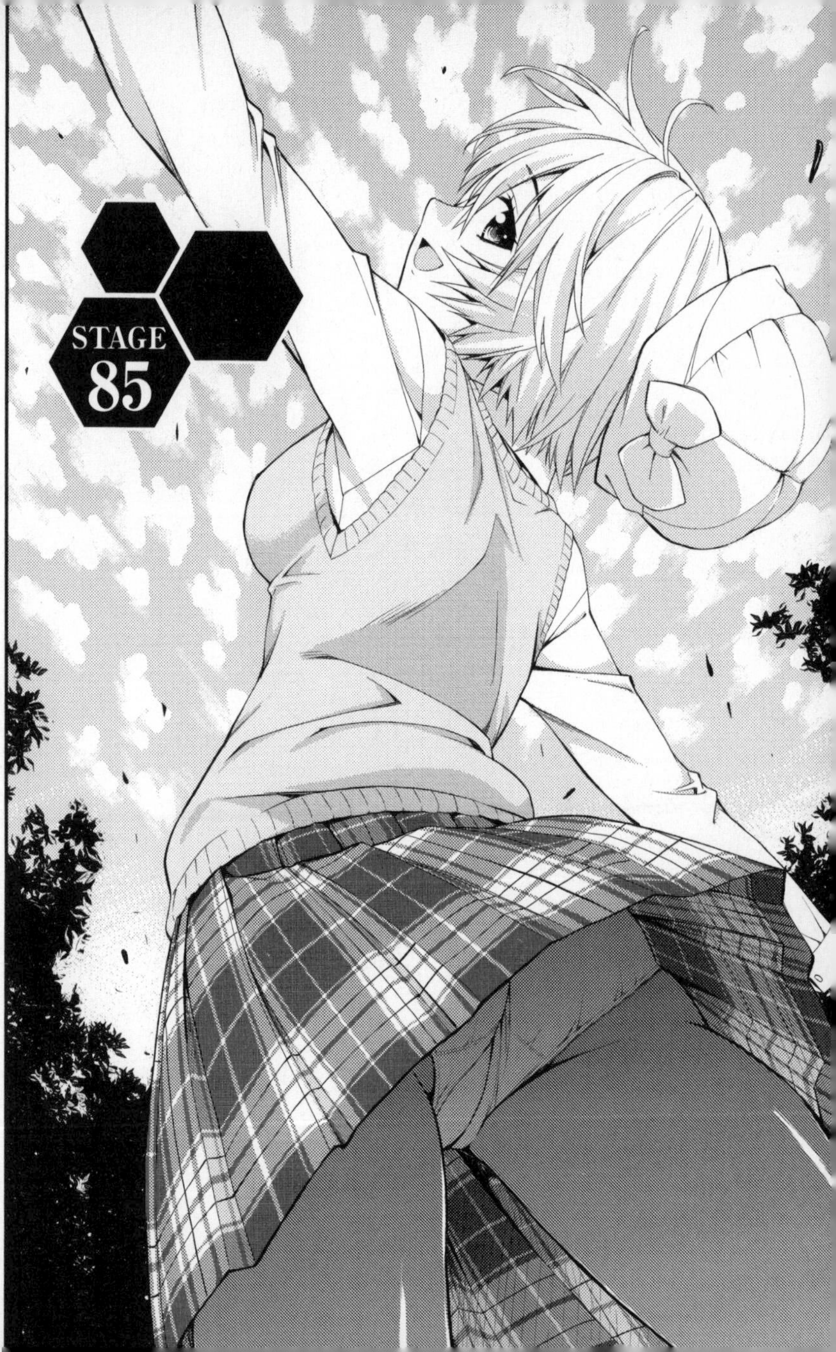
STAGE
85

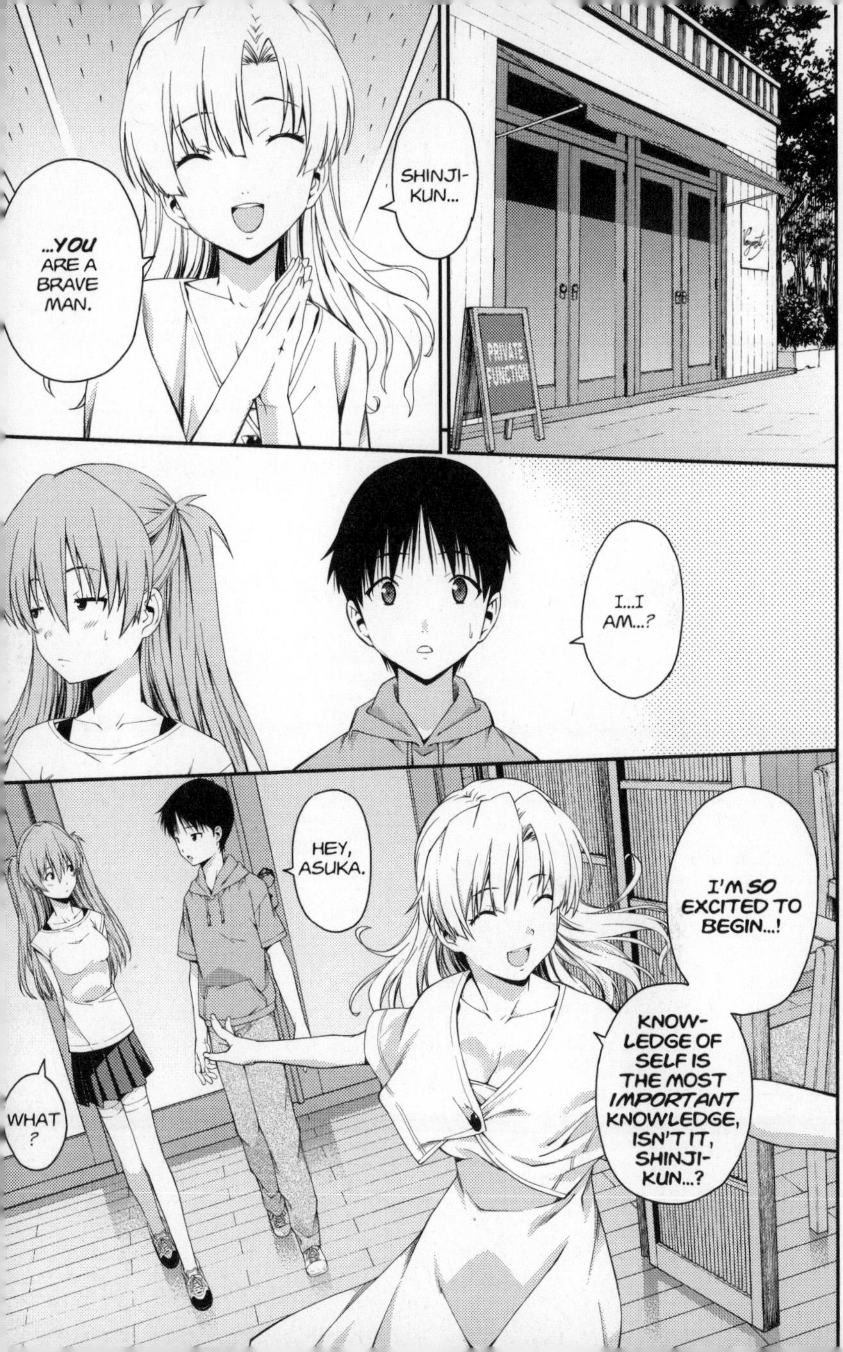
PRIVATE FUNCTION
SHINJI-KUN...
...YOU ARE A BRAVE MAN.
I...I AM...?
I'M SO EXCITED TO BEGIN...!
HEY, ASUKA.
KNOW-LEDGE OF SELF IS THE MOST IMPORTANT KNOWLEDGE, ISN'T IT, SHINJI-KUN...?
WHAT?

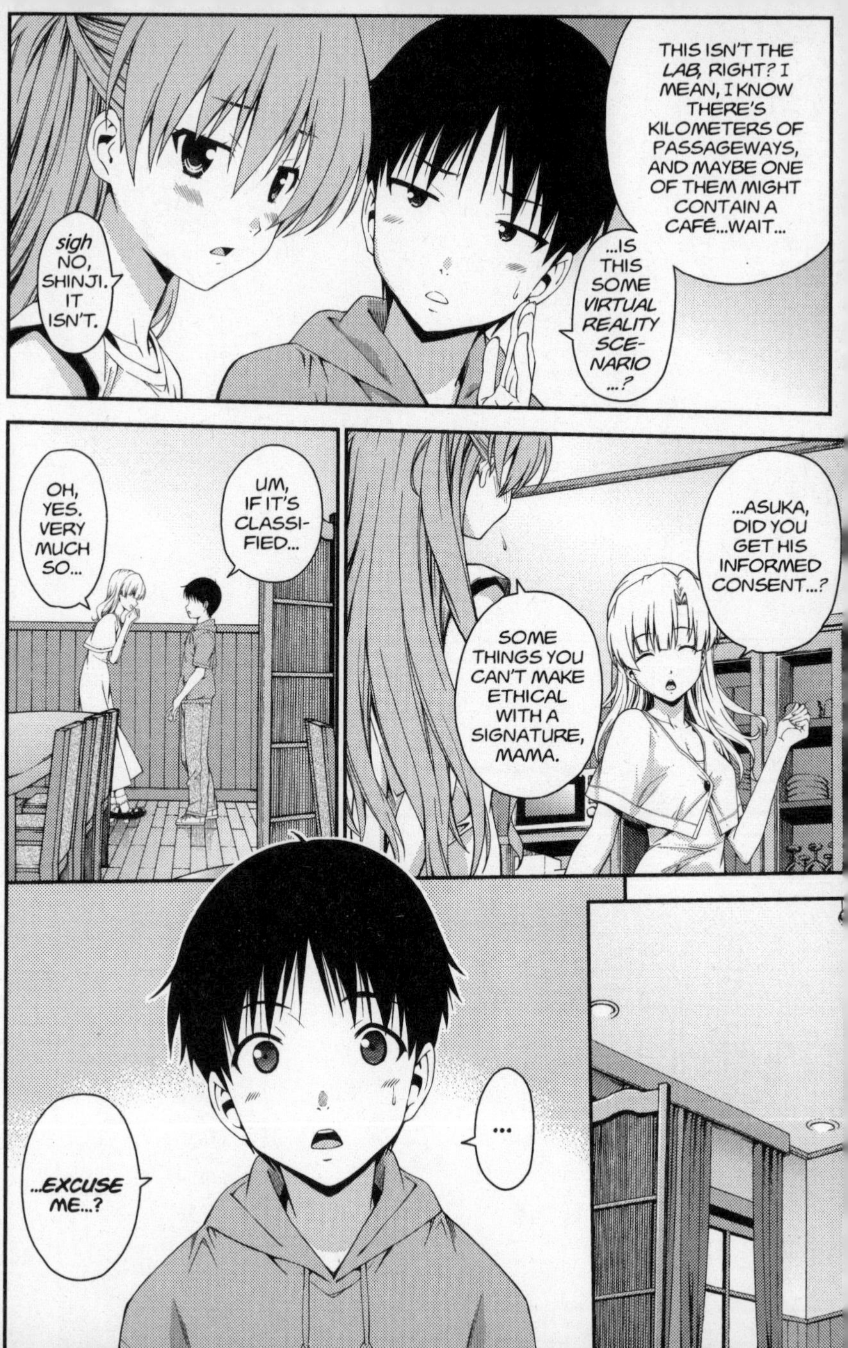
THIS ISN'T THE *LAB*, RIGHT? I MEAN, I KNOW THERE'S KILOMETERS OF PASSAGEWAYS, AND MAYBE ONE OF THEM MIGHT CONTAIN A CAFÉ...WAIT...
...IS THIS SOME *VIRTUAL REALITY* SCE-NARIO ...?
sigh NO, SHINJI. IT ISN'T.
...ASUKA, DID YOU GET HIS INFORMED CONSENT...?
SOME THINGS YOU CAN'T MAKE ETHICAL WITH A SIGNATURE, MAMA.
UM, IF IT'S CLASSI-FIED...
OH, YES. VERY MUCH SO...
...
...*EXCUSE* ME...?

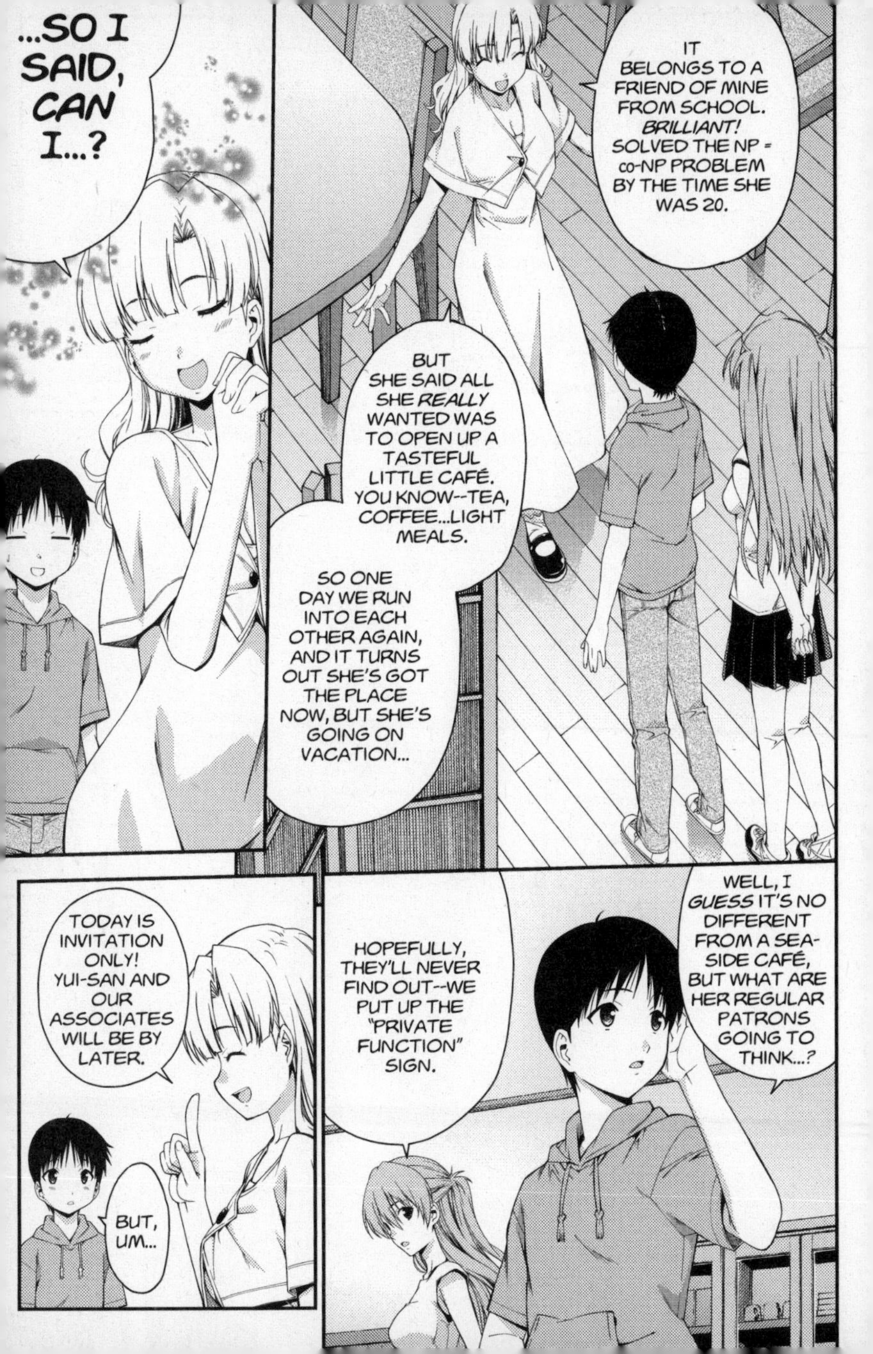
IT BELONGS TO A FRIEND OF MINE FROM SCHOOL. *BRILLIANT!* SOLVED THE NP = co-NP PROBLEM BY THE TIME SHE WAS 20.
BUT SHE SAID ALL SHE *REALLY* WANTED WAS TO OPEN UP A TASTEFUL LITTLE CAFÉ. YOU KNOW--TEA, COFFEE...LIGHT MEALS.
SO ONE DAY WE RUN INTO EACH OTHER AGAIN, AND IT TURNS OUT SHE'S GOT THE PLACE NOW, BUT SHE'S GOING ON VACATION...
...SO I SAID, CAN I...?
WELL, I *GUESS* IT'S NO DIFFERENT FROM A SEA-SIDE CAFÉ, BUT WHAT ARE HER REGULAR PATRONS GOING TO THINK...?
HOPEFULLY, THEY'LL NEVER FIND OUT--WE PUT UP THE "PRIVATE FUNCTION" SIGN.
TODAY IS INVITATION ONLY! YUI-SAN AND OUR ASSOCIATES WILL BE BY LATER.
BUT, UM...

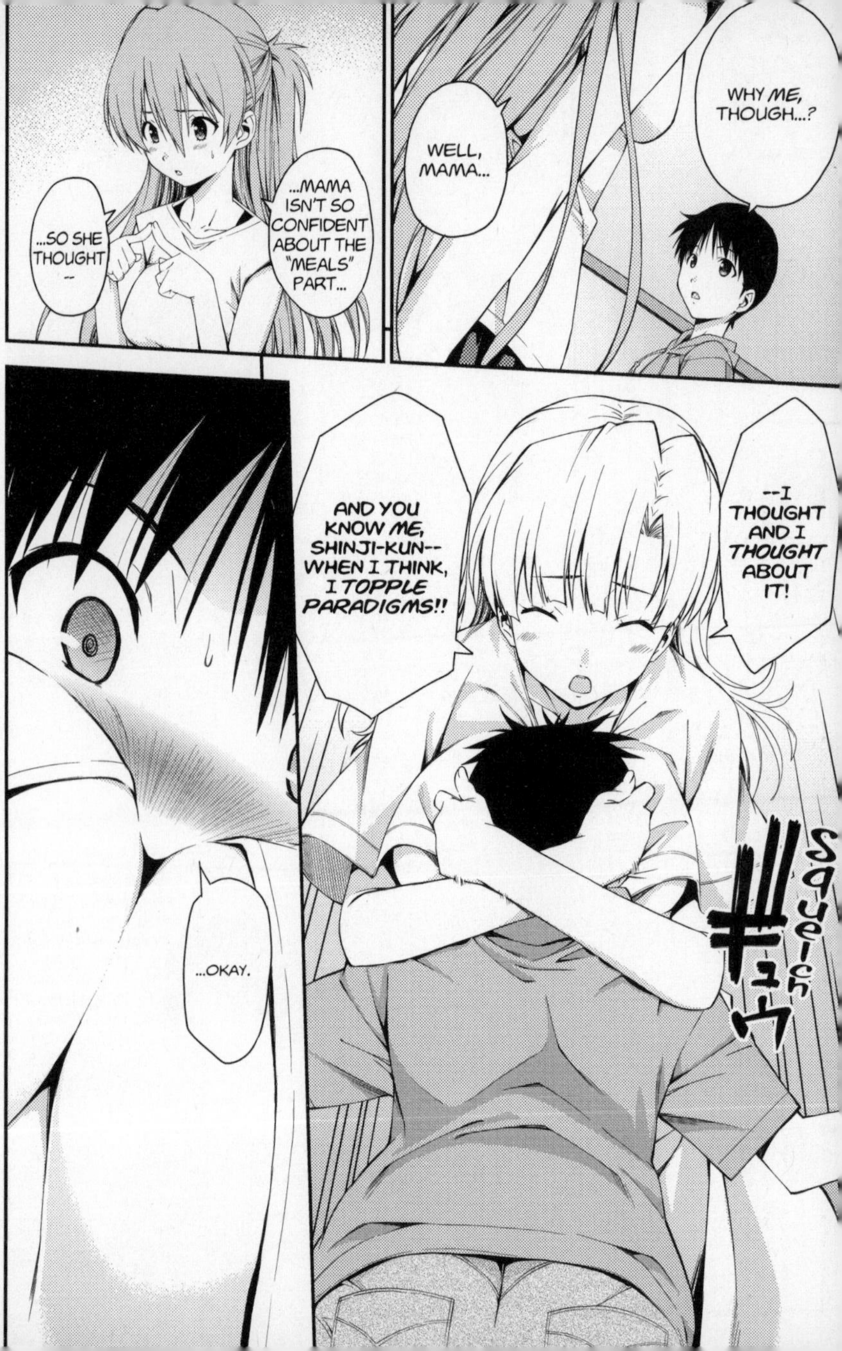
WHY *ME*, THOUGH...?
WELL, MAMA...
...MAMA ISN'T SO CONFIDENT ABOUT THE "MEALS" PART...
...SO SHE THOUGHT --
--I THOUGHT AND I *THOUGHT* ABOUT IT!
AND YOU KNOW *ME*, SHINJI-KUN-- WHEN I THINK, I *TOPPLE PARADIGMS*!!
squeeeze
...OKAY.

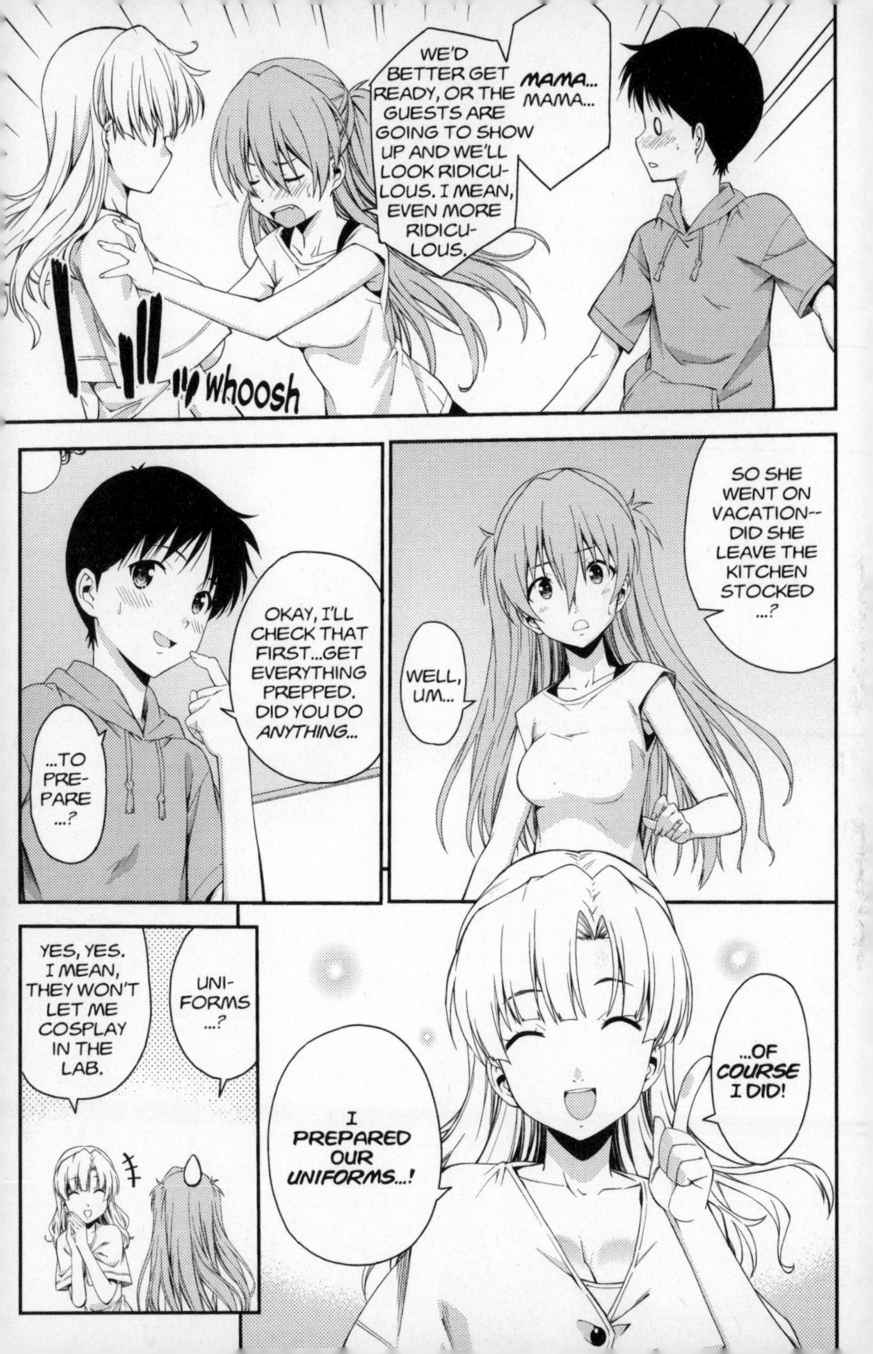
MAMA... MAMA...
WE'D BETTER GET READY, OR THE GUESTS ARE GOING TO SHOW UP AND WE'LL LOOK RIDICU-LOUS. I MEAN, EVEN MORE RIDICU-LOUS.
whoosh
SO SHE WENT ON VACATION--DID SHE LEAVE THE KITCHEN STOCKED...?
WELL, UM...
OKAY, I'LL CHECK THAT FIRST...GET EVERYTHING PREPPED. DID YOU DO *ANYTHING*...
...TO PRE-PARE...?
...OF *COURSE* I DID!
I PREPARED OUR *UNIFORMS*...!
UNI-FORMS...?
YES, YES. I MEAN, THEY WON'T LET ME COSPLAY IN THE LAB.

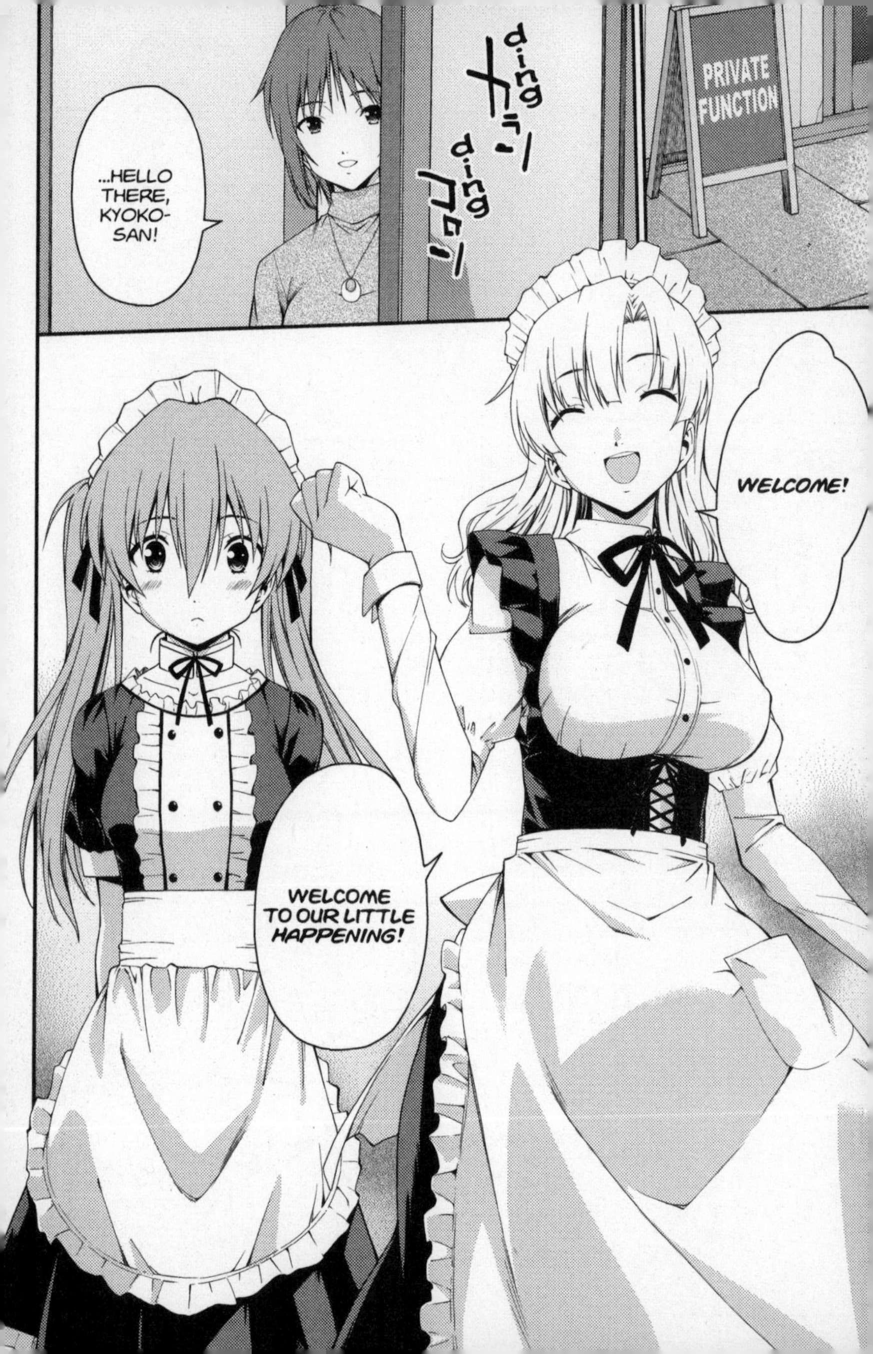
PRIVATE FUNCTION
ding
ding
...HELLO THERE, KYOKO-SAN!
WELCOME!
WELCOME TO OUR LITTLE HAPPENING!

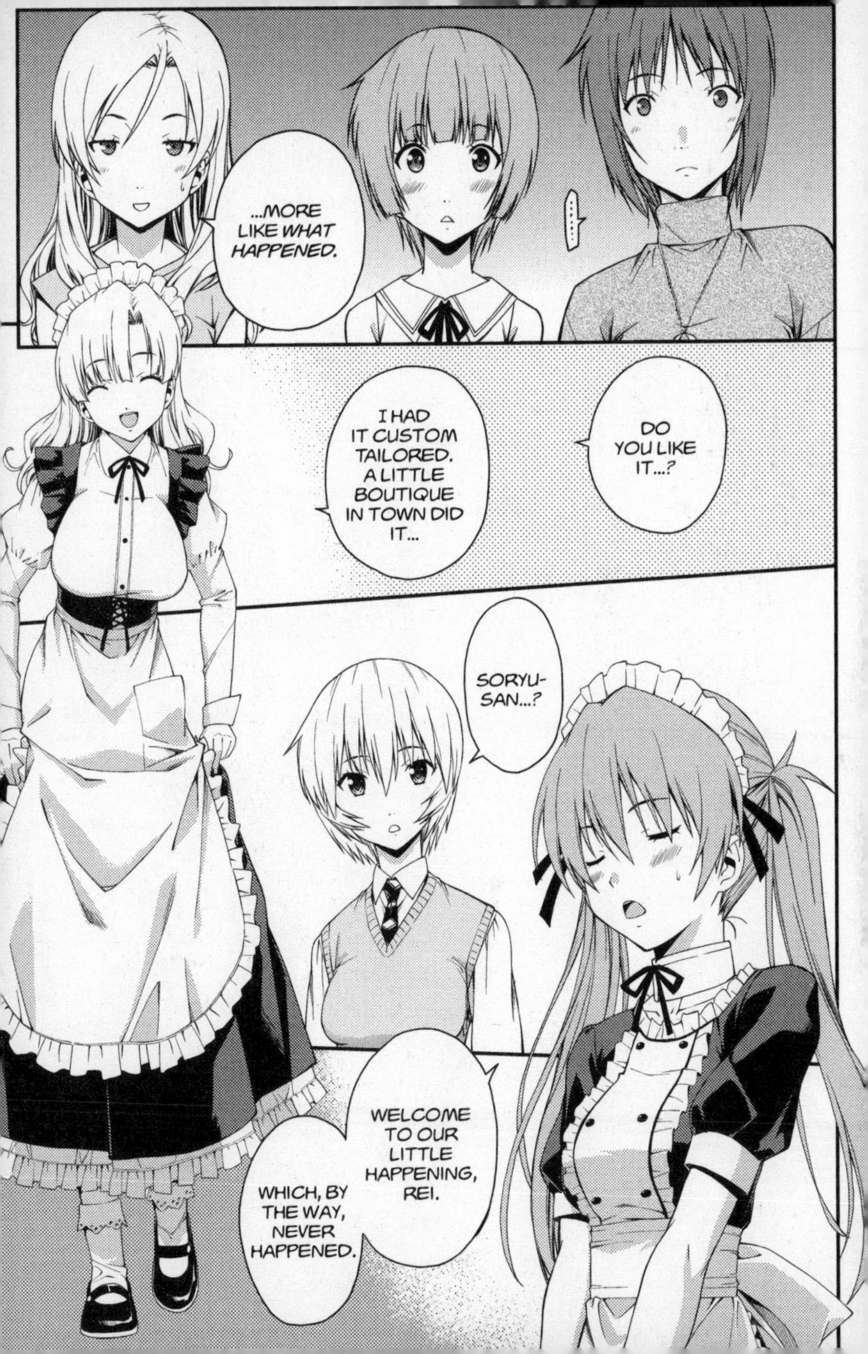
......
...MORE LIKE WHAT HAPPENED.
DO YOU LIKE IT...?
I HAD IT CUSTOM TAILORED. A LITTLE BOUTIQUE IN TOWN DID IT...
SORYU-SAN...?
WELCOME TO OUR LITTLE HAPPENING, REI.
WHICH, BY THE WAY, NEVER HAPPENED.

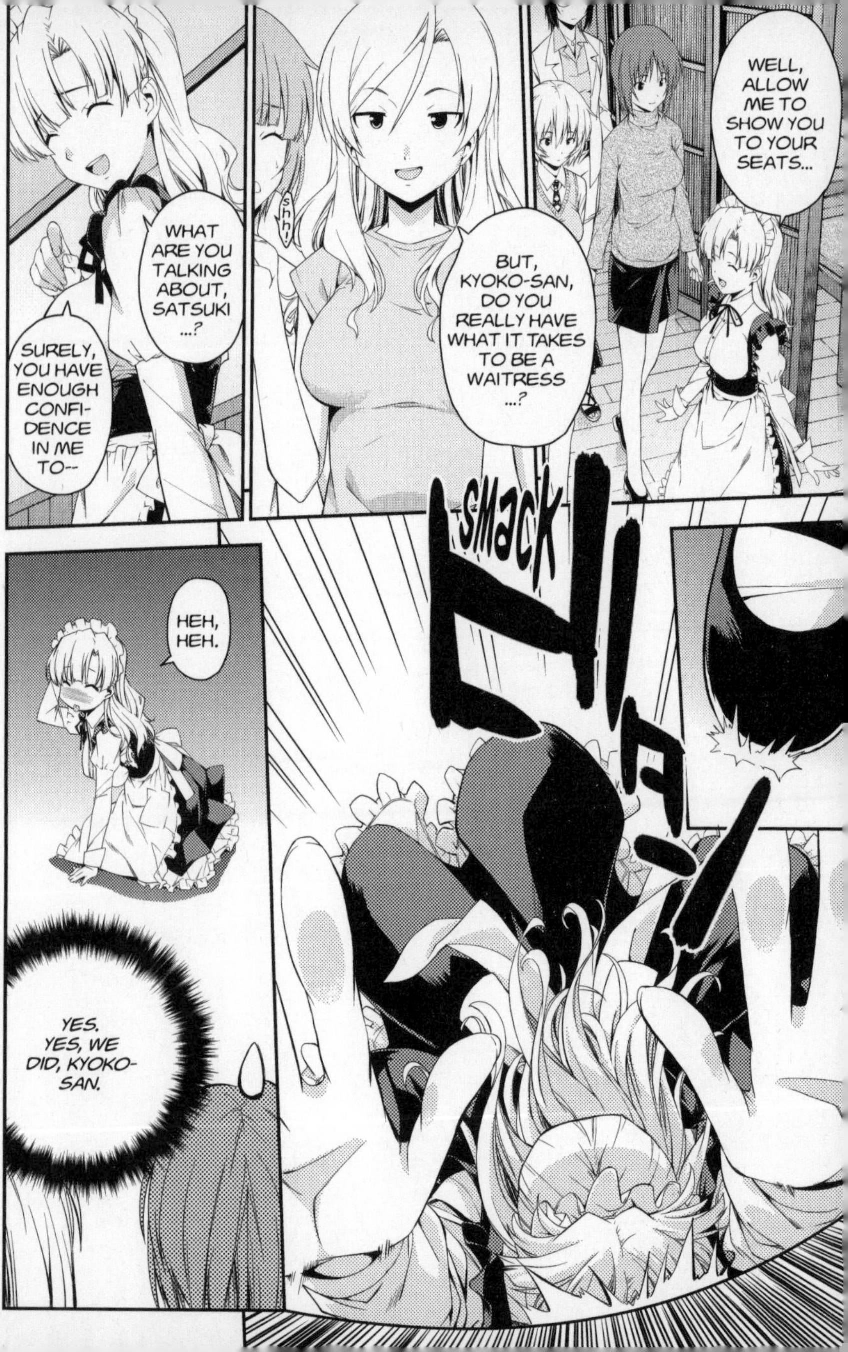
WELL, ALLOW ME TO SHOW YOU TO YOUR SEATS...
BUT, KYOKO-SAN, DO YOU REALLY HAVE WHAT IT TAKES TO BE A WAITRESS ...?
shh!
WHAT ARE YOU TALKING ABOUT, SATSUKI ...?
SURELY, YOU HAVE ENOUGH CONFI-DENCE IN ME TO--
SMACK
HEH, HEH.
YES. YES, WE DID, KYOKO-SAN.

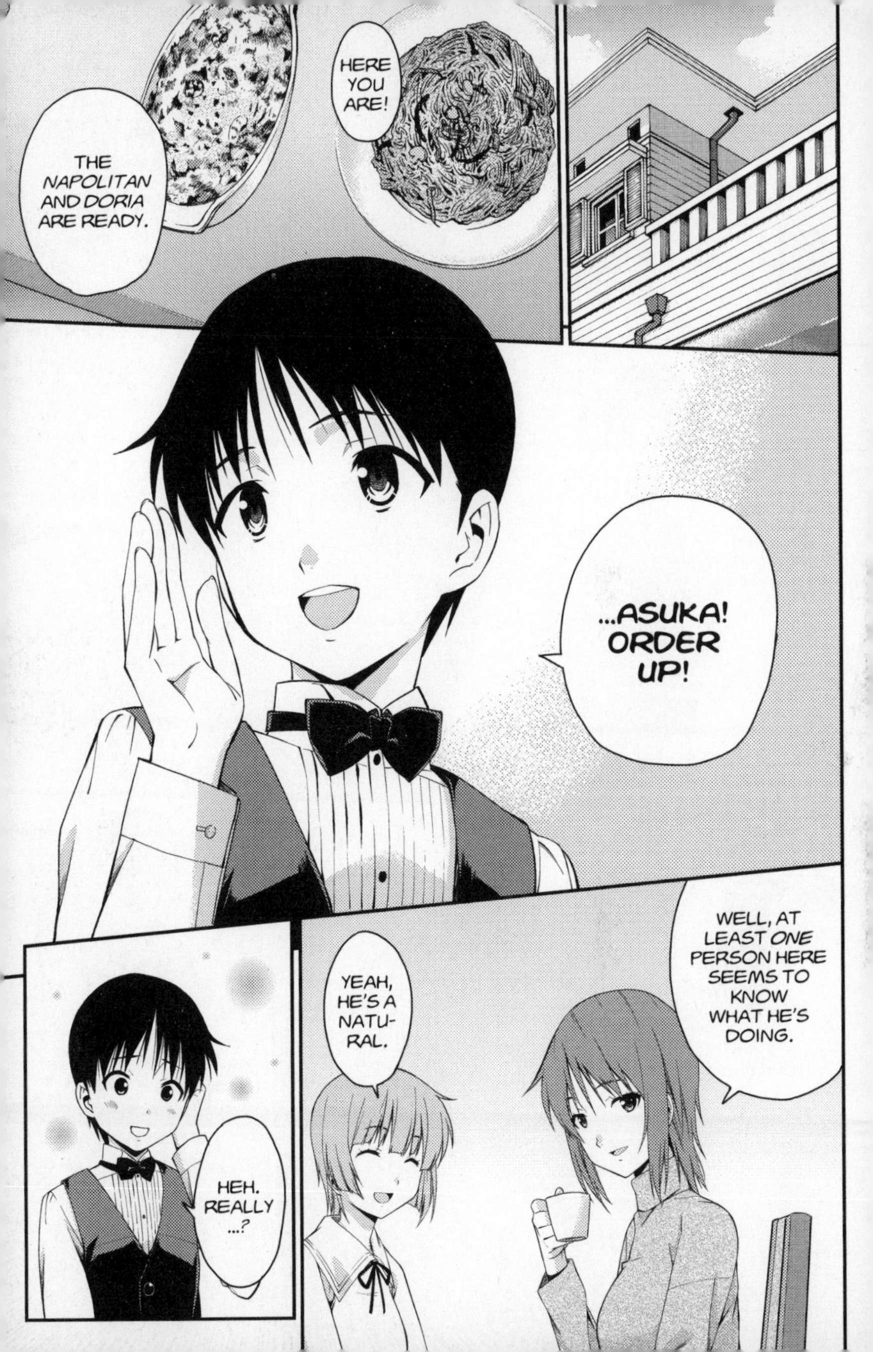
HERE YOU ARE!
THE *NAPOLITAN* AND *DORIA* ARE READY.
...ASUKA! ORDER UP!
WELL, AT LEAST *ONE* PERSON HERE SEEMS TO KNOW WHAT HE'S DOING.
YEAH, HE'S A NATU-RAL.
HEH. REALLY ...?

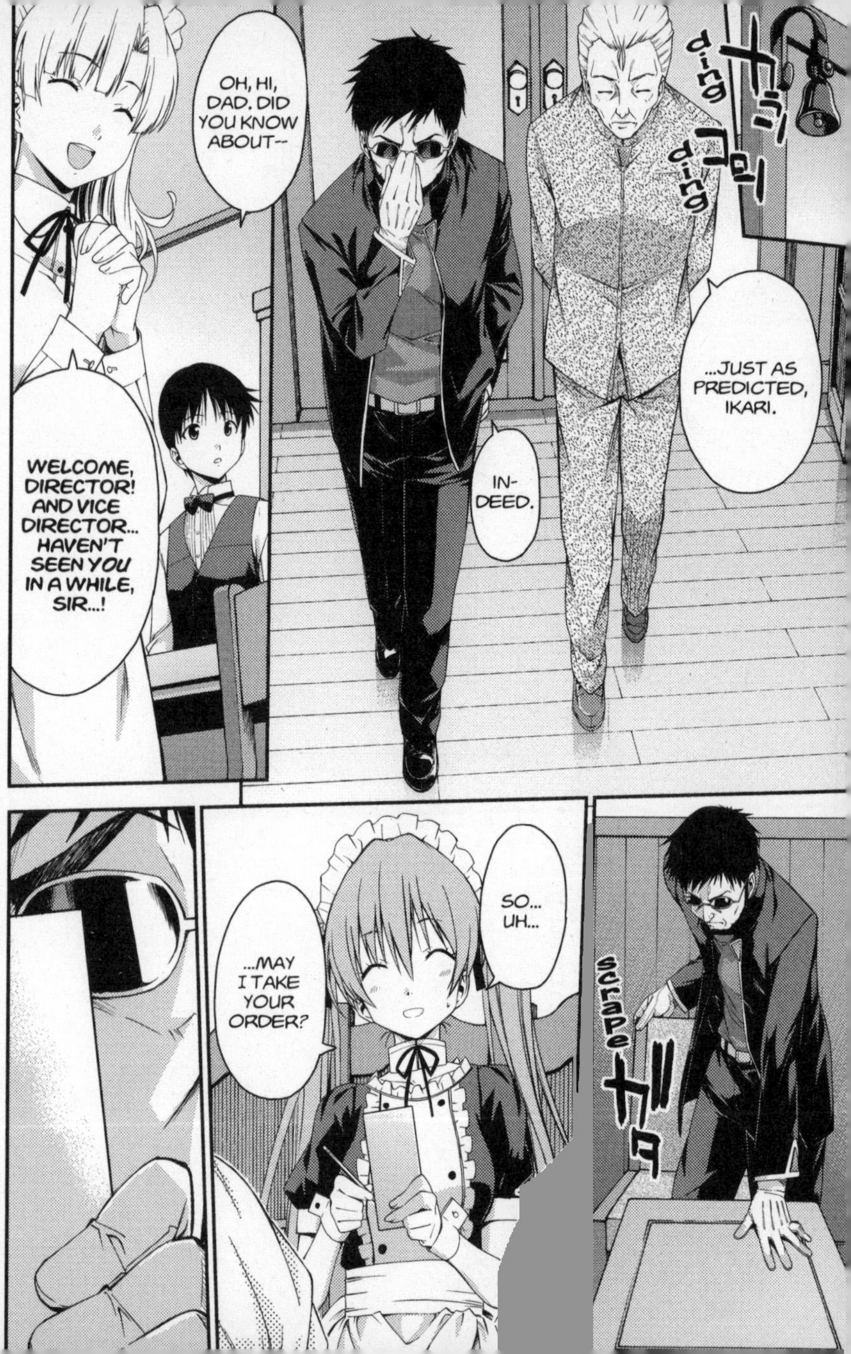
ding
ding
...JUST AS PREDICTED, IKARI.
IN-DEED.
OH, HI, DAD. DID YOU KNOW ABOUT--
WELCOME, DIRECTOR! AND VICE DIRECTOR... HAVEN'T SEEN YOU IN A WHILE, SIR...!
scrape
SO... UH...
...MAY I TAKE YOUR ORDER?

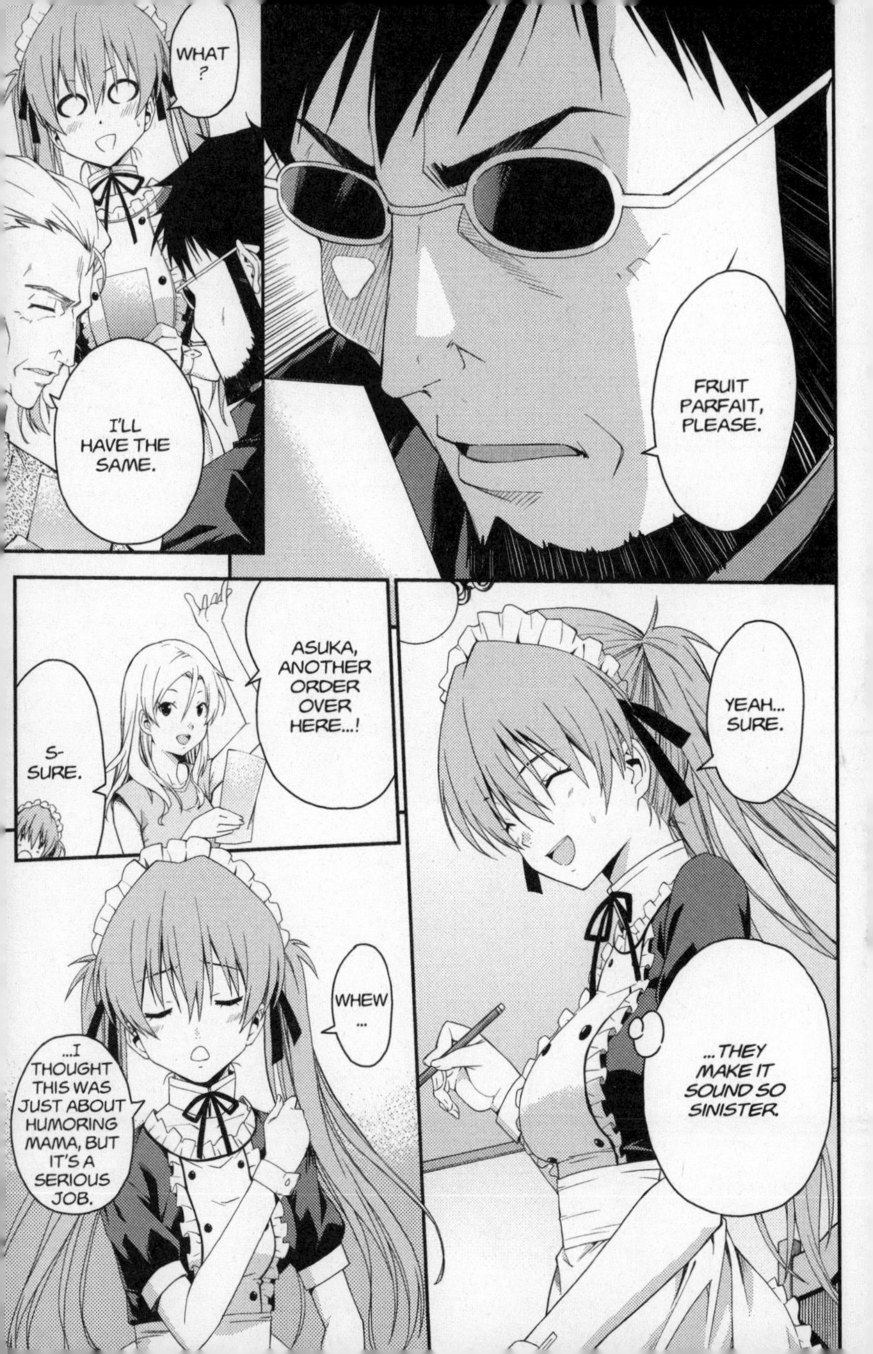
FRUIT PARFAIT, PLEASE.
WHAT ?
I'LL HAVE THE SAME.
YEAH... SURE.
...THEY MAKE IT SOUND SO SINISTER.
ASUKA, ANOTHER ORDER OVER HERE...!
S- SURE.
WHEW ...
...I THOUGHT THIS WAS JUST ABOUT HUMORING MAMA, BUT IT'S A SERIOUS JOB.

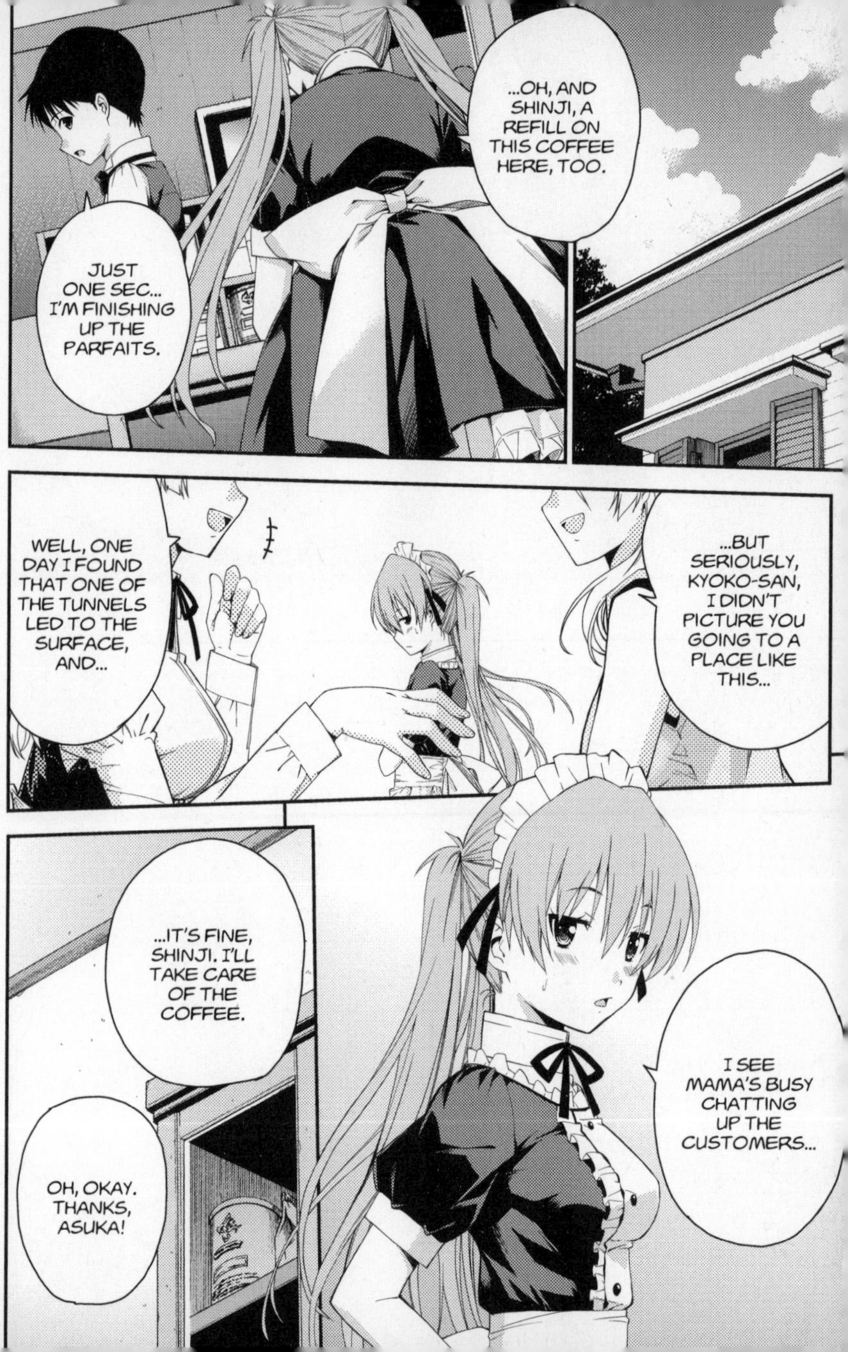
...OH, AND SHINJI, A REFILL ON THIS COFFEE HERE, TOO.
JUST ONE SEC... I'M FINISHING UP THE PARFAITS.
...BUT SERIOUSLY, KYOKO-SAN, I DIDN'T PICTURE YOU GOING TO A PLACE LIKE THIS...
WELL, ONE DAY I FOUND THAT ONE OF THE TUNNELS LED TO THE SURFACE, AND...
I SEE MAMA'S BUSY CHATTING UP THE CUSTOMERS...
...IT'S FINE, SHINJI. I'LL TAKE CARE OF THE COFFEE.
OH, OKAY. THANKS, ASUKA!

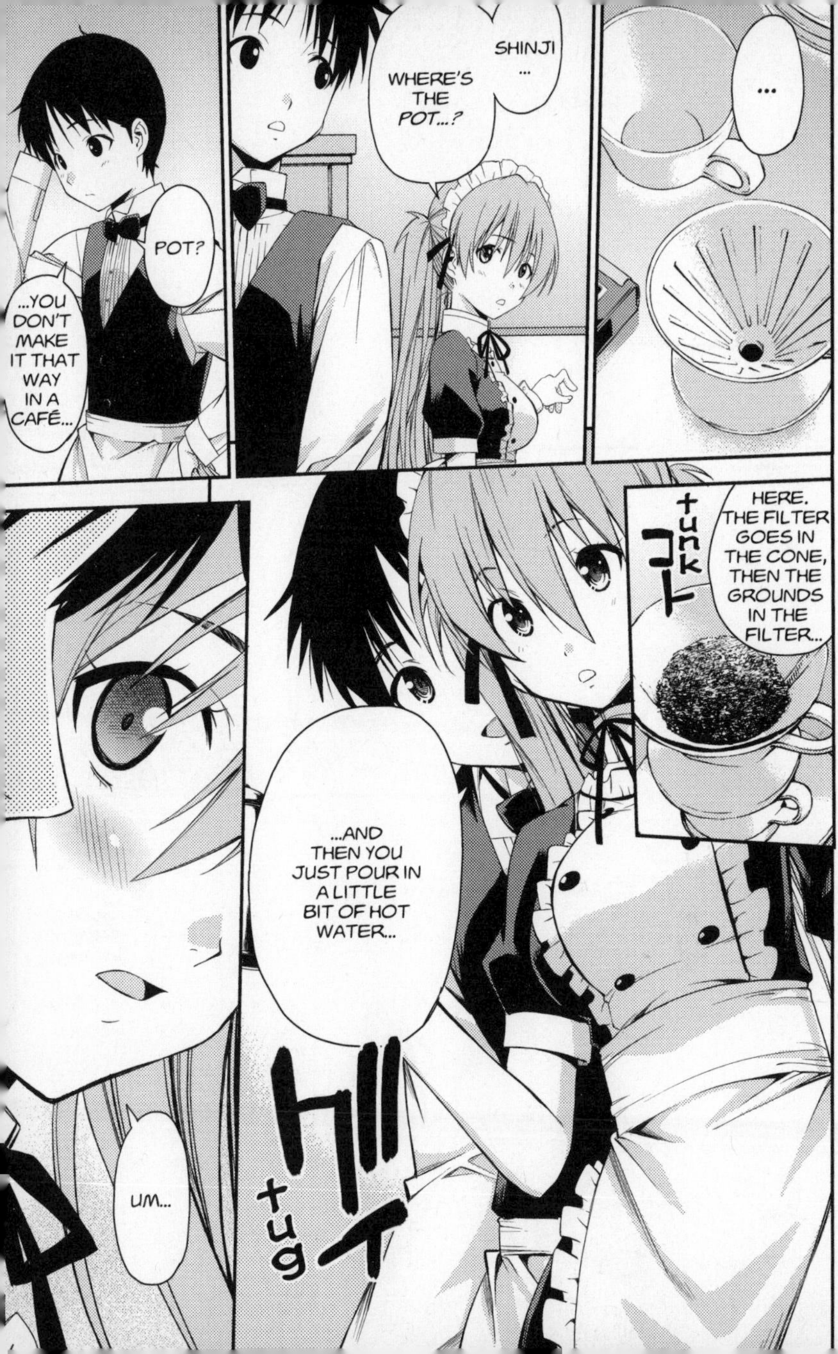
...
SHINJI ...
WHERE'S THE POT...?
POT?
...YOU DON'T MAKE IT THAT WAY IN A CAFÉ...
tunk
HERE. THE FILTER GOES IN THE CONE, THEN THE GROUNDS IN THE FILTER...
...AND THEN YOU JUST POUR IN A LITTLE BIT OF HOT WATER...
tug
UM...

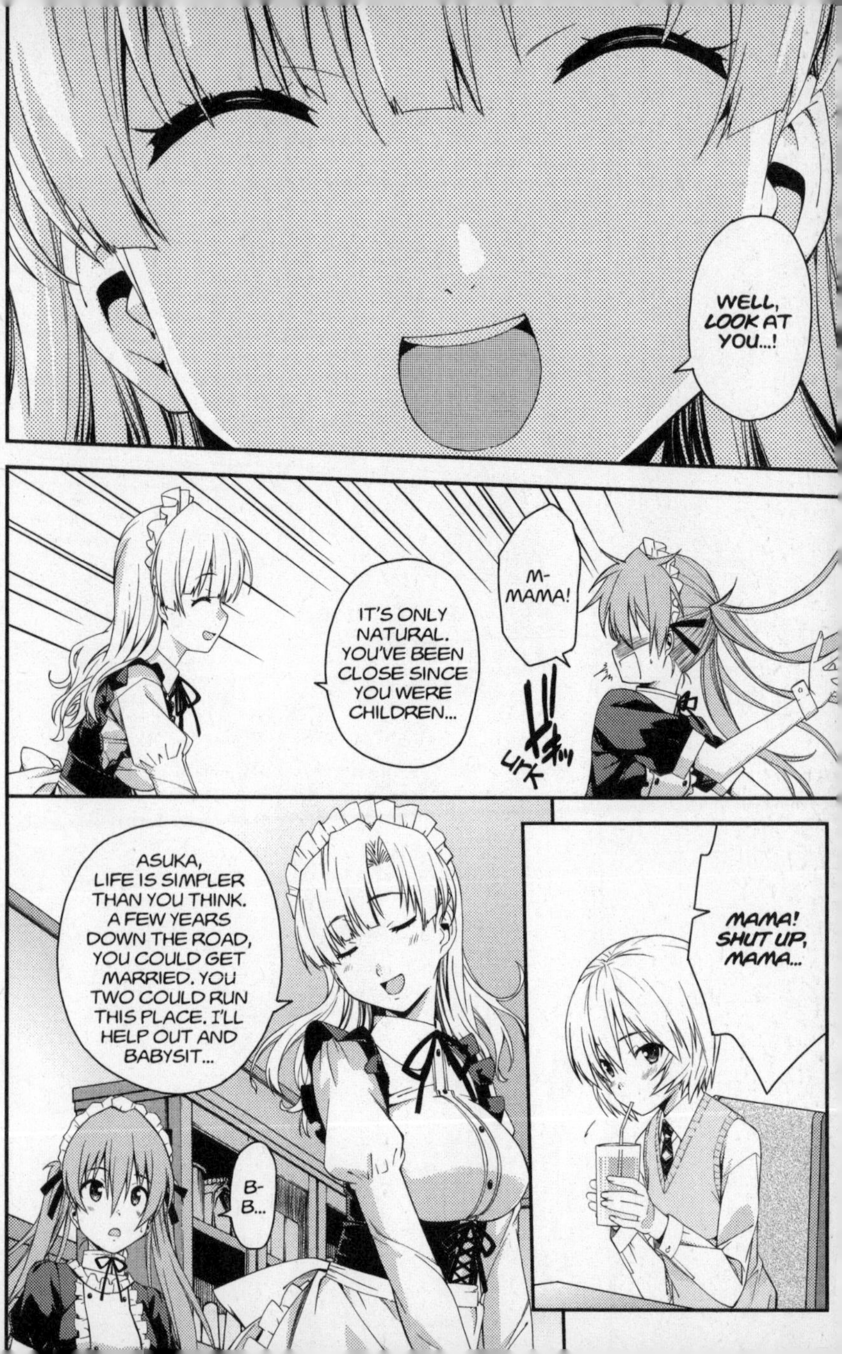

WELL, LOOK AT YOU...!
M-MAMA!
ドキッ
URK
IT'S ONLY NATURAL. YOU'VE BEEN CLOSE SINCE YOU WERE CHILDREN...
MAMA! SHUT UP, MAMA...
ASUKA, LIFE IS SIMPLER THAN YOU THINK. A FEW YEARS DOWN THE ROAD, YOU COULD GET MARRIED. YOU TWO COULD RUN THIS PLACE. I'LL HELP OUT AND BABYSIT...
B-B...

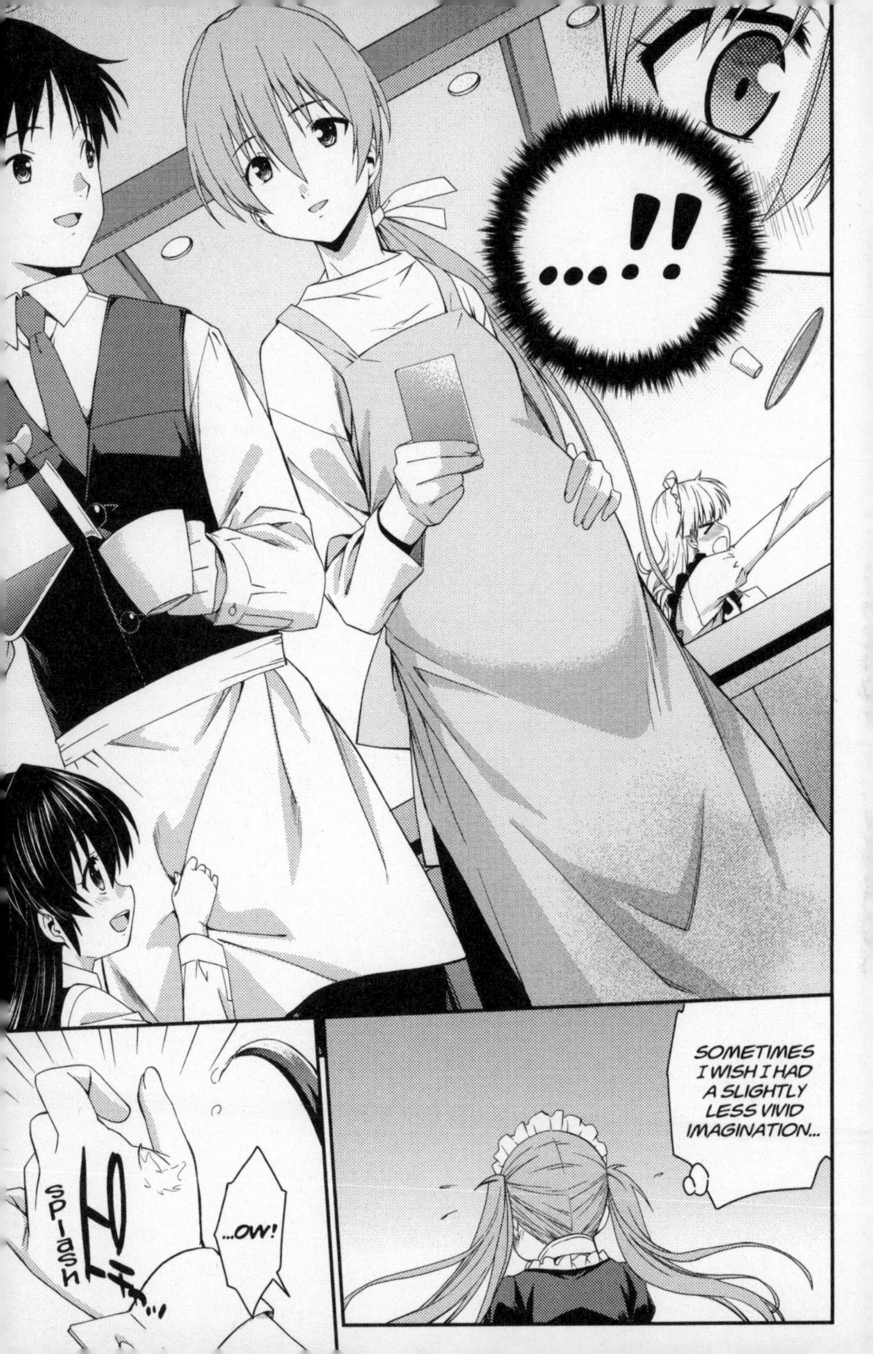
...!!
SOMETIMES I WISH I HAD A SLIGHTLY LESS VIVID IMAGINATION...
...OW!
splash

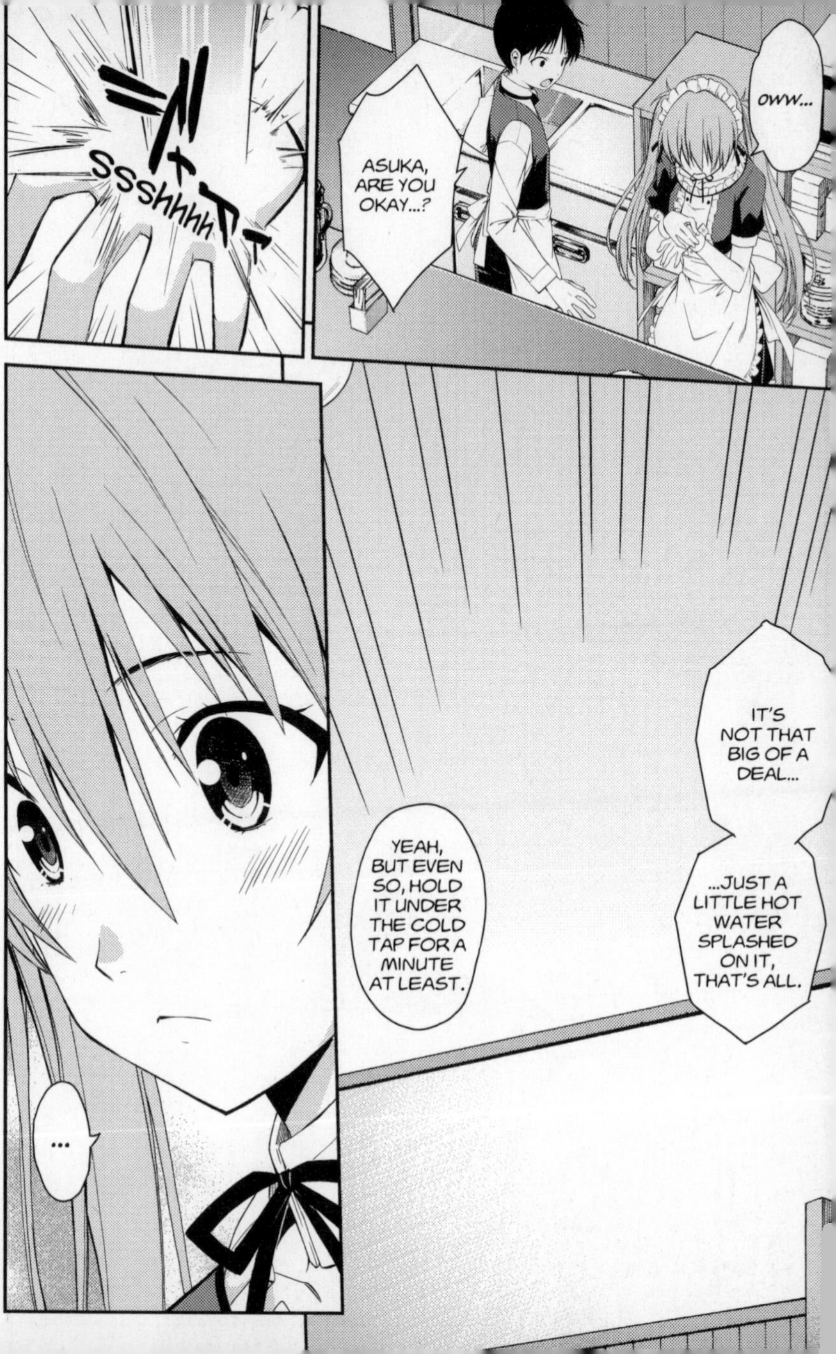
OWW...
ASUKA, ARE YOU OKAY...?
SSShhhh
IT'S NOT THAT BIG OF A DEAL...
...JUST A LITTLE HOT WATER SPLASHED ON IT, THAT'S ALL.
YEAH, BUT EVEN SO, HOLD IT UNDER THE COLD TAP FOR A MINUTE AT LEAST.
...

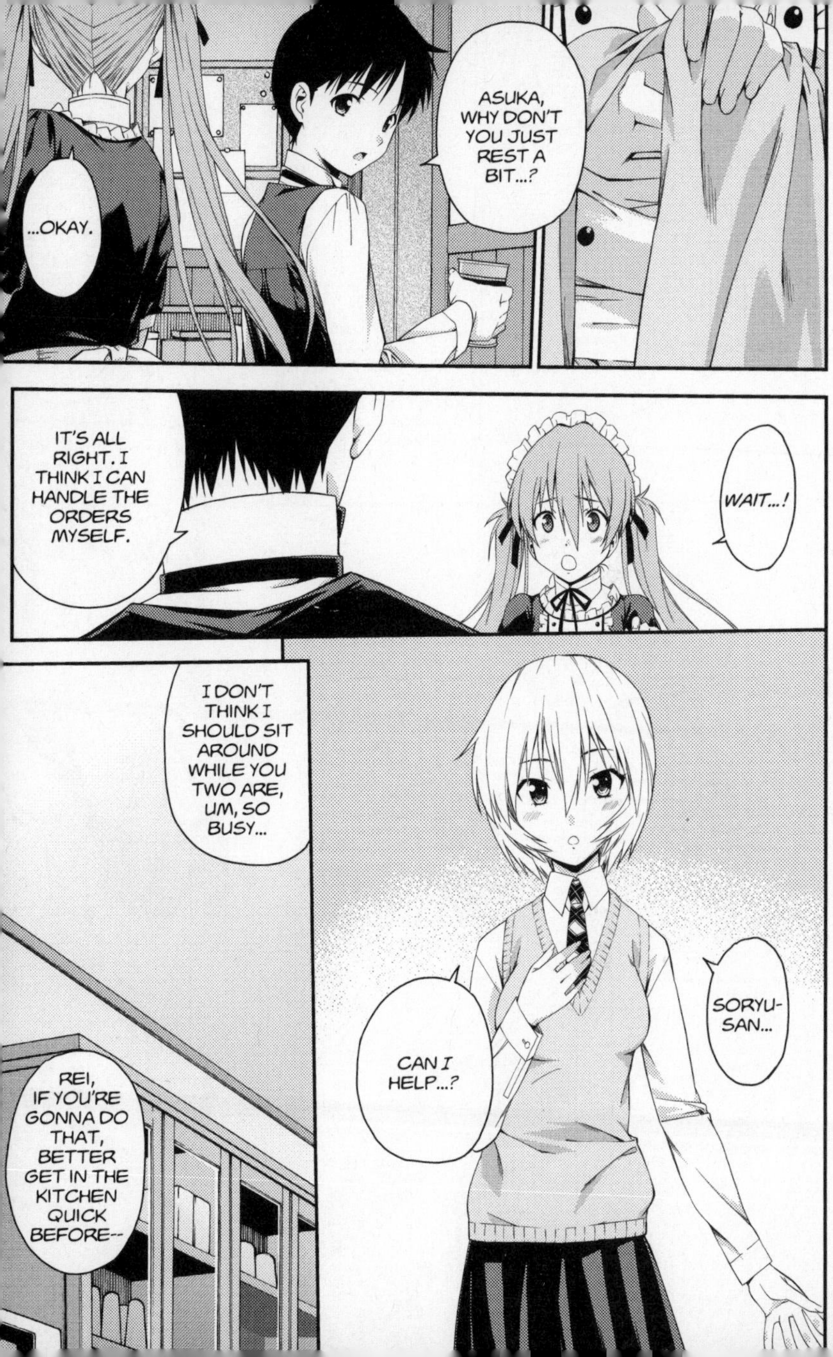
ASUKA, WHY DON'T YOU JUST REST A BIT...?
...OKAY.
WAIT...!
IT'S ALL RIGHT. I THINK I CAN HANDLE THE ORDERS MYSELF.
SORYU-SAN...
CAN I HELP...?
I DON'T THINK I SHOULD SIT AROUND WHILE YOU TWO ARE, UM, SO BUSY...
REI, IF YOU'RE GONNA DO THAT, BETTER GET IN THE KITCHEN QUICK BEFORE--

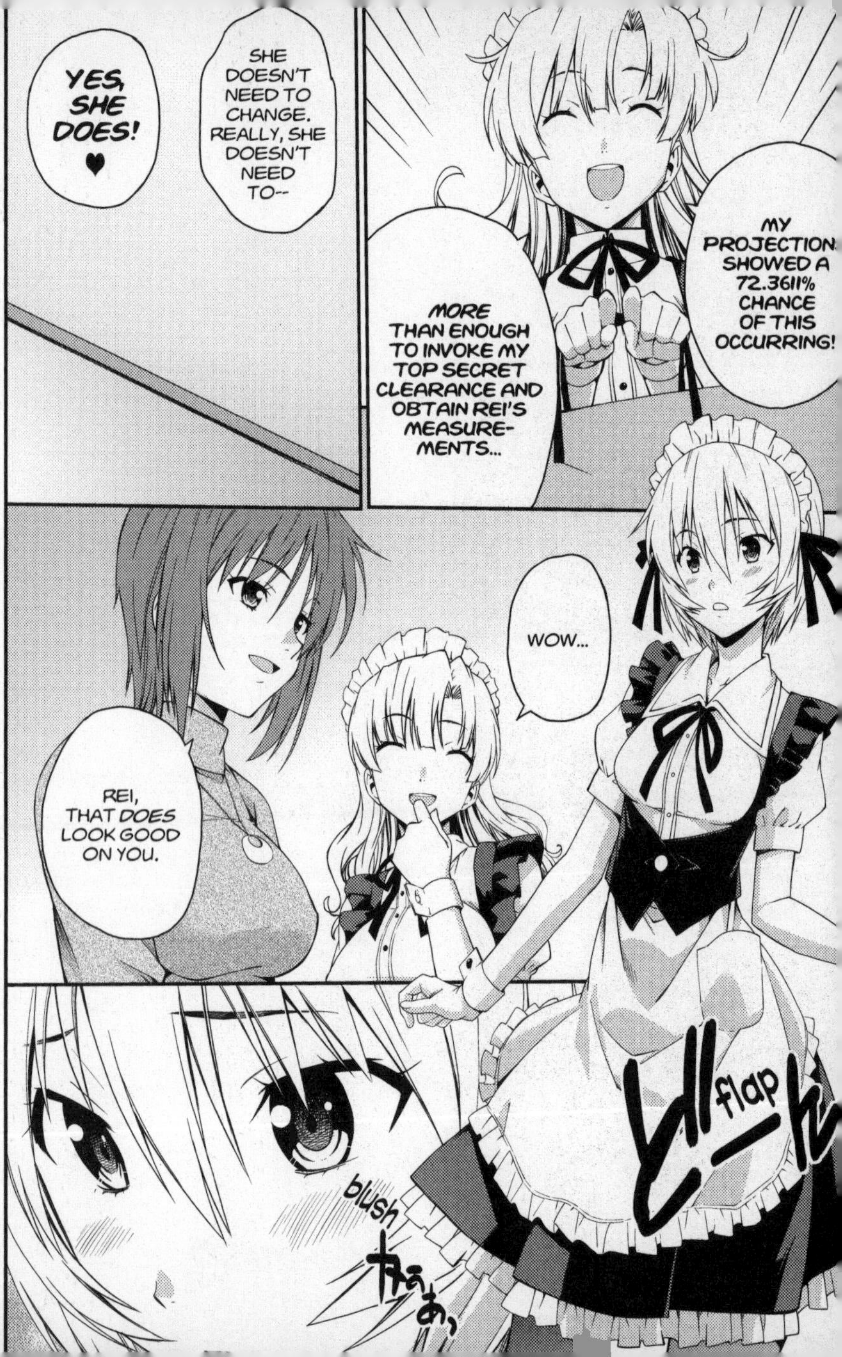
MY PROJECTION SHOWED A 72.3611% CHANCE OF THIS OCCURRING!
MORE THAN ENOUGH TO INVOKE MY TOP SECRET CLEARANCE AND OBTAIN REI'S MEASURE-MENTS...
SHE DOESN'T NEED TO CHANGE. REALLY, SHE DOESN'T NEED TO--
YES, SHE DOES! ♥
WOW...
flap
REI, THAT DOES LOOK GOOD ON YOU.
blush

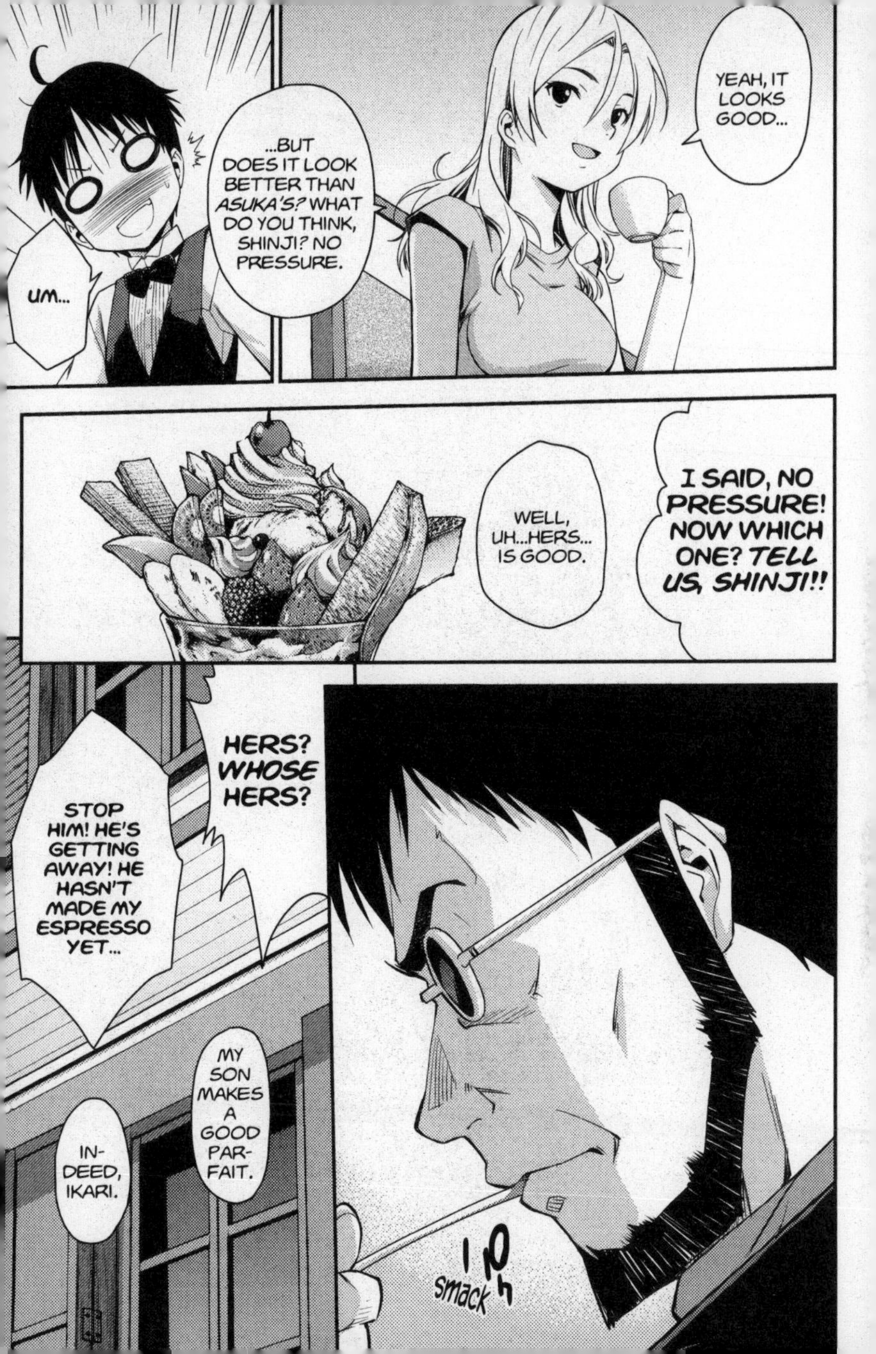
YEAH, IT LOOKS GOOD...
...BUT DOES IT LOOK BETTER THAN *ASUKA'S?* WHAT DO YOU THINK, SHINJI? NO PRESSURE.
UM...
I SAID, NO PRESSURE! NOW WHICH ONE? *TELL US, SHINJI!!*
WELL, UH...HERS... IS GOOD.
smack
HERS? WHOSE HERS?
STOP HIM! HE'S GETTING AWAY! HE HASN'T MADE MY ESPRESSO YET...
MY SON MAKES A GOOD PAR-FAIT.
IN-DEED, IKARI.

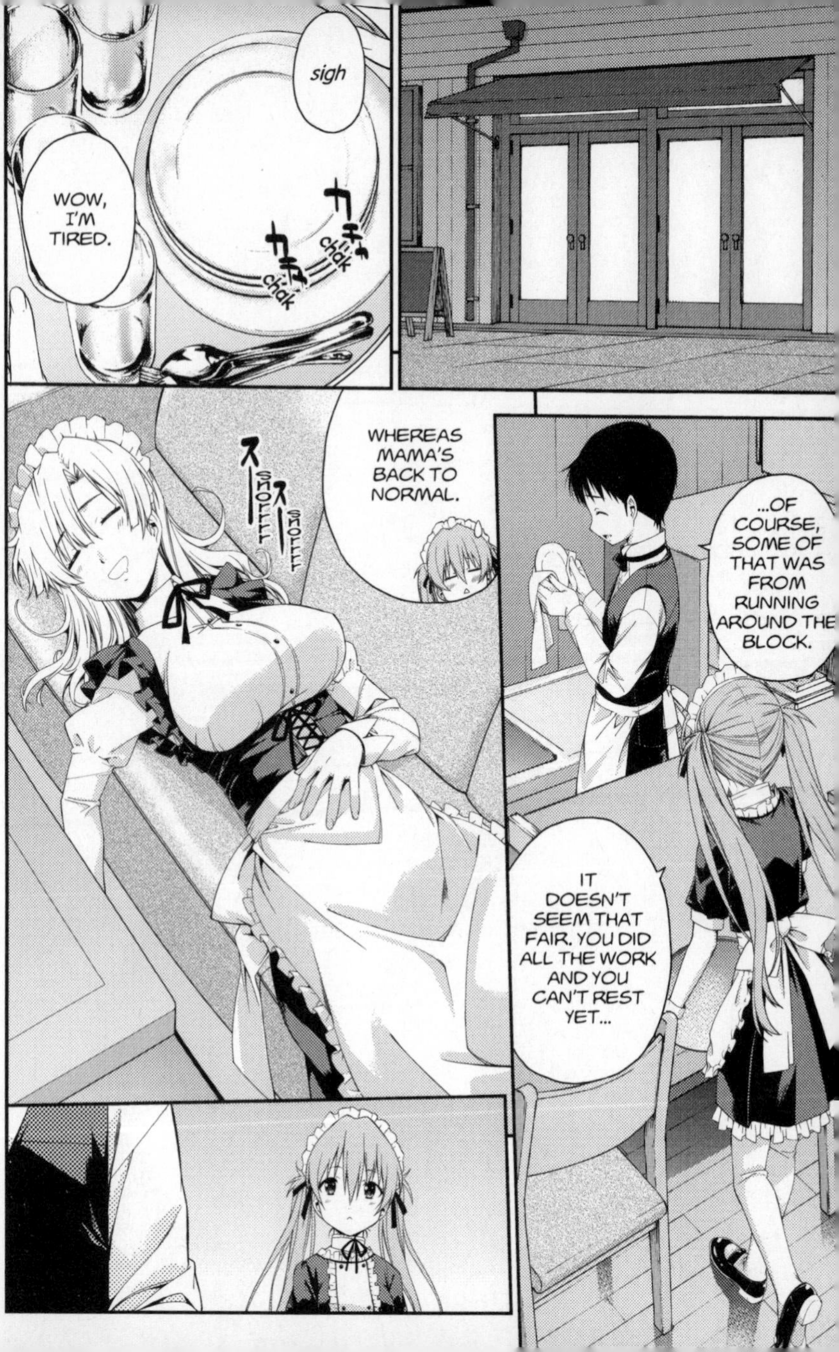
sigh
WOW, I'M TIRED.
カチャ chak
カチャ chak
...OF COURSE, SOME OF THAT WAS FROM RUNNING AROUND THE BLOCK.
IT DOESN'T SEEM THAT FAIR. YOU DID ALL THE WORK AND YOU CAN'T REST YET...
WHEREAS MAMA'S BACK TO NORMAL.
スー snorrrr
スー snorrrr

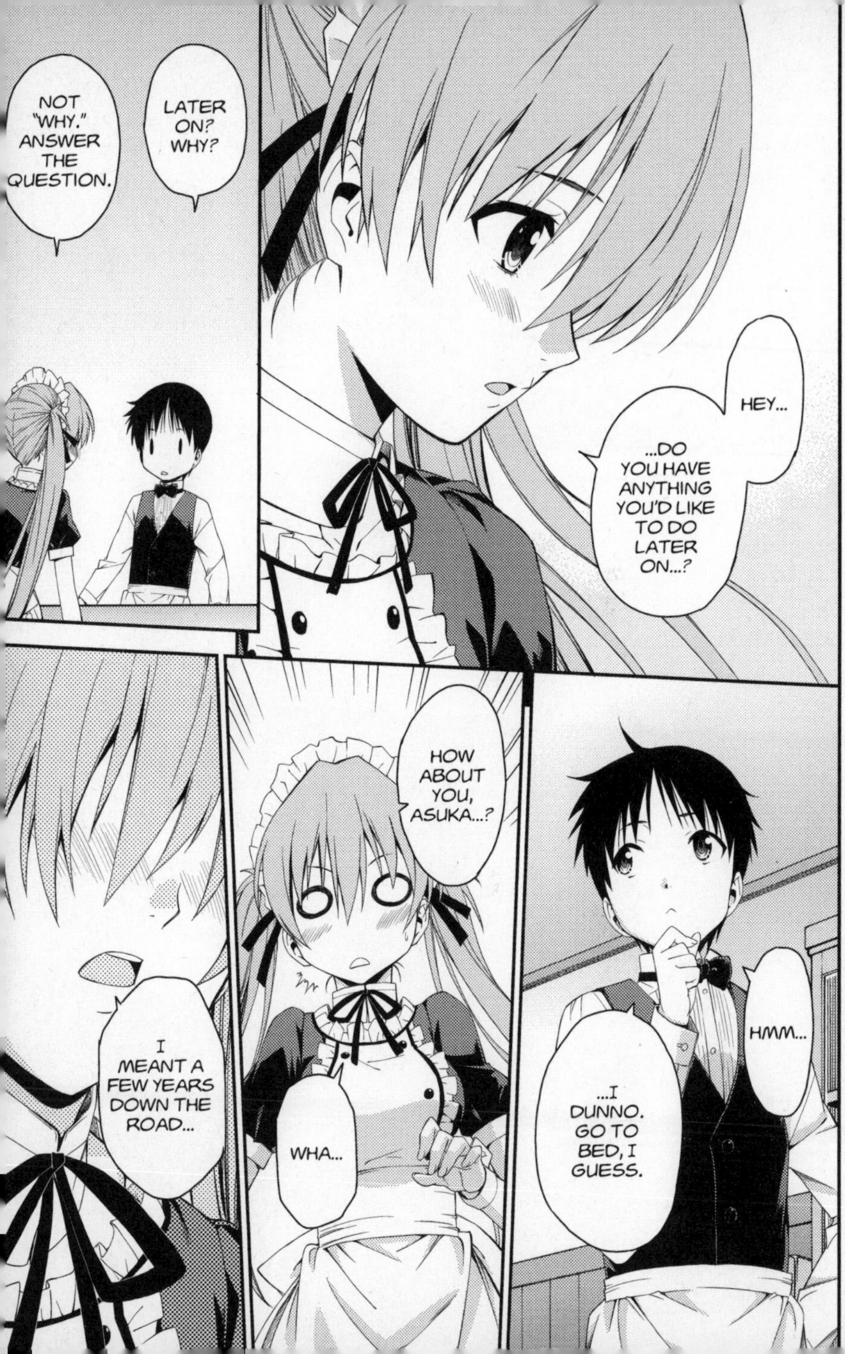
HEY...
...DO YOU HAVE ANYTHING YOU'D LIKE TO DO LATER ON...?
LATER ON? WHY?
NOT "WHY." ANSWER THE QUESTION.
HMM...
...I DUNNO. GO TO BED, I GUESS.
HOW ABOUT YOU, ASUKA...?
WHA...
I MEANT A FEW YEARS DOWN THE ROAD...

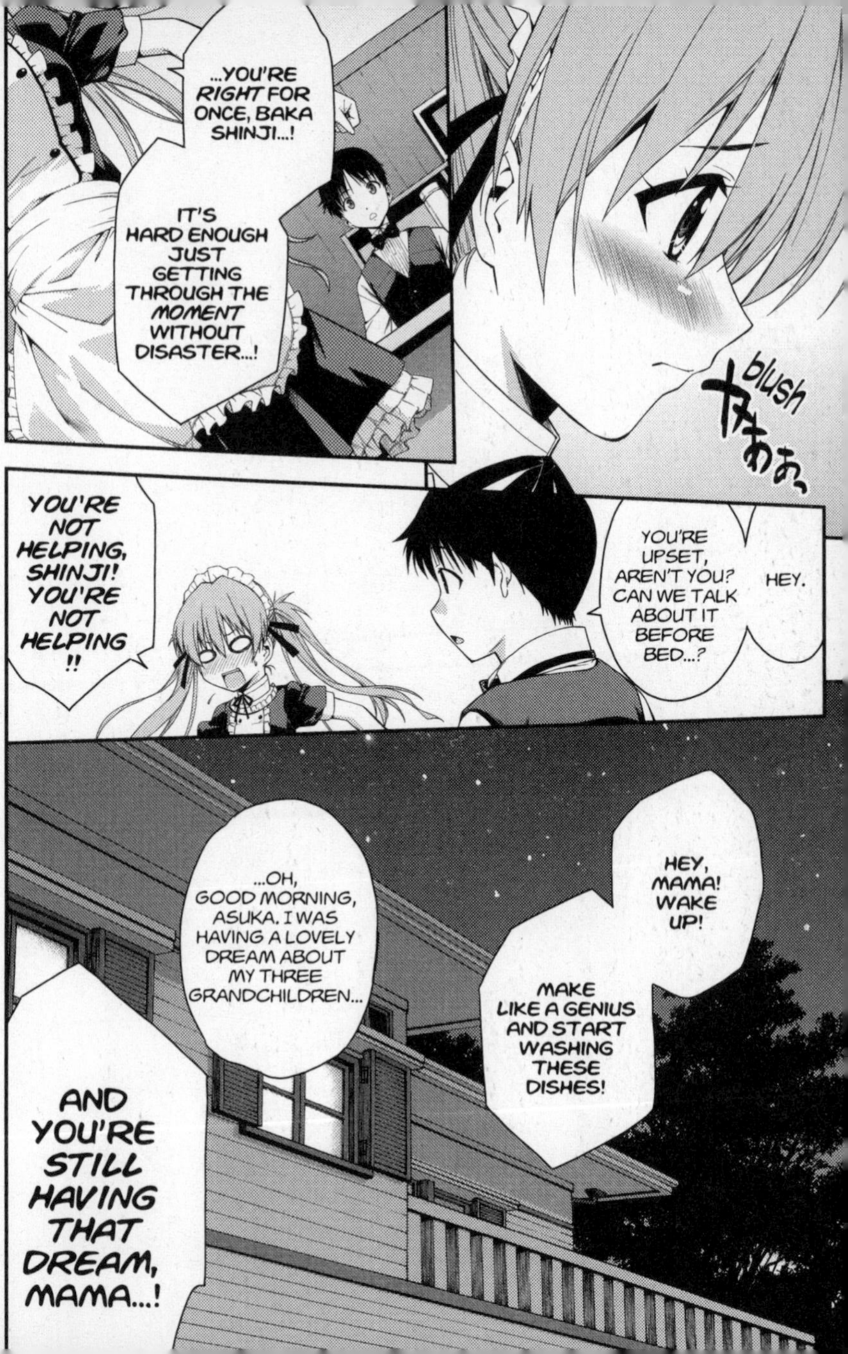
blush
...YOU'RE RIGHT FOR ONCE, BAKA SHINJI...!
IT'S HARD ENOUGH JUST GETTING THROUGH THE MOMENT WITHOUT DISASTER...!
HEY.
YOU'RE UPSET, AREN'T YOU? CAN WE TALK ABOUT IT BEFORE BED...?
YOU'RE NOT HELPING, SHINJI! YOU'RE NOT HELPING!!
HEY, MAMA! WAKE UP!
MAKE LIKE A GENIUS AND START WASHING THESE DISHES!
...OH, GOOD MORNING, ASUKA. I WAS HAVING A LOVELY DREAM ABOUT MY THREE GRANDCHILDREN...
AND YOU'RE STILL HAVING THAT DREAM, MAMA...!

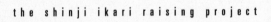
the shinji ikari raising project

NEON GENESIS EVANGELION

THE SHINJI IKARI RAISING PROJECT

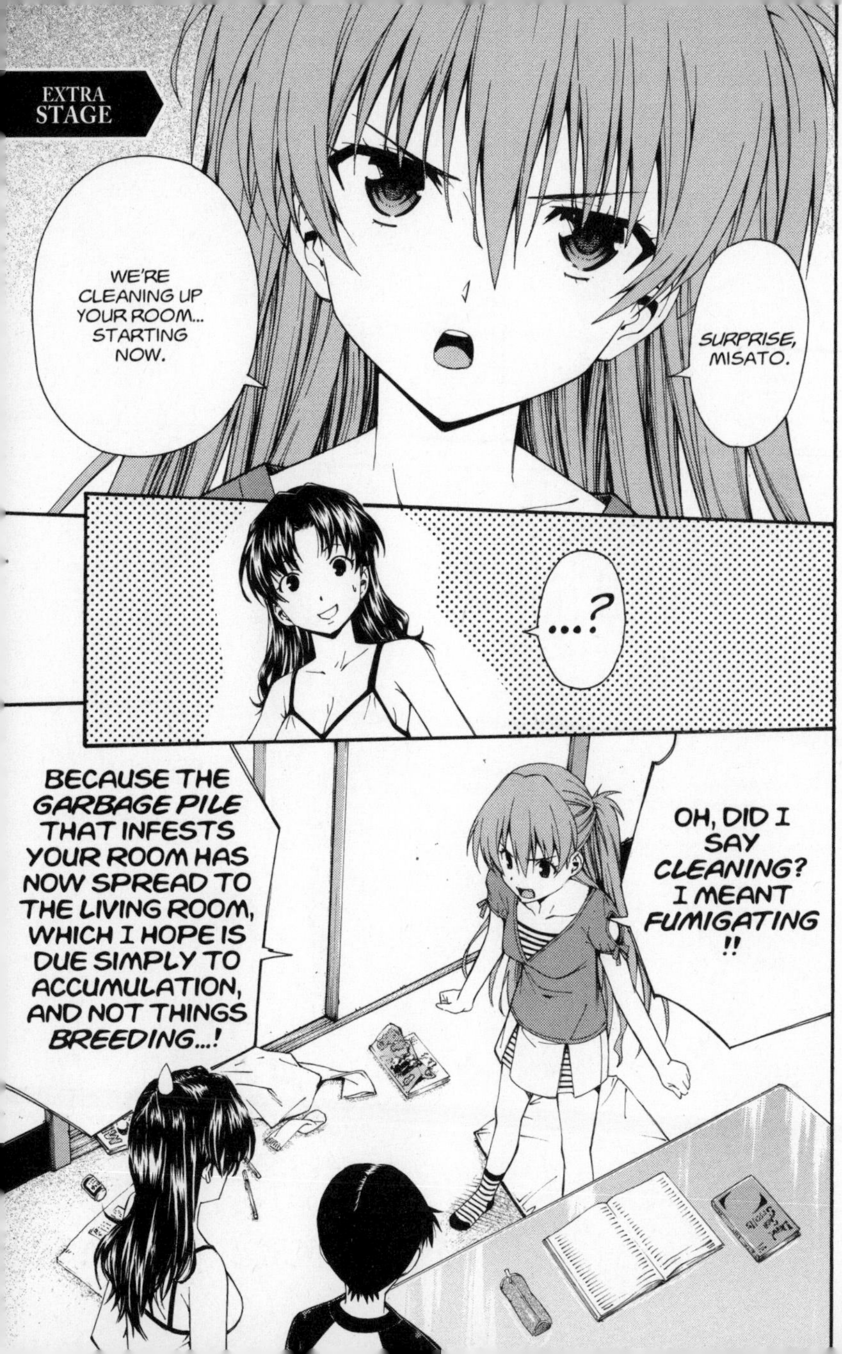
EXTRA STAGE
SURPRISE, MISATO.
WE'RE CLEANING UP YOUR ROOM... STARTING NOW.
...?
OH, DID I SAY *CLEANING*? I MEANT *FUMIGATING*!!
BECAUSE THE *GARBAGE PILE* THAT INFESTS YOUR ROOM HAS NOW SPREAD TO THE LIVING ROOM, WHICH I HOPE IS DUE SIMPLY TO ACCUMULATION, AND NOT THINGS *BREEDING*...!

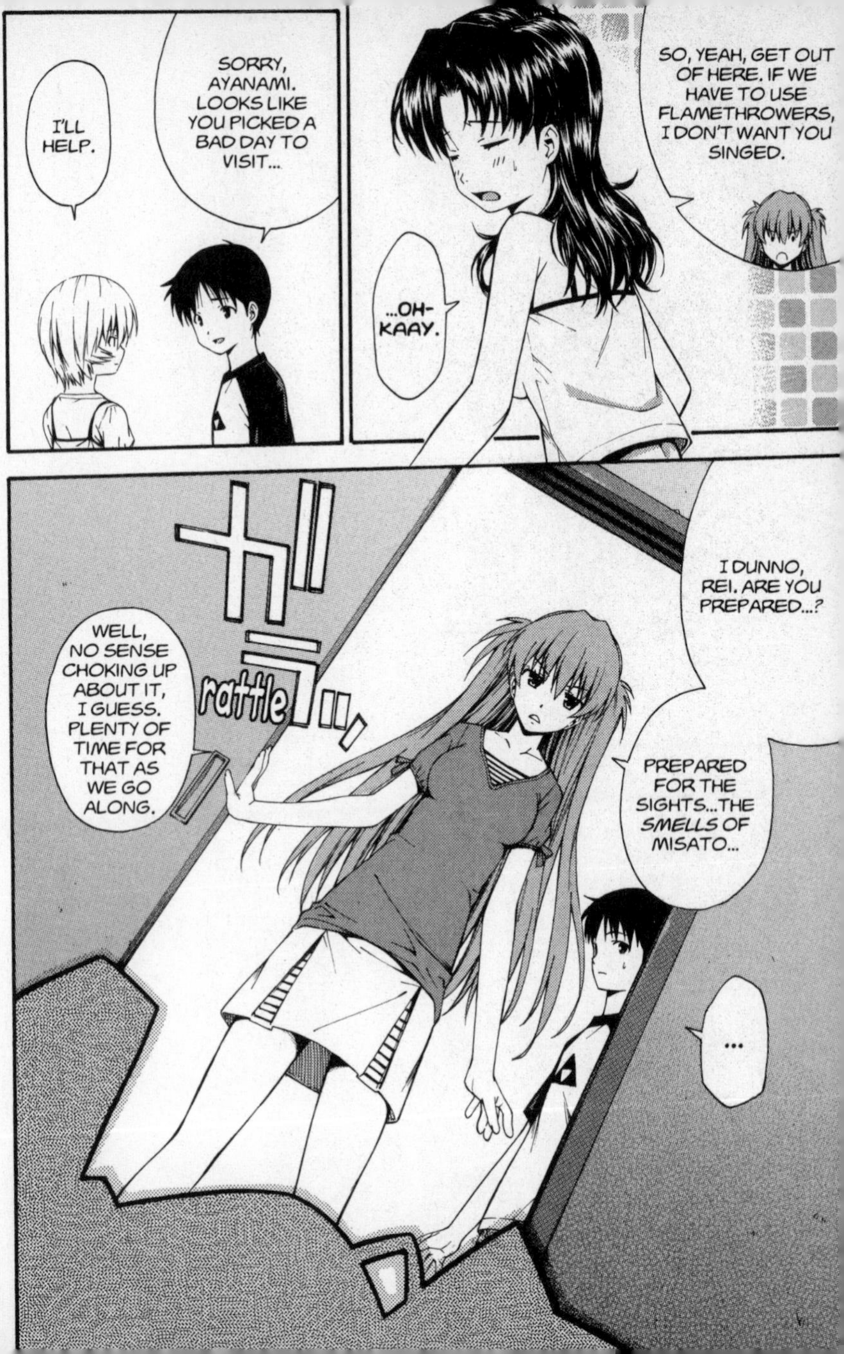
SO, YEAH, GET OUT OF HERE. IF WE HAVE TO USE FLAMETHROWERS, I DON'T WANT YOU SINGED.
...OH-KAAY.
SORRY, AYANAMI. LOOKS LIKE YOU PICKED A BAD DAY TO VISIT...
I'LL HELP.
I DUNNO, REI. ARE YOU PREPARED...?
PREPARED FOR THE SIGHTS...THE *SMELLS* OF MISATO...
WELL, NO SENSE CHOKING UP ABOUT IT, I GUESS. PLENTY OF TIME FOR THAT AS WE GO ALONG.
rattle
...

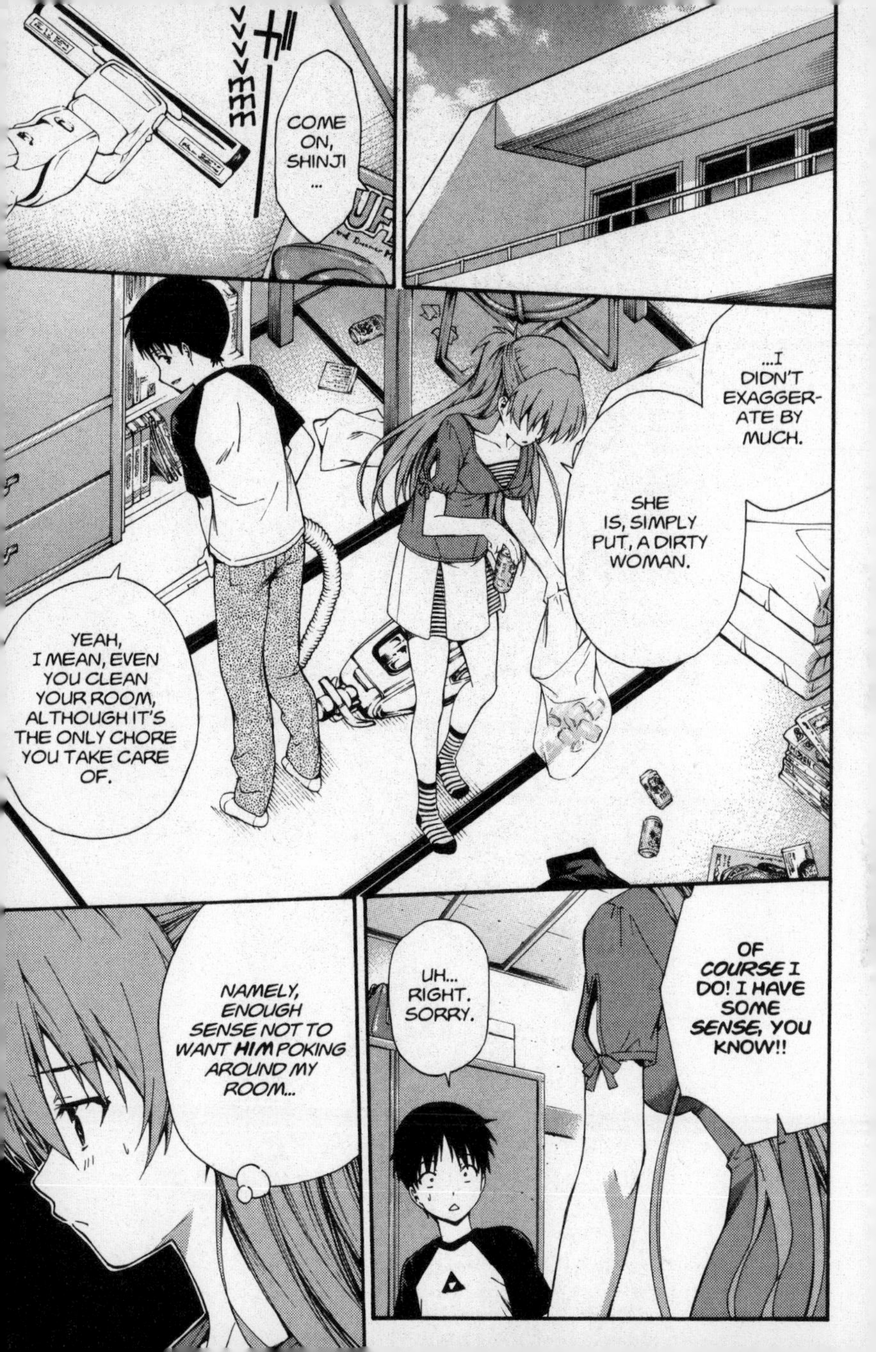
VVVVVMMM
COME ON, SHINJI ...
...I DIDN'T EXAGGERATE BY MUCH.
SHE IS, SIMPLY PUT, A DIRTY WOMAN.
YEAH, I MEAN, EVEN YOU CLEAN YOUR ROOM, ALTHOUGH IT'S THE ONLY CHORE YOU TAKE CARE OF.
OF COURSE I DO! I HAVE SOME SENSE, YOU KNOW!!
UH... RIGHT. SORRY.
NAMELY, ENOUGH SENSE NOT TO WANT HIM POKING AROUND MY ROOM...

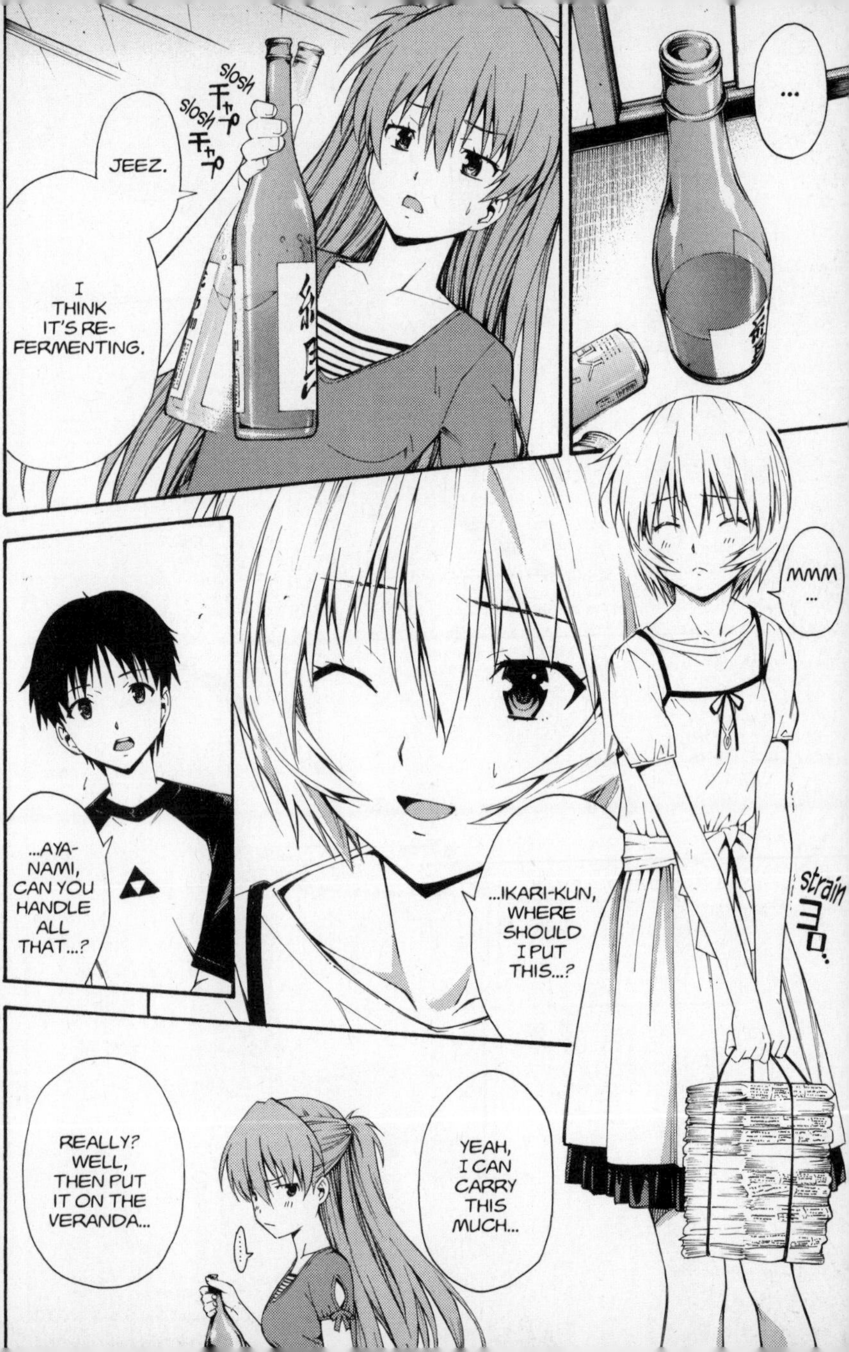
...
slosh チャプ
slosh チャプ
JEEZ.
I THINK IT'S RE-FERMENTING.
MMM...
strain ヨロ..
...IKARI-KUN, WHERE SHOULD I PUT THIS...?
...AYA-NAMI, CAN YOU HANDLE ALL THAT...?
YEAH, I CAN CARRY THIS MUCH...
REALLY? WELL, THEN PUT IT ON THE VERANDA...
......

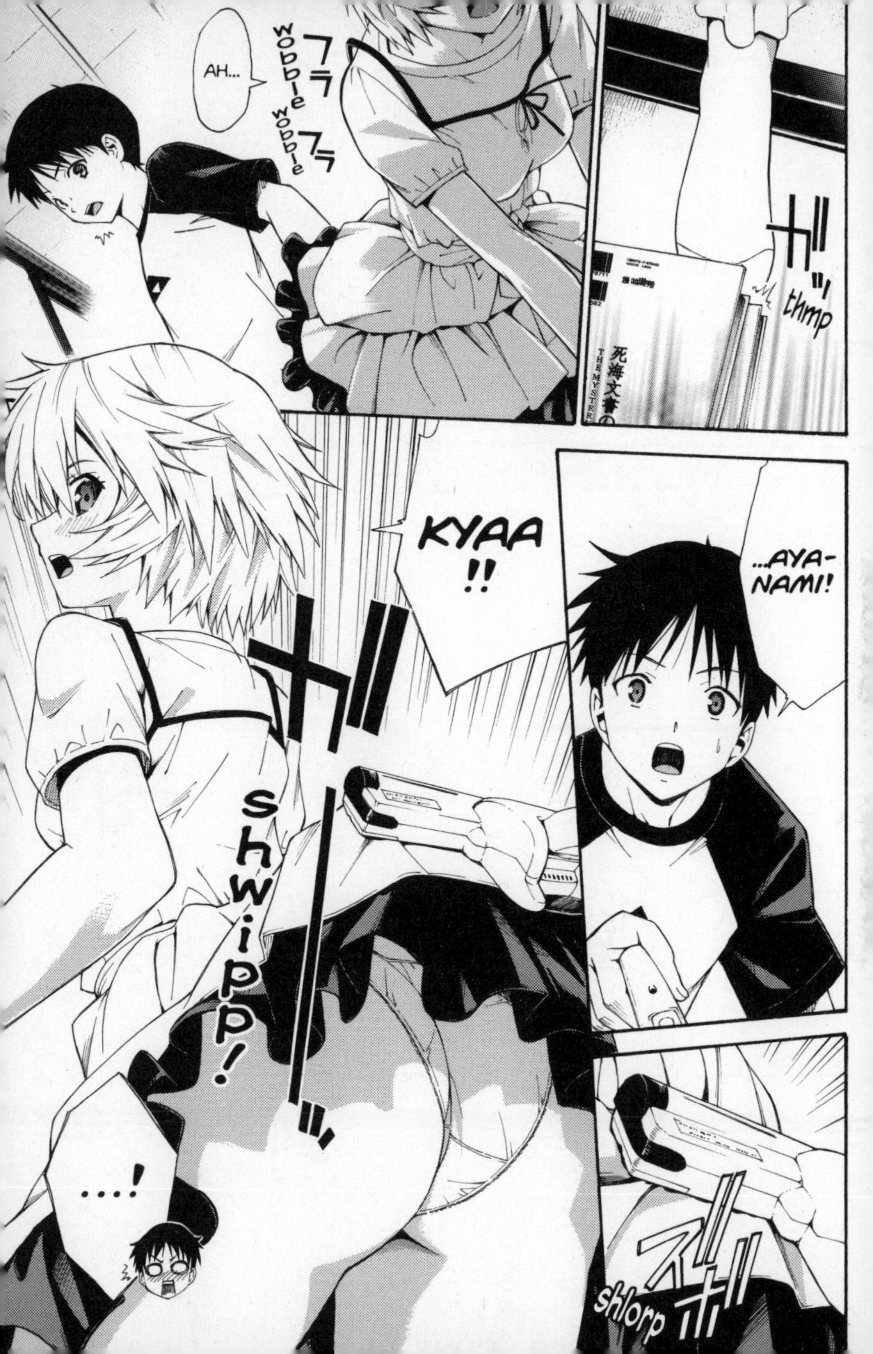

ガッ
thmp
死海文書の
THE MYSTER
AH...
フラ
wobble wobble
フラ
...AYA-NAMI!
KYAA!!
ガッ
shwipp!
...!
shlorp

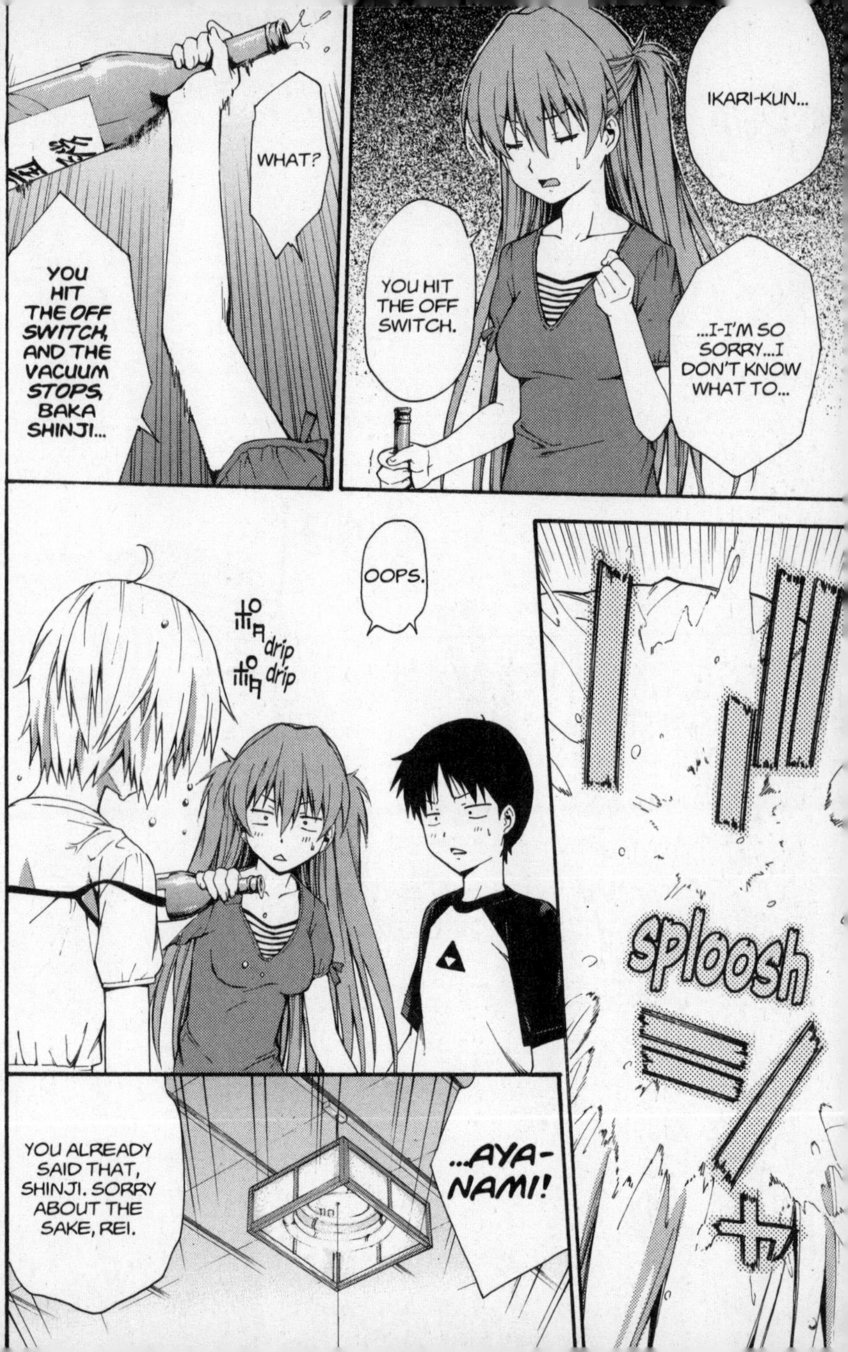
IKARI-KUN...
...I-I'M SO SORRY...I DON'T KNOW WHAT TO...
YOU HIT THE OFF SWITCH.
WHAT?
YOU HIT THE OFF SWITCH, AND THE VACUUM STOPS, BAKA SHINJI...
sploosh
OOPS.
drip drip
...AYA-NAMI!
YOU ALREADY SAID THAT, SHINJI. SORRY ABOUT THE SAKE, REI.

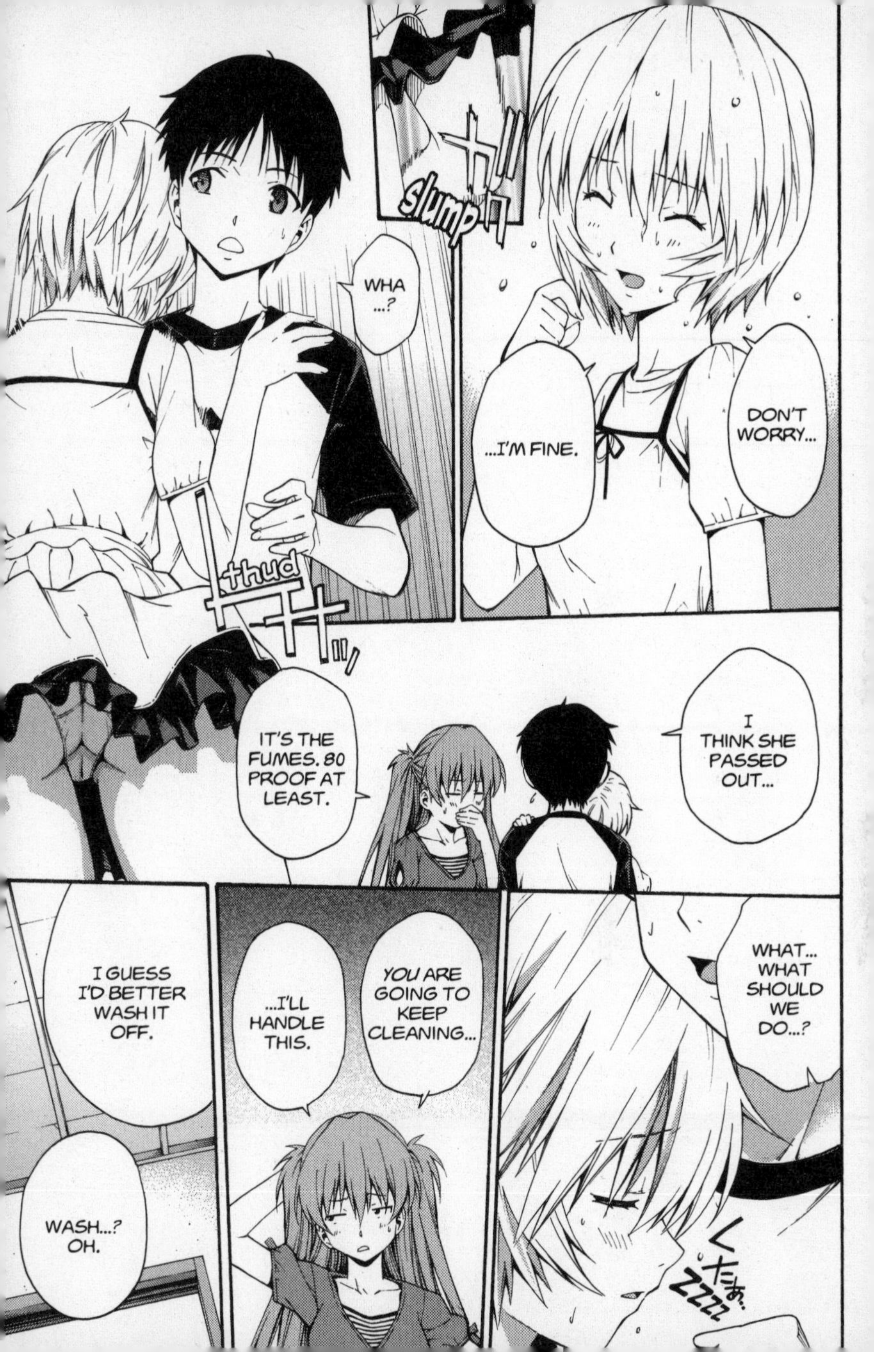
DON'T WORRY...
...I'M FINE.
slump
WHA ...?
thud
I THINK SHE PASSED OUT...
IT'S THE FUMES. 80 PROOF AT LEAST.
WHAT... WHAT SHOULD WE DO...?
ZZZZ
YOU ARE GOING TO KEEP CLEANING...
...I'LL HANDLE THIS.
I GUESS I'D BETTER WASH IT OFF.
WASH...? OH.

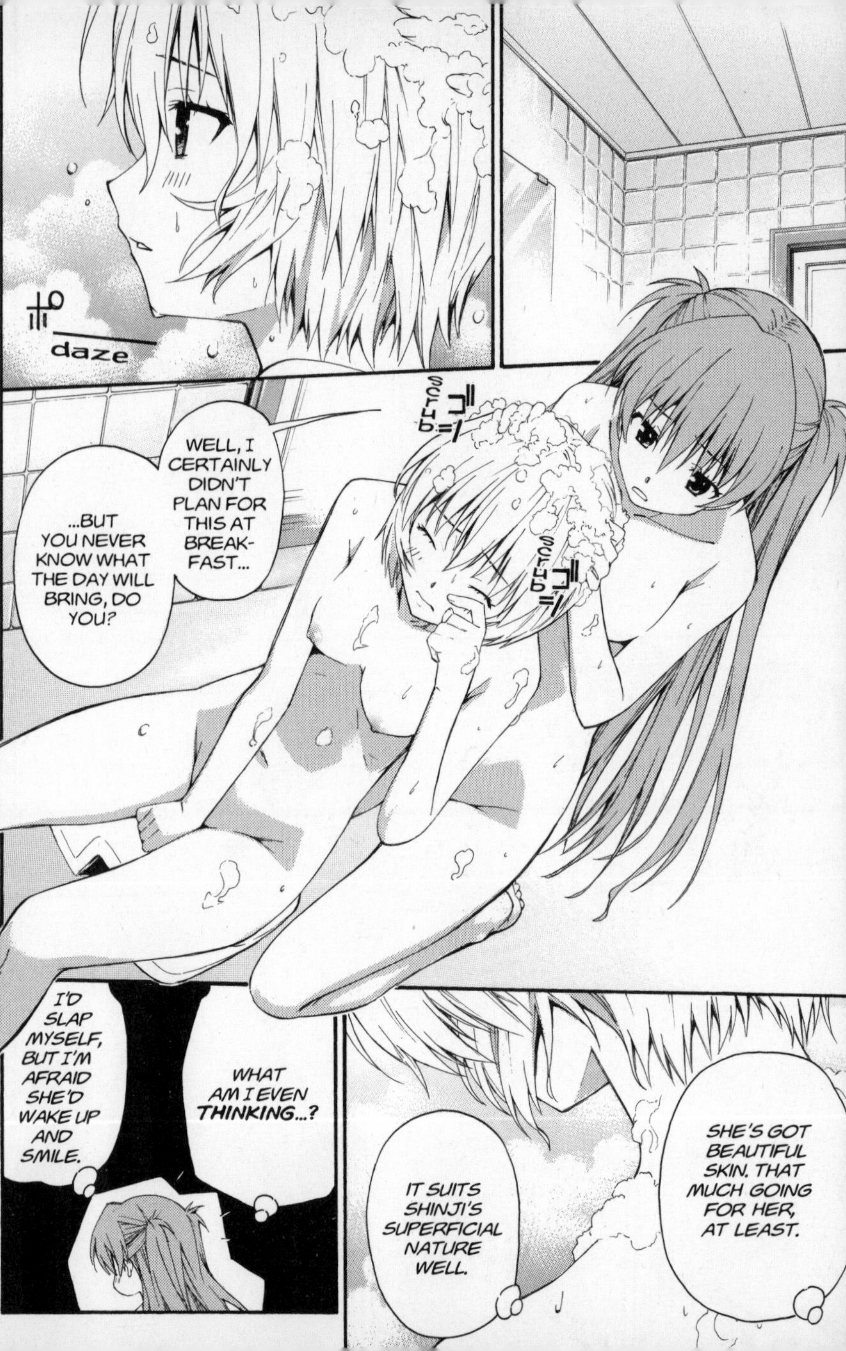
daze
scrub
scrub
WELL, I CERTAINLY DIDN'T PLAN FOR THIS AT BREAK-FAST...
...BUT YOU NEVER KNOW WHAT THE DAY WILL BRING, DO YOU?
SHE'S GOT BEAUTIFUL SKIN. THAT MUCH GOING FOR HER, AT LEAST.
IT SUITS SHINJI'S SUPERFICIAL NATURE WELL.
WHAT AM I EVEN **THINKING**...?
I'D SLAP MYSELF, BUT I'M AFRAID SHE'D WAKE UP AND SMILE.

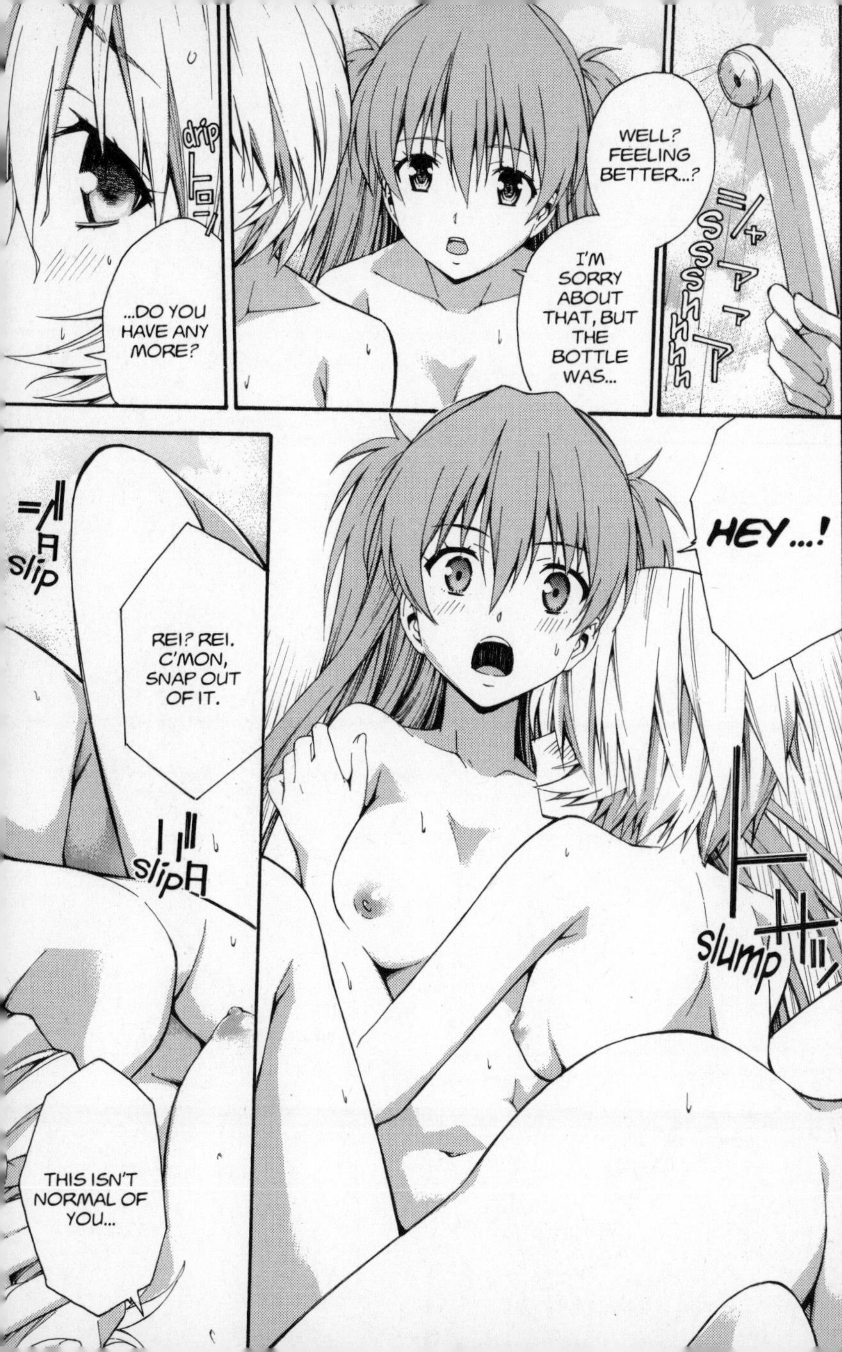
sssshhh
WELL? FEELING BETTER...?
I'M SORRY ABOUT THAT, BUT THE BOTTLE WAS...
drip
...DO YOU HAVE ANY MORE?
HEY...!
slump
slip
REI? REI. C'MON, SNAP OUT OF IT.
slip
THIS ISN'T NORMAL OF YOU...

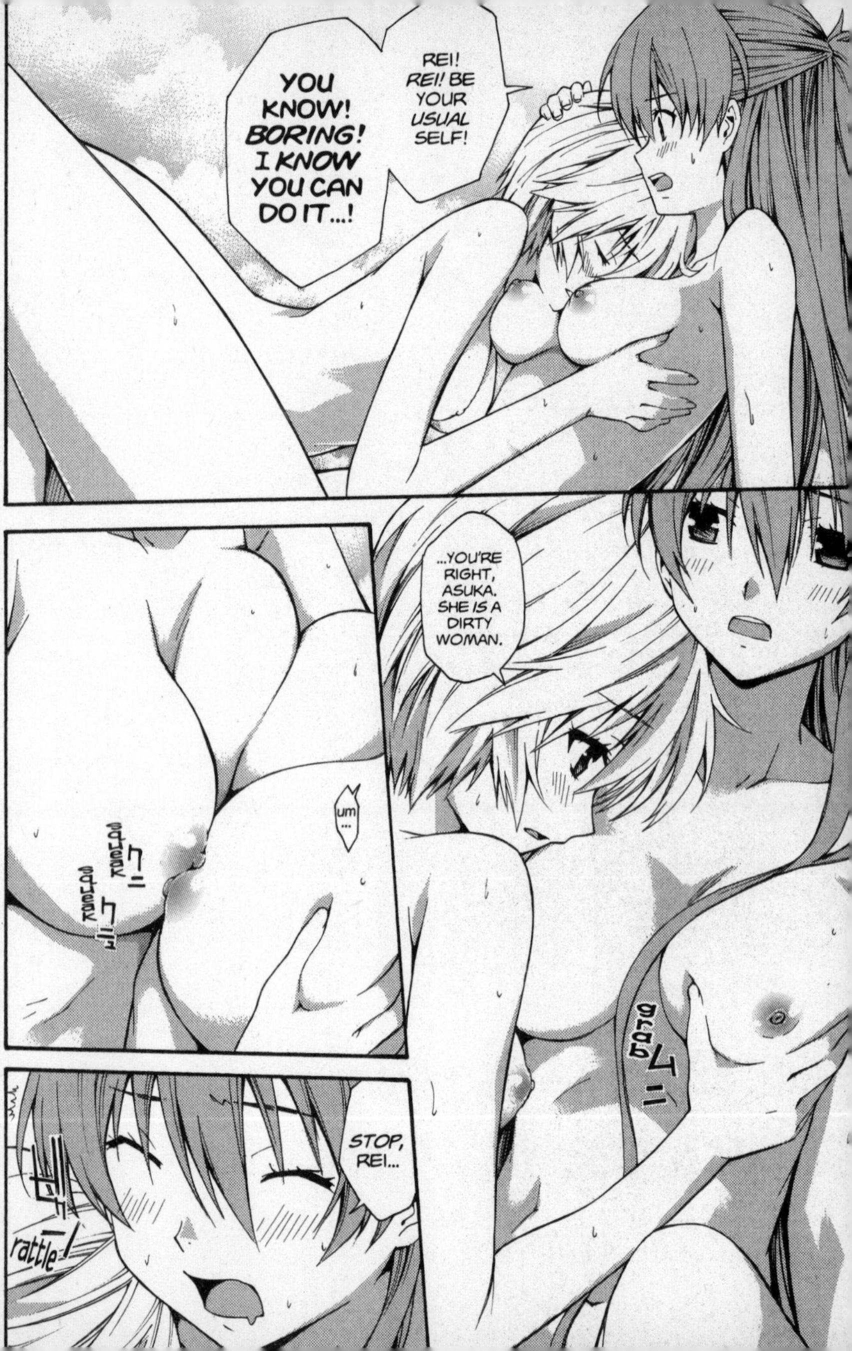
REI! REI! BE YOUR USUAL SELF!
YOU KNOW! BORING! I KNOW YOU CAN DO IT...!
...YOU'RE RIGHT, ASUKA. SHE IS A DIRTY WOMAN.
grab
um...
squeak
squeak
STOP, REI...
rattle!

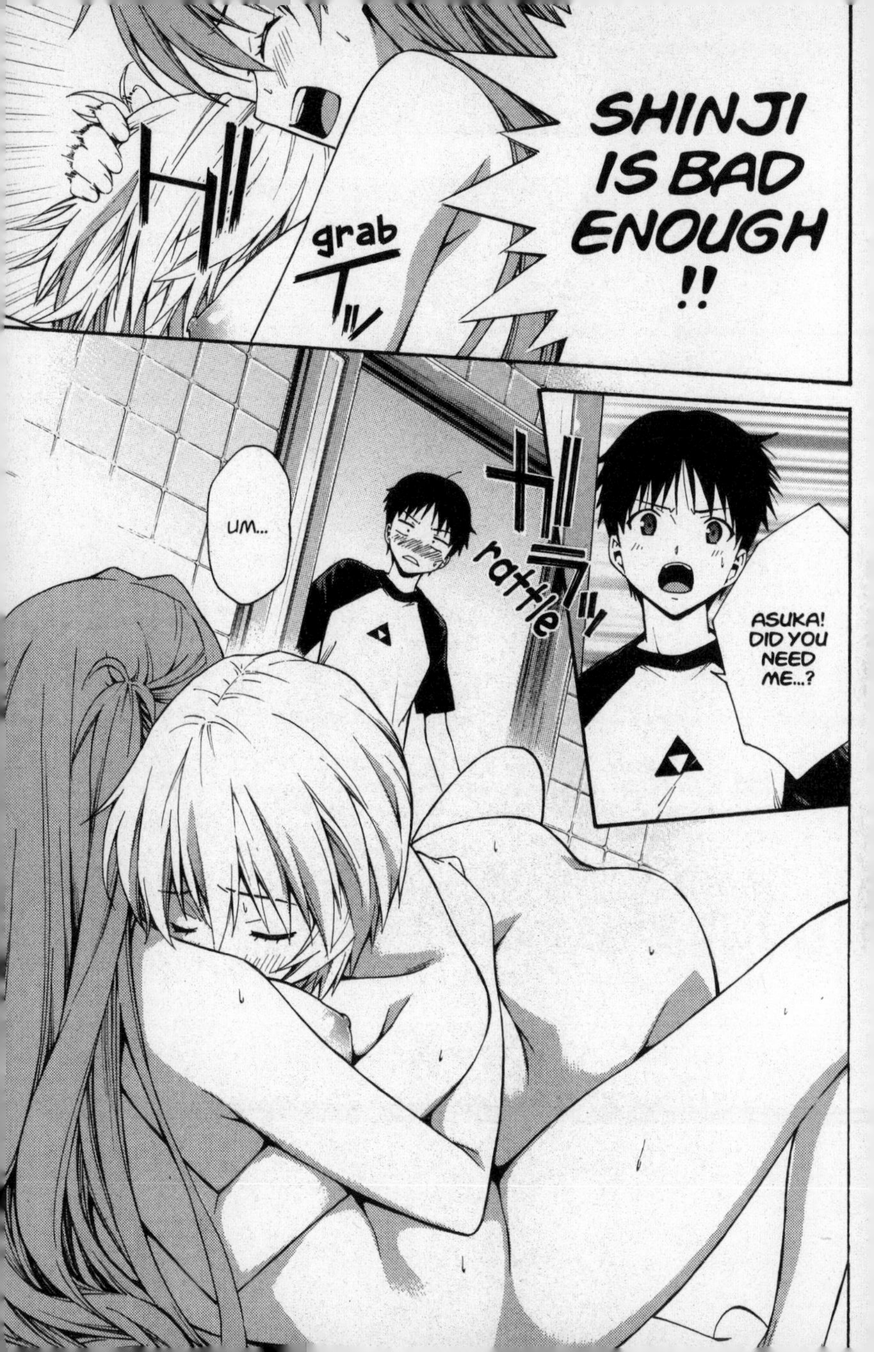
SHINJI IS BAD ENOUGH!!
grab
ASUKA! DID YOU NEED ME...?
rattle
UM...

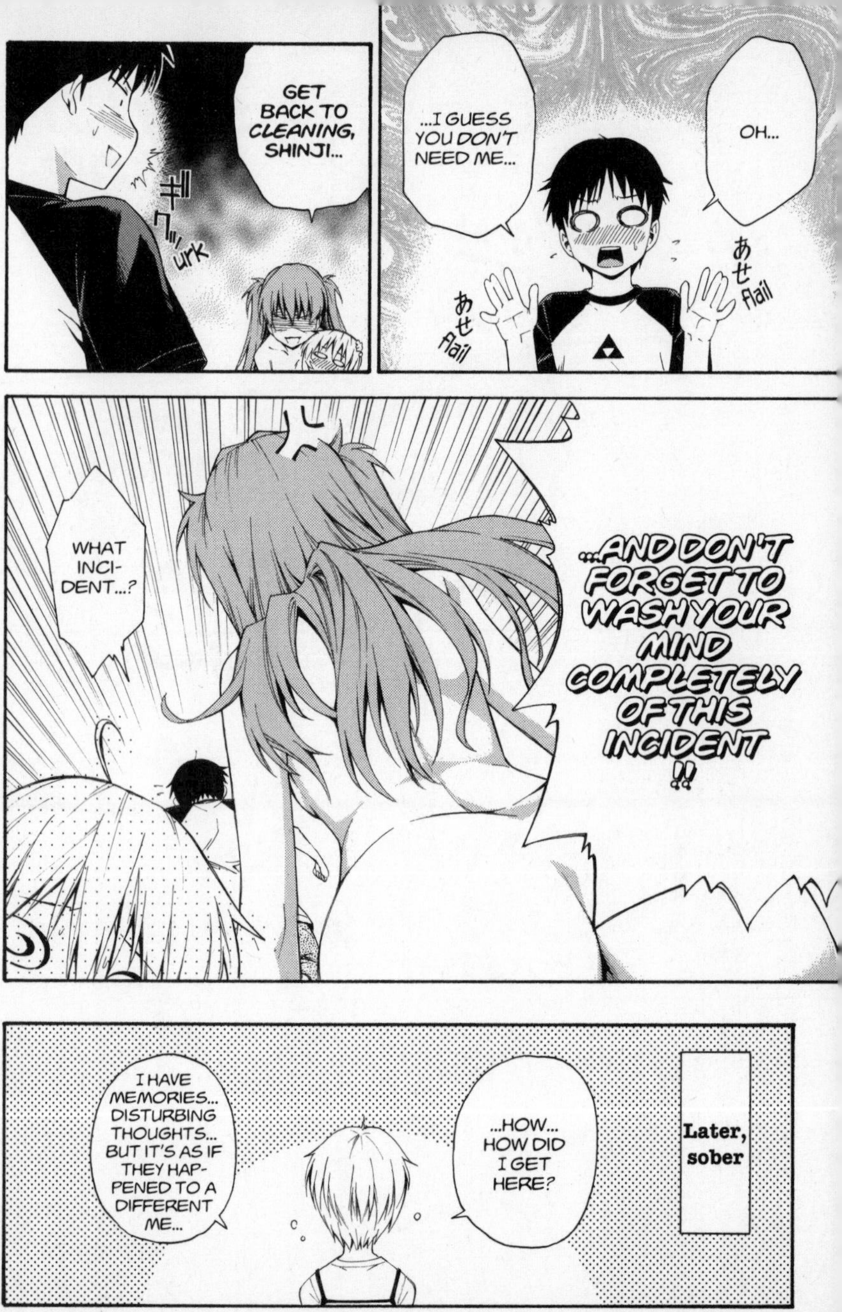
OH...
...I GUESS YOU DON'T NEED ME...
あせ flail
あせ flail
GET BACK TO CLEANING, SHINJI...
ギクッ urk
...AND DON'T FORGET TO WASH YOUR MIND COMPLETELY OF THIS INCIDENT!!
WHAT INCI-DENT...?
Later, sober
...HOW... HOW DID I GET HERE?
I HAVE MEMORIES... DISTURBING THOUGHTS... BUT IT'S AS IF THEY HAP-PENED TO A DIFFERENT ME...

AFTERWORD

In the middle of this volume, I finally took the plunge and started producing the art digitally. I had held off, thinking I would go digital at the start of a volume, but instead I found myself saying, "Why not now?" and just took the plunge!

-Osamu Takahashi

~STAFF~

Miki

Mitogawa Wataru

and many others

COVER DESIGN

Seki Shindo

See you in vol. 15...

EDITOR
CARL GUSTAV HORN

DESIGNER
KAT LARSON

PUBLISHER
MIKE RICHARDSON

English-language version produced by Dark Horse Comics

Neon Genesis Evangelion: The Shinji Ikari Raising Project Vol. 14

st published in Japan as NEON GENESIS EVANGELION IKARI-SHINJI IKUSEI KEIKAKU Volume 14. © OSAMU TAKAHASHI 2012 © GAINAX • khara.
ited by KADOKAWA SHOTEN. First published in Japan in 2012 by KADOKAWA CORPORATION. Tokyo. English translation rights arranged with KADO-
WA CORPORATION, Tokyo, through TOHAN CORPORATION, Tokyo. This English-language edition © 2014 by Dark Horse Comics, Inc. All other material

Published by
Dark Horse Manga
A division of Dark Horse Comics, Inc.
10956 SE Main Street
Milwaukie, OR 97222

DarkHorse.com

To find a comics shop in your area, call the Comic Shop Locator Service toll-free at 1-888-266-4226

First edition: June 2014
ISBN 978-1-61655-432-3

1 3 5 7 9 10 8 6 4 2
Printed in the United States of America

MISATO'S FAN SERVICE CENTER

c/o Dark Horse Comics • 10956 SE Main Street • Milwaukie, OR 97222 • evangelion@darkhorse.com

DARK HORSE rolled in force to the Hollywood Theatre in Portland this last January to catch the one-night-only showing of *Evangelion: 3.0 You Can (Not) Redo* (of course, on home video it's called *3.33* rather than *3.0*). And it was a good thing we arrived early, because it was a full house even though it's a big room, with a fifty-foot screen.

Portland is both a film town and an anime town (in fact, Hayao Miyazaki's Oscar-nominated *The Wind Rises* was chosen as one of the two films that kicked off the opening night of our recent two-week international film festival) and we have several vintage movie theaters that our residents support. The Hollywood is one of them, built in 1926; its marquee was recently rebuilt to look the way it did back in the 1920s. All of a sudden I had a vision of the cast of *Baccano!* showing up there to see a movie back in the days of Prohibition. I also had a sudden vision of Ladd Russo as Asuka, piloting Unit-02 in *The End of Evangelion* as he gore stomps the Angels.

But this was a different movie we had come to see, *Evangelion: 3.0 You Can (Not) Redo*. Hopefully it's okay to say a few spoilers by the time this book comes out (if it isn't, please skip straight to the cosplay photo). This was the second time I'd seen the film (the first time was at Kumoricon last year, courtesy of Sarah Sullivan from Funimation), and it was as grim as I remembered. If *The End of Evangelion* was the story in apocalypse mode, you might say *Evangelion: 3.0* is its postapocalypse.

Watching the movie, I was reminded how much humor and fun there was in the original *Evangelion* TV series, even if it did of course get progressively darker toward the end. Maybe this grim tone from the films is one of the reasons *The Shinji Ikari Raising Project* has proven to be the longest-running of the *Evangelion* spinoff manga—even longer than Yoshiyuki Sadamoto's original *Eva* manga, which will only have fourteen volumes (volume 15 of *The Shinji Ikari Raising Project* is already out in Japan). Could it be that fans want some sort of counterbalance? In *The Shinji Ikari Detective Diary*, I was struck by its artist, Takumi Yoshimura, saying that their motivation to create *Detective Diary* was to give all the characters from the anime a happy ending.

However, I did feel that *3.0* advanced the *Evangelion* saga not only through its new tory elements, but through that dreaded phrase, *character growth.* ^_^ Namely, much of the cast realized that wherever NERV was leading them, it wasn't to anywhere good, and mutinied to form WILLE. Misato was always independent minded, but the big surprise for me was Ritsuko, who seems to have found a way to grow beyond Gendo and move ahead with her life (as opposed to the murder-suicide she had intended in *The End of Evangelion*). Even if WILLE turns out to be ultimately under the manipulation of Gendo, I have to admire them for at least trying.

By the way, we were privileged to have Rei and Asuka show up in person to the Dark Horse booth at the aforementioned Kumoricon! You know how on the covers of *The Shinji Ikari Raising Project* they're always acting like best friends? They said that's just for marketing purposes, and in reality, they don't socialize much outside of NERV.

—CGH

NEON GENESIS EVANGELION

Dark Horse Manga is proud to present new original series based on the wildly popular *Neon Genesis Evangelion* manga and anime! Continuing the rich story lines and complex characters, these new visions of *Neon Genesis Evangelion* provide extra dimensions for understanding one of the greatest series ever made!

NEON GENESIS EVANGELION Campus Apocalypse

STORY AND ART BY MINGMING

VOLUME 1
ISBN 978-1-59582-530-8 | $10.99

VOLUME 2
ISBN 978-1-59582-661-9 | $10.99

VOLUME 3
ISBN 978-1-59582-680-0 | $10.99

VOLUME 4
ISBN 978-1-59582-689-3 | $10.99

NEON GENESIS EVANGELION COMIC TRIBUTE

STORY AND ART BY VARIOUS CREATORS

ISBN 978-1-61655-114-8 | $10.99

NEON GENESIS EVANGELION The Shinji Ikari Detective Diary

STORY AND ART BY TAKUMI YOSHIMURA

VOLUME 1
ISBN 978-1-61655-225-1 | $9.99

VOLUME 2
ISBN 978-1-61655-418-7 | $9.99

NEON GENESIS EVANGELION
THE SHINJI IKARI RAISING PROJECT

STORY AND ART BY OSAMU TAKAHASHI

VOLUME 1
ISBN 978-1-59582-321-2 | $9.99

VOLUME 2
ISBN 978-1-59582-377-9 | $9.99

VOLUME 3
ISBN 978-1-59582-447-9 | $9.99

VOLUME 4
ISBN 978-1-59582-454-7 | $9.99

VOLUME 5
ISBN 978-1-59582-520-9 | $9.99

VOLUME 6
ISBN 978-1-59582-580-3 | $9.99

VOLUME 7
ISBN 978-1-59582-595-7 | $9.99

VOLUME 8
ISBN 978-1-59582-694-7 | $9.99

VOLUME 9
ISBN 978-1-59582-800-2 | $9.99

VOLUME 10
ISBN 978-1-59582-879-8 | $9.99

VOLUME 11
ISBN 978-1-59582-932-0 | $9.99

VOLUME 12
ISBN 978-1-61655-032-2 | $9.99

VOLUME 13
ISBN 978-1-61655-315-9 | $9.99

VOLUME 14
ISBN 978-1-61655-432-3 | $9.99

Each volume of *Neon Genesis Evangelion* features bonus color pages, your *Evangelion* fan art and letters, and special reader giveaways!

FROM THE CREATOR OF
TRIGUN AND *GUNGRAVE*!

YASUHIRO
NIGHTOW

3
BLOOD BLOCKADE
BATTLEFRONT

Three years ago, a gateway between Earth and the Beyond opened over New York City. In one terrible night, New York was destroyed and rebuilt, trapping New Yorkers and extradimensional creatures alike in an impenetrable bubble. New York is now Jerusalem's Lot, a paranormal melting pot where magic and madness dwell alongside the mundane, where human vermin gather to exploit other-worldly assets for earthly profit. Now someone is threatening to breach the bubble and release New Jerusalem's horrors, but the mysterious superagents of Libra fight to prevent the unthinkable.

Trigun creator Yasuhiro Nightow returns with *Blood Blockade Battlefront*, an action-packed supernatural science-fiction steamroller as only Nightow can conjure.

VOLUME ONE
ISBN 978-1-59582-718-0 | $10.99

VOLUME FOUR
ISBN 978-1-61655-223-7 | $12.99

VOLUME TWO
ISBN 978-1-59582-912-2 | $10.99

VOLUME FIVE
ISBN 978-1-61655-224-4 | $12.99

VOLUME THREE
ISBN 978-1-59582-913-9 | $10.99

AVAILABLE AT YOUR LOCAL COMICS SHOP OR BOOKSTORE To find a comics shop in your area, call 1-888-266-4226 For more information or to order direct: • On the web: DarkHorse.com E-mail: mailorder@darkhorse.com • Phone: 1-800-862-0052 Mon.- Fri. 9 AM to 5 PM Pacific Time.

DARK HORSE MANGA

STOP!

止 ま れ

THIS IS THE BACK OF THE BOOK!

This manga collection is translated into English, but arranged in right-to-left reading format to maintain the artwork's visual orientation as originally drawn and published in Japan. If you've never read comics this way before, take a look at the diagram below to give yourself an idea of how to go about it. Basically, you'll be starting in the upper-right-hand corner, and will read each word balloon and panel moving right to left. It may take a little getting used to, but you should get the hang of it very quickly. Have fun! If this is the millionth manga you've read this way, never mind.

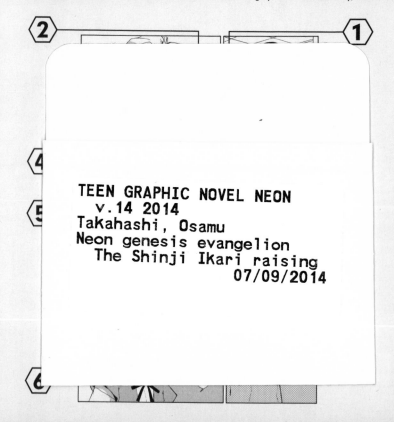